The Best of Woman's Day Crochet

A Treasury of Classic and Contemporary Crochet Patterns

SIMON AND SCHUSTER   NEW YORK

*Copyright © 1971, 1972, 1973, 1974, 1975, 1976 by Fawcett Publications, Inc.
All rights reserved
including the right of reproduction
in whole or in part in any form
Published by Simon and Schuster
A Gulf+Western Company
Rockefeller Center, 630 Fifth Avenue
New York, New York 10020*

*Designed by Elizabeth Woll
Manufactured in the United States of America*

1   2   3   4   5   6   7   8   9   10

*Library of Congress Cataloging in Publication Data
Main entry under title:*

The Best of Woman's Day crochet.

*1. Crocheting—Patterns.   I. Woman's day.
TT825.B4   746.4'34   76-2460
ISBN 0-671-22225-2*

Contents

INTRODUCTION   **9**

How to Crochet   11

Crochet Hooks, 13   *Materials,* 14   *Gauge,* 14   *Abbreviations and Terms,* 15   *To Begin Crochet,* 15
Basic Stitches, 16   *Basic Techniques,* 19   *Special Stitches,* 21   *Finishing Your Work,* 23

For Women   25

HALTERS, VESTS AND SMALL TOPS	**27**	**LONG-SLEEVED AND SPORTY PULLOVERS**	**51**
Short-Story Tunic	27	Trumpet-Sleeved Tunic	51
Mosaic Vest	29	Shawl-Collared Pullover	55
Pink Popcorn Tank Top	32	Kimono Sweater	57
Diagonal Pull-On Top	33		
Rainbow Halter	34		
Scoop Halter	35	**SWEATER SETS AND JACKETS**	**58**
		Contemporary Sweater Duo	58
SHORT-SLEEVED SWEATERS	**38**	Super Sweater Set	62
A Little-Bit-of-Everything Sweater	38	Scalloped Sweater Set	65
Pansy Sweater	40	Boldly Striped Sweater Set	67
Cap-Sleeved Shrink Top	42	Tailored Blazer and Hat	70
Powder-Pink Pullover	43	Distaff Flight Jacket	73
Pineapple Pull-On	44	Yellow Jacket	74
Three-Toe Sweater	46	Yellow Smock	77
Side-Wrap Sweater	48		

DRESSY SWEATERS	**80**	Classic Wraparound Suit	124
How to Block Linen Garments	80	Mix-and-Match Blazer Suit	128
Old-Fashioned Peplum Camisole	81	Romantic Coatdress	132
Charming Square-Neck Pullover and Cloche	83	Turtleneck Poncho and Matching Beret	135
Side-Tie Sweater	86		
Extraordinary Sparkle Sweater	88	**ACCESSORIES**	**137**
Sensational Rust Jacket	90	Head-Warmers Supreme	137
		Sporty Fedora	138
LONG SKIRTS, DRESSES, SUITS AND WRAPS	**93**	Classic Cloche for Summer	139
		Three Winter Hats	140
Romantic Wedding Dress	93	Double-Strap Backpack	146
Breezy Beach Cover-Ups	98	Stretchy Tote	147
Spiraling Swirl Skirt	103	Musette Shoulder Pouch	148
Tank Top and Plaid Skirt	105	Four Fluffy Bags	149
One-Piece-Look Dress	108	Carry-All Shopping Net	153
Sweater Dress	110	Fluffy Seven-Footer	154
V-Neck Ruffle Dress	112	Espadrilles	155
Yoked Dress	115	Lacy Cobweb Shawl	158
Layered-Look One-Piece Dress	117	Gold and Silver Circular Shawl	159
Capelet	120	Delicate Triangular Shawl	160
Casual Coat	122	Baby Doll Bikini	161

For Children 165

CLOTHES	**167**	Drawstring Skirt	188
Baby Helmet	167		
Baby Jacket	168	**ACCESSORIES**	**190**
Baby Bonnet	169	Snappy Envelope	190
Infanta Bonnet	171	Shoulder Bag	191
Summer-Cool Baby Romper and Hat	172	Watchband	192
Jumper	174	Funny Puppet Mittens	192
Vest	176		
Pinafore	177	**TOYS**	**195**
Scarlet Bib Jumper	178	Four Soft Foam-Filled Blocks	195
Pretty Poncho	179	Zoo Animals to Cuddle	197
Toddler's Shorts	180	Panda Bear	199
Toddler's Jumper	181	Tootsie Turtle	201
Tyrolean Smock	183	Mr. Mouse	202
Girl's Sweater Set	185	The Three Bears	204
Boy's Sweater Set	186	Porky Pig	207

For Men 209

SWEATERS	**211**	Casual Coat	216
Sweatermates for Men	211	Zip-Front Battle Jacket	217
Lumber Jacket	214	Vest in Basket-Weave Stitch	219

Decorating with Crochet 221

Extravagant Afghan	223	Bed-Linen Decorations	240
Superwarm Afghan	225	Filet Café Curtain	241
Hexagon Afghan	226	Café Curtains and Valance	243
Bedspread	227	Rug-in-the-Round	244
Cozy Afghan	229	Coasters	246
Crossover Granny Pillow	229	Candy Pockets	246
Pyramid and Zigzag Pillows	230	Cat Nest	247
Pink Scallops	232	Fruit Centerpiece	248
Chair Seat	233	Cachepot	251
Special Setting to Fit Round Tables	235	Room Divider	252
Four Fruits Tablecloth	237	Rag Rug	253
Elegant Tablecloth	238	Romantic Mirror Frame	254

YARN SOURCES 255 **CREDITS** 256

Introduction

Crochet, which derives its name from the French word for "little hook," has been practiced since the dawn of civilization all over the world. Today women are rediscovering this simplest and freest of handcrafts—its infinite variations, the personalized look of each project, the ease and speed of its technique. Especially in recent years crochet has experienced a new and booming popularity. Along with the charming, ever popular doilies and edgings of yesteryear there is also a whole new, almost sculptural, dimension in crochet.

The editors of *Woman's Day* have selected from their extensive library the best and most exciting crochet projects for you to make and enjoy, all of which have appeared over the years in the pages of the magazine.

You will find something for everyone, beginner and experienced needlewoman alike.

Here's what lies ahead for you to make:
To Wear: For the whole family: sweaters, ponchos, blazers, tunics, halter tops, skirts, vests, hats, shawls, bags, and espadrilles and more.
For the Home: Rugs, pillows, curtains, tablecloths, sheet borders, afghans, a cachepot, room divider, mirror frame, chair seat, a bedspread and a flower basket.
Toys: Three little bears to hug and hold, baby blocks, and a flowered piggy; an elephant, a tiger, and a not so cowardly lion, Mr. Mouse, Panda Bear, and Tootsie Turtle also join the menagerie.

You will also find complete information on hooks, yarns, and crochet terms and their abbreviations; detailed instructions for holding hook and yarn in your hands; clear and precise directions and illustrative drawings for the basic stitches and techniques; descriptions of afghan, shell, knot, popcorn, and star stitches; instructions for finishing; hints on laundering, blocking, and sewing your work.

With this book in hand, anyone can learn how to crochet, and spend many enjoyable hours making something practical and pretty.

How to Crochet

Crochet is essentially a process of drawing one loop through another.

The basic stitches in crochet are simple enough for the beginner to master, and yet these same simple stitches can be worked in an almost endless variety of patterns to present a challenge to the novice and experienced needlewoman alike.

Here are step-by-step directions and detailed drawings to teach you all the basic stitches, plus the five most popular special stitches—afghan, shell, knot, popcorn, and star stitches.

Crochet Hooks

Crochet hooks come in a variety of sizes, materials, and lengths.

Steel crochet hooks are usually used for cotton thread and come in sizes 00, the largest, through 14, the smallest.

Aluminum and plastic hooks, recommended for beginners, are used for both wool and cotton yarn. They are sized in different ways by different manufacturers, so it is wise to select from widely distributed, well-known brand names. Some manufacturers size them by letter, some by number, and others by both letter and number. Aluminum and plastic hooks usually come in sizes B through K, K being the largest; or they may come numbered from 1 through 10½, the latter being the largest.

Wooden rug hooks are made in large sizes only.

Afghan hooks are manufactured especially for the afghan stitch and are meant to hold a large number of stitches. They are about the length of knitting needles, either 9" or 14" long, and come in the same sizes as other crochet hooks.

Because the sizing of hooks is not the same in the United States as in England and Canada a listing of comparative sizes is given.

Aluminum/Plastic Hooks	
American	England/Canada
B 1	14
C 2	13
D 3	12
E 4	11
F 5	10
G 6	9
H 7	8
I 8	7
J 9	6
K 10½	4

Steel Hooks	
American	England/Canada
00	
0	
1	0
2	1
3	1½
4	2
5	2½
6	3
7	3½
8	4
9	4½
10	5
11	5½
12	6
13	6½
14	7

Materials

In Grandmother's time crochet was mostly associated with cotton—that was in the days of doilies and fine laces—but today the sky is the limit. Anything that can be looped with a hook may be used. Wool in new and exciting weights and textures and metallic and synthetic yarns in an endless variety of colors are often used for wearables and decorating accessories such as afghans and pillows. Synthetics, because of their machine washability, are a good choice for children's and baby clothes. Heavy cotton, wool, and jute yarns are used for rugs, plant hangers, sturdy tote bags, and even espadrilles. We have seen fine wire used for crocheted jewelry.

Buy all the thread or yarn you need to complete a project at one time so as to be sure of having the same dye lot, and check that the dye-lot numbers are all the same. (A dye-lot number refers to a quantity of yarn dyed at the same time in the same dye bath.). Despite modern dyeing processes there is always some variation—no matter how slight—between two dye lots, which may spoil the appearance of your work.

The materials mentioned in the directions have been especially selected to suit the projects. If at all possible, do *not* substitute another yarn for the one recommended for making a garment unless you are very experienced. The directions have been written specifically for the yarn named, which has been crocheted to a certain gauge on a certain size hook to obtain a particular *size* garment.

Gauge

At the beginning of all directions a gauge is given. It is very important that you crochet to the gauge specified so that your finished article will be the correct size.

Gauge means *the number of stitches to one inch* and *the number of rows to one inch*.

To check *your gauge*—because everybody has a different tension in working—make a practice piece at least 2" square, using the hook and materials specified in the directions. With a ruler, measure the number of stitches you have to 1", as in Diagram 1. If your number of stitches does not correspond to the gauge given, try a hook of a different size.

If you have *more* stitches to the inch than specified, you should use a *larger* hook. If you have *fewer* stitches to the inch, use a *smaller* hook.

Keep changing the size hook until your gauge is exactly the same as that specified. The size hook used is not important as long as you obtain the correct gauge.

Diagram 1

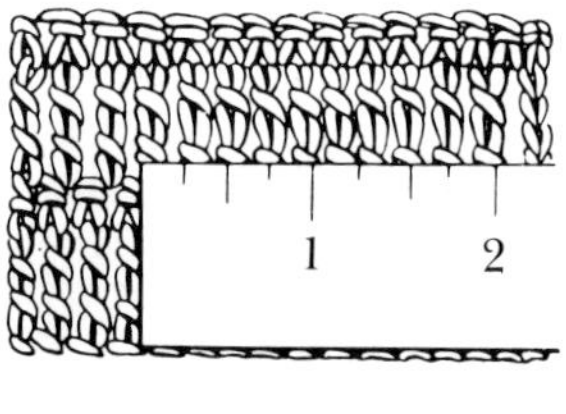

How to Crochet

ample: "(ch 5, sc in next sc) 5 times" means to make all that is in parentheses 5 times in all.

Abbreviations and Terms

Here are the common abbreviations and an explanation of the terms and symbols most frequently used in crochet:

beg	beginning
bl	block
ch	chain
cl	cluster
dec	decrease
dc	double crochet
d tr	double treble
h dc	half double crochet
inc	increase
incl	inclusive
lp	loop
p	picot
rnd	round
sc	single crochet
sk	skip
sl	slip
sl st	slip stitch
sp	space
st	stitch
sts	stitches
tog	together
tr	treble
tr tr	triple treble
y o, o	yarn (thread) over hook

Asterisk means repeat the instructions following the asterisk as many times as specified, in addition to the first time.

[ ] *Brackets* are used to designate changes in size when directions are given, as they often are, for more than one size. The figure preceding the brackets refers to the smallest size.

Even: When directions say "work even," this means to continue working without increasing or decreasing.

Multiple of Stitches: A pattern often requires an exact number of stitches to be worked correctly. When directions say "multiple of," it means the number of stitches must be divisible by this number. For example: "(multiple of 6)" would be 12, 18, 24, etc.; "(multiple of 6 plus 3)" would be 15, 21, 27, etc.

( ) *Parentheses* mean repeat instructions in parentheses as many times as specified. For ex-

To Begin Crochet

The following diagrams show you how to make a slipknot, which anchors the yarn on the hook, positions for holding yarn and hook, and how to do the chain stitch, which is the foundation for other stitches.

Make a practice piece of each new stitch and work until you are familiar with it. Use knitting worsted and a size G aluminum or plastic hook.

While you learn, hold your hands in the positions shown in the diagrams. There really is no one "right" way to hold your hook. We think that whatever way is most comfortable for you is correct for you, and we show you two ways (Diagrams 2 and 3).

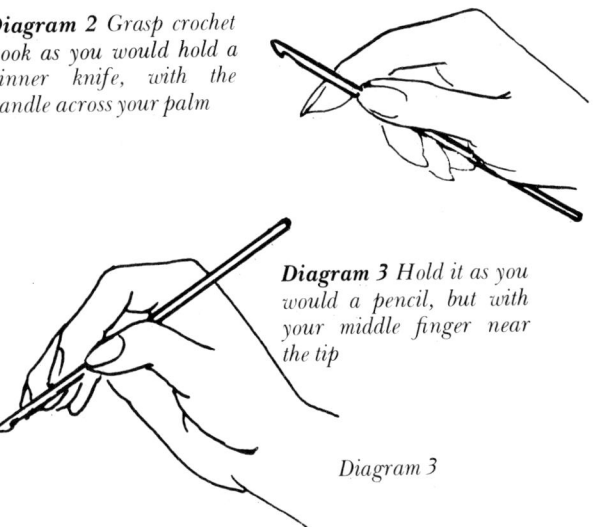

Diagram 2 *Grasp crochet hook as you would hold a dinner knife, with the handle across your palm*

Diagram 3 *Hold it as you would a pencil, but with your middle finger near the tip*

Left-handed crochet work comes out in reverse. If you are left-handed, try to crochet with your right hand—directions are mostly written for right-handed crocheters, and you'll find it easier to follow more complex patterns and shaping later on. However, if using your right hand is impossible, hold diagrams in front of a mirror to reverse hands.

THE FIRST LOOP (Slipknot)

1. Make a loop at the end of thread and hold loop in place with thumb and forefinger

of left hand. Diagram 4. (At left is short end of thread; at right is the long, or working, thread.)

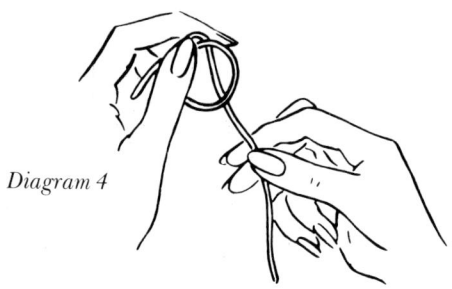
Diagram 4

2. With right hand grasp the crochet hook as you would a pencil and put hook through loop, catch working thread and draw it through. Diagram 5.

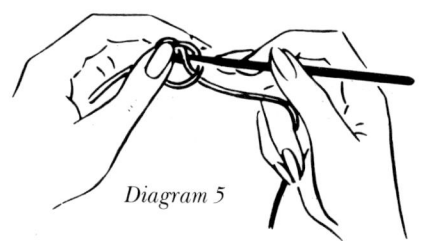
Diagram 5

3. Pull short end and working thread in opposite directions to bring loop close around the end of hook. Diagram 6.

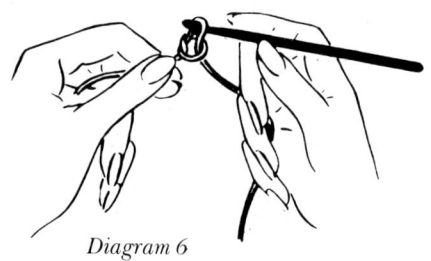
Diagram 6

TO HOLD THREAD

1. Measure down working thread about 4" from loop on hook.

2. At this point insert thread between ring finger and little finger of left hand. Diagram 7.

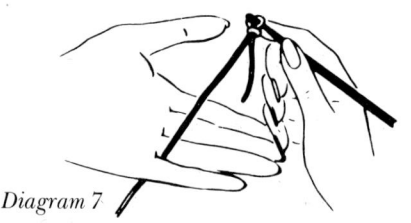
Diagram 7

3. Weave thread toward back, under little and ring fingers, over middle finger, and under forefinger toward you. Diagram 8.

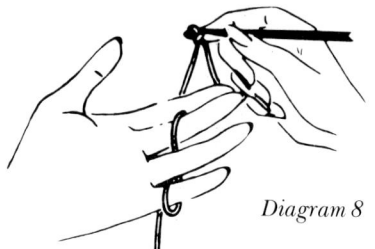
Diagram 8

4. Grasp hook and loop with thumb and forefinger of left hand. Gently pull working thread so that it is taut but not tight. Diagram 9.

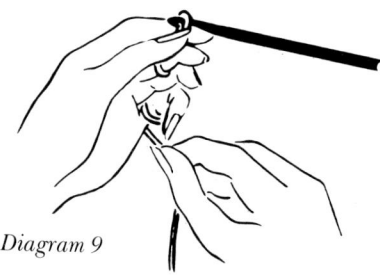
Diagram 9

TO HOLD HOOK

In order to begin working, hold hook as in Diagram 3 and adjust fingers of left hand as in Diagram 10. The middle finger is bent so it can

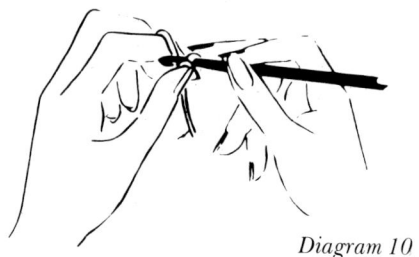
Diagram 10

control the tension, while the ring and little fingers prevent the thread from moving too freely. As you practice you will become familiar with the correct tension. Now you are ready to begin the chain stitch.

Basic Stitches

CHAIN STITCH (CH)

1. Pass hook under thread and catch thread with hook (this is called thread over—O). Diagram 11.

How to Crochet 17

Diagram 11

2. Draw thread through loop on hook. This makes one chain. Diagram 12.

Diagram 12

3. Repeat steps 1 and 2 until you have as many chain stitches as you need. One loop always remains on hook. Keep thumb and forefinger of your left hand near stitch on which you are working. Practice making chains until they are uniform. Diagram 13.

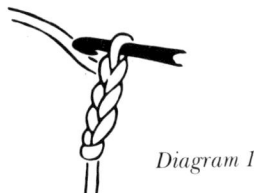
Diagram 13

SINGLE CROCHET (SC)

Make a foundation chain of 20 stitches for practice piece.

1. Insert hook from the front under 2 top threads of 2nd chain from hook. Diagram 14.

Diagram 14

2. Thread over hook. Diagram 15.

Diagram 15

3. Draw through stitch. There are now 2 loops on hook. Diagram 16.

Diagram 16

4. Thread over. Diagram 17. Draw thread through 2 loops on hook. One loop remains on hook. One single crochet now is completed. Diagram 18.

Diagram 17

Diagram 18

5. For next single crochet, insert hook under 2 top threads of next stitch. Diagram 19. Repeat steps 2, 3, and 4. Repeat until you have made a single crochet in each chain.

Diagram 19

6. At end of row of single crochet, chain 1. Diagram 20.

7. Turn work so reverse side is facing you. Diagram 21.

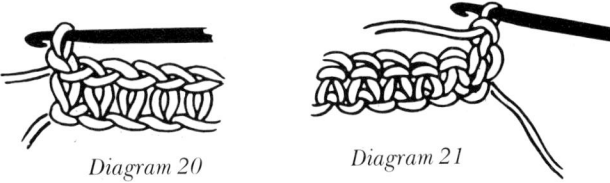
Diagram 20   *Diagram 21*

8. Insert hook under 2 top threads of first single crochet. Repeat steps 2, 3, 4, 5, 6, and 7. Continue working single crochet in this manner until work is uniform and you feel familiar with the stitch. On last row do not make a turning chain. Clip thread about 3″ from work, bring loose end through the one remaining loop on hook and pull tight. Diagram 22.

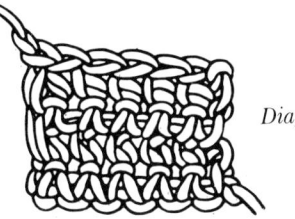
Diagram 22

Now you have completed your practice piece of single crochet.

Note: In all crochet, pick up the 2 top threads of every stitch unless otherwise specified. When only one thread is picked up, a different effect is produced.

DOUBLE CROCHET (DC)

Make a foundation chain of 20 stitches for practice piece.

1. Thread over, insert hook under the 2 top threads of 4th chain from hook. Diagram 23.

Diagram 23

2. Thread over, draw through stitch. There are now 3 loops on hook.

3. Thread over. Diagram 24. Draw through 2 loops. Two loops remain on hook.

Diagram 24

4. Thread over again. Diagram 25. Draw through the 2 remaining loops. One loop remains on hook. One double crochet is now completed. Diagram 26.

Diagram 25    *Diagram 26*

5. For next double crochet, thread over, insert hook under the 2 top threads of next stitch and repeat steps 2, 3, and 4. Repeat until you have made a double crochet in each stitch.

6. At end of row, chain 3 and turn work. Diagram 27.

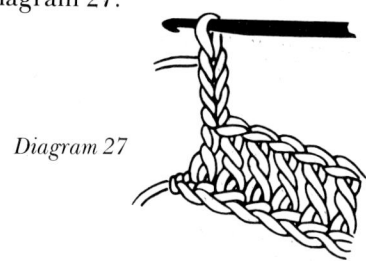

Diagram 27

7. On next row, thread over, skip first double crochet, insert hook under the 2 top threads of 2nd double crochet. Repeat steps 2, 3, 4, 5, 6, and 7. Diagram 28.

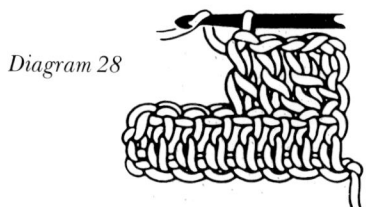

Diagram 28

8. Continue working double crochet in this manner until work is uniform and you feel familiar with the stitch. On last row, do not make a turning chain. Clip thread about 3" from work, bring loose end through the one remaining loop on hook and pull tight.

HALF DOUBLE CROCHET (H DC)

To make half double crochet, repeat steps 1 and 2 under Double Crochet but insert hook in 3rd chain from hook. At this point there are 3 loops on hook. Thread over and draw through all 3 loops at once. Diagram 29. Half double crochet now is completed. At end of row, chain 2 to turn.

Diagram 29

TREBLE CROCHET (TR)

Make a foundation chain of 20 stitches for practice piece.

1. Thread over twice, insert hook under 2 top threads of 5th chain from hook.

2. Thread over and draw a loop through the chain. There are now 4 loops on hook.

3. Thread over again. Diagram 30. Draw through 2 loops on hook (3 loops remain on hook).

4. Thread over again. Diagram 31. Draw through 2 loops (2 loops remain on hook).

5. Thread over again. Diagram 32. Draw

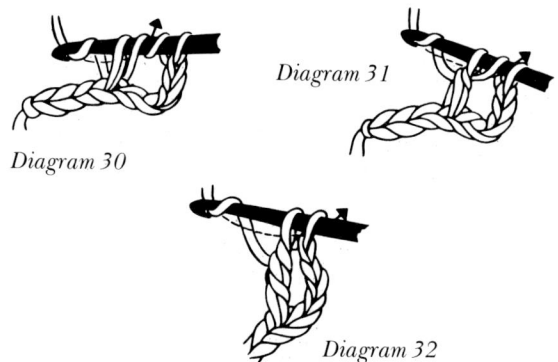

Diagram 30   *Diagram 31*

Diagram 32

through 2 remaining loops (one loop remains on hook). One treble crochet now is completed. At end of row, chain 4 to turn. On second and subsequent rows, make first treble crochet in second stitch from beginning of row, counting ch-4 as first stitch. Continue making

How to Crochet

treble crochet in this manner until you are familiar with the stitch. Finish piece same as other pieces.

DOUBLE TREBLE (D TR)

Thread over hook 3 times, insert hook under 2 top threads of 6th chain from hook and draw a loop through the chain (5 loops on hook). Thread over and draw through 2 loops at a time 4 times. A double treble now is completed. Diagram 33. At end of row, chain 5 to

Diagram 33

turn. On second and subsequent rows, make first double treble crochet in second stitch from beginning of row, counting ch-5 as first stitch.

TRIPLE TREBLE (TR TR)

Thread over hook 4 times, insert hook under 2 top threads of 7th chain from hook and draw a loop through the chain (6 loops on hook). Thread over and draw through 2 loops at a time 5 times. A triple treble now is completed. Diagram 34. At end of row, chain 6 to

Diagram 34

turn. On second and subsequent rows, make first triple treble crochet in second stitch from beginning of row, counting ch-6 as first stitch.

Basic Techniques
TO TURN WORK

You will notice that stitches vary in length. Each uses a different number of chain stitches to turn at the end of a row. Below is a table showing the number of chain stitches required to make a turn for each stitch.

Single crochet (sc)	Ch 1 to turn
Half double crochet (h dc)	Ch 2 to turn
Double crochet (dc)	Ch 3 to turn
Treble crochet (tr)	Ch 4 to turn
Double treble (d tr)	Ch 5 to turn
Triple treble (tr tr)	Ch 6 to turn

A Helpful Hint: When you are designing your own project, here is a little rule of thumb to help you figure out how many chain stitches you need on your foundation chain to get a particular number of stitches:

Chain 10: sc in 2nd chain from hook and in each chain across will give you 9 sc.

Chain 10: dc in 4th chain from hook and in each chain across will give you 8 dc, counting the turning chain as 1 dc (the turning chain is the 3 stitches you skipped at the beginning).

Chain 10: dc in 3rd chain from hook and in each chain across will also give you 8 dc, *not* counting the turning chain as 1 dc.

TO DECREASE (DEC) SINGLE CROCHET

1. Work one single crochet to point where 2 loops are on hook. Draw up a loop in next stitch. Diagram 35.

Diagram 35

2. Thread over, draw thread through 3 loops at one time. One decrease made. Diagram 36.

Diagram 36

TO DECREASE (DEC) DOUBLE CROCHET

1. Work one double crochet to point where 2 loops are on hook. Begin another double crochet in next stitch and work until 4 loops are on hook. Diagram 37.

Diagram 37

2. Thread over, draw through 2 loops. Diagram 38.

Diagram 38

3. Thread over, draw through 3 loops. Diagram 39. One decrease made.

Diagram 39

TO INCREASE (INC)

When directions call for an increase, work 2 stitches in one stitch. This forms one extra stitch.

TO CHANGE COLORS

Always change colors within a row as follows: Work to within last st of old color, work last st until there are 2 loops of old color on hook, pick up new color and draw loop of new color through both loops on hook. Continue with new color, holding color not in use across top of piece and crocheting over it, concealing it within sts of new color.

When changing colors at end of row, break off old color, leaving a 3″ end. Tie on new color and work over ends as before.

When a design is not repeated continuously across a row a bobbin of yarn is attached, where specified in the directions, to crochet each color of the motif. Do not carry colors not in use across the wrong side of work. Instead, cut off old color, leaving 4″ end. Weave all ends through back of garment.

To Make Yarn Bobbins: To minimize tangling, wind yarn into small balls that pull from the center. Wind balls as follows:

Step 1: Hold yarn in left hand with thumb and index finger in position shown in drawing.

Step 2: While holding end A firmly in left hand, with right hand wind yarn around index finger about 4 times, then wind yarn around finger 6 times more at a slightly different

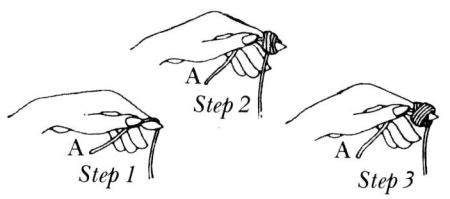

angle. **Step 3:** With right hand wind yarn 4 times at an angle over strands on finger, being careful not to catch end A. Remove ball of yarn from index finger and, holding it between thumb and index finger, continue to wind ball, turning it every 4 or 5 winds, being careful not to catch end A into winding. Break off and tuck outside end into last winding. Use end A; ball will now pull from center.

Note: After most of yarn is used, balls will become loose, drop down, and need rewinding. **To Rewind:** Without breaking ball from work, starting with end of yarn that is attached to work, rewind ball following original directions.

SLIP STITCH (SL ST)

Make a foundation chain of 20 stitches for practice piece.

Insert hook under top thread of 2nd chain from hook, thread over. With one motion draw through stitch and loop on hook. Insert hook under top thread of next chain, then thread over and draw through stitch and loop on hook. Diagram 40.

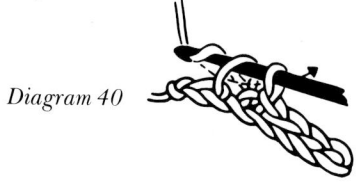
Diagram 40

Repeat until you have made a slip stitch in each chain.

A chain with slip stitch is often used for ties on bonnets, sacques, etc. Rows of slip stitch worked in the back loop of each stitch produce a ribbed effect.

SLIP STITCH FOR JOINING

When directions say "join," always use a slip stitch.

1. Insert hook through the 2 top threads of stitch. Diagram 41.

2. Thread over and with one motion draw through stitch and loop on hook. Diagram 42.

Diagram 41

Diagram 42

WORKING AROUND THE POST

The "post" or "bar" is the vertical or upright section of a stitch. When directions say to make a stitch around the post or bar of a stitch in a

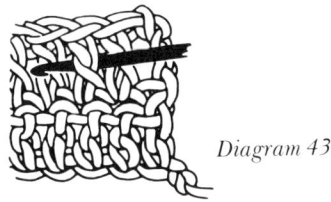
Diagram 43

previous row, insert the hook *around* stitch instead of in top of stitch. See Diagram 43 for placement of hook.

Special Stitches

AFGHAN STITCH

This stitch requires a long hook in order to hold a number of stitches at one time. Though the name of the stitch implies that it is used primarily for afghans, it is equally effective for crocheting sweaters, scarves, and other woolen articles.

Make a foundation chain of 20 stitches for practice piece.

1. Insert hook under 2 top threads of 2nd chain from hook; thread over and draw a loop through chain.

2. Retaining all loops on hook, draw up a loop in each remaining chain. Diagram 44.

Diagram 44

3. When all loops are on hook, thread over, draw through one loop; thread over, draw through 2 loops.

4. Thread over, draw through next 2 loops. Diagram 45. Repeat this across row. The loop which remains on hook at end of row always counts as the first stitch of next row. Do not turn.

Diagram 45

5. To begin 3rd and all uneven rows, insert hook in the front thread of the 2nd vertical bar. Diagram 46.

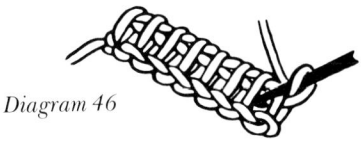
Diagram 46

6. Draw up a loop. Retaining all loops on hook, draw up a loop in the front thread of each vertical bar across to within last vertical bar. Diagram 47. Insert hook in front thread of last vertical bar and the stitch directly behind it and draw up a loop. This gives a firm edge to this side.

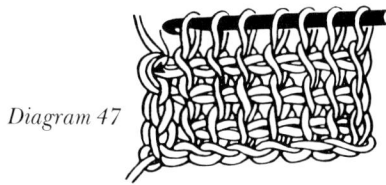
Diagram 47

7. Work off loops as in 2nd row, drawing through one loop first and then through 2 loops across row. On last row of work, make a slip stitch in each vertical bar to keep edge from curling.

To Increase Afghan Stitch: To increase one stitch, draw up a loop in chain between vertical bars.

To Decrease Afghan Stitch: To decrease one stitch, insert hook under 2 vertical bars and draw up one loop.

Cross-Stitch over Afghan: Because afghan stitch forms almost perfect squares, when an article is completed it is often embroidered with cross-stitch. Diagram 48.

Diagram 48
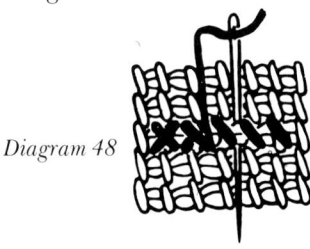

BASIC SHELL STITCH

This is one of the many varieties of shell stitch. Once you have learned this basic stitch, you'll find directions for the others easy to follow.

Make a foundation chain (multiple of 6 stitches plus 4) for practice piece.

1st row: Work 2 dc in 4th ch from hook (half shell), skip 2 ch, sc in next ch, * skip 2 ch, 5 dc in next ch (shell made), skip 2 ch, sc in next ch. Repeat from * across, ending with 3 dc in last ch (another half shell). Ch 1, turn.

2nd row: Sc in first dc, * skip 2 dc, shell (5 dc) in next sc, skip 2 dc, sc in center dc of next shell. Repeat from * across, ending with sc in top of half shell. Ch 3, turn.

3rd row: Work 2 dc in first sc, * sc in center dc of next shell, shell in next sc. Repeat from * across, ending with 3 dc in last sc. Ch 1, turn.

Repeat 2nd and 3rd rows for desired length. Diagram 49.

Diagram 49

KNOT STITCH

Make a foundation chain of 20 stitches (multiple of 5 sts) for practice piece.

1st row: Draw up a long loop (about ¾"), O (Diagram 50), draw this loop through long loop; insert hook between long loop and single strand (Diagram 51), O, and draw loop through, O (Diagram 52), and draw loop through 2 loops on hook (single knot st made). Draw up a long loop, O (Diagram 53), draw this loop through long loop; insert hook between long loop and single strand, O, and draw loop through, O, and draw loop through 2 loops on hook (double knot st made). Skip 4 ch, sc in next ch; * work double knot st, skip 4 ch; sc in next ch. Repeat from * across, ending sc in last ch. Make 1 double and 1 single knot st to turn.

2nd row: * Sc over 2 top strands of first loop of double knot st of previous row (to right of knot), sc over next 2 top strands of 2nd loop of double knot st (to left of same knot), make a double knot st. Repeat from * across, ending sc on each side of last double knot st. Make 1 double and 1 single knot st to turn.

Repeat 2nd row for desired length. Diagram 54.

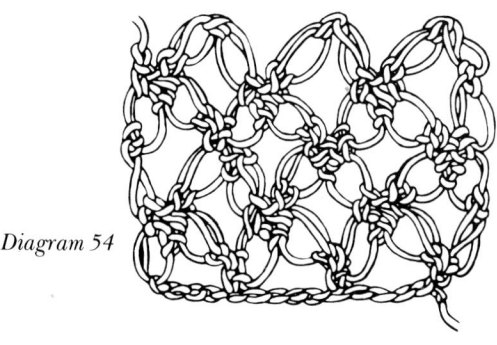
Diagram 54

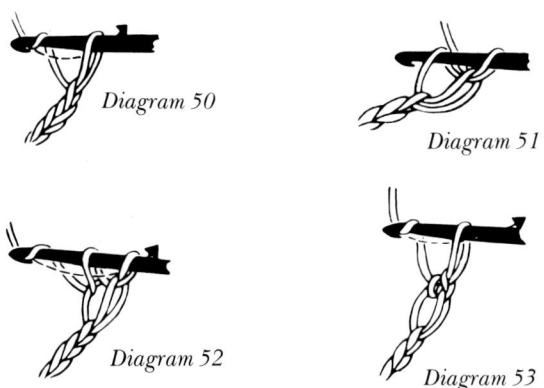
Diagram 50
Diagram 51
Diagram 52
Diagram 53

STAR STITCH

Make a foundation chain of 19 stitches (uneven number) for practice piece.

1st row: Draw up a loop in 2nd ch from hook, draw up a loop in next 3 ch (5 loops on hook), O, draw through all loops on hook (Diagram 55); ch 1 to form eye (one star st made), * draw

Diagram 55

up a loop in eye of star st just completed, in back of last loop of same star st and in next 2 ch (Diagram 56); O, draw through all 5 loops on

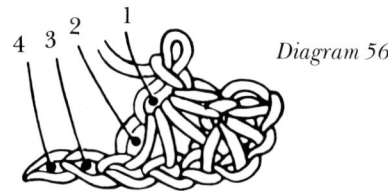
Diagram 56

hook, ch 1 for eye (another star st made). Repeat from * across. Turn.

2nd row: Work 2 sc in eye of each star st across

to last star st, sc in eye of last star st, sc in first ch of foundation chain. Ch 3, turn.

3rd row: Draw up a loop in 2nd and 3rd ch from hook and in first and 2nd sc, O, draw through all 5 loops on hook, ch 1 for eye, * draw up a loop in eye of last st, in back loop of same st and in next 2 sc; O, draw through all 5 loops on hook, ch 1 for eye. Repeat from * across. Turn.

4th row: Work 2 sc in eye of each star st across to last star st, sc in eye of last star st, sc in first ch of turning chain. Ch 3, turn.

Repeat 3rd and 4th rows for desired length.

POPCORN STITCH

Make a foundation chain of 16 stitches for practice piece.

1st row: Sc in 2nd ch from hook and in each remaining ch across (15 sc on row). Ch 3, turn.

2nd row: Skip first sc, work popcorn as follows: * Work 5 dc all in next sc, remove hook from loop, insert hook in top of first dc of this 5-dc group plus the dropped loop (Diagram

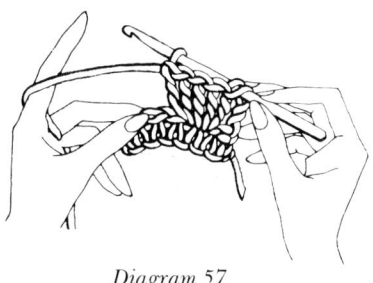

Diagram 57

57). Draw dropped loop through, ch 1 to fasten; popcorn made; dc in each of next 3 sc. Repeat from * across to last 2 sc, work popcorn in next sc, dc in last sc. Ch 1, turn.

3rd row: Sc in first dc, * sc in ch-1 of popcorn, sc in each of next 3 dc between popcorns. Repeat from * across to last popcorn, sc in ch-1 of popcorn, sc in top st of turning ch. Be sure to have 15 sc at end of row. Ch 3, turn.

4th row: Skip first sc, dc in each of next 2 sc, * popcorn in next sc, dc in each of next 3 sc. Repeat from * across. Ch 1, turn.

5th row: Sc in each dc and each popcorn across, working last sc in turning ch (15 sc). Ch 3, turn. Repeat 2nd through 5th rows for pattern.

Finishing Your Work

FASTENING ENDS

After you have completed an article, thread each loose end of thread or yarn in a needle and darn in through a solid part of the crochet to fasten it securely. Cut off remaining thread close to the work. Be sure to leave starting ends long enough to be fastened off.

LAUNDERING

If your work has become soiled, wash it by hand before blocking. Launder cotton-thread work in thick suds of a mild soap and lukewarm water; wash woolens with cold-water soap or mild soap and lukewarm water. Squeeze but do not wring the article. Rinse in lukewarm water several times until soap is thoroughly removed. Roll in a bath towel to absorb some of the moisture.

BLOCKING

This is the process of steaming or pressing and shaping a garment or article before sewing it together.

If an article is made up of several pieces, block them before sewing together. In the case of a garment, two similar pieces, such as back and front or both sleeves, should be blocked together before sewing seams.

First, lay piece to be blocked face down, or if two similar pieces, with right sides facing each other, on a padded board. Insert *rustproof* (important) pins about ¼" apart at outer edges of pieces, adjusting the pieces to desired proportions (blocking measurements) by giving a tuck here and there. Ribbed portions should be stretched in direction of rib so ribs lie close together to give the greatest elasticity.

Place a damp cloth over the pieces. On smooth surfaces, such as single crochet, press hot iron very gently on damp cloth, and do it quickly enough not to dry out the pressing cloth. Remove cloth and let pieces dry thoroughly before unpinning them.

Pieces worked in any raised pattern or fluffy yarn should of course never be pressed, but steamed. Pin pieces out as before. Hold steam iron as close as possible above work without touching it. Move it around above entire piece. Unpin when dry.

Sometimes it is convenient not to have to use an iron at all, and often it just isn't necessary. Pin out pieces, and with a spray bottle or plant mister, dampen them well. Again, let them dry well before you unpin them. And that's all you'll have to do.

SEWING SEAMS

Seams should be sewn so that they are as nearly invisible as possible.

Pin together edges to be sewn, being careful to match pattern rows, stitch rows, or stripes. Use the yarn with which the item was made unless it is very bulky or directions specify otherwise and use a blunt-tipped large-eyed tapestry needle. Sometimes it is possible to split yarn (e.g., knitting worsted consists of 4 strands of yarn that are twisted together—that's what 4-ply means). Untwist the strands and use 2 strands together to sew with.

To begin sewing, do not knot thread but take several over and over stitches, darning them, if possible, through a solid part of the crochet. Sew straight even edges with a whipped stitch, placing it at edges of the work. Sew slanting or uneven edges, caused by increasing or decreasing, with a backstitch, placing it just inside edges of work. On woolen articles leave stitches loose enough to match elasticity of garment.

When sewing is completed, press seams on the wrong side and give article a light final blocking.

For Women

Halters, Vests and Small Tops

Short-Story Tunic

Sunshine and fluffy clouds decorate the front. The dark night is pictured on the back, complete with moonshine and stars. Single crochet worked in knitting worsted, with a touch of angora.

SIZES: 6–8 [10–12]. Vest measures approximately 14½" [15½"] across front from underarm to underarm, 20" [20½"] from shoulder to lower edge. Measurements given while working front and back do not include side panels. Panels are worked later and will complete measurements for finished garment.

MATERIALS: Knitting worsted, 2 ounces each light green (color A), dark green (B), light blue (C), royal blue (D), yellow (E), 1 ounce each red (F), burgundy (G), small amounts each magenta (H), brown (I), tan (J), purple (K), white angora (L), and pale yellow sport yarn (M); aluminum crochet hook size H (or Canadian hook No. 8) *or the size that will give you the correct gauge.*

GAUGE: 4 sc = 1"; 14 rows = 3".

For Women

To Change Colors: see page 20.

DAY (FRONT OF TUNIC): Starting at lower edge with A, ch 17; attach E and ch 9; attach another ball A and ch 13 (39 sts; chain should measure about 10½"). **1st row (right side):** With A sc in 2nd ch from hook and in each of next 11 ch, changing to E on last sc, with E sc in next 9 ch, changing to A on last sc, with A sc in next 17 ch (38 sc, to measure 10"); ch 1, turn. **2nd row:** With A sc in next 18 sc, with E sc in next 8 sc, with A sc in next 12 sc; ch 1, turn.

Starting with 3rd row of chart, follow chart until it has been completed, reading from right to left on right-side rows and from left to right on wrong-side rows. After last row of chart has been completed, continue with C until piece measures 16" [16½"] from beg, or 4" less than desired length to shoulders. Do not break off but ch 1, turn.

Shoulder Straps: Continuing on bodice, work straps as follows: **First Strap:** With C, sc in next 9 sc; ch 1, turn. Working only on these 9 sc, continue in rows of sc until strap measures 4" [4½"] or desired length. Break off. **Second Strap:** Skip center 20 sc on front neck edge; attach C by working a sc in next st, then sc in next 8 sc; ch 1, turn. Complete as for first strap. Break off.

NIGHT (BACK OF TUNIC): Starting at lower edge with B, ch 17; attach J and ch 9; attach another ball B and ch 13 (39 sts; chain should measure about 10½"). Working in sc as for front and starting with first row of Night chart, follow chart until it has been completed, then continue with D until piece measures same as Day.

Shoulder Straps: With D, work as for Day shoulder straps.

SIDE PANELS (make 2): Starting at side edge with E, crochet a chain to measure 11½" [12½"]. **1st row:** Sc in 2nd ch from hook and in each ch across to measure 11" [12"]; ch 1, turn. **2nd row:** Sc in each sc across; ch 1, turn. Repeat 2nd row until piece measures 4½" [5½"]. Break off.

FINISHING: With tapestry needle and E, sew side panels between Night and Day, matching ends of panels with lower edge of front and back. With C, seam straps.

Edging: With matching colors, work 1 row sc around armholes and neck.

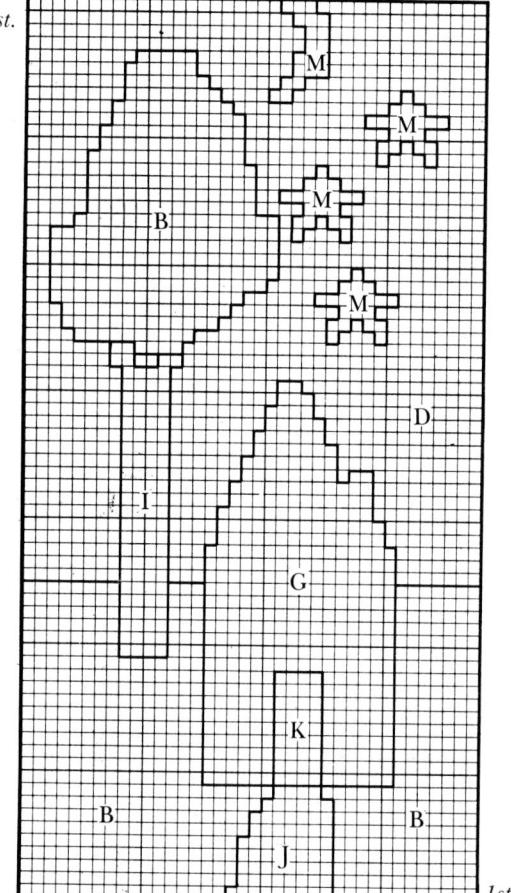

Each square = 1 st.

Night — 1st row

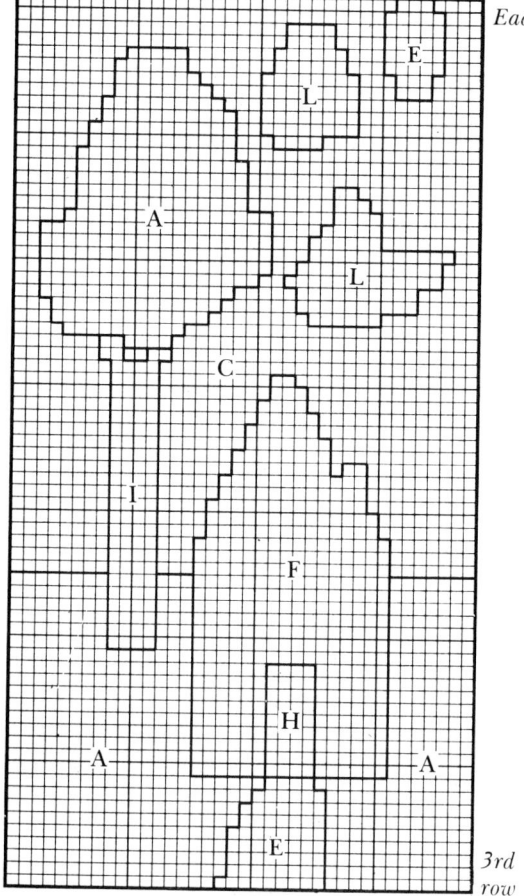

Each square = 1 st.

Day — 3rd row

Mosaic Vest

Inspired by the rich colors and design motifs of North African tapestries. Granny squares joined in diamond shape with single crochet.

SIZES: 8–10 [12–14]. Vest measures 16" [18"] across back at underarms, 21" from top of shoulder to lower edge.

MATERIALS: Bucilla Perlette (Dupont Orlon acrylic), 3 (1¾-ounce) balls purple No. 20 (color P), 2 balls each strawberry (pink) No. 16 (S), spearmint (green) No. 9 (G), and bright yellow No. 11 (Y); aluminum crochet hook size F (or Canadian hook No. 10) *or the size that will give you the correct gauge.*

GAUGE: 9 sc = 2"; 5 rows = 1".

To Change Colors: see page 20.

FRONT: Front of vest is worked in separate motifs which are sewn together, then small sections are added later. Back of vest is crocheted in one piece, then sewn to adjacent motifs at sides. Mark each completed motif with sticker or tag; this will be helpful in joining.

Center Front Motif: Starting at center with G, ch 4; join with sl st to form ring. **1st rnd:** Work 5 sc in ring; join with sl st in first sc. **2nd rnd:** Ch 4, dc in same place as sl st, (ch 1, dc in next sc, ch 1, dc in same sc) 4 times; ch 1, sl st in 3rd ch of ch-4 (10 dc, counting starting ch as 1 dc). Break off G. **3rd rnd:** With P, sl st in any dc on 2nd rnd, ch 4, dc in same place as sl st, ch 1, * dc in next dc, ch 1, dc in same dc, ch 1. Repeat from * around; sl st in 3rd ch of ch-4 (20 dc, counting starting ch as 1 dc). Drop P, attach S and ch 1. **4th rnd:** Work 2 sc in top of ch-4 of last rnd and in each dc around, sl st in ch-1. Break off S, pick up P, ch 1. **5th rnd:** With P, * working over S sts of last rnd, insert hook into next ch-1 sp of previous rnd and work 1 sc, ch 1. Repeat from * around; join with sl st to first sc. Piece should measure 2⅛" across. Break off P, attach Y and ch 1. **6th rnd:** Sc in first ch-1 sp, (ch 11, skip next 4 ch-1 sps, sc in next ch-1 sp) 3 times; ch 11, skip next 4 ch-1 sps; join with sl st in ch-1. **7th rnd:** Ch 1, * sc in next sc, in next ch-11 lp work 1 dc and 2 tr, then ch 2 and sl st in top of last tr, work 3 tr in same lp, ch 4 and sc in 4th ch from hook, work 3 tr in same lp, ch 2, sl st in top of last tr, work 2 tr and 1 dc in same lp. Repeat from * around; join in first ch-1. Break off Y, attach P and sl st in same ch-1. **8th rnd:** Ch 5, * sc in next ch-2 lp, ch 3, skip next 3 tr, 3 dc in sp before next ch-4 lp, sc in ch-4 lp, 3 dc in same sp after ch-4 lp, ch 3, sc in next ch-2 lp, ch 3, h dc in next sc, ch 3. Repeat from * 3 times more, ending last repeat with sl st in 2nd ch of starting ch-5, omitting h dc and last ch-3. **9th rnd:**

Ch 1, * 3 sc in next ch-3 sp, sc in next sc, 3 sc in next ch-3 sp, sc in each of next 3 dc, sc in next sc (mark this sc for corner), sc in each of next 3 dc, 3 sc in next ch-3 sp, sc in next sc, 3 sc in next ch-3 sp, sc in next h dc. Repeat from * 3 times more, ending last repeat with sl st in starting ch-1 (instead of sc in next h dc). Motif should measure about 5" across. Break off P, attach Y. **10th rnd:** Ch 1, * sc in each sc to within corner, work 5 dc in corner (mark center dc for corner). Repeat from * 3 times more; sc in each remaining sc, ending with sl st in starting ch-1. Break off Y, attach P. **11th rnd:** Ch 1, * sc in each st to within corner, work sc, ch 1 and sc in corner. Repeat from * 3 times more; sc in each remaining st, ending with sl st in ch-1. Break off P, attach G. **12th rnd:** With G, * sc in each sc to within next ch-1 sp, work sc, ch 1 and sc in ch-1 sp. Repeat from * 3 times more; sc in each remaining sc. Break off G, attach P, sl st in starting ch-1. **13th through 18th rnds:** Repeat 12th rnd, working 1 rnd each in P, S, P, Y, P, and G. Break off. Finished motif measures about 9" across.

Center Front Fill-In Cluster: With Y, form a lp on hook. Working along 5 sts of any corner of center front motif (2 sc, ch 1 and 2 sc) with right side facing you, work cluster as follows: Leaving last lp of each st on hook, tr in each of next 5 sts, y o hook and draw through all 6 lps on hook. Break off. Use this cluster at the top edge of vest when joining motifs later.

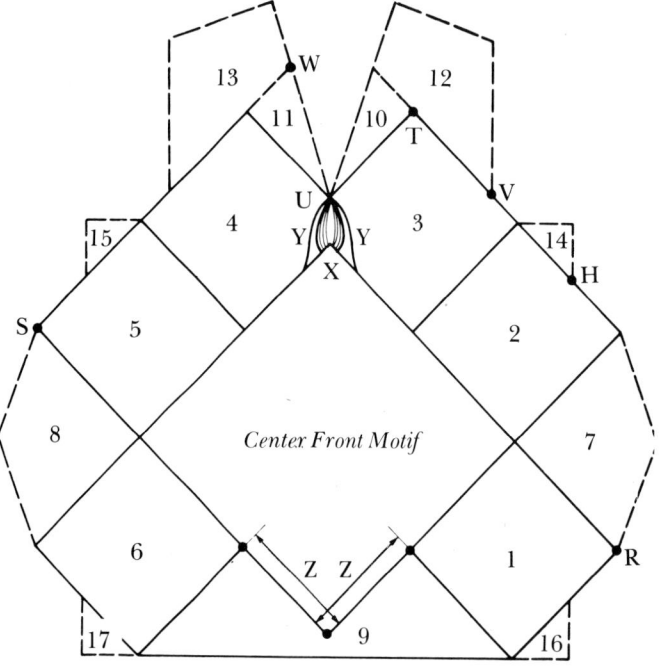

Mosaic Vest

Outer Front Motif (make 6): Starting at center with G, ch 5; join with sl st to form ring. **1st rnd:** (Ch 6, sc in 3rd ch from hook, h dc in each of next 2 ch, sc in next ch, sl st in ring) 4 times (4 petals made). Break off. **2nd rnd:** Attach P with sl st to ch-2 sp at tip of any petal, ch 1 and sc in same place, ch 3; y o hook, insert hook in ring between petals and draw lp through up to ½", (y o hook and draw through 2 lps on hook) twice (long dc made); work another long dc in same place, * ch 3, sc in sp at tip of next petal, ch 3, work 2 long dc in ring. Repeat from * twice more; ch 3, sl st in starting ch-1. **3rd rnd:** Ch 1, * work sc, ch 1 and sc in next sc, 3 sc in next ch-3 sp, sc in each of next 2 long dc, 3 sc in next ch-3 sp. Repeat from * 3 times more; join with sl st to ch-1. Break off P, attach S. **4th rnd:** Ch 1, sc in each sc around, working sc, ch 1 and sc in each of the 4 ch-1 corner sps; join as before. Break off S, attach P and sl st in starting ch-1. **5th through 11th rnds:** Repeat 4th rnd, working 1 rnd each in P, Y, P, G, P, S, and P. Break off. Finished motif should measure about 5" across.

Following diagram, sew the 6 motifs (Nos. 1 through 6) to center motif, leaving 1 additional sc free along each side of cluster at top of center front motif (X on diagram), 6 sc free along each center front edge of motifs No. 3 and No. 4 (Y), and 14 sts free along each side of lower corner of center front motif (Z). With P, sew tip of cluster and corresponding corners of motifs No. 3 and No. 4 together.

Left Side Motif: (No. 7 on diagram) Starting at outer corner of motif No. 1 at R, form a lp on hook with Y. **1st row:** Sc in first sc following corner ch-1 and in each sc to within 1 sc of joined corner (25 sc); dec 1 sc over last sc on same motif and first sc on next motif as follows: (Insert hook in next sc, y o hook and draw lp through) twice; y o hook and draw through all 3 lps on hook (1 sc dec); sc in each sc to within next corner ch-1 (51 sc). Break off Y, attach P; ch 1, turn. **2nd row:** Sc in each sc to within 2 sc of decreased sc (center sc), dec 1 sc, sc in next sc, dec 1 sc, sc in each sc across (49 sc). Break off P, attach G; ch 1, turn. **3rd row:** Sc in each sc to within 1 st of center st; (insert hook in next sc and pull lp through) 3 times; y o hook and draw through all 4 lps on hook (2 sc dec), sc in each sc across. Break off G; attach

P; ch 1, turn. **4th row:** Dec 1 sc over first 2 sc, sc in each sc to within 1 st of center st; (insert hook in next sc and pull lp through) 3 times; y o hook and draw through all 4 lps on hook (2 sc dec), sc in each sc to within last 2 sc, dec 1 sc (43 sc). Break off P, attach S; ch 1, turn. Repeat 2nd through 4th rows 5 times more, continuing in stripe pattern of 1 row each of S, P, Y, P, G, and P as already established (3 sc remain). Break off.

Right Side Motif: (8) Starting at outer corner of motif No. 5 (S on diagram), work as for left side motif.

Lower Front Fill-In: (9) Starting at lower edge with Y, ch 54 to measure about 12". **1st row:** Sc in 2nd ch from hook and in each ch across (53 sc). Break off Y, attach P; ch 1, turn. Working in stripe pattern of 1 row each of P, G, P, S, P, and Y, dec 1 sc at beg and end of every row 6 times (41sc); ch 1, turn. **First point: 1st row:** Dec 1 sc, sc over next 18 sc (19 sc); ch 1, turn. Continuing in stripe pattern as established, dec 1 sc at beg and end of every row 8 times (3 sc remain). Break off. **Second point:** Skip center st on last full row worked. With P, form a lp on hook and sc in each of next 18 sc, dec 1 sc (19 sc); ch 1, turn. Complete as for first point.

With right side facing you and using P, work 1 row of sc along diagonal sides of fill-in, working 3 sc at tip of each point. Sew fill-in motif in place.

Left Front Neck Fill-In: (10) With right side facing you, starting at upper corner of motif No. 3 (T on diagram) with Y, form lp on hook. **1st row:** Sc in each sc to next corner (26 sc). Break off Y, turn. **2nd row:** Skip first 2 sts, form lp on hook with P and sc in each sc across. Break off P, attach G; ch 1, turn. **3rd row:** Sc in each sc to within last 2 sc. Break off G, turn. Continue to dec 2 sts at neck edge every row, working in stripe pattern of 1 row each of P, S, P, Y, P and G until 2 sts remain. Break off.

Right Front Neck Fill-In: (11) With right side facing you, starting at center front corner of motif No. 4 (U on diagram), work to correspond to left front neck fill-in (dec 2 sts at neck edge in same manner).

Left Front Shoulder Fill-In: (12) With right side facing, skip 11 sc along upper side edge of motif No. 3. With Y, form lp on hook. **1st row:** Sc in next sc (V on diagram) and in each sc to next corner ch-1 (15 sc), then work 14 sc along free edge of left front neck fill-in (29 sc). Break off Y, attach P; ch 1, turn. **2nd row (neck edge):** 2 sc in first sc, sc in each sc across to within last 3 sc (armhole edge). Break off P, attach G; ch 1, turn. **3rd row:** Sc in each sc across. Break off G, attach P; ch 1, turn. Continuing in stripe pattern of 1 row each of P, S, P, Y, P, and Y, repeat 2nd and 3rd rows 5 times more (17 sts remain).

Shoulder Shaping: At neck edge sl st over first 5 sts, sc in each sc across; ch 1, turn.

Following row: Sc in each sc to within last 5 sc. Break off.

Right Front Shoulder Fill-In: (13) With right side facing you, using Y, form lp on hook, and starting at upper corner of right front neck fill-in (W on diagram), work to correspond to left front shoulder fill-in (inc at neck edge and dec at armhole edge).

Left Underarm Fill-In: (14) With right side facing you, using Y, form lp on hook. **1st row:** Sc in 10th sc from upper corner along side edge of motif No. 2 (H on diagram), sc in each of next 9 sc. Break off Y, attach P; ch 1, turn. Continuing in stripe pattern of 1 row each of P, G, P, and S, dec 1 sc at beg and end of every row 4 times. Break off.

Right Underarm Fill-In: (15) Work to correspond to left underarm fill-in.

Work 2 more fill-ins (16 and 17) in same manner along outer lower sides of lower corners of motifs No. 1 and No. 6.

BACK: Work in stripe pattern of 1 row each of Y, P, G, P, S, and P throughout. Starting at lower edge with Y, ch 74 [84] to measure about 16" [18"]. **1st row:** Sc in 2nd ch from hook and in each ch across (73 [83] sc). Break off Y, attach P; ch 1, turn. Work even on 73 [83] sc for 8 rows more. Dec 1 sc at beg and end of next row, then every other row 14 times more (43 [53] sc). Inc 1 st at beg and end of next row, then every other row 14 times more, omitting ch-1 at end of last row (73 [83] sc). Work even, if necessary, until piece is about 13" from beg.

To Shape Armholes: 1st row: Sl st over first 4 [5] sc, sc in each sc to within last 4 [5] sc; turn. **2nd row:** Sl st over first 2 sc, sc in each sc to within last 2 sc; turn. Repeat 2nd row 2 [3] times more. Work even on 53 [57] sc until armholes measure 7" from beg, omitting ch-1 at end of last row.

To Shape Shoulders: 1st row: Sl st over first 4 sc, sc in each sc to within last 4 sc; turn. Repeat first row twice more. Break off.

With right side facing you, using P, work 1 row sc evenly spaced along side edges of back.

FINISHING: Sew shoulder and side seams. With right side facing you, using P, work 1 rnd sc around neck and lower edge and 2 rnds sc around each armhole.

Pink Popcorn Tank Top

In flattering shades of pink, peach, red, and lavender, finished in single crochet edgings.

SIZES: Small size stretches to fit 30" to 32" bust [medium size stretches to fit 34" to 36"]. Garment measures about 14½" [15½"] across, unstretched, and 12½" long, not including shoulder straps. Length is adjustable.

MATERIALS: D.M.C. Pearl Cotton No. 5, 9 (53-yard) balls red No. 350 (color A), 8 balls purple No. 553 (B), 4 balls each pink No. 893 (C) and peach No. 353 (D); aluminum crochet hook size C (or Canadian hook No. 13) *or the size that will give you the correct gauge.*

GAUGE: 2 popcorns = 1"; 2 stripes (4 rows of popcorns) = 1¼".

BACK: Starting at lower edge with B, ch 114 [122] to measure about 16" [17"]. **1st row:** Sc in 2nd ch from hook and in each ch across (113 [121] sc); ch 1, turn. **2nd row (right side):** Sc in first sc, ch 1, work 4 dc in next sc, drop lp from hook, insert hook from front to back in first dc and draw dropped lp through (popcorn will form on right side of work); * ch 1, skip next sc, sc in next sc, ch 1, skip next sc, work popcorn in next sc. Repeat from * across to within last 3 sc, ch 1, skip next sc, sc in each of last 2 sc (28 [30] popcorns); ch 1, turn. **3rd row:** Sc in each of first 2 sc, * ch 1, sc in next popcorn, ch 1, sc in next sc. Repeat from * across; ch 1, turn. **4th row:** Sc in first sc, * ch 1, sc in next sc (over popcorn 2 rows below), ch 1, work popcorn in next sc. Repeat from * across, ch 1, sc in last sc; ch 1, turn. **5th row:** Sc in first sc, * ch 1, sc in next popcorn, ch 1, sc in next sc. Repeat from * across, ending ch 1, insert hook in last sc and draw up lp; break off B, attach color A and draw through both lps on hook and tighten B end (always change colors in this manner); ch 1, turn. **6th row:** Sc in first sc, * ch 1, popcorn in next sc, ch 1, sc in next sc (over popcorn). Repeat from * across, sc in last sc; ch 1, turn.

Working 4 rows of a color in each stripe, repeat 3rd through 6th rows for pattern and work in color stripes as follows: (A, C, D, A, B, A, B) twice; A, C, D, A, B. Piece should measure about 12½" from beg. For a longer tank top, continue in pattern for desired length. Break off.

FRONT: Work as for back.

STRAPS (make 2): With B, ch 10. **1st row:** Repeat first pattern row (9 sc); ch 1, turn. **2nd row:** Sc in first sc, ch 1, popcorn in next sc, ch 1, skip next sc, sc in next sc, ch 1, skip next sc, popcorn in next sc, ch 1, skip next sc, sc in each of last 2 sc (2 popcorns); ch 1, turn. **3rd row:** Repeat 3rd pattern row. **4th row:** Repeat 4th pattern row. **5th row:** Repeat 5th pattern row, changing to D. **6th row:** Repeat 6th pattern row. Continue in established pattern, finishing D stripe. Continue in stripes of (C, B, A, B, A, D) twice; C, B, A, B. For longer straps, continue in pattern for desired length. Break off.

FINISHING: Sew side seams. Slip on top and mark position of straps. Remove top and sew straps in place.

With right side facing you, with B, work 1 row sc evenly across front and back neck, along straps and around armholes.

Diagonal Pull-On Top

This sweater, of single and double crochet stripes, leaves one shoulder bare. Lovely for evening with a long skirt.

SIZES: Small (6–8) [medium (10–12)]. Sweater measures 14″ [15″] across back at underarms for snug fit.

MATERIALS: Lily Sugar-'n'-Cream cotton yarn, 3 [4] (125-yard) balls cream No. 3 (color A), 1 ball each medium green No. 61 (B), orange No. 20 (C), and dark rose No. 44 (D); aluminum crochet hook size G (or Canadian hook No. 9) *or the size that will give you the correct gauge.*

GAUGE: 7 sc = 2″; 8 average sc and dc rows = 3″.

Note: Work front and back in same color sequence. Be sure that colors B, C, and D rows are sc rows. To change colors, at end of row always break off old color and attach new before working the turning chain.

BACK: Starting at lower edge with A, ch 56 [60] to measure about 16″ [17″]. **1st row (wrong side):** Sc in 2nd ch from hook and in each ch to within last 2 ch, dec 1 sc as follows: Draw up lp in each of next 2 sts, y o hook and draw through all 3 lps on hook (54 [58] sc); ch 3, turn. **2nd row (right side):** Skip first sc, dc in each sc across (54 [58] dc, counting turning ch as 1 dc); ch 1, turn. **3rd row:** Work 2 sc in first dc, sc in each dc to within last 2 sts, dec 1 sc (in last dc and in top of ch-3); ch 3, turn. **4th row:** Skip first sc, dc in each sc across; break off A, attach B, ch 1, turn. **5th row:** With B, repeat 3rd row; break off B, attach A, ch 3, turn.

Working in the following color sequence, repeat 2nd through 5th rows 3 times more: 3 rows A, 1 C, 3 A, 1 D, 3 A, 1 B, ending last row with ch-1, turn.

The next 12 rows (including armhole shaping) are all sc rows. Work them in the following color sequence: (1 row C, 1 D, 1 B) 4 times. **18th row:** Sc in each sc across; ch 1, turn. **19th row:** Work 2 sc in first sc, sc in each sc to within last 2 sts, dec 1 sc; ch 1, turn. **20th row:** Repeat 18th row (54 [58] sc). Piece should measure about 7" from beg.

To Shape Armhole: Mark beg of next row for arm edge. **21st row:** Dec 1 sc, sc in each sc to within last 2 sc, dec 1 sc; ch 1, turn. **22nd row (right side):** Sc in each sc to within last sc, dec 1 sc; ch 1, turn. **23rd row:** Dec 1 sc, sc in each sc across; ch 1, turn. **24th row:** Repeat 21st row. **25th row:** Repeat 23rd row. **26th row:** Repeat 22nd row. Repeat 21st through 23rd rows once more (42 [46] sc); with A, ch 3, turn.

The next 14 rows are alternating dc and sc rows as before. Work them in the following color sequence: 3 rows A, 1 D, 3 A, 1 C, 3 A, 1 B, and 2 A. **30th row:** Skip first sc, dc in each sc across; ch 18 for shoulder, turn. **31st row:** Dec 1 sc in 2nd and 3rd ch from hook, sc in each of next 15 ch, sc in each dc to within last 2 sts, dec 1 sc (57 [61] sc); ch 3, turn. **32nd row:** Skip first sc, dc in each dc across; ch 1, turn. **33rd row:** Dec 1 sc, sc in each dc to within last 2 sts, dec 1 sc; ch 3, turn. Repeat last 2 rows 5 times more, omitting ch-3 at end of last row (45 [49] sc). Break off.

FRONT: Starting at lower edge with A, ch 56 [60] to measure about 16" [17"]. **1st row (wrong side):** Dec 1 sc in 2nd and 3rd ch from hook, sc in each remaining ch across (54 [58] sc); ch 3, turn. **2nd row:** Skip first sc, dc in each sc across (54 [58] dc, counting turning ch as 1 dc); ch 1, turn. **3rd row:** Dec 1 sc, sc in each dc to within turning ch, work 2 sc in top of turning ch-3; ch 3, turn.

Work entire front in same color sequence as for back. Repeat 2nd and 3rd rows 7 times more, ending last row with ch-1 instead of ch-3. **18th row:** Sc in each sc across; ch 1, turn. **19th row:** Dec 1 sc, sc in each sc to within last sc, work 2 sc in last sc; ch 1, turn. **20th row:** Repeat 18th row (54 [58] sc).

To Shape Armhole: 21st row: Dec 1 sc, sc in each sc to within last 2 sc, dec 1 sc; ch 1, turn. **22nd row:** Dec 1 sc, sc in each remaining sc across; ch 1, turn. **23rd row:** Sc in each sc to within last 2 sc, dec 1 sc; ch 1, turn. **24th row:** Repeat 21st row. **25th row:** Repeat 23rd row. **26th row:** Repeat 22nd row. Repeat 21st through 23rd rows once more (42 [46] sc); ch 3, turn. **30th row:** Skip first sc, dc in each sc across; ch 1, turn. With another ball of A, ch 17, sl st to top of turning ch-3 at beg of 30th row. Break off. **31st row:** Dec 1 sc in each dc across, sc in each of next 15 ch, dec 1 sc in last 2 ch (57 [61] sc); ch 3, turn. **32nd row:** Skip first sc, dc in each sc across; ch 1, turn. **33rd row:** Dec 1 sc, sc in each dc to within last 2 sts, dec 1 sc; ch 3, turn. Repeat last 2 rows 5 times more, omitting ch-3 at end of last row (45 [49] sc). Break off.

FINISHING: Sew side and shoulder seams, matching stripes.

Rainbow Halter

Tied at the neck and at back, this sunny halter top goes equally well with shorts or skirts. The ribbed midriff band is crocheted first; then the rainbow pattern is worked over it.

SIZE: One size fits 6 through 10.
MATERIALS: Kentucky All Purpose (rayon) yarn, 2 (100-yard) skeins royal blue No. 719 (color B), 1 skein each emerald green No. 723 (E), gold No. 711 (G), orange No. 708 (O), red No. 733 (R), and purple No. 714 (P); aluminum crochet hook size E (or Canadian hook No. 11) *or the size that will give you the correct gauge.*
GAUGE: 9 dc = 2"; 4 dc rows = 1¾".
MIDRIFF BAND: Starting at one end of tie with B, ch 81 to measure about 18". **1st row:** Sc

in 2nd ch from hook and in each ch across to within last ch, work 3 sc in last ch; ch 1, turn. (**Note:** From now on work in back lp only of each st on band.) **2nd row:** Work 2 sc in first sc, sc in next sc, 2 sc in last sc (5 sc); ch 1, turn. **3rd row:** Work 2 sc in first sc, sc in each sc to within last sc, 2 sc in last sc (7 sc); ch 1, turn. **4th row:** Repeat 3rd row (9 sc). **5th row:** Sc in each sc across (9 sc); ch 1, turn. Repeat 5th row until band measures 20" from base of tie. **Next row:** Draw up lp in each of next 2 sc, y o and draw through all 3 lps on hook (1 sc dec), sc in each sc to within last 2 sc, dec 1 sc; ch 1, turn. Repeat last row twice more (3 sc).

Following row: Draw up lp in each of next 3 sc, y o and draw through all 4 lps on hook; do not break off. Ch 81 to measure about 18" for other tie. Sc in 2nd ch from hook and in each ch across, sl st in last st of band. Break off.

HALTER: Mark center of upper edge of band and work along this edge as follows: Attach E with sl st to edge of band ¼" to right of marker, ch 6, join with sl st in band ¼" to left of marker; ch 3, skip ⅜" of band edge, sl st in edge; turn. **1st row:** Work 7 dc in ch-6 lp (8 dc, counting turning ch as 1 dc); sl st in edge, ch 3, skip ⅜" of edge, sl st in edge; turn. **2nd row:** Dc in first dc, 2 dc in each of next 7 dc (16 dc); join to edge, ch 3, skip ⅜", join to edge; turn. **3rd row:** Skip first dc, 2 dc in next dc, * dc in next dc, 2 dc in next dc. Repeat from * 6 times more (24 dc); join. Break off E; attach G, ch 3, join to edge; turn. **4th row:** Skip first dc, dc in next dc, 2 dc in next dc, * dc in each of next 2 dc, 2 dc in next dc. Repeat from * 6 times more (32 dc); join, ch 3, join to edge; turn. Last 4 rows should measure 1¾" straight up from center of starting ch-6 lp.

Continuing in striped pattern and joining as before, work 2 more rows G, 3 rows each O and R, and 2 rows P, increasing 6 dc as evenly spaced as possible on each row (92 dc). Work 1 row even with P and 1 with B; then with B, dec 8 dc, evenly spaced, on next row (to dec 1 dc, y o, insert hook in next st and draw up lp, y o and draw through 2 lps on hook, y o, insert hook in following st and draw up lp, y o and draw through 2 lps on hook, y o and draw through all 3 lps on hook). Break off.

NECK TIES: Place 2 pins on edge of halter to mark position of ties. With B, ch 81. Sc in 2nd ch from hook and in each ch across; sl st in edge of halter at one of the pins. Break off. Make and attach other tie.

Scoop Halter

Halter top slips over your head, ties in back. An ingenious arrangement of single and double crochet stitches.

SIZE: 17" wide, 14½" long.
MATERIALS: Kentucky All Purpose Yarn. 1 (100-yard) skein each orchid No. 713 (color A), dusty rose No. 729 (B), and antique gold No. 712 (C); aluminum crochet hook size F (or Canadian hook No. 10) *or the size that will give you the correct gauge.*
GAUGE: 4 sts (dc or sc) = 1".

LEFT FRONT: Starting at lower edge

(above waistband) with B, ch 31 loosely to measure about 7½". **1st row (right side):** Dc in 4th ch from hook and in each ch across (29 dc, counting turning ch as 1 dc); ch 1, turn. **2nd row (wrong side):** Skip first dc, work a post dc over next dc in following manner: y o hook, insert hook under post of next dc (dc is over the hook), y o hook, draw lp back under post (3 lps on hook), (y o hook, draw through 2 lps) twice (a large ridge is formed on right side of work); work a post dc over each dc across, dc in turning ch; ch 3, turn. **3rd row:** Skip first dc, dc in each dc across, dc in turning ch. Break off B, attach C; ch 3, turn. **4th row:** With C, repeat 2nd row, ending ch-1 instead of ch-3 to turn. **5th row (dec row):** Working in back lps only, draw up a lp in each of next 2 sts, y o hook and draw through 3 lps on hook (1 sc dec), sc in each dc to within last 2 sts, dec 1 sc (27 sc). Break off C, attach A; ch 4, turn. **6th row:** Skip first 2 sc, dc in next sc, * ch 1, skip next sc, dc in next sc. Repeat from * across; ch 1, turn. **7th row:** Sc in first dc, * sc in next sp, sc in next dc. Repeat from * across, ending with sc in first 2 sts of turning ch (27 sc); ch 3, turn. **8th row (dec row):** Working in front lps only, skip first sc, (y o hook, insert hook in next st, y o hook and draw through st, y o hook and draw through 2 lps on hook) twice; y o hook, draw through all 3 lps on hook (1 dc dec), dc in each sc to within last 2 sts, dec 1 dc (25 dc). Break off A, attach B; ch 1, turn. **9th row:** Working through back lps only, sc in each dc across, sc in turning ch; ch 1, turn. **10th row:** Working through front lps only, dec 1 sc, sc in each sc to within last 2 sts, dec 1 sc (23 sc); ch 3, turn. **11th row:** Skip first sc, dc in each sc across; ch 3, turn. **12th row:** Repeat 2nd row, ending ch-1 instead of ch-3; turn. **13th row:** Sc in each dc across, sc in turning ch; ch 1, turn. **14th row:** Working in front lps only, dec 1 sc, sc in each sc to within last 2 sc, dec 1 sc (21 sc); ch 4, turn. **15th row:** Repeat 6th row, omitting ch-1 to turn. Break off B, attach A; ch 1, turn. **16th row:** Sc in first dc, * sc in next ch-1 sp, sc in next dc. Repeat from * across, ending with sc in first 2 sts of turning ch (21 sc). Break off A, attach C; ch 1, turn. **17th row:** Dec 1 sc, sc in each sc to within last 2 sts, dec 1 sc (19 sc); ch 1, turn. **18th row:** Working in front lps only, dec 1 sc, sc in each sc to within last 2 sts, dec 1 sc (17 sc); ch 4, turn. **19th row:** Repeat 6th row. **20th row:** Repeat 16th row (17 sc). Break off C, attach A; ch 3, turn. **21st row:** Working in back lps only, skip first sc, dec 1 dc, dc in each sc to within last 2 sc, dec 1 dc (15 dc); ch 3, turn. **22nd row:** Repeat 2nd row, ending ch-1 instead of ch-3 to turn. **23rd row:** Dec 1 sc, sc to within last 2 sts, dec 1 sc (13 sc); ch 4, turn. **24th row:** Skip first 3 sc, dc in next sc, (ch 1, skip next sc, dc in next sc) 3 times; ch 1, skip next 2 sc, dc in last sc; ch 3, turn. **25th row:** Skip first dc and ch-1, (dc in next dc, dc in ch-1 sp) 3 times; skip ch-1, dc in turning ch (9 dc); ch 1, turn. **26th row:** Repeat 2nd row. **27th row:** Working in back lps only, skip first dc, dec 1 dc, dc to within last 2 dc, dec 1 dc (7 dc); ch 3, turn. **28th row:** Working in front lps only, repeat 27th row (5 dc). **29th row:** Skip first dc, dc in each dc across, dc in turning ch; ch 3, turn. Repeat last row twice more, omitting ch-3 on last row. Piece should measure 13½" from beg. Break off.

RIGHT FRONT: Work same as left front.
FINISHING: Sew last row of both pieces together for center back neck seam. Both long edges of sides are the same. Neck edging is

worked along one edge and back edging is worked along the other.

Neck Edging: Always work with right side facing you. With right side facing, attach C at center back neck seam. **1st rnd:** Sc evenly spaced along left neck edge to lower edge. Mark last sc with pin for center front, then join as follows to right side: Starting at lower edge continue to sc along right neck edge (from lower edge) to center back. **2nd rnd:** Working in back lps only, sc in each sc to within marked sc of center front; skip next 2 sc, sc in each sc around. Repeat 2nd rnd twice more; always skip 2 sc at center front join. Break off.

Back Edging: With right side facing you, attach B to lower left corner of back edge of left side. **1st row:** Sc evenly spaced across back edges of left side and right side, ending at lower edge of right side; ch 1, turn. **2nd row:** Working in front lps only, sc in each sc across; ch 1, turn. **3rd row:** Working in back lps only, sc in each sc across. Break off.

Waistband: With right side facing, attach A to lower corner of right front edging, sc evenly spaced along lower edge of right front, work 2 sc across neck edging, then sc evenly spaced along lower edge of left front and edging; ch 1, turn. Work 4 more rows sc, working in front lps on wrong-size rows and back lps on right-side rows. Break off.

Ties (make 2): With A, make a chain to measure about 13″. Sc in 2nd ch from hook and in each ch across. Break off. Sew one end of each tie to side edge of waistband.

Slip on over your head and tie ends in bow at back.

Short-Sleeved Sweaters

A Little-Bit-of-Everything Sweater

Worked in simple crochet and chain-one pattern, and embroidered with chain-stitch motifs. Appliqués, in double crochet, are sewn on afterwards. Worked with two strands of yarn throughout.

SIZES: Small (6–8) [medium (10–12)—large (14–16)]. Snug-fitting garment measures 15" [16"—17"] across bust from side seam to side seam.

MATERIALS: Bucilla Perlette (100% Orlon acrylic), 4 (1¾-ounce) balls rust No. 19, 3 balls burnt orange No. 10; Bucilla Melody (50% mohair, 50% acrylic), 1 (1-ounce) ball black No. 6; aluminum crochet hook size J (or English hook No. 6) *or the size that will give you the correct gauge;* aluminum crochet hook size H, for appliqué only; tapestry needle.

GAUGE: 1 sc, ch 1 and 1 sc = 1"; 2 rows = 1".

Note: Work with 2 strands of yarn held together throughout.

To Change Colors: Work in pattern to within last sc with old color, insert hook in last sc, draw up lp of old color (2 lps on hook); y o with new color and draw through both lps on hook to complete st. Do not break off old color but bring to back of work. Continue in pattern with new color.

BACK: Starting at lower edge with rust, ch 46 [50—54] to measure about 15″ [16″—17″]. **1st row (right side):** Sc in 2nd ch from hook, * ch 1, skip next ch, sc in next ch. Repeat from * across (45 [49—53] sts); ch 1, turn. **2nd row:** Sc in first sc, * ch 1, skip ch-1, sc in next sc. Repeat from * across; ch 1, turn.

Repeating 2nd row for pattern, work even until piece measures 10½″ from beg, or desired length to underarm. Break off. Turn work.

To Shape Armholes: 1st row (dec row): With orange, make lp on hook, work sc in 3rd [3rd—5th] sc on last row. Work in pattern across each of next 12 [14—14] sts, changing to rust on last sc. Drop orange; with rust continue to work in pattern across each of next 14 sts, changing to separate ball of orange on last sc. Drop rust; with orange continue to work in pattern across next 14 [16—16] sts (2 [2—4] sts dec at beg and end of row—41 [45—45] sts); ch 1, turn.

2nd row: Work even in pattern across row, matching colors of previous row; ch 1, turn. Work even in pattern as established across 41 [45—45] sts until armholes measure 6¾″ [7″—7¼″]. Break off.

FRONT: Work same as for back to underarm. Do not break off; ch 1, turn.

To Shape Armholes: 1st row (dec row): Sl st across 2 [2—4] sts, ch 1, continue across row in pattern to within last 2 [2—4] sts (41 [45—45] sts; ch 1, turn. Work even in pattern as established until armholes measure 2¾″ [3″—3¼″]. Break off. Turn work.

To Shape Neck: 1st row: With orange, make lp on hook, work sc in first sc, work in pattern across next 12 [14—14] sts. Do not work over remaining sts; ch 1, turn. Working on one side only, work even in pattern on 13 [15—15] sts until armhole measures same as back armhole. Break off.

For other side, skip 15 sts at center front; with orange work the 13 [15—15] sts of other side to correspond.

SLEEVES: Starting at lower edge with orange, ch 28 [30—32] to measure about 9½″ [10″—10½″]. Work even in pattern as for back on 27 [29—31] sts for 2 rows. **Next row (inc row):** Work 1 sc, ch 1 and 1 sc in first sc, * ch 1, skip next ch-1, work 1 sc, ch 1 and 1 sc in next sc. Repeat from * across (55 [59—63] sts); ch 1, turn. Work even in pattern for 3 rows.

To Shape Cap: 1st row: Sl st across first 4 sts (4 sts dec), ch 1, work in pattern across row to last 4 sts (47 [51—55] sts); ch 1, turn. **2nd row (dec row):** Sl st across first 2 sts, ch 1, work in pattern across remaining sts (45 [49—53] sts); ch 1, turn. Repeat dec row 12 [13—14] times more (21 [23—25] sts); ch 1, turn.

Next row (dec row): Sc in first sc, * skip next ch-1, sc in next sc. Repeat from * across (11 [12—13] sc); ch 1, turn. **Following row (dec row):** * Draw up a lp in each of next 2 sc, y o hook and draw through 3 lps on hook (dec made). Repeat from * across. Break off.

FINISHING: Sew shoulder, side, and sleeve seams. Sew sleeves in place.

Neck Edging: Make lp on hook with orange. With right side of work facing you, work sc in first orange st at corner of right front neck opening, * ch 1, skip ¼″ of edge and work sc in edge. Repeat from * along right front, back of neck, and left front, leaving center front sts unworked. Break off.

APPLIQUÉ MOTIF (make 2): Working with size H hook and using single strand of black Melody, ch 4. **1st row:** Work 9 dc in 4th ch from hook; join with sl st to top of ch-3 (10 dc, counting turning ch as 1 dc); ch 3, turn. **2nd row:** Dc in same place as turning ch, work 2 dc in each of next 9 dc (20 dc). Do not join, ch 3, turn. **3rd row:** Skip first dc, * work 2 dc in next dc, dc in next dc. Repeat from * around, ending with 2 dc in top of turning ch (30 dc); ch 1, turn. **4th row:** Sc in each dc across. Break off.

Following photograph for position, sew motifs in place.

EMBROIDERY: Lower Edge: Following photograph, using double strand of Melody and tapestry needle, work chain stitch (see stitch diagram) over sc's vertically across 6 rows. Work 11 stripes in all in this manner, spacing them about 1" apart. Work in same manner across back.

Center Motif: At center front starting about 4" above lower edge, work chain stitch center motif as shown in photograph.

Chain Stitch

Pansy Sweater

Pansies are crocheted in, using bobbins of various colors to work each design unit. Worked in single crochet throughout with acrylic sport yarn.

SIZES: 10–12 [14–16]. Sweater measures 16½" [18½"] across back at underarms; 20½" [21½"] from shoulder to lower edge.

MATERIALS: Brunswick Fore-'n-Aft acrylic sport yarn, 2 [3] (2-ounce) skeins white No. 6000 (color W), 3 skeins tiger No. 6004 (T), 1 skein each powder blue No. 6011 (B), maize No. 60031 (M), lime No. 6093 (G), lilac heather No. 6038 (L), and purple No. 6014 (P); aluminum crochet hook size F (or Canadian hook No. 10) *or the size that will give you the correct gauge.*

GAUGE: 9 sc = 2"; 11 rows = 2".

To Change Colors: see page 20.

FRONT: Starting at lower edge with W, ch 75 [83] to measure about 16½" [18½"]. **1st row (right side):** Sc in 2nd ch from hook and in each ch across; ch 1, turn. **2nd row:** Sc in each sc across; ch 1, turn. Repeat 2nd row until piece measures 3" [4"] from beg, ending with a wrong-side row.

Continuing in sc pattern, starting with 1st row of Chart 1, follow chart through 85th row, working right-side rows from right to left and wrong-side rows from left to right. (**Note:** At end of 49th row piece should measure about 11" [12"] from lower edge.)

To Shape Neck: 86th row (wrong side): Continuing to follow chart, work across first 30 [34] sts; turn. Shaping one side of neck only, continue as follows: **87th row:** Sl st across first 2 sts at neck (2-st dec made at neck edge), ch 1, work across in pattern to arm edge; ch 1, turn. **88th row:** Work across first 26 [30] sts (2 sts dec at neck edge); turn. Continue to follow chart, decreasing 1 st at neck edge every row 4 times. Working even on 22 [26] sts, follow chart to top. Break off.

With wrong side facing you, skip center 14 sts at front neck edge. Following other side of chart, sc in next st and work across. Shaping other side of neck, follow chart to top. Break off.

BACK: Work as for front through 6th row of Chart 1, then repeat 6th row 42 times more, ending with a wrong-side row. Piece should measure about 11" [12"] from beg.

Starting with 1st row of Chart 2, follow chart

Short-Sleeved Sweaters

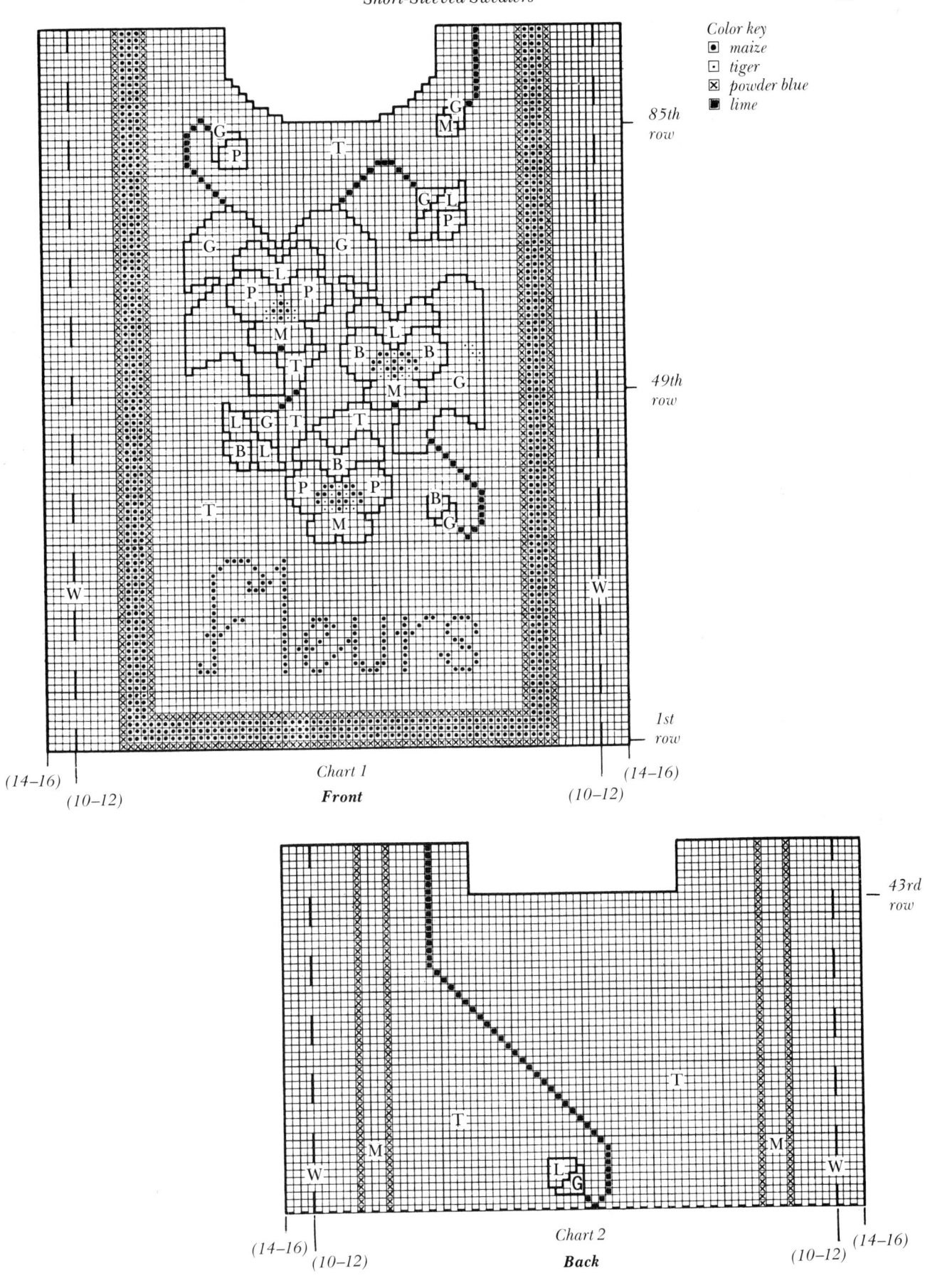

Color key
- ● maize
- · tiger
- ⊠ powder blue
- ■ lime

Chart 1
Front

Chart 2
Back

through 43rd row, working right-side rows from right to left and wrong-side rows from left to right.

To Shape Neck: Next row (wrong side): Continuing to follow Chart 2, work across first 22 [26] sts; ch 1, turn. Shaping one side of neck only, follow chart to top. Break off.

With wrong side facing you, skip center 30 sts at back neck edge. Following other side of chart, sc in next st and work across. Follow chart to top. Break off.

Block pieces, Sew front to back at shoulders.

SLEEVES: Place markers 8" [8½"] from shoulders on front and back at side edges.

Left Sleeve: With right side facing you, using W, begin in marked st on front and work sc over each st along edge to within 1 st of shoulder seam; draw up lp in st before seam, draw up lp in st after shoulder seam, y o and draw through all 3 lps (joined sc made); sc over each st along edge to marker on back; ch 1, turn. **Next row:** Sc in each sc across; ch 1, turn. Repeat last row until sleeve measures 2½" [3"] from beg. Break off.

Right Sleeve: With right side facing you, begin in marked st on back and, working to marker on front, work as for left sleeve.

Neck Trim: 1st rnd: With right side facing you, make lp on hook with T and, starting at center back neck edge, work sc in each sc to within 1 sc of corner; in corner work joined sc as follows: Draw up lp in next sc, draw up lp over st at edge on other side of corner, y o and pull through all 3 lps on hook; sc over each st at edge to shoulder seam; at seam work joined sc as on sleeves; sc evenly along front neck edge; work joined sc at other shoulder seam; sc over each st at edge to corner; work joined sc in corner; sc in each sc across; join with sl st to 1st sc. Break off. **2nd rnd:** Make lp on hook with W, sc in 1st sc, sc in each sc around, working joined sc's at back corners; join, ch 1. Repeat last rnd once more. Break off.

Sew side and sleeve seams.

Cap-Sleeved Shrink Top

In multicolored double and half-double crochet stripes. A delectable way to use up leftover knitting worsted-weight yarn.

SIZE: 6–8 [10–12].

MATERIALS: Knitting worsted-weight yarns, 6 ounces in assorted colors (we used small amounts of rust, aqua, maroon, red, gold, white, olive green, purple, powder blue, apple green, and medium rose); aluminum crochet hook size H (or Canadian hook No. 8) *or the size that will give you the correct gauge.*

GAUGE: 3 dc = 1"; 3 h dc = 1".

To Change Colors: Make lp on hook with new color and draw it through lp of old color. Break off old color, leaving a 3" end. Conceal ends in work by crocheting over them.

BACK: Starting at lower edge, ch 41 [44] to

measure about 13" [14"]. **1st row (right side):** Dc in 4th ch from hook and in each ch across (39 [42] dc, counting ch-3 as 1 dc); ch 2, turn. **(Note:** Change colors every row.) **2nd row:** H dc in 2nd dc and in each dc across; ch 3, turn. **3rd row:** Skip first h dc, dc in each h dc across; ch 2, turn.

Repeat 2nd and 3rd rows until piece measures 12" from beg. Mark beg and end of last row for armhole edge.

Continue to repeat 2nd and 3rd rows until piece measures 13" from beg, ending with h dc row.

To Shape Shoulder: 1st row: Dc in 2nd h dc and in each of next 9 [10] h dc; ch 2, turn. **2nd row:** H dc in 2nd dc and in each dc across; ch 3, turn.

Continue to work in pattern on 11 [12] sts until shoulder measures 4". Break off. Skip next 17 [18] sts (back neck) and work other shoulder to correspond. Break off.

FRONT: Work as for back.

Sew shoulder seams. Sew side seams up to armhole markers.

SLEEVES: 1st rnd: Starting at side seam at one underarm edge, work 36 sc evenly spaced around arm opening. **2nd rnd:** Sl st in first st, ch 2, h dc in each st around; join with sl st to top of ch-2. **3rd rnd:** Ch 3, dc in each h dc around, increasing 2 dc evenly spaced. **4th rnd:** Repeat 2nd rnd. **5th rnd:** Repeat 3rd rnd.

Repeat 4th and 5th rnds until sleeve measures about 3½" from beg; join.

Sleeve Edging: * Ch 4, sc in next dc. Repeat from * around. Break off.

Work other sleeve to correspond.

Neck Edging: With right side facing you, work 2 rnds sc around neck edge. Break off.

Powder-Pink Pullover

With elbow-length sleeves, crocheted in alternating bands of single crochet and V-stitches in scrumptious mohair.

SIZES: 6–8 [(10–12)—(14–16)]. Pullover measures about 16" [18"—20"] across back at underarms, about 17" [17½"—18"] from back of neck to lower edge.

MATERIALS: Bucilla Melody mohair and acrylic yarn, 7 [7–8] (1-ounce) balls powder pink No. 16; aluminum crochet hook size I (or Canadian hook No. 7) *or the size that will give you the correct gauge.*

GAUGE: 7 sc = 2"; 4 rows sc = 1".

BACK: (Note: Waistband is worked separately and vertically.) Starting at one end of waistband, ch 11. **1st row:** Sc in 2nd ch from hook and in each ch across (10 sc); ch 1, turn. **2nd row:** Working in back lp of each st, sc in each sc across; ch 1, turn. Repeat 2nd row until piece measures 14" [16"—18"]. Break off; set aside.

Body of Sweater: Starting at lower edge, ch 60 [66—72] loosely to measure about 16″ [18″—20″]. **1st row:** Sc in 2nd ch from hook and in each ch across (59 [65—71] sc); ch 1, turn. **2nd row:** Working in both lps of each st, sc in each sc across; ch 1, turn. Repeat last row until piece measures 2½″ from beg, ending last row with ch 3, turn.

To Establish V-stitch Pattern: 1st row: Skip first 2 sc, in next sc work dc, ch 1 and dc (V-st made), * skip 2 sc, V-st in next sc. Repeat from * across to within last 2 sc, skip next sc, dc in last sc (19 [21—23] V-sts across, with 1 dc at beg and end of row, counting turning ch-3 as 1 dc); ch 3, turn. **2nd row:** Work V-st in each ch-1 sp across, dc in turning ch; ch 3, turn. Repeat 2nd row 5 times more, ending last row with ch 1, turn.

Next row: Work sc in each dc and ch-1 sp across (59 [65—71] sc); ch 1, turn. Work even in sc for 3″, ending last row with ch 3, turn.

Next row: Repeat first row of V-st pattern, ending ch 1, turn.

To Shape Raglan Armhole: 1st row (dec row): Sl st across to 1st [1st—2nd] ch-1 sp, sl st in sp, ch 3, work V-st in next sp and in each sp across to last 1 [1—2] ch-1 sp, dc in next ch-1 sp (do not work across last 1 [1—2] V-sts), 17 [19—19] V-sts; ch 3, turn. Continuing in V-st pattern, dec 1 V-st at beg and end of every other row 2 [3—3] times more (13 V-sts). Work 1 [0—1] row even. Break off.

FRONT: Work same as for back.
SLEEVES: Starting at lower edge, ch 57 [57—60] to measure about 16″ [16″—17″]. **1st row:** Sc in 2nd ch from hook and in each ch across (56 [56—59] sc); ch 1, turn. Work even in sc until piece measures 2½″ from beg, ending last row with ch 3, turn.

Work in V-st pattern as for back for 7 rows on 18 [18—19] V-sts, ending last row with ch 1, turn. **Next row:** Sc in each dc and ch-1 sp across; ch 1, turn. Work 2 rows even on 56 [56—59] sts. Continuing in sc, dec 1 st at beg and end of next row (to dec 1 sc, draw up lp in each of 2 sts, y o and draw through all 3 lps on hook), then every 1″ twice more (50 [50—53] sts). **Next row:** Repeat first row of V-st pattern, ending ch 1, turn.

To Shape Raglan Cap: 1st row (dec row): Sl st across to first ch-1 sp, sl st in sp, ch 3, V-st in next sp and in each sp across to within last ch-1 sp, dc in last sp (14 [14—15] V-sts). Continuing in V-st pattern, repeat dec row every other row twice more, then work 1 [2—3] rows even on 10 [10—11] V-sts. Break off.

FINISHING: Sew waistband to lower edges of front and back, stretching to fit. Sew raglan, underarm, and side seams.

Neckband: 1st row: Starting at right back raglan seam, * work 3 sc in ch-1 sp of next V-st, work 2 sc in each sp across to within one V-st of next seam, 3 sc in next ch-1 sp. Repeat from * 3 times more (100 [100—104] sts), ch 1, turn. **2nd row:** Sc in each sc across, decreasing 1 sc before and after each raglan seam (8 sts dec); ch 1, turn. Repeat last row 3 times more (68 [68—72] sts). Break off. Sew seam.

Pineapple Pull-On

Design consists of eight squares. It is worn inside out for a more interesting texture.

SIZES: 10–12 [14—16]. Finished garment measures 16″ [18″] square. The change in size is obtained by using different size hooks.
MATERIALS: J. & P. Coats Knit-Cro-Sheen mercerized crochet cotton, 4 (250-yard) balls ecru No. 61; steel crochet hook No. 2 [No. 0]; ⅝ yard 45″-wide lightweight knitted fabric for lining (optional).
GAUGE: Each motif measures 8″ [9″] square, blocked.
Note: Always join motifs with right sides facing you.
FIRST MOTIF: Starting at center, ch 8. Join with sl st to form ring. **1st rnd (right side):** Ch 4, work 27 tr in ring. Join with sl st to top of ch-

4 (28 tr, counting ch-4 as 1 tr). **2nd rnd:** Ch 5, * tr in next tr, ch 1. Repeat from * around, ending with sl st in 4th ch of ch-5. Piece should measure 2¼" [2¾"] in diameter at end of 2nd rnd. **3rd rnd:** Sl st in first ch-1 sp, ch 1 and sc in same sp, * ch 3, sc in next sp. Repeat from * around, ending ch 3, sl st in first sc (28 lps made). **4th rnd:** Sl st in first lp. Ch 3, dc in same lp as sl st, * ch 5, skip next 2 lps, work 9 dc in next lp, ch 5, skip next 2 lps; holding back on hook the last lp of each dc, work 2 dc in next lp, y o hook, draw through all 3 lps on hook (joined dc made), ch 3, joined dc in next lp. Repeat from * around, ending last repeat with joined dc in last lp, ch 3, sl st to top of ch-3. **5th rnd:** Sl st in next dc, ch 3, dc in same place as sl st, * ch 5, (tr in next dc, ch 1) 8 times; tr in next dc, (ch 5, joined dc in next joined dc) twice. Repeat from * around, ending last repeat with ch 5, joined dc in last joined dc, ch 5; join as for last rnd. **6th rnd:** Sl st in next dc, ch 3, dc in same place as sl st, * ch 5, (sc in next ch-1 sp, ch 3) 7 times; sc in next ch-1 sp, ch 5, joined dc in next joined dc, ch 7, joined dc in next joined dc (ch-7 corner lp made). Repeat from * around, ending last repeat with ch-7 corner lp; join. **7th rnd:** Sl st in next dc, ch 3, dc in same place as sl st, * ch 5, (sc in next ch-3 lp, ch 3) 6 times; sc in next lp, ch 5, joined dc in next joined dc, ch 5; in next ch-7 lp work (2 dc, ch 5) twice; joined dc in next joined dc. Repeat from * around, ending last repeat with 2 dc, ch 5 and 2 dc in last lp, ch 5; join. **8th rnd:** Sl st in next dc, ch 3, dc in same place as sl st, * ch 5, (sc in next ch-3 lp, ch 3) 5 times; sc in next lp, ch 5, joined dc in next joined dc, ch 5, dc in each of next 2 dc; in next ch-5 lp work 2 dc, ch 5 and 2 dc; dc in each of next 2 dc, ch 5, joined dc in next joined dc. Repeat from * around, ending ch 5; join. **9th rnd:** Sl st in next dc, ch 3, dc in same place as sl st, * ch 5, (sc in next ch-3 lp, ch 3) 4 times; sc in next lp, ch 5, joined dc in next joined dc, ch 5, dc in each of next 4 dc; in next ch-5 lp work 2 dc, ch 5 and 2 dc; dc in each of next 4 dc, ch 5, joined dc in next joined dc. Repeat from * around, ending with dc in next 4 dc, ch 5; join. **10th rnd:** Sl st in next dc, ch 3, dc in same place as sl st; * ch 9, holding back on hook last lp of each tr, work 1 tr in each of next 4 ch-3 lps, y o and draw through all 5 lps on hook, ch 9, joined dc in next joined dc, ch 5, dc in each of next 4 dc, ch 5, skip next 2 dc; in next ch-5 lp work 2 dc, ch 7 and 2 dc; ch 5, skip next 2 dc, dc in each of next 4 dc, ch 5, joined dc in next joined dc. Repeat from * around, ending with dc in each of last 4 dc, ch 5; join. **11th rnd:** Ch 1, * sc in next lp, ch 6, sc in 4th ch from hook for p, ch 2, sc in same lp (p lp made), ch 6, make p, ch 2. Repeat from * around; join with sl st to first sc. Break off (56 p lps). Be sure motif measures 8" [9"] when pinned on flat surface.

SECOND MOTIF: Work as for first motif through 10th rnd. **11th rnd:** Ch 1, * sc in next lp, ch 6, make p, ch 2, sc in same lp (p lp made), ch 6, make p, ch 2. Repeat from * to within corner lp.

TO JOIN 2 MOTIFS: Sc in corner lp, ch 4, sl st in any corner p lp on first motif, * ch 1, sc in 3rd ch of ch-4 on 2nd motif, ch 2, sc in same lp on 2nd motif, ch 4, sl st in next p lp on first motif, ch 1, sc in 3rd ch of ch-4 on 2nd motif, ch 2, sc in next lp on 2nd motif, ch 4, sl st in next p lp on first motif. Repeat from * across to within next corner p lp, ch 1, sc in 3rd ch of ch-4 on 2nd motif, ch 2, sc in corner lp on 2nd motif, ch 4, sl st in next corner p lp on first motif, ch 1, sc in 3rd ch of ch-4 on 2nd motif, ch 2, sc in same corner lp on 2nd motif—joining completed. Ch 6, sc in 4th ch from hook; ch 2. Starting from * on 11th rnd of first motif, complete as for first motif. Break off.

Work 3rd motif and join to 2nd. Work 4th

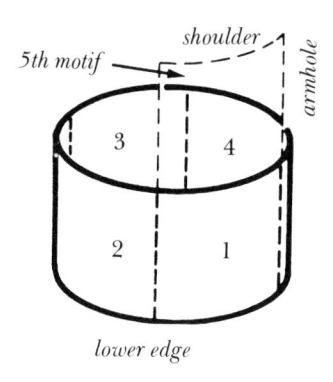

motif and join to 3rd and to first to form ring (see diagram).

Work 5th motif and join to top of first motif (see broken lines on diagram).

Work 6th motif and join to 2nd (the opening between 5th and 6th forms front V-neck).

Work 7th motif and join to 3rd; also join to top of 6th to form shoulder, but leave last lp free at back neck. Work 8th motif and join to 4th and 7th; also join to top of 5th to form shoulder, leaving last lp free at back neck. Openings between 5th and 8th motifs and between 6th and 7th are armholes.

Block garment to size, pinning it out on a padded board and steaming it under a wet cloth. Do not remove until thoroughly dry.

Note: We turned our top inside out, using the wrong side as the right side for a more interesting texture.

LINING: Cut one lining piece each for front and back, ½" larger on all sides than garment. Seam sides and shoulders. Insert in garment and pin in place. Slash front neck opening. Turn in all edges and blindstitch.

Three-Toe Sweater

Front and back of this boldly colored sweater are worked horizontally, yoke and sleeves vertically in two halves. Mostly in double crochet. Zip front. Three-toed pocket is appliquéd on.

SIZES: Small (6–8) [medium (10–12)—large (14–16)]. Snug-fitting sweater measures 15" [16"—17"] across at underarms, 21" [21½"—22"] from back of neck to lower edge.

MATERIALS: Reynolds Classique (100% wool), 2 [2—3] (1¾-ounce) balls blue bic No. 2592; 1 ball each prune No. 2510, cyclamen (dark rose) No. 2597, rubis No. 2540, flamant rose (light rose) No. 2596, rose boull (red-orange) No. 2598, abricot (apricot) No. 2505, blanc (white) No. 2500; small amount black sports yarn; aluminum crochet hook size H (or Canadian hook No. 8) *or the size that will give you the correct gauge;* 14" red separating zipper.

GAUGE: 4 dc = 1"; 2 dc rows = 1".

GENERAL DIRECTIONS: Stripes: Work in pattern of 6 rows each abricot, rose boull, flamant rose, rubis, and cyclamen and 5 [9—7] rows prune.

To Change Colors: Work turning ch in new color as follows: At end of row break off old color, leaving a 3" end, and knot this end with new color, keeping knot close to work. Ch 3 with new color; turn.

Front and back are worked horizontally. Yoke and sleeves are worked vertically in two halves. **To dec 1 dc:** (y o hook, insert hook in next dc, y o hook and draw lp through st, y o hook and draw through 2 lps on hook) twice, y o and draw through all 3 lps on hook.

BACK: Starting at lower edge with abricot, ch 74 [78—82] to measure about 18" [19"—20"]. **1st row:** Dc in 4th ch from hook and in each ch across (72 [76—80] dc, counting turning ch as 1 dc); ch 3, turn. **2nd row (dec row):** Skip first dc (ch-3 counts as first dc), dc in each of next 4 [6—8] dc, (dec 1 dc, dc in each of next 18 dc) 3 times; dec 1 dc, dc in each of remaining 5 [7—9] dc, ending with dc in top of turning ch (68 [72—76] dc); ch 3, turn. **3rd row:** Skip first dc, dc in each dc across, decreasing 1 dc over each dec of previous row (64 [68—72] dc); ch 3, turn.

4th and 5th rows: Skip first dc, dc in each dc across; ch 3, turn. **6th row:** Skip first dc, dc in each dc across, decreasing 9 dc as evenly spaced as possible (55 [59—63] dc). Piece should measure 3" from beg. Change colors to establish stripe pattern. Work 1 row even (see 4th row). **8th row:** Skip first dc, dec 1 dc, work across to within last 3 sts, dec 1 dc, dc in top of turning ch (53 [57—61] dc); ch 3, turn. Work 6 rows even, maintaining stripe pattern.

15th row (inc row): Work 1 dc in first dc (1 dc inc), work across to last st, work 2 dc in top of turning ch (55 [59—63] dc); ch 3, turn. **16th row:** Work even. Repeat 15th and 16th rows once; then repeat 15th row once more (59 [63—67] dc). Work 10 rows even, ending ch 1, turn.

To Shape Armholes: 1st row: Sl st in first 4 [4—5] dc, ch 3, skip next dc, dc to within last 4 [4—5] sts (do not work over these sts); ch 3, turn. Work even on 51 [55—57] dc for 5 [6—7] rows. Break off.

RIGHT FRONT: Starting at lower edge with abricot, ch 38 [40—42] to measure about 9" [9½—10"]. **1st row (right side):** Dc in 4th ch from hook and in each ch across (36 [38—40] dc); ch 3, turn. **2nd row:** Skip first dc, dc in each of next 4 [6—8] dc, dec 1 dc, dc in each of next 18 dc, dec 1 dc, dc in each of remaining 9 dc (34 [36—38] dc); ch 3, turn. **3rd row:** Skip first dc, dc in each dc across, decreasing 1 dc over each dec of previous row 32 [34—36] dc; ch 3, turn. Work 2 rows even. **6th row:** Skip first dc, dc in each dc across, decreasing 4 dc as evenly spaced as possible. Piece should measure 3" from beg. Change colors to establish stripe pattern and work 1 row even. **8th row:** Skip first dc, dec 1 dc, dc in each dc across; ch 3, turn. Work 6 rows even. **15th row (inc row):** Work across to last st, work 2 dc in top of turning ch; ch 3, turn. **16th row:** Work even. Repeat 15th and 16th rows once more; then repeat 15th row again (30 [32—34] dc). Work 10 rows even, ending ch 1, turn.

To Shape Armhole and Neck: 1st row: Sl st in first 4 [4—5] dc, ch 3, skip next dc, work across to within last 2 sts, dec 1 dc at neck edge; ch 3, turn. **2nd row:** Skip first dc, dec 1 dc, dc in each dc across; ch 3, turn. **3rd row:** Work across to within last 2 sts, dec 1 dc (23 [25—26] dc); ch 3, turn.

Repeat 2nd and 3rd rows 1 [1—2] times more. Then repeat 2nd row 0 [1—0] times more. **Last row (for small and large sizes only):** Skip first dc, (dec 1 dc) twice, dc in each dc across (19 [20] dc). Break off. **Last row (for medium size only):** Work across to within last 4 sts, (dec 1 dc) twice at neck edge (20 dc). Break off.

LEFT FRONT: Work same as for right front; pieces are reversible.

LEFT RAGLAN SLEEVE AND YOKE: Starting at lower edge of sleeve with blue bic, ch 42 [44—46]. **1st row:** Dc in 4th ch from hook and in each ch across (40 [42—44] dc); ch 3, turn. **2nd row:** Work even. **3rd row:** Dc in each dc across, increasing 1 dc at beg and end of row; ch 3, turn. **4th row:** Dc in each dc across, increasing 6 dc as evenly spaced as possible (48 [50—52] dc); ch 1, turn.

To Shape Cap: 1st row: Sl st in each of first 3 dc, ch 3, skip next dc, work across to within last 3 sts; ch 3, turn. **2nd row:** Skip first dc, dec 1 dc, work across to within last 2 sts, dec 1 dc; ch 3, turn. Repeat 2nd row 0 [1—2] times more. **Next row (dec row):** Skipping first dc, (dec 1 dc) 3 times; work across to within last 6 sts, dec 3 dc; ch 3, turn. Repeat last dec row twice more. Then work 9 [10—10] rows even over 22 dc for yoke (this even section fits over shoulder; shoulder seam is omitted); ch 3, turn. **Next row:** Skipping first dc, dc in each of next 10 dc for back of yoke (11 [11—11] dc). Remaining sts on row are side neck edge; ch 3, turn. Repeat last row 3 times more for back yoke. Break off (center back).

RIGHT RAGLAN SLEEVE AND YOKE: Work to correspond to left side.

FINISHING: Sew center back seam of yoke. Sew yoke and raglan sleeves to back and fronts. Sew sleeve and side seams.

Front and Neck Edging: Make lp on hook with abricot. With right side of work facing you, sl st at lower right front edge. Sc evenly spaced along right front, neck edge, and left front, changing colors to match pattern. Sew zipper in place. **Appliqué Pocket (make 2):** Starting at top edge with white, ch 9. **1st row:** Sc in 2nd ch from hook and in each ch across (8 sc); ch 1, turn. **2nd row (inc row):** Work 2 sc in first sc, sc in each sc across to last sc, work 2 sc in last sc (10 sc); ch 1, turn. Repeat 2nd row 4 times more (18 sc). **7th row:** Sc in each sc across; ch 1, turn. Repeat 7th row twice more. Then repeat 2nd inc row once more (20 sc). **11th row:** Sc in each of next 3 sc, * ch 12 for post, sc in 2nd ch from hook and in each ch across (11 sc, first post made), sc in each of next 7 sc. Repeat from * once more. Work one more post, sc in each of last 3 sc (3 posts made); turn. **12th row:** Skip first 3 sc, dc in each of 10 sc of first post, * work 7 dc in next sc; working down opposite side of post, dc in base of each of next 10 sc, skip next 3 sc, sl st in next sc, skip next 3 sc, dc in each of next 10 sc of next post. Repeat from * once more. Work 7 dc in next sc; working down opposite side of last post, dc in base of each of next 10 sc, skip next 2 sc, sl st in last st. Do not break off but work completely around piece as follows: **1st rnd:** Ch 1, sc evenly around, increasing 1 sc at tip of each post; join with sl st to first ch-1. Break off. Mark center of tip of each post. **2nd rnd:** With black, make lp on hook, with right side of work facing you, sc in same place as last sl st, sc in each sc to within 2 sc before marker, * work 2 sc in each of next 4 sc, slipping marker, work 1 dc in each of next 3 sc, sc in each sc to within 5 sc before next marker, work 1 dc in each of next 3 sc. Repeat from * once more. Work 2 dc in each of next 4 dc, slipping marker, sc in each sc to end. Join and break off. Following photograph for position, sew pockets in place, leaving tops open.

Side-Wrap Sweater

A timeless surplice design spruced up in new stitches and soft, misty colors, with a dash of bright orange and lime. It is worked vertically in shell stitch and chain-one and single crochet. The ribbed waistband is worked in single crochet—its texture is obtained by working in the back loop of each stitch.

SIZES: Small (8–10) [medium (12–14)]. Garment measures 16″ [18″] across back from side seam to side seam and 17″ [17½″] from back neck to lower edge.

MATERIALS: Brunswick Germantown knitting worsted, 3 [4] (4-ounce) skeins helio No.

438 (color A), 1 skein each dusty pink No. 436 (B), persimmon No. 4060 (C), medium lime No. 4272 (D), and orange No. 406 (E); aluminum crochet hook size H (or Canadian hook No. 8) *or the size that will give you the correct gauge;* snaps.

GAUGE: 7 sts = 2″; pattern repeat (19 rows) = about 6″.

Note: Sweater and waistband are worked vertically.

RIGHT BACK: Starting at sleeve edge with color A, ch 22. **1st row:** Sc in 2nd ch from hook, * ch 1, skip 1 ch, sc in next ch. Repeat from * across (11 sc); ch 1, turn. **2nd row:** Sc in first sc, * ch 1, sc in next sc. Repeat from * across. Drop A; attach B; ch 1, turn. **3rd row:** With B, repeat 2nd row. Drop B; attach C; ch 1, turn. **4th row:** With C, repeat 2nd row. Break off C; attach D; ch 1, turn. **5th row:** With D, work sc, ch 1 and sc in first sc (inc made), * ch 1, sc in next sc. Repeat from * across, ending ch 1, work sc, ch 1 and sc in last sc (another inc made). Break off D; attach E; ch 1, turn. **6th row:** With E, sc in first sc, * ch 1, insert hook in next B sc *3 rows below* (this is same place as C sc was worked) and work sc (long sc made), ch 1, sc in next sc. Repeat from * across. Break off E; pick up A; sl st along side edge to level of 7th row, ch 1, turn. **7th row:** With A, sc in first sc, * ch 1, sc in next long sc, ch 1, sc in next sc. Repeat from * across; ch 1, turn. **8th row:** With A, repeat 2nd row. Drop A; do not turn work but pick up B at righthand edge, sl st along side edge to level of 8th row, ch 1. **9th row:** With B, sc in first sc, ch 1, sc in next sc, * ch 3, skip 1 sc, sc in next sc. Repeat from * across, ending ch 1, sc in last sc. Drop B; pick up A; ch 1, turn. **10th row:** With A, work long sc in first sc 2 rows below, * ch 1, sc in next sc, ch 1, work long sc in skipped sc 2 rows below. Repeat from * across, ending ch 1, work long sc in last sc 2 rows below; ch 1, turn. **11th row:** With A, work sc, ch 1 and sc in first long sc (inc made), * ch 1, sc in next sc, ch 1, sc in next long sc. Repeat from * across, ending with sc, ch 1, and sc in last long sc (another inc). Drop A; pick up B; ch 1, turn. **12th row:** Repeat 9th row. Drop B; do not turn work but pick up A; ch 1. **13th row:** Repeat 10th row. **14th row:** With A, sc in first long sc, * ch 1, sc in next sc, ch 1, sc in next long sc. Repeat from * across. Drop A; do not turn work but pick up B; ch 1. **15th row:** With B, sc in first sc, * ch 3, skip next sc, sc in next sc. Repeat from * across. Break off B; pick up A; ch 1, turn. **16th row:** With A, work sc, ch 1 and sc in first sc (inc), * ch 1, work long sc in skipped sc 2 rows below, ch 1, sc in next sc. Repeat from * across, ending with sc, ch 1 and sc in last sc (inc); ch 1, turn. **17th row:** With A, sc in first sc, * work 3 dc in next sc (shell made), sc in next long sc. Repeat from * across, ending with sc in last sc. Drop A; do not turn work but attach E at beg of last row; ch 1. **18th row:** With E, work long sc in first sc 2 rows below (this is same place as A sc was worked), * sc in each dc of next shell, work long sc in next sc 2 rows below. Repeat from * across, ending with long sc in last sc 2 rows below. Break off E; attach D; ch 3, turn. **19th row:** With D, work 2 dc in first long sc, * skip 1 sc, sc in next sc, work 3-dc shell in next long sc. Repeat from * across, ending with 2 dc in last long sc. Break off D; do not turn work but pick up A; sl st along side edge to level of 20th row, ch 1. **20th row:** With A, work sc, ch 1 and sc in top of ch-3 (inc), * ch 1, sc in next sc, ch 1, sc in center dc of next shell. Repeat from * across, ending with sc, ch 1 and sc in last dc (inc); ch 1, turn. Repeat 2nd through 8th rows once more (21 sc). Drop A; do not turn work but pick up B; sl st along side edge to level of next row, ch 11 for side edge. **Next row:** With B, sc in 2nd ch from hook, (ch 1, skip 1 ch, sc in next ch) 4 times; then ch 3, skip last ch and first sc of previous row, sc in next sc, * ch 3, skip 1 sc, sc in next sc. Repeat from * across, ending with ch 1, sc in last sc. Drop B; pick up A; ch 1, turn. **Next row:** With A, work as for 10th row across to last ch-3, work long sc in skipped sc 2 rows below, (ch 1, sc in next sc) 5 times (26 sc and long sc); ch 1, turn. **Next row:** With A, sc in first sc, (ch 1, sc in next sc) 4 times, * ch 1, sc in long sc, ch 1, sc in next sc. Repeat from * across, ending sc, ch 1 and sc in last sc (inc made—27 sc). Drop A; pick up B; ch 1, turn. Now, working in same manner as for 12th pattern row, work even in pattern, keeping continuity of pattern as established. Make no new increases and work all previously added sts in pattern. Work even until piece measures about 8″ [9″] from side edge. Break off.

LEFT BACK: Work same as for right back until 26 rows have been completed (21 sc). **Next row:** Repeat 8th row of pattern across, then ch 10 for side edge. Drop A; do not turn work but pick up B; ch 1. Mark beg of 8th row for top edge. **Next row:** Work as for 9th row across, ending with ch 3, skip last sc and first ch of attached chain, sc in next ch, (ch 3, skip 3 ch, sc in next ch) twice. Complete to correspond to right back, working one more inc at top edge on 11th row.

RIGHT FRONT: Work same as for left back until piece measures 4½" [5"] from side edge, ending at neck edge (27 sc).

To Shape Neck: Starting at neck edge, sl st in first sc, sl st in next ch; complete row in pattern as established. Continue to sl st across first 2 sts at neck edge every other row until piece measures 16" [18"] from side edge when slightly stretched. Break off.

LEFT FRONT: Work same as for right back until piece measures 4½" [5"] from side edge, ending at neck edge. Shape neck same as for right front until piece measures 10" [11"] from side edge. Break off.

WAISTBAND: With A, ch 15 [19]. **1st row:** Sc in 2nd ch and in each remaining ch across; ch 1, turn. **2nd row:** Working in back lp only, sc in each sc across (14 [18] sc); ch 1, turn. Repeat 2nd row until piece measures 24" [28"] from beg when slightly stretched. Break off.

FINISHING: Block to measurements. Sew back seam, then sew shoulder, side and underarm edges. **Edging:** Attach A to one sleeve edge at underarm seam. With right side of work facing you, work a row of sc around sleeve edge, then work a row of reverse sc (work from left to right—see diagram on page 66) around sleeve edge. Break off. Work edging on other sleeve edge. Attach A to front edge and work edging along decreased front edges and around neck edge.

Overlap surplice fronts as shown in photograph and pin lower edges together. Sew narrow ends of waistband together; with seam matching one side seam on sweater, sew waistband to lower edge of sweater, catching both layers of overlapping fronts. Sew snaps along front edge as needed.

Long-Sleeved and Sporty Pullovers

Trumpet-Sleeved Tunic

In textured stripes of various shades of blue, worked in single and double crochet, plus shell stitch.

SIZE: 10–12 [(14–16)—(18–20)]. Tunic measures 17" [19"—21"] across back at underarms, about 25" from back of neck to lower edge.

MATERIALS: Bernat Berella "4" (knitting-worsted weight), 2 [3—3] (4-ounce) balls each gobelin mix No. 8906 and totem blue No. 8964, 1 [2—2] ball each tartan mix No. 8976, myrtle green No. 8985, and flag blue No. 8963; aluminum crochet hook size F for size 10–12, H hook for size 14–16, I hook for size 18–20 (or Canadian hook No. 10 [8—7]) *or the size that will give you the correct gauge.*

GAUGE: 4 sc = 1" on size F hook.
7 sc = 2" on size H hook.
10 sc = 3" on size I hook.

Note: It is important to get the exact gauge. Change hook if necessary.

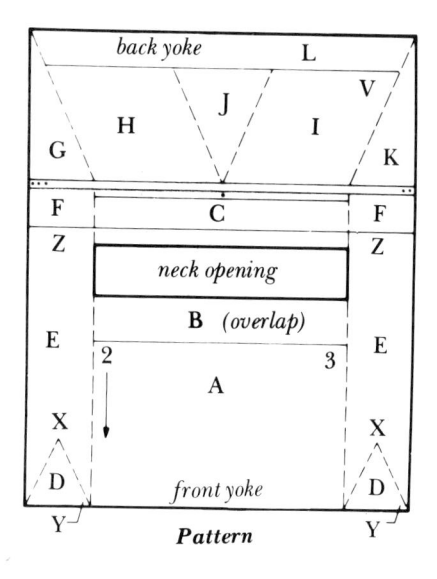

FRONT YOKE: Section A: With gobelin, ch 22 to measure about 5½" [6"—6¾"]. **1st row (right side):** Sc in 2nd ch from hook and in each ch across (21 sc); ch 1, turn. Mark this row for bottom edge of panel. **2nd row:** Sc in each sc across; ch 1, turn. Repeat 2nd row 15 times more, omitting ch-1 at end of last row. Break off gobelin.

Note: Work with right side of work facing you unless otherwise specified.

With totem, work dc over post of last sc on last sc row (No. 2 on diagram), dc over post of each sc along side edge in direction of arrow to within 1 post of marked row, 2 dc over last post (18 dc); ch 1, work 2 dc into opposite side of first ch st of starting chain, dc in opposite side of each ch of starting chain to within last st, work 2 dc in last st (23 dc); ch 1, work 2 dc over post of next row along side edge, dc over post of each sc of next 16 rows (18 dc; mark last dc worked). Break off. Top edge of Section A is left free.

Section B: 1st row: With myrtle, work 2 sc over post of marked dc (No. 3 on diagram), sc in each sc across to within last dc, work 2 sc over last dc (25 sc); ch 1, turn. **2nd row:** Sc in each sc across; ch 1, turn. **3rd through 7th rows:** Repeat 2nd row, marking 5th sc row. **8th row:** Sc in each of first 12 sc, work 3 sc in center sc, sc in each of remaining 12 sc (27 sc); ch 1, turn. **9th through 11th rows:** Repeat 2nd row, omitting ch-1 at end of last row. Break off.

Overlap: 1st row: Attach myrtle to beg of first sc of first myrtle row. Fold Section B to right side at marked row to form double thickness. Working through both thicknesses, work 5 sc evenly spaced along side edge, ch 57 and, being careful not to twist chain, work 5 sc along other short side of Section B, sl st in next st. Break off. Mark 16th ch from beg of chain for left shoulder edge, skip next 25 ch for back neck edge, mark 42nd ch for right shoulder edge.

Section C: Back Neck Edge: 1st row: With totem, sc in opposite side of each of 25 ch of back neck; ch 1, turn. **2nd row:** Sc in each sc across; ch 1, turn. **3rd row:** Repeat 2nd row. Break off totem; attach gobelin; ch 1, turn. **4th row:** With gobelin, sc in each sc across; turn. **5th row:** Sl st in sc, ch 3 (ch-3 counts as 1 dc), dc in each of next 4 sc, * skip next 2 sc, work 5 dc in next sc (5-dc shell made), skip 2 sc, work dc in each of next 5 sc. Repeat from * once more; ch 1, turn. **6th row:** Sc in each dc across (25 sc). Break off.

With totem, sl st in center st of last sc row (dot on diagram), sc in each of remaining 12 sc, ch 3 (mark this ch), sc over post of next gobelin row along side edge, 2 sc over post of next dc, work sc over post of each of next 3 rows, sc in each of 16 shoulder ch, work sc in each of next 5 sc of overlap edge of Section B, (* ch 1, skip next dc of front panel of Section A, sc in next dc. Repeat from * to within corner ch-1 of Section A, ch 3, sc in next dc) 3 times, omitting corner ch-3 sp on last repeat; sc in next dc, sc in each of next 5 sc of overlap, sc in each of next 16 ch, sc over post of each st along side edge of next 3 rows, work 2 sc over post of next dc, sc in post of next row, ch 3 (mark this ch), sc in each of first 12 sc to within center sl st, sl st in sl st (dot on diagram). Break off.

With myrtle, sc in first marked ch-3 sp, sc in each totem sc along neck side edge, shoulder edge, and in each of next 5 sc of overlap edge, (* dc over next ch-1 of Section A, sc in next sc. Repeat from * to within unmarked ch-3 sp, work 5 dc in same sp, sc in next sc) twice, then ** dc over next ch-1 sp, sc in next sc. Repeat from **, ending dc over last ch-1 sp, sc in each of next 5 sc of overlap edge. Continue as for other side, ending with sc in 2nd marked ch-3 sp. Sections A, B, and C completed. Set piece aside.

Front and Back Shoulder Panels: Front Tri-

angle Section D: With flag, ch 12. **1st row:** Sc in 2nd ch from hook and in each ch across (11 sc); ch 1, turn. **2nd row (dec row):** Y o hook, draw up lp in each of next 2 sts, y o and draw through all 3 lps on hook (1 sc dec), sc in each sc to end of row; ch 1, turn. Repeat 2nd row until 1 st remains. Mark this st (X on Section D). Break off.

Section E: Attach myrtle at X, ch 29. Break off.

With totem, sl st in last ch worked, skip next ch, * work 5-dc shell in next ch, skip next 2 ch, dc in next ch, skip next 2 ch. Repeat from * 3 times more, work 5-dc shell in next ch, skip last 2 ch, sc over post of last sc worked on triangle (X on diagram) and over post of each sc to within starting row, work 2 sc over post of sc on starting row (12 sc); ch 1; 2 sc in opposite side of first ch at base of triangle, sc in each ch across to within last ch, 2 sc in last ch (13 sc), ch 1, 2 sc over first sc row along opposite side of triangle, sc over post of each remaining row (12 sc), skip 2 ch, work shell row in opposite side of ch-29 to correspond to other side, ending with sl st in same ch as first sl st. Break off. Section E completed.

Edging: With myrtle, sl st in same place as first totem sl st. Ch 3, * h dc in first dc of 5-dc shell, sc in each of next 3 dc, h dc in next dc, dc in next dc. Repeat from * 4 times more, ending with dc in sc at point of triangle. Break off. Beginning with ch 3 in sc on other side of point of triangle, work to correspond to opposite side, ending with ch 3, sl st in unworked sl st.

With flag, sc in top of first myrtle ch-3 and in each myrtle edging st (31 sc), dc in next totem sc along side of triangle, h dc in next totem sc, sc in next sc. Break off. Work other side to correspond.

With gobelin, sc in first flag sc, ch 1, skip next sc, * sc in next sc, ch 1, skip next sc. Repeat from * to end of totem row, dc in next sc along side of triangle, h dc in next sc, sc in next sc. Break off. Work other side to correspond.

With tartan, sc in first gobelin sc, dc over next flag ch-1 sp 2 rows below, * sc in next gobelin sc, dc over next flag ch-1 sp 2 rows below. Repeat from * to within last 3 gobelin sts on side of edging, sc in each of these 3 sts, dc in next sc along side of triangle, h dc in next sc, sc in next sc. Break off. Work other side to correspond.

Attach gobelin to corner ch-1 of triangle (Y on diagram), ch 1, h dc in next sc, dc in next sc. Continue to sc in each remaining tartan st, then work 14 sc evenly spaced across short edge of panel (Z on diagram), then sc in each remaining tartan st along other side of panel to within remaining 2-sc on side of triangle, sc in next sc, h dc in next sc, sc in corner ch-1. Break off.

Section F: 1st row: With wrong side facing you and using gobelin, sc in each sc along short Z edge of Section E; ch 1, turn. Work even in sc for 5 more rows. Break off. Front and back shoulder panel is completed. Work other panel is same manner. With wrong sides of Sections A, B, and C and front and back shoulder panels facing, whipstitch pieces together with tapestry needle and yarn following broken lines on diagram.

BACK YOKE: With totem and right side of back neck edge facing you, starting at 2 dots on last completed row of Section F, sc in each gobelin sc across F (14 sc), sc over post of next myrtle sc, sc over next totem ch-3 sp, sc in each of next 25 totem sts, sc over next ch-3 sp, sc over post of next myrtle sc, sc in each of next 14 gobelin sc (57 sc—3 dots on diagram); ch 1, turn.

Section G: 1st row: Sc in each of next 12 sc; draw up a lp in each of next 2 sc, y o hook and draw through all 3 lps on hook (1 sc); ch 1, turn. **2nd row:** Sc in each sc across; ch 1, turn. **3rd row:** Sc in each sc across to within last 2 sc, dec 1 sc; ch 1, turn. Repeat 2nd and 3rd rows until 1 st remains. Break off. Section G completed.

Section H: 1st row: With myrtle, sc in next free totem sc of back, sc in each of next 13 sc; ch 1, turn. **2nd row:** Dec 1 sc, sc in each of next 11 sc, work 2 sc in last sc (14 sc); ch 1, turn. **3rd row:** Sc in each sc across; ch 1, turn. Repeat 2nd and 3rd rows 8 times more. Break off.

Section I: Skip next free totem st of back (mark this st). **1st row:** With myrtle, sc in each of next 14 free totem sc; ch 1, turn. **2nd row:** Work 2 sc in first sc, sc in each sc across to within last 2 sc, dec 1 sc; ch 1, turn. **3rd row:** Sc in each sc across; ch 1, turn. Complete to correspond to Section H. Break off.

Section J: With tartan, ch 20. **1st row:** Sc in 2nd ch from hook and in each ch across (19 sc);

ch 1, turn. Continue to work as for 2nd row (dec row) of front triangle (Section D on diagram) until 1 st remains. Break off.

With wrong sides of Sections G, H, and I facing you, place point of Section J directly below marked sc of Section I. With tapestry needle and yarn, whipstitch the 4 sections together as indicated by the broken lines on diagram.

Section K: 1st row: With totem, draw up lp in each of next 2 totem sc, y o hook and draw through all 3 lps (1 sc dec), sc in each of remaining 12 sc; ch 1, turn. **2nd row:** Sc in each sc across; ch 1, turn. **3rd row:** Dec 1 sc, sc in each sc across; ch 1, turn. Repeat 2nd and 3rd rows until 1 st remains. Break off. Whipstitch Section K to remaining free edge of Section I (see diagram).

Section L: 1st row: With gobelin, work 2 sc in first sc of last Section I row (V on diagram), sc in each of next 13 myrtle sc, sc in each of next 19 tartan sts, sc in each of next 13 myrtle sc, work 2 sc in last sc (49 sc); ch 1, turn. **2nd row:** Sc in each sc across; ch 1, turn. **3rd row:** Work 2 sc in first sc, sc in each sc across to within last sc, work 2 sc in last sc. Repeat 2nd and 3rd rows twice more (55 sc). Break off. Mark center st. Whipstitch remaining free edges of Sections G and K to short edges of Section L.

With totem, sc in marked center st of last row of Section L, sc in each of next 27 gobelin sc, and in point of Section G, ch 11 (mark this chain for underarm gusset), then sc over post of next gobelin st of free edge of front shoulder panel, sc in each of next 13 totem sts at base of D triangle, sc over post of next gobelin st, sc in next 2 corner myrtle dc of free edge of Section A, sc in each of next 23 sts to within last 2 corner dc, sc in each of next 2 dc, sc over post of next gobelin st on other front shoulder panel, sc in each of next 13 sc, sc over post of next gobelin st, ch 11 (mark this chain for underarm gusset), sc in point of Section K and in each remaining st to within center back sc, sl st in this sc (138 sts, including each st of each ch-11). Break off. Yoke completed.

BODY: 1st rnd: With totem, sc in opposite side of each ch of a ch-11, sc in each sc across last totem sc row to within next ch-11, sc in opposite side of each ch, sc in each st around to within first sc, sl st in first sc (138 sc). **2nd rnd:** Ch 1, sc in same place as sl st, sc in each sc around; join with sl st to first sc. Repeat 2nd rnd 6 times more.

Body Pattern: 1st rnd: With totem, sc in same place as sl st, ch 1, skip next sc, * sc in next sc, ch 1, skip next sc. Repeat from * around, ending sl st in first sc. Break off totem; attach gobelin. **2nd rnd:** Sc in sl st, dc over next ch-1 sp in sc of row below, * sc in next sc, dc over ch-1 sp in sc of row below. Repeat from * around; join. Break off gobelin, attach tartan. **3rd rnd:** Ch 1, sc in sl st, sc in each sc and dc around; join. Break off tartan; attach totem. **4th rnd:** Ch 1, * draw up lp in each of next 2 sc, y o hook and draw through all 3 lps on hook, ch 1. Repeat from * around; join. Break off totem; attach myrtle. **5th rnd:** Ch 1, sc in sl st, sc in each sc and over each ch-1 sp around; join. Break off myrtle; attach totem. **6th rnd:** Ch 3, in same place as sl st, work 4 dc (5-dc shell made—ch-3 counts as 1 dc), * skip 2 sc, sc in next sc, skip 2 sc, 5-dc shell in next sc. Repeat from * around, ending last repeat by skipping next 2 sc, sc in next sc, skip last 2 sc, sl st in top of ch-3. Break off totem, attach gobelin. **7th rnd:** Ch 1, sc in first sl st, sc in each of next 3 dc, * work dc in next tartan sc 2 rows below, h dc in next sc, work dc in next tartan sc 2 rows below, dc in center 3 dc of next 5-dc shell. Repeat from *, ending dc in next tartan sc, h dc in next dc, dc over next tartan sc; join with sl st in first sc. Break off gobelin, attach myrtle. **8th rnd:** Ch 1, sc in same place as sl st, sc in each st around, including last sl st; do not join. Break off myrtle; attach flag. **9th rnd:** With flag, skip first sc, sl st in next sc, ch 3, work dc in skipped sc, * skip next sc, dc in next sc, dc in skipped sc (crossed-dc group made). Repeat from * around, ending with sl st in top of ch-3. Break off flag; attach tartan. **10th rnd:** Sc in space between first 2 dc, * sc in next space between 2 dc. Repeat from * around; join. Break off tartan; attach totem. Repeat 1st through 10th rnds of pattern 3 times more. **Next rnd:** Repeat 1st rnd. **Following rnd:** Repeat 2nd rnd. Do not break off gobelin. With gobelin only, repeat 1st and 2nd rnds until piece measures 15″ from underarm. Break off.

Armhole Shaping: 1st rnd: With right side

of piece facing you, using totem, sc in center ch of left ch-11 underarm gusset, sc in each of next 4 ch; draw up lp in next ch and in first gobelin st of front shoulder panel and dec 1 sc (mark this st), work 73 sc evenly spaced around armhole edge as follows: Sc in each gobelin sc along remainder of long edge of panel to within Section F, sc over post of each sc of Section F and each totem st along Section K to within last totem st; draw up lp in last st and in next ch of ch-11 and dec 1 sc (mark this st—73 sts between marked sts), sc in each ch to within first sc, sl st in first sc. **2nd rnd:** Ch 1, sc in same place as sl st, sc in each sc of underarm gusset to within last sc; draw up lp in last sc, in marked sc and in next sc, y o hook and draw through all 4 lps (2 sc dec—always mark dec st). Sc in each sc to within last sc before next marked sc; draw up lp in last sc, in marked sc and in next sc, dec 2 sc, sc in remaining sc to beg of rnd; join. **3rd through 5th rnds:** Repeat 2nd rnd. **6th rnd:** Work as for 2nd rnd to within last marked sc of previous rnd, draw up lp in marked sc, remaining sc of gusset and next marked sc, dec 2 sc (mark this st, removing all other markers). **7th rnd:** Sc in each sc around to within 1 sc of marked sc, draw up lp in next sc, marked sc and next sc, dec 2 sc. Repeat 7th rnd twice more, always working sc before and after marked sc together with marked sc, as 1 st (60 sts remain). **Following rnd (Sleeve):** Following pattern for body of sweater, repeat first through 10th rnds 5 times. Repeat 1st and 2nd rnds once more, then, with gobelin only, repeat same 2 rnds twice more. Break off. Work other sleeve to correspond.

Shawl-Collared Pullover

Crocheted in tweedy raspberry yarn, with cuffs and collar striped in burgundy and tan.

SIZES: 6–8 [(10–12)—(14–16)—(18–20)]. Pullover measures 16" [17"—19"—21"] across back below armholes and 24¼" [24½"—24¾"—25"] from shoulder to lower edge.

MATERIALS: 4 [5—5—5] (4-ounce) skeins Four Seasons (Orlon acrylic knitting worsted-weight yarn by Yarn Industries) raspberry tweed No. 10 (color A); Yarn Industries Carrousel (Orlon acrylic knitting worsted-weight yarn), 1 (4-ounce) skein each burgundy No. 714 (B) and tan No. 715 (C); aluminum crochet hook size I (or Canadian hook No. 7) *or the size that will give you the correct gauge.*

GAUGE: 4 sts (sc's and ch-1's) = 1"; 6 rows = 2".

BACK: Starting at lower edge with A, ch 64 [68—76—84] to measure about 16" [17"—19"—21"]. **1st row:** Sc in 2nd ch from hook, * ch 1, skip next ch, sc in next ch. Repeat from *

across (63 [67—75—83] sts); ch 1, turn. **2nd row:** Sc in first sc, * ch 1, skip next ch, sc in next sc. Repeat from * across; ch 1, turn. Repeating 2nd row for pattern, work even until piece measures 17", or desired length to underarms, omitting ch-1 on last row; turn.

To Shape Armholes: 1st row: Sl st in first 4 sts, work in pattern to last 4 sts; turn. **2nd row:** Sl st in first 2 sts, work in pattern to last 2 sts; turn. Repeat last row 0 [1—2—3] times more. Work even on 51 [51—55—59] sts until armholes measure 7" [7¼"—7½"—8"], omitting ch-1 on last row.

To Shape Shoulders: 1st row: Sl st in first 4 [4—4—6] sts, work to last 4 [4—4—6] sts; turn. Repeat last row 2 [2—1—1] times more. **Next row:** Sl st in next 0 [0—6—4] sts, work to last 0 [0—6—4] sts (27 sts). Break off.

FRONT: Work as for back until piece measures 15", or 2" less than desired length to underarms, ending on wrong side; ch 1, turn.

To Shape Neck: 1st row: Working on left side only, work in pattern over next 15 [17—21—25] sts; ch 1, turn. Work even on 15 [17—21—25] sts until piece measures same as back to underarm, ending at side edge and omitting ch-1 on last row.

To Shape Armhole: 1st row: Sl st in first 4 sts, work across; ch 1, turn. **2nd row:** Work across first 9 [11—15—19] sts; ch 1, turn. **3rd row:** Sl st in first 0 [2—2—2] sts, work across; ch 1, turn. **4th row:** Work across first 9 [9—11—15] sts; ch 1 [1—1—0], turn. **5th row:** Sl st in first 0 [0—0—2] sts; work across; ch 1, turn. Work even on 9 [9—11—13] sts until armhole measures same as back to shoulder, ending at arm edge and omitting ch-1 on last row.

To Shape Shoulder: 1st row: Sl st in first 4 [4—4—6] sts, work across; ch 1, turn. **2nd row:** Work across first 1 [1—3—1] sts. Break off.

Skip center 33 sts, attach A to next sc and work other side to correspond.

SLEEVES: Starting at lower edge above cuff with A, ch 60 [62—64—66]. Work even in pattern on 59 [61—63—65] sts until piece measures 6". Dec 2 sts at beg and end of next row (to dec 1 st, pull up a lp in each of 2 sc, y o hook and draw through all 3 lps on hook); 4 sts dec in row. Dec 4 sts every 3" twice more, then work even on 47 [49—51—53] sts until piece measures 15" [15"—15½"—15½"].

To Shape Cap: 1st row: Sl st in first 4 sts, work to last 4 sts; turn. **2nd row:** Sl st in first 2 sts, work to last 2 sts; turn. **3rd row:** Work even. Repeat 2nd and 3rd rows 5 times more, then repeat 2nd row twice more. Break off.

FINISHING: Sew shoulder and side seams.

Collar: 1st row: Starting at lower right front corner of neck in first end sc, with right side facing you, using A, work in sc, ch-1 pattern evenly spaced along right front neck edge 19 [21—21—22] times, ending at shoulder with sc (39 [41—43—45] sts); break off A. Attach B in last st; ch 1, turn. **2nd row:** Sc in first sc, * ch 1, sc in next sc. Repeat from * across; ch 1, turn. Repeating 2nd row for pattern, work in stripes of 1 additional row B, 2 rows C, 1 row A, and 1 row B, increasing 2 sts at shoulder edge on 2nd C row (41 [43—45—47] sts). Break off.

Starting at shoulder edge of left front, work other side to correspond. Mark first sc at front neck on last row worked. Sew shoulder seams.

8th row: With wrong side facing you, with B, starting at marked sc, work in pattern along left front, (work ch-1 and sc) 13 times along back of neck, ch 1, work in pattern along right front (109 [113—117—121] sts).

Working along entire collar edge, continue in stripes of (2 rows C, 1 row A, 2 rows B) 4 times, increasing 2 sts evenly spaced along back of collar on first row of last C stripe. Break off.

Lap right collar over left and sew lower edges to center front neck edge.

Cuffs: 1st row: With right side facing you, using A and working along lower edge, sc in first sc, * ch 1, draw up a lp in each of next 2 sc, y o hook and pull through all 3 lps on hook (1 st dec). Repeat from * to last sc, ch 1, sc in last sc (31 [32—33—34] sts). Break off A. Starting with wrong side facing you and working in sc and ch-1 pattern, work in stripes of 2 rows B, (2 rows C, 1 row A, 2 rows B) twice. Break off.

Sew sleeve seams. Sew sleeves in place.

Kimono Sweater

The mood is Oriental. Kimono sweater in brilliant rectangles of color, very simple in double crochet. With patch pocket and shawl collar.

SIZES: Small (8–10) [medium (12–14)]. Pullover measures 16½" [18½"] across back at underarms, 20½" [21½"] from shoulder to lower edge.

MATERIALS: Brunswick Windrush (Orlon acrylic, knitting worsted-weight), 1 (4-ounce) skein each purple No. 9014 (color P), tender green No. 90710 (G), orange No. 9006 (O), persimmon (light orange) No. 9004 (L), saffron (yellow) No. 9008 (Y), China rose No. 9029 (R), shamrock No. 9043 (S), and dark cherry No. 9099 (C); aluminum crochet hook size J (or Canadian hook No. 6) *or the size that will give you the correct gauge.*

GAUGE: 3 dc = 1".

BACK: Starting at lower edge with P, ch 52 [58] loosely to measure about 16½" [18½"]. **1st row:** Dc in 4th ch from hook and in each ch across (50 [56] dc, counting turning ch as 1 dc); ch 3, turn. **2nd row:** Skip first dc, dc in next dc and in each dc across; ch 3, turn. Repeat 2nd row for pattern until piece measures 12½" [13"] from beg, omitting ch-3 on last row. Break off P.

To Shape Armholes: With G, form lp on hook. **Next row:** Skip first 5 [6] dc, dc in next dc and in each dc across to within last 5 [6] dc (40 [44] dc); ch 3, turn. Work even in pattern until armholes measure 8" [8½"]. Break off G.

FRONT: With O, work as for back to armholes. Break off O.

To Shape Armhole and Neck: With Y, form lp on hook. **Next row:** Skip first 5 [6] sts, dc in each of next 11 [12] dc (mark next st for start of front neck); ch 3, turn. Work even in pattern until armhole measures same as back armhole. Break off Y. Starting with marked st, skip center 18 [20] sts for front neck edge. With Y, form lp on hook, dc in next dc and in each dc across to within last 5 [6] sts (11 [12] dc); ch 3, turn. Work even in pattern until armhole measures same as back armhole. Break off Y.

SLEEVES: Starting at armhole edge with S, ch 60 [63] loosely to measure about 19" [20"]. Work as for back on 58 [61] dc until piece measures 7½" from beg, omitting ch-3 on last row. Break off S, attach P, ch 3, turn. Work in pattern for 3½" with P, 8½" with L and 1½" with C. Break off.

COLLAR: With R, ch 20 [22] to measure about 6" [6½"]. Work as for back on 18 [20] dc for 22" [23½"]. Break off.

POCKET: With Y, ch 19 to measure about 5". Work as for back for 6". Break off.

FINISHING: Sew shoulder, side, and sleeve seams. Sew in sleeves, easing to fit at armhole. Sew collar in place, lapping left end over right at center front. Following photograph, sew pocket on front.

Sweater Sets and Jackets

Contemporary Sweater Duo

In charcoal, medium gray, and white. Mostly double crochet. U-neck vest echoes zigzag stripe pattern of cardigan. Jacket is belted, buttoned, and collared.

SIZES: 6–8 [(10–12)—(14–16)—(18–20)]. Cardigan measures 16" [17"—19"—21"] across back at underarms and 17" [17½"—18"—18½"] from underarm to lower edge. Pullover measures 16" [17"—18"—20"] across back at underarms and 14" [14"—14½"—14½"] from underarm to lower edge.

MATERIALS: Spinnerin Germantown Deluxe (Orlon acrylic knitting worsted-weight yarn). **For Cardigan and Vest:** 4 [4—5—5] (4-ounce) skeins dark charcoal gray No. 3282 (color D), 3 [3—4—4] skeins medium gray No. 3283 (M) and 1 skein white No. 3200 (W).

Cardigan only: 4 [4—5—5] skeins No. 3282 (color D), 1 [1—2—2] skein No. 3283 (M) and 1 skein No. 3200 (W); 3 buttons ¾" in diameter.

Vest only: 1 skein each No. 3282 (D) and No. 3200 (W) and 2 skeins No. 3283 (M).

Crochet Hooks: For Cardigan: Aluminum crochet hook size I [J—I—J] (or Canadian hook No. 7 [6—7—6]). **For Vest:** Aluminum crochet hook size H [I—H—I] (or Canadian hook No. 8 [7—8—7]) *or the size that will give you the correct gauge.*

GAUGE: For Cardigan: With size I hook: 3 dc = 1". With size J hook: 8 dc = 3".

For Vest: With size H hook: 10 dc = 3". With size I hook: 3 dc = 1".

Cardigan

BACK: Starting at lower edge with color D and size I [J—I—J] crochet hook, ch 60 [60—68—68] to measure about 16" [17"—19"—21"]. **1st row:** Sl st in 2nd ch from hook, sl st in next ch, * sc in each of next 2 ch, h dc in each of next 2 ch, dc in each of next 2 [2—3—3] ch, tr in next ch, dc in each of next 2 [2—3—3] ch, h dc in each of next 2 ch, sc in each of next 2 ch, sl st in next ch. Repeat from * across, sl st in last ch; ch 3, turn. **2nd row:** Skip first st, as turning ch counts as one dc, (y o hook, insert hook in next st, y o and draw lp through, y o and draw through 2 lps on hook) twice; y o and draw through all 3 lps on hook (2-joined dc made—1 dc dec), * dc in each of next 5 [5—6—6] sts, work a shell of dc, tr and dc in next tr, dc in each of next 5 [5—6—6] sts, (y o hook, insert hook in next st, y o and draw lp through, y o hook and draw through 2 lps on hook) 3 times; y o and draw through all 4 lps on hook (a 3-joined dc made—2 dc dec). Repeat from * across to last 3 sts, work a 2-joined dc in next 2 sts, dc in last sl st; ch 3, turn.

3rd row: Skip first st, work a 2-joined dc in next 2 dc, * dc in each of next 5 [5—6—6] dc, work shell in tr, dc in each of next 5 [5—6—6] dc, work a 3-joined dc in next 3 sts. Repeat from * across to last 3 sts, work a 2-joined dc in next 2 dc, dc in top of ch-3; ch 3, turn.

Next row: Repeat 3rd row 1 [2—3—4] times more, but do not ch 3 at end of last row. Break off D; attach M and ch 3, turn. Always change colors in this manner.

Repeating 3rd row for pattern, work in color pattern of 4 rows each M, W, M, D, M, then work 2 rows W, omitting ch-3 on last row. Break off W. Turn. Piece should measure about 17" [17½"—18"—18½"] from beg.

To Shape Armholes: Skip first 4 [4—5—5] sts, with W make lp on hook and dc in each of next 4 dc, work 2 dc in next tr for first point, work across row in pattern as established to last 9 [9—10—10] sts, work 2 dc in next tr for last point, dc in each of next 4 dc; ch 3, turn.

Working 1 row more with W, then 2 rows with M, work as follows: Dec 1 dc at both ends of next 3 rows and, *at the same time,* work 2 dc each in first and last points.

Work even in pattern on 45 [45—51—51] sts, working 2 rows more with M, then 3 rows with D, omitting ch-3 at end of last row. **To work even:** Skip first st, 2 dc in next st, work across row in pattern as established to last 2 sts, work 2 dc in next st, dc in turning ch; ch 3, turn. Use only D from now on.

Next row: Sl st across first 2 sts, * sc in each of next 2 sts, h dc in each of next 2 sts, dc in each of next 2 [2—3—3] sts, tr in next st, dc in each of next 2 [2—3—3] sts, h dc in each of next 2 sts, sc in each of next 2 sts, sl st in next st. Repeat from * across, ending sl st in turning ch; ch 3, turn. **Following row:** Skip first st, dc in each st across; ch 3, turn. Repeat last row 1 [1—2—2] times more, omitting ch-3 on last row. Armhole should measure about 7" [7½"—7½"—8"] from beg.

To Shape Shoulders: Sl st across first 6 [6—8—8] sts, sc in next st, h dc in next st, dc in each of next 5 sts. Break off.

Work other side as follows: Skip center 19 [19—21—21] sts and attach D in next st, ch 3, dc in each of next 4 sts, h dc in next st, sc in next st, sl st in each remaining st to end of row. Break off.

LEFT FRONT: Work as for back in same stitch and color pattern throughout. Starting at lower edge with D and size I [J—I—J] crochet hook, ch 32 [32—36—36] to measure about 8" [8½"—9½"—10½"]. Starting with first row, work as for back until 2nd row of third color M stripe is completed, ending at side edge.

Neck Shaping: Next row: Work across in pattern to within last 4 sts, (work a 2-joined dc across next 2 sts) twice (1 extra dc dec at neck edge); ch 3, turn.

Being careful to keep pattern as established,

dec 1 dc at neck edge every other row twice more, then every row 8 [8—9—9] times more and, *at the same time,* when front is same length as back to underarm (center of second color W stripe), end at side edge, break off W for beg of armhole shaping. Turn.

To Shape Armhole: Starting at side edge skip first 4 [4—5—5] sts, with W make lp on hook and dc in each of next 4 dc, work 2 dc in next tr for first point, work across row in pattern. Dec 1 dc at armhole edge of next 3 rows and, *at the same time,* work 2 dc in first point (as for back).

Working as for back, work even, if necessary, on 13 [13—15—15] sts until armhole is 7" [7½"—7½"—8"] from beg. Shape shoulder same as for back.

RIGHT FRONT: Work as for left front, reversing shaping.

SLEEVES: Use color D throughout. Starting at lower edge with size I [J—I—J] crochet hook, ch 30. **1st row:** Dc in 4th ch from hook and in each ch across (28 dc, counting ch-3 as one dc); ch 3, turn. **2nd row:** Skip first st, dc in each st across, dc in top of turning ch (28 dc); ch 3, turn.

Repeating 2nd row for pattern, inc 1 st at beg and end of row every 1½" 7 [7—8—8] times. Work even on 42 [42—44—44] dc until sleeve is 16½" from beg or 1½" less than desired length to underarm, omitting ch-3 on last row.

To Shape Cap: Sl st in first 5 sts, work across row to within last 5 sts; ch 3, turn. Continue in dc and dec 1 dc at beg and end of next 7 [7—8—8] rows, then dec 2 dc at beg and end of next 2 rows. Break off.

FINISHING: Sew shoulder, side, and sleeve seams. Sew in sleeves.

Border: 1st rnd: With right side of work facing you, using size I [J—I—J] hook, attach D to right side seam at lower edge of cardigan. Sc evenly across lower edge of right front, work 2 sc in corner st, continue in sc along front edge, back neck edge, other front edge, work 2 sc in corner st, work sc along lower edge of left front and back. Join with sl st to first sc. Drop D.

2nd rnd: Using W and working loosely, sl st in back lp of each sc, working a ch-1 at each corner. Join and break off. **3rd rnd:** Using M and working in back lp of sl st, repeat 2nd rnd. **4th rnd:** Using D, sc in back lp of each st around.

Mark right front edge for 3 buttonholes. Place first marker 1½" from lower edge, the 2nd one 11½" from lower edge, the 3rd one centered between.

Sc in both lps of each st to complete border as follows: **5th rnd (buttonhole rnd):** With D, sc in each st around, working 2 sc in each corner and working each buttonhole as follows: Sc to within 1 sc of marker, ch 2, skip 2 sc. **6th rnd:** Sc in each sc around, working 2 sc over each ch-2 lp for buttonholes and increasing at corners. **7th rnd:** Sc in each sc around. Join and break off.

Repeat same 7-rnd border around lower edge of each sleeve, omitting corners and buttonholes.

COLLAR: Starting at neck edge with size I [J—I—J] hook and D, ch 24. **1st row:** Sc in 2nd ch from hook and in each ch across (23 sc); ch 14, turn. **2nd row:** Sc in 2nd ch from hook and in each of next 12 ch, sc in each of next 23 sc; ch 14, turn. **3rd row:** Sc in 2nd ch from hook and in each of next 12 ch, sc in each sc across (49 sc); ch 3, turn. **4th row:** Dc in each sc across; ch 3, turn.

Working in dc, inc 1 dc at beg and end of next 4 rows. Break off.

Border: Working in rows instead of rnds, and working along 3 sides of collar (do not work along neck edge), repeat 1st through 4th rnds of border, increasing at corners.

Center and pin collar to neck edge, then sew in place. Sew on buttons.

BELT: With D, ch 156. **1st row:** Dc in 4th ch from hook and in each ch across; ch 3, turn. Work 1 row more of dc, then work 1 row of sc around all edges of belt, working 2 sc in each corner st. Break off.

Block lightly.

U-Neck Vest

BACK: Use color M throughout. Starting at lower edge with size H [I—H—I] hook, ch 55 [55—61—61] to measure about 16" [17"—18"—20"]. **1st row:** Dc in 4th ch from hook and in each ch across; ch 3, turn. **2nd row:** Skip first st, dc in each dc across, dc in top of turning ch (53 [53—59—59] dc, counting ch-3 as one dc); ch 3, turn.

Repeating 2nd row for pattern, work even until piece measures 13" [13"—13½"—13½"] or 1" less than desired length to underarm, omitting ch-3 at end of last row.

To Shape Armholes: 1st row: Sl st across first 5 dc, ch 3, dc across to within last 5 dc; ch 3, turn. **2nd row (dec row):** Skip first dc and dec 1 dc over next 2 sts as follows: (y o hook, insert hook in next st, y o hook and draw lp through st, y o and draw through 2 lps) twice, y o hook and draw through all 3 lps on hook (1 dc dec); work across to within last 2 sts, dec 1 dc; ch 3, turn. Repeat dec row twice more.

Work even on 37 [37—43—43] dc until armholes measure 7" [7"—7½"—7½"] from beg, omitting ch-3 at end of last row.

To Shape Shoulders: Sl st across first 3 [3—5—5] dc, h dc in next dc, dc in each of next 3 dc. Break off. Skip center 23 [23—25—25] sts and work other side to correspond.

FRONT: Work as for back on 53 [53—59—59] sts until piece measures 8" [8"—8½"—8½"] from beg, omitting ch-3 at end of last row. Break off M, attach D; ch 1, turn. Work stripe pattern as follows:

1st row: With D, sl st in first st, sc in each of next 2 sts, h dc in next st, dc in next st, * tr in next st, dc in each of next 2 [2—3—3] sts, h dc in each of next 2 sts, sc in each of next 2 sts, sl st in next sc, sc in each of next 2 sts, h dc in each of next 2 sts, dc in each of next 2 [2—3—3] sts. Repeat from * twice more; tr in next st, dc in next st, h dc in next st, sc in each of next 2 sts, sl st in last st; ch 3, turn.

Note: See 2nd row of back of cardigan for working a 2-joined dc (1 st dec), a shell and a 3-joined dc (2 sts dec).

2nd row: Skip first st, as turning ch counts as one dc, work a 2-joined dc in next 2 sts, dc in each of next 2 sts, * shell in next tr, dc in each of next 5 [5—6—6] sts, work a 3-joined dc in next 3 sts, dc in each of next 5 [5—6—6] sts. Repeat from * twice more, shell in next tr, dc in each of next 2 sts, work a 2-joined dc in next 2 sts, dc in last st. Drop D, attach W; ch 3, turn.

Repeating 2nd row for pattern, work 2 rows with W, then 2 rows with D. Break off D, attach M; ch 3, turn.

7th row: With M, skip first st, dc in next st, h dc in next st, sc in each of next 2 sts, * sl st in next st, sc in each of next 2 sts, h dc in each of next 2 sts, dc in each of next 2 [2—3—3] sts, tr in next st, dc in each of next 2 [2—3—3] sts, h dc in each of next 2 sts, sc in each of next 2 sts. Repeat from * twice more, sl st in next st, sc in each of next 2 sts, h dc in next st, dc in next st, dc in turning ch; ch 3, turn.

Work even in dc until piece is same length as back to underarm, omitting ch-3 at end of last row.

To Shape Armholes: Repeat 1st and 2nd rows of back armhole shaping (41 [41—47—47] dc); ch 3, turn.

To Shape Neck and Armhole: Next row: Skip first dc, dec 1 dc over next 2 dc, work across next 9 [9—11—11] dc; ch 3, turn. Dec 1 dc at beg and end of next row; ch 3, turn. Work 2 rows more, decreasing 1 dc at neck edge only. Work even on 7 [7—9—9] dc until armhole is same length as back armhole to shoulder, ending at arm edge, then repeat shoulder shaping of back of vest.

Skip center 17 [17—19—19] sts and work other side to correspond.

FINISHING: Sew shoulder and side seams. Work all borders with right side facing you. **Lower Edge Border: 1st rnd:** Using size H [I—H—I] hook, attach W at side seam at lower edge and, working loosely, sl st in each st of starting ch. Join and break off. **2nd rnd:** With M, sl st in back lp of each st around. Join and break off. **3rd rnd:** With D, sc in back lp of each sl st. Join. With D, work 3 more rnds sc, working in both lps of each sc around. Break off at end of last rnd.

Armhole Border: Working as for lower border with M, work 1 rnd of sc evenly around armhole. Join and break off. With W, sl st in back lp of each sc around. Join and break off. Repeat 2nd and 3rd rnds of lower border. Break off.

Repeat armhole border around other armhole and around neckline. Block lightly.

Super Sweater Set

A whole new look is created by giving the cardigan a vestlike appearance and coordinating its short striped sleeves with the long-sleeved patterned turtleneck sweater under it. Patterned areas are worked in shell stitch and single crochet, solid area is worked in a chain-one and single crochet pattern, ribs are in single crochet.

SIZES: Small (8–10) [medium (12–14)—large (16–18)]. Pullover measures 16" [18"—20"] across back from side seam to side seam and about 22" [22½"—22¾"] from back neck to lower edge. Vest measures 17" [19"—21"] across back from side seam to side seam and 24" [24½"—25"] from back neck to lower edge.

MATERIALS: Brunswick Germantown knitting worsted, 4 [5—6] (4-ounce) skeins sandstone No. 430 (color A) for pullover, 3 [4—5] skeins cinnamon No. 429 (B) for vest; for design area amounts specified are enough to work both sweaters: 1 skein each Danish blue No. 484 (C), peach glow No. 485 (D), old rose No. 419 (E), helio No. 438 (F), medium lime No. 4272 (G), and absinthe heather No. 471 (H); aluminum crochet hook size H (or Canadian size No. 8) *or the size that will give you the correct gauge;* six ¾"-diameter buttons.

GAUGE: 4 sts (sc, ch 1, sc and ch 1) = 1"; 7 rows = 2".

Pullover

BACK: Starting at waist ribbing with color A, ch 9. **1st row:** Sc in 2nd ch from hook and in each remaining ch across (8 sc); ch 1, turn. **2nd row:** Sc in back loop only of each sc across; ch 1, turn. Repeat 2nd row for ribbing pattern until piece measures 15½" [17½"—19½"] from beg when slightly stretched. Do not break off; turn ribbing piece sideways to work across one long edge. Working into edge of work, crochet a row of 65 [73—81] sc evenly spaced across; ch 1, turn. **2nd row:** Sc in first sc, * ch 1, skip next sc, sc in next sc. Repeat from * across (33 [37—41] sc); ch 1, turn. **3rd row:** Sc in first sc, * ch 1, sc in next sc. Repeat from * across; ch 1, turn. Repeat last row for main pattern st. Work even in pattern st until piece measures 10", including ribbing. Break off A; attach C; ch 1, turn.

Design Pattern: 1st row: With C, sc in first sc, * ch 3, skip 1 sc, sc in next sc. Repeat from * across. Break off C; attach D; ch 1, turn. **2nd row:** With D, sc in first sc, * ch 1, insert hook into skipped sc *2 rows below* and work sc (long sc made), ch 1, sc in next sc. Repeat from * across. Drop D; attach E; ch 3, turn. **3rd row:** With E, work dc in first sc, * sc in next long sc, work 3 dc in next sc (shell made). Repeat from * across, ending with 2 dc in last sc. Break off E; do not turn work but pick up D; ch 1. **4th row:** With D, sc in top of ch-3, * ch 1, work a long sc in next long sc 2 rows below (this is same place where E sc was worked), ch 1, sc in center dc of next shell. Repeat from * across, ending sc in last dc; ch 1, turn. **5th row:** With D, sc in first sc, * ch 1, sc in next long sc, ch 1, sc in next sc. Repeat from * across. Break off D; attach F; ch 1, turn. **6th row:** With F, sc in first sc, * ch 1, sc in next sc. Repeat from * across. Break off F; attach G; ch 1, turn. **7th row:** With G, repeat 6th row. Break off G; attach A; ch 1, turn. **8th row:** With A, work long sc in first sc 2 rows below, * ch 1, sc in next sc, ch 1, work long sc in next sc 2 rows below. Repeat from * across. Break off A; attach H; ch 1, turn. **9th row:** With H, sc in first long sc, * ch 3, skip next sc, sc in next long sc. Repeat from * across. Break off H; attach D; ch 1, turn. **10th row:** With D, repeat 2nd row. Drop D; do not turn work but attach E to beg of row just completed; ch 3. **11th row:** With E, repeat 3rd row. Break off E; pick up D; ch 1, turn. **12th row:** With D, sc in first dc, * ch 1, work long sc in next long sc 2 rows below, ch 1, sc in center dc of next shell. Repeat from * across, ending with sc in top of ch-3; ch 1, turn. **13th row:** Repeat 5th row. Break off D; attach C; ch 1, turn. **14th row:** With C, repeat 6th row. Break off C; attach F; ch 1, turn. **15th row:** With F, repeat 6th row. Break off F; attach A to 3rd [5th—5th] sc from end; ch 1, turn.

To Shape Armhole: 16th row: With A, work long sc in sc 2 rows below where yarn was attached, * ch 1, sc in next sc, ch 1, work long sc in next sc 2 rows below. Repeat from * across, ending with long sc worked 2 rows below in 3rd [5th—5th] sc from end (29 [29—33] sc and long sc). Break off A; attach C; ch 1, turn. **17th row:** With C, repeat 9th row. Break off C; attach D; ch 1, turn. **18th through 24th rows:** Repeat 2nd through 8th rows once more. This completes design pattern.

With A only, work even in main pattern st until armholes measure 7¼" [7¾"—8"].

To Shape Shoulder: Next row: Sl st across first 6 sts, sc in 4th sc from beg, work across in main pattern, ending with sc in 4th sc from end; ch 1, turn. Repeat last row once more. **Next row:** Sl st across 4 [4—6] sts, sc in 3rd [3rd—4th] sc from beg, work across in main pattern, ending with sc in 3rd [3rd—4th] sc from end. 13 [13—15] sc remain for back neck edge. Break off.

FRONT: Work same as for back until armholes measure 5¾" [6"—6¼"] (29 [29—33] sc).

To Shape Neck: Mark center sc. **Next row:** Work in pattern until 12 [12—13] sc are completed (last sc worked in 3rd [3rd—4th] sc before marked sc); ch 1, turn. **Next row:** Sl st across first 4 sts, work in pattern to end; ch 1, turn. **Next row:** Work in pattern until 8 [8—9] sc are completed; ch 1, turn. Work even in pattern on one side only until piece measures same as back to shoulder, ending at arm edge.

To Shape Shoulder: Next row: Starting at arm edge, sl st across first 6 sts, sc in 4th sc from beg, work across in pattern; ch 1, turn. **Next row:** Work in pattern across, ending with sc in 4th sc from end. Break off. To work other side, attach yarn to 3rd [3rd—4th] sc on opposite side of marker (leaving center 5 [5—7] sc unworked) and work to end of row (12 [12—13] sc); ch 1, turn. **Next row:** Work in pattern across, ending sc in 3rd sc from end; ch 1, turn. **Next row:** Sl st across first 4 sts, work in pattern to end (8 [8—9] sc). Complete to correspond to first.

SLEEVES: With A, ch 15. Work same as for back waist ribbing until piece measures 7" [7½"—8"] from beg. Do not break off; turn ribbing piece sideways to work across one long edge. Working into edge of work, crochet a row of 57 [61—65] sc evenly spaced across; ch 1, turn. **2nd row:** Sc in first sc, ch 1, skip next sc, sc in next sc. Repeat from * across (29 [31—33] sc); ch 1, turn. **3rd row: (Main Pattern):** Sc in first sc, * ch 1, sc in next sc. Repeat from * across. Break off A; attach C; ch 1, turn.

Design Pattern: Work even in design pattern same as for back, but omitting decreases on 16th row (work same as for 16th row of sleeves for Vest). When 24 rows of design pattern have been completed, continue with A only as follows: **Next row:** Sc in first sc, work (ch 1, sc in next sc) 0 [2—4] times, * ch 1, skip 1 sc, sc in next sc, (ch 1, sc in next sc) twice. Repeat from * across (22 [24—26] sc). Work even in main pattern st for 2". **Next row (inc row):** Work sc, ch 1, and sc in first sc (inc made), * ch 1, sc in next sc. Repeat from * across, ending work sc, ch 1 and sc in last sc (another inc). Continue in main pattern st and repeat inc row every 2" twice more (28 [30—32] sc). Work even in pattern until sleeve measures 18½", or length desired to underarm.

To Shape Cap: Next row (dec row): Sl st across first sc and ch, work across in pattern, ending with sc in next to last sc (2 sc dec); ch 1, turn. Repeat dec row 2 [3—3] times more. * Work even in pattern for 2 rows. Repeat dec row. Repeat from * 2 [2—3] times more. Work even in pattern for 1 row. Then repeat dec row 4 times more (8 sc). Break off.

TURTLENECK: With A, ch 21. Work same as for back waist ribbing until piece measures 16" [17"—18"] when slightly stretched. Break off.

FINISHING: Block to measurements. Sew shoulder, side, and sleeve seams. Sew sleeves in place. Sew together narrow ends of turtleneck; sew turtleneck to neck edge.

Vest

BACK: With B, ch 68 [76—84]. **1st row:** Sc in 2nd ch from hook, * ch 1, skip 1 ch, sc in next ch. Repeat from * across (34 [38—42] sc); ch 1, turn. **2nd row:** Sc in first sc, * ch 1, sc in next sc. Repeat from * across; ch 1, turn. Repeat 2nd row for pattern. Work even in pattern until piece measures 16" from beg or length desired to underarm.

To Shape Armholes: Next row: Sl st across sc and ch, sc in next sc, work in pattern across, ending with sc in next to last sc (2 sc dec); ch 1, turn. Repeat last row 2 [3—4] times more (28 [30—32] sc). Work even in pattern until armholes measure 7½" [8"—8½"].

To Shape Shoulders: Next row: Sl st across first 4 sts, work in pattern across, ending sc in 3rd sc from end (4 sc dec); ch 1, turn. Repeat last row twice more. **Next row:** Sl st across first 4 [6—6] sts, work in pattern across, ending sc in 3rd [4th—4th] sc from end (12 [12—14] sc remain for back neck). Break off.

LEFT FRONT: With B, ch 36 [40—44]. Work same as for back on 18 [20—22] sc until piece measures 10½" from beg or 5½" less than back to underarm. End at front edge.

To Shape V-Neck: Next row: Starting at front edge, sl st across first sc and ch (one sc dec), work across in pattern. Continue to dec 1 sc at front edge in this manner every 6th row 6 [6—7] times more and, *at the same time,* when piece measures same as back to underarm, shape armhole.

To Shape Armhole: Work decreases in same manner as for back armhole, decreasing one sc at arm edge every row 3 [4—5] times. When neck decreases are completed, work even in pattern on 8 [9—9] sc until piece measures same as back to shoulder.

To Shape Shoulder: Work decreases in same manner as for back shoulder, decreasing 2 sc at arm edge every row 3 times. Break off.

RIGHT FRONT: Work to correspond to left front, reversing all shaping.

SLEEVES: With B, ch 58 [62—66]. **1st row:** Sc in 2nd ch from hook, * ch 1, skip 1 ch, sc in next ch. Repeat from * across (29 [31—33] sc).

Design Pattern: Work same as design pattern of pullover back for 8 rows. **9th row:** With H, sl st in first long sc and ch, sc in next sc, ch 1, * sc in next long sc, ch 3, skip next sc. Repeat from * across, ending sc in next to last long sc, ch 1, sc in last sc (2 sc dec). Break off H; attach D; ch 1, turn. **10th row:** With D, repeat 8th row of design pattern for pullover. Drop D; do not turn work but attach E to beg of row just completed; ch 1. **11th row:** With E, sc in first long sc, * work 3-dc shell in next sc, sc in next long sc. Repeat from * across. Break off E; pick up D; ch 1, turn. **12th row:** With D, work long sc in first long sc 2 rows below, * ch 1, sc in center dc of next shell, ch 1, work long sc in next long sc 2 rows below. Repeat from * across; ch 1, turn. **13th row:** With D, sc in first long sc, * ch 1, sc in next sc, ch 1, sc in next long sc. Repeat from * across. Break off D; attach C to next to last sc; ch 1, turn. **14th row:** With C, sc in same place as C was attached, * ch 1, sc in next sc. Repeat from * across, ending with sc in next to last sc (2 sc dec). Drop C; attach F; ch 1, turn. **15th row:** Work same as 6th row of design pattern for pullover. Break off F; attach A; ch 1, turn. **16th row:** With A, work long sc in first sc 2 rows below, * ch 1, sc in next sc, ch 1, work long sc in next sc 2 rows below. Repeat from * across. Break off A; pick up C; ch 1, turn. **17th row:** With C, repeat 9th row of design pattern for pullover. Break off C; attach D; ch 1, turn. **18th through 21st rows:** Work same as for 2nd through 5th rows of design pattern for pullover. **22nd row:** With F, sl st in first sc and ch, sc in next sc, * ch 1, sc in next sc. Repeat from * across, ending with sc in next to last sc (2 sc dec). Break off F; attach G; ch 1, turn. **23rd row:** With G, work same as for 6th row of design pattern for pullover. **24th row:** With A, sc in first sc, * ch 1, long sc in next sc 2 rows below; ch 5, sc in next sc. Repeat from * across. Break off A; attach H; ch 1, turn. **25th row:** With H, sc in first sc, ch 1, * sc in next long sc, ch 3, skip next sc. Repeat from * across, ending with sc in last long sc, ch 1, sc in last sc. Break off H; attach D; ch 1, turn. **26th and 27th rows:** Repeat 10th and 11th rows above. **28th row:** With D, sl st in first sc and dc, sc in center dc of first shell, * ch 1, work long sc in next long sc 2 rows below, ch 1, sc in center dc of next shell. Repeat from * across, ending with sc in center of last shell (2 sc dec); ch 1, turn. **29th row:** Work same as for 5th row of design pattern for pullover. Break off. Sleeve should measure about 8½" from beg.

FINISHING: Block to measurements. Sew shoulder, side, and sleeve seams. Sew sleeves in place, gathering top edge to fit armholes. **Edging:** Attach B to right front edge at lower corner. With right side of work facing you, work a row of sc up front edge, around neck edge and down left front edge, spacing sc to keep edge flat and smooth; ch 1, turn. Work sc in each sc around to right front corner. Break off. Sew six buttons evenly spaced along left front edge below V-neck. To form buttonholes, push buttons through ch-1 spaces in right front opposite buttons. If desired, reinforce buttonholes by whipstitching around buttonholes with A yarn.

Scalloped Sweater Set

In delicious sherbet colors of cream, pink, and yellow. Sleeveless shell zigzags along in single and double crochet. Long-sleeved cardigan goes straight in double crochet.

SIZES: 6–8 [(10–12)—(14–16)]. Snug-fitting slipover measures 15" [16"—17"] across back at underarms, 16" [16¼"—16½"] from shoulder to lower edge. Cardigan measures 16" [17"—18"] across back at underarms, 18" [18½"—19"] from back of neck to lower edge.

MATERIALS: Brunswick Windrush (100% Orlon acrylic). **For set:** 3 [4—4] (4-ounce) skeins ecru (color A), 3 skeins each light dusty rose No. 9010 (B) and saffron No. 9008 (C); for cardigan in all sizes use aluminum crochet hook size H; for slipover use H hook for size 6–8, I hook for size 10–12, J hook for size 14–16, or Canadian hook No. 8 [7—6] *or the size that will give you the correct gauge.* **For cardigan:** 2 [3—3] skeins ecru (A), 2 skeins each light dusty rose (B) and saffron (C). **For slipover:** 1

skein each ecru (A), light dusty rose (B), and saffron (C).

GAUGE: For cardigan: On size H hook, 7 dc = 2″; 2 rows = 1″. **For slipover:** On size H hook, 1 scallop = 2½″. On size I hook, 1 scallop = 2⅝″. On size J hook, 1 scallop = 2⅞″.

Cardigan

BODY: Border: (Note: Border is worked vertically. Body of cardigan is worked in one piece without side seams.)

Starting at side edge with A, ch 9. **1st row:** Sc in 2nd ch from hook and in each ch across (8 sc); ch 1, turn. **2nd row:** Working in back lp of each st, sc in first sc and in each sc across; ch 1, turn. Repeat 2nd row until piece measures 30″ [32″—34″] when slightly stretched. Do not break off or turn, but work along one long edge (top edge) of border and start body of cardigan as follows: **1st row:** Ch 1, work 105 [112—119] sc evenly spaced along top edge of border. Break off A; attach B; ch 3, turn. **2nd row:** Skip first st, dc in each st across (105 [112—119] dc, counting ch-3 as 1 dc); ch 3, turn. Repeating 2nd row and working in stripe pattern of 2 rows each B, C, and A, work even until piece measures 11″, or 1″ less than desired length to underarms.

To Divide for Front and Back: Place markers on 23rd [25th—27th] st, 29th [31st—33rd] st, 76th [81st—86th] st and 82nd [87th—92nd] st. Moving markers up on the next 2 rows worked, begin neck and armhole shaping as follows:

To Shape Neck and Armholes: 1st row (dec row): Skip first dc, dec 1 dc over next 2 sts as follows: (y o hook, insert hook in next st, y o hook and draw lp through st, y o and draw through 2 lps) twice, y o hook and draw through all 3 lps on hook (1 dc dec); work across to within last 2 sts, dec 1 dc; ch 3, turn. **2nd row:** Work even.

LEFT YOKE: Next row: Dec 1 dc, work across to first marker (arm edge); ch 3, turn. Work on left front only as follows: At neck edge dec 1 dc every other row twice, then every row 5 [6—7] times and, *at the same time,* at arm edge dec 1 dc every row 4 times. Work even on 10 [11—12] sts until armhole measures 6″ [6½″—7″], ending at arm edge; ch 1, turn.

To Shape Shoulder: Next row: Sc in each of first 3 dc, h dc in each of next 3 dc, dc in each of last 4 [5—6] dc. Break off.

RIGHT YOKE: Attach yarn to 82nd [87th—92nd] (marked) st, ch 3 and work to correspond to left front.

BACK YOKE: Attach yarn to 29th [31st—33rd] (marked) st. **Next row:** Ch 3, dec 1 dc over next 2 sts, work across to within 2 sts of 76th [81st—86th] (marked) st, dec 1 dc over next 2 sts; ch 3, turn. Dec 1 dc at beg and end of next 2 rows, then work even on 41 [44—47] sts until armholes measure same as fronts; ch 1, turn.

To Shape Shoulders: Next row: Sc in each of first 3 dc, h dc in each of next 3 dc, dc in each of next 29 [32—35] dc, h dc in each of next 3 dc, sc in last 3 dc. Break off.

SLEEVES: Cuff: (Note: Cuff is worked vertically.) With A, ch 7. Work same as border on lower edge until cuff measures 6″ when stretched slightly. Do not break off or turn, but work along one long edge (top edge) of border as follows: **1st row:** Ch 1, work 28 sc evenly spaced along top edge of cuff. Break off A; attach B; ch 3, turn. Working in stripe pattern as on back, inc 1 st at beg and end of row every 1½″ [1″—1″] 7 [9—11] times. Work even on 39 [43—47] sts until sleeve measures 14½″, or desired length to underarm, ending on same stripe row as body of sweater.

To Shape Cap: 1st row: Sl st in first 3 sts, ch 3, work across to within last 2 sts (4 sts dec); ch 3, turn. Dec 1 st at beg and end of every row 7 [8—9] times, then repeat first row twice more. Break off.

FINISHING: Sew shoulder and sleeve seams. Sew in sleeves. **Neckband: 1st row:** With A, starting at lower right front edge, work row of sl sts evenly spaced along entire right front, neck, and left front edge; ch 1, turn. **2nd row:** Sc in top lp only of each sl st across; ch 1, turn. **3rd row:** Sc in each sc across; ch 1, turn. Repeat 3rd row once more. **4th row:** Sl st in each sc across. Break off.

Slipover

BODY: (Note: Body of sweater is worked in rounds in one piece without side seams.)

Starting at lower edge with A, ch 120 to measure about 30" [32"—34"]. Being careful not to twist sts, join with sl st to form ring. **1st rnd:** Ch 3 (counts as 1 dc), dc in next ch; make joined dc as follows: * y o hook, insert hook in next ch, y o and draw through, y o and draw through 2 lps on hook *, skip next 3 sts. Repeat from * to * once more, y o and draw through all 3 lps on hook (joined dc made); dc in each of next 2 ch, 5 dc in next ch (shell made), ** dc in each of next 2 ch, work joined dc, dc in each of next 2 ch, work shell in next ch. Repeat from ** 10 times more; join with sl st in top of ch-3. Break off A. **2nd rnd:** Attach C to 4th dc of last shell of last rnd, ch 3, dc in next dc, work joined dc, dc in each of next 2 dc, work shell in next dc (center of shell on last rnd), * dc in each of next 2 dc, work joined dc, dc in each of next 2 dc, shell in next dc. Repeat from * 10 times more; join. Break off C; with A, repeat 2nd rnd, then continue in stripe pattern of 1 rnd each A, B, and C until piece measures 9", or desired length to underarms, ending with a B rnd. Break off B.

BACK YOKE: To Shape Armholes: 1st row: Attach C to center dc of next shell, ch 3, work 2 dc in same place, dc in each of next 2 dc, work joined dc, dc in each of next 2 dc, * work shell in next dc (center of shell), dc in each of next 2 dc, work joined dc, dc in each of next 2 dc. Repeat from * 3 times more; work 3 dc in next dc (center dc of shell). Break off C; attach A; ch 3, turn. **2nd row:** Work 2 dc in first dc, dc in each of next 2 dc, work joined dc, dc in each of next 2 dc, * work shell, dc in each of next 2 dc, work joined dc, dc in each of next 2 dc. Repeat from * 3 times more; work 3 dc in next dc. Break off A; attach C; ch 3, turn. Repeat 2nd row once more. Break off C; attach B and repeat 2nd row once more; then break off B; ch 1, turn. **5th row:** Sc in each of first 2 dc, * h dc in each of next 2 dc, work joined dc skipping 1 dc instead of 3 dc, h dc in each of next 2 dc, sc in each of next 3 dc. Repeat from * across, ending last repeat with sc in last dc, sc in top of ch-3; ch 1, turn. **6th row:** Sc in first st, * ch 1, skip next st, sc in next st. Repeat from * across; ch 1, turn. **7th row:** Sc in first sc, * ch 1, sc in next sc. Repeat from * across; ch 1, turn. Repeat 7th row 5 [6—7] times more, omitting ch-1 on last row. Break off.

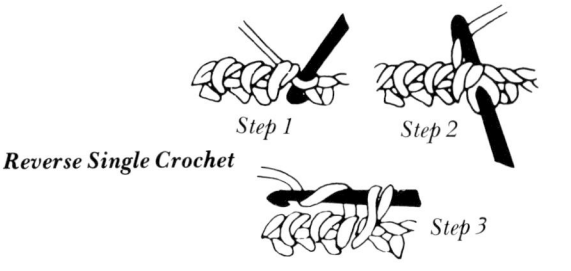

FRONT YOKE: Attach C to center dc of next shell on last B rnd (9 sts are left unworked on each side of piece for armholes) and work as for back until 5th row of yoke has been completed.

To Shape Neck: 1st row: Sc in first st, (ch 1, sc in next st) 7 times; turn. **2nd row:** Sl st in first sc and ch-1, sc in next sc, * ch 1, sc in next sc. Repeat from * across; ch 1, turn. **3rd row:** Sc in first sc, * ch 1, sc in next sc. Repeat from * across. Repeat 2nd row once, then repeat 3rd row 3 [4—5] times. Break off.

FINISHING: Sew shoulder seams. With A, work reverse sc (see diagram, p. 66) working from *left to right* around neck and armholes. With right side facing you, using A, * work sc into foundation ch at bottom of shell, (sc over sp between each of next 2 dc) 3 times; work 3 sc in next ch-3 sp, (sc over sp between next 2 dc) 3 times. Repeat from * around; join. Break off.

Reverse Single Crochet — Step 1, Step 2, Step 3

Boldly Striped Sweater Set

Turquoise jacket, with pockets and roll-up cuffs, pairs off with raglan pullover in forest green and white stripes. Waist and neckband worked in same yarn as jacket.

SIZES: 6–8 [(10–12)—(14–16)]. Pullover measures 15½" [17"—18½"] across back at underarms, 22" [22½"—23"] from shoulder to lower edge. Cardigan measures 17" [18½"—20"] across back at underarms, 24" [24½"—25"] from shoulder to lower edge.

MATERIALS: For Set: Bucilla Soufflé (90% acrylic, 10% vinyon), 10 [10—11] (1¾-ounce) balls turquoise No. 469 (color A); Bear Brand Winsom, 4 (2-ounce) skeins each winter white No. 330 (B) and Scotch green No. 90 (C). **For Pullover:** Bucilla Soufflé, 2 balls turquoise No. 469 (A); Bear Brand Winsom, 4 skeins each winter white No. 330 (B) and Scotch green No. 90 (C). **For Cardigan:** Bucilla Soufflé, 8 balls turquoise No. 469 (A). **For Both Garments:** aluminum crochet hook size H (or Canadian hook No. 8) *or the size that will give you the correct gauge.*

GAUGE: 4 sts = 1″; 4 rows = 1″.

Pullover

BACK: Ribbing: (Note: Ribbing is worked vertically.) Starting at side edge with A, ch 26. **1st row:** Sc in 2nd ch from hook and in each ch across (25 sc); ch 1, turn. **2nd row:** Working in back lp of each st, sc in each sc across; ch 1, turn. Repeat 2nd row until border measures 15″ [16½″—18″] when stretched slightly. Break off A. Attach C and ch 1. Do not turn, but work along one long edge (top edge) of border and start body of pullover as follows: **Body of Pullover: 1st row:** Sc in same place as last sc; (work ch 1 and sc) 30 [33—36] times evenly spaced along top edge of border (61 [67—73] sts); ch 1, turn. **2nd row:** Sc in first sc, * ch 1, sc in next sc. Repeat from * across; ch 1, turn. Repeating 2nd row for pattern, work in stripes of 6 rows each C and B until piece measures 9″, or desired length to underarm, above ribbing.

To Shape Armholes: 1st row: Sl st over first 2 sts, work in pattern to last 2 sts; turn. Repeat last row 2 [2—3] times more. Work even on 49 [53—57] sts until armholes measure 5½″ [6″—6½″].

To Shape Neck: 1st row: Work across first 13 [15—17] sts; turn. **2nd row:** Sl st over first 2 sts, work across; ch 1, turn. **3rd row:** Work across to last 2 sts; turn. **4th row:** Repeat 2nd row. Work even on 7 [9—11] sts until armhole measures 7″ [7½″—8″]. Break off.

Skip center 23 [25—23] sts, attach yarn to next st; ch 1, sc in same place; work other side of neck to correspond.

FRONT: Work as for back until armholes measure 3½″ [4″—4½″].

To Shape Neck: Work as for back neck shaping.

SLEEVES: Starting at lower edge with C, ch 50 [52—54] to measure about 12½″ [13″—13½″]. **1st row:** Sc in 2nd ch from hook, * ch 1, skip next ch, sc in next ch. Repeat from * across (49 [51—53] sts); ch 1, turn. **2nd row:** Sc in first sc, * ch 1, sc in next sc. Repeat from * across; ch 1, turn. Repeating 2nd row for pattern, work even in stripes as for body of back until piece measures 17″ or desired length to underarm.

To Shape Cap: 1st row: Sl st over first 2 sts, work across to last 2 sts. Repeat last row 6 times more. Break off.

FINISHING: Sew shoulder, side, and sleeve seams. Sew in sleeves. **Neckband:** With A, ch 9. Work as for ribbing on back until piece, when stretched slightly, fits around neck. Sew ends together to form ring. Sew neckband in place.

Cardigan

BACK: Starting at lower edge with A, ch 69 [75—81] to measure about 17″ [18½″—20″]. **1st row:** Sc in 2nd ch from hook, dc in next ch, * sc in next ch, dc in next ch. Repeat from * across (68 [74—80] sts); ch 1, turn. **2nd row:** * Sc in next dc, dc in next sc. Repeat from * across; ch 1, turn. Repeating 2nd row for pattern, work even until piece measures 16½" or desired length to underarm.

To Shape Armholes: 1st row: Sl st over first 3 sts, ch 1, work across to last 3 sts; ch 1, turn. **2nd row:** Draw up a lp in each of first 2 sts, y o and draw through all 3 lps on hook (1 st dec), work across in pattern to last 2 sts, draw up a lp in each of last 2 sts, y o and draw through all 3 lps on hook (another st dec). Repeat 2nd row 5 [6—7] times more. Work even on 50 [54—58] sts until armholes measure 5½" [6"—6½"], ending at arm edge.

To Shape Neck: 1st row: Work in pattern over first 16 [18—20] sts; turn. Work on 1 side only. **2nd row:** Starting at neck edge, sl st over first 2 sts, ch 1, work in pattern across; ch 1, turn. **3rd row:** Work in pattern to last 2 sts; ch 1, turn. Repeat 2nd and 3rd rows once more, then work even on 8 [10—12] sts until armhole measures 7½" [8"—8½"], ending at arm edge.

To Shape Shoulder: 1st row: Sl st over first 2 [3—3] sts, ch 1, work across; ch 1, turn. **2nd row:** Work across first 4 [5—6] sts; turn. **3rd row:** Sl st over first 2 [3—3] sts, ch 1, work across remaining 2 [2—3] sts. Break off.

Skip center 18 sts, attach yarn to next st, and work other side to correspond, reversing shaping.

POCKET LINING (make 2): Ch 23 to measure about 5¾". Work in pattern on 22 sts as for back for 4". Break off.

LEFT FRONT: Starting at lower edge with A, ch 31 [34—37] to measure about 7¾" [8¼"—8¾"]. Work as for back on 30 [33—36] sts until piece measures 5½", ending at side edge.

Pocket Opening: Mark 6th and 28th sts from front edge on last row. **Next row:** Work in pattern to first marked st, work sc (in back lps) across 22 sts of last row of pocket lining; then, starting with other marked st, continue in pattern across, ch 1, turn. Work even on 30 [33—36] sts until piece measures same as back to underarm, ending at side edge.

To Shape Armhole: 1st row: Sl st over first 3 sts, ch 1, work across; ch 1, turn. **2nd row:** Work across to last 2 sts, dec 1 st over last 2 sts; ch 1, turn. **3rd row:** Dec 1 st over first 2 sts, work across; ch 1, turn. Repeat 2nd and 3rd rows 2 [2—3] times, then repeat 2nd row 0 [1—0] times more. Work even on 21 [23—25] sts until armhole measures 3", ending at side edge.

To Shape Neck: 1st row: Work across first 16 [18—20] sts; turn. **2nd row:** Starting at neck edge, sl st over first 2 sts, ch 1, work in pattern across; ch 1, turn. **3rd row:** Work in pattern to last 2 sts; turn. Dec 1 st at neck edge every row 4 times, then work even on 8 [10—12] sts until armhole measures 7½" [8"—8½"], ending at arm edge.

To Shape Shoulder: Work as for back shoulder shaping.

RIGHT FRONT: Work to correspond to left front, reversing all shaping.

SLEEVES: Starting at lower edge with A, ch 53 [55—57] to measure about 13¼" [13¾"—14¼"]. Work even in pattern on 52 [54—56] sts as for back until piece measures 14½" or desired length to underarm.

To Shape Cap: 1st row: Sl st over first 2 sts, ch 1, work across to last 2 sts; ch 1, turn. Dec 1 st at beg and end of every other row 5 times, then every row twice more. **Next row:** Sl st over first 2 sts, ch 1, work across to last 2 sts; turn. Repeat last row once more. Break off.

FINISHING: Sew shoulders, side, and sleeve seams. Sew in sleeves. Sew pockets in place. **Neckband:** With A, ch 9. Work as for ribbing on pullover back until piece, when stretched slightly, fits around neck. Sew in place. **Front Band (make 2):** Work as for neckband until piece, when stretched slightly, fits front edge. Sew in place. With right side facing you, with A, work 1 row sc evenly spaced around lower edge of sleeves. Starting at one side seam, with right side facing you, using A, work 1 row sl st around entire lower, front, and neck edges, easing neck so ribbing will lie flat. Turn up sleeves to form cuffs.

Tailored Blazer and Hat

A sophisticated combination of wine and eggshell knitting worsted worked in long single crochet, with hat to match.

SIZES: 8 [(10–12)—(14–16)—(18–20)]. The blazer measures 16" [17"—19"—21"] across bust for a snug fit. Finished length is 16" [16½"—17"—17½"] from underarm to lower edge.

MATERIALS: Coats & Clark's knitting worsted: **For Blazer:** 3 [4—4—4] (4-ounce) skeins wine rose No. 760 (color R) and 4 [5—5—5] skeins of eggshell No. 111 (E); **For Hat:** 1 skein of each color. **For Blazer and Hat:** use aluminum crochet hooks sizes F and H (or Canadian hooks No. 10 and No. 8) *or the size that will give you the correct gauge;* 3 buttons ¾" in diameter.

GAUGE: In pattern st: With size F hook, 4 sts = 1"; 11 rows = 2". With size H hook, 7 sts = 2"; 5 rows = 1".

Note: When increasing and decreasing in pattern, if the first or last stitch of any row should be a long sc, work a regular sc instead.

Blazer

BACK: Starting at lower edge with R and size H hook, ch 64 [68—76—84] loosely to measure about 18" [19"—21"—23"]. **1st row (right side):** Sc in 2nd ch from hook and in each ch across (63 [67—75—83] sc); ch 1, turn. **2nd row:** Sc in each sc across. Drop R; attach E; ch 1, turn.

3rd row: With E, * sc in each of next 3 sc, insert hook in next R st 2 rows below (in foundation ch) and work sc (long sc made). Repeat from * across, ending with sc in each of last 3 sc; ch 1, turn. **4th row:** With E, sc in each sc and in each long sc across. Drop E; pick up R; ch 1, turn. **5th row:** With R, sc in first sc, * work long sc in next sc 2 rows below (in same place as E sc was worked), sc in each of next 3 sc. Repeat from * across, ending with long sc in next sc 2 rows below, sc in last sc, ch 1, turn. **6th row:** With R, sc in each sc and in each long sc across. Drop R; pick up E.

Repeating 3rd through 6th rows for pattern, work even in pattern for 3 [5—7—9] rows.

Next row (dec row): Draw up lp in each of first 2 sts, y o and draw through all lps on hook (1 st dec made), sc across row to within last 2 sts, draw up lp in each of last 2 sts, y o and draw through all lps on hook (another 1 st dec made) (2 sts dec on row).

Continue in pattern as established, repeating

dec row every 4th row 3 times more (55 [59—67—75] sts). Work even in pattern for 3 rows.

Next row (dec row): Place 2 safety pins as markers in work, each one marking the nearest long sc possible 4" [4½"—4¾"—5"] from beg of row and 4" [4½"—4¾"—5"] from end of row. * Sc across to within 3 sts of pin, (draw up lp in next sc, skip next sc, draw up lp in next sc, y o and draw through all 3 lps on hook) twice (4 st dec made). Repeat from * once more; work to end of row—8 sc dec on row (47 [51—59—67] sts). Keep pins in work.

Change to size F hook and use to complete back. Work even in pattern as established for 1½".

Keeping increased sts in pattern, inc 1 sc at beg and end of every 4th row 4 times (55 [59—67—75] sts). Work even until piece measures 13" from beg, then on the next sc row (work across to within 2 sc of pin below, work 2 sc in each of next 4 sc) twice; work to end of row (8 sts inc in all).

Being careful to work increased sts in pattern, work even on 63 [67—75—83] sts until piece measures 15" [15½"—16"—16½"] from beg (1" border is added later).

To Shape Armholes: Keeping pattern as established, work as follows: **1st row:** Sl st across first 4 [4—5—6] sts, ch 1, work across row to within last 4 [4—5—6] sts; ch 1, turn. Dec 1 sc at beg and end of every other row 3 [4—5—5] times. Work even on 49 [51—55—61] sts until armholes measure 7" [7¼"—7½"—7¾"] from beg.

To Shape Shoulder: Sl st across first 3 [4—6—8] sts, ch 1, work across next 10 sts; ch 1, turn. Work even for 1 row; then at shoulder edge sl st across first 5 sts, ch 1, work across 5 remaining sts. Work 1 row even. Break off.

Skip center 23 [23—23—25] sts for neck, attach yarn and work to end of row (13 [14—16—18] sts). Work to correspond to first shoulder shaping.

RIGHT FRONT: Starting at lower edge with R and size H crochet hook, ch 32 [34—38—42] loosely to measure about 9" [9½"—10½"—11½"]. **1st row:** Sc in 2nd ch from hook and in each ch across (31 [33—37—41] sc); ch 1, turn. **2nd row:** Sc in each sc across. Drop R; attach E; ch 1, turn. **3rd row:** With E, sc in each of next 3 [1—1—1] sc, * work long sc in next sc, sc in each of next 3 sc. Repeat from * across; ch 1, turn. **4th row:** With E, sc in each sc and in each long sc across. Drop E; pick up R; ch 1, turn. **5th row:** With R, sc in first 1 [3—3—3] sc, * work long sc in next sc, sc in each of next 3 sc. Repeat from * across, ending with long sc in next sc, sc in last sc; ch 1, turn. **6th row:** With R, sc in each sc and in each long sc across. Drop R; pick up E; ch 1, turn.

Repeating 3rd through 6th rows for pattern, work even in pattern for 3 [5—7—9] rows. Mark end of last row for side edge. **Next row:** Dec 1 st at beg of row, work to end of row.

Continuing in pattern as established, dec 1 st at side edge every 4th row 3 times more. Work even in pattern for 3 rows.

Mark with safety pin the long sc nearest to the center of last row. Continue in pattern and dec 4 sts (as for back) at pin. Keep pin in work.

Change to size F hook and use to complete front. Work even in pattern as established on 23 [25—29—33] sts for 1½", then inc 1 sc at side edge every 4th row 4 times (27 [29—33—37] sts). Work even until piece measures 13" from beg, then on next sc row, inc 4 sc above pin below (4 sts inc). Work even until piece measures same as back to underarm, ending at side edge (31 [33—37—41] sts).

To Shape Armhole and V-Neck: Sl st in first 4 [4—5—6] sts, ch 1, work to end of row; ch 1, turn. Mark this edge of work for beg of collar. Working in pattern, dec 1 sc at beg and end of every other row 3 [4—5—5] times; then dec 1 st at neck edge only, every other row until 13 [14—16—18] sts remain. Work even if necessary until armhole measures same as back armhole to shoulder, ending at arm edge.

To Shape Shoulder: Repeat shoulder shaping of back.

LEFT FRONT: Work as for right front until 2nd row is completed. **3rd row:** With E, * sc in each of next 3 sc, work long sc in next sc. Repeat from * across, ending with sc in each of last 3 [1—1—1] sc; ch 1, turn.

Continue in pattern as established and complete to correspond to right front.

SLEEVES: Starting at lower edge with E and size F hook, ch 36 loosely to measure about 10". Repeat first row of back (35 sc). Work even in sc for 3 rows more; then, with R, work 2 rows of sc. Starting with 3rd row of pattern, work even as for back on 35 sts for 3". Keeping increased sts in pattern, work 2 sc in first and last sts of next sc row and repeat this 2-st inc every 4" [3½"—2½"—2"] 2 [3—4—5] times more. Work even on 41 [43—45—47] sts until sleeve measures 17" [17"—17½"—17½"] or desired length to underarm.

To Shape Cap: 1st row: Repeat first row of back armhole shaping. Dec. 1 sc at beg and end of every other row 12 [12—13—13] times; then dec every row 4 [5—4—5] times. Break off.

FINISHING: Sew shoulder, side, and sleeve seams. Sew sleeves in place.

Shawl Collar: 1st row: With right side of work facing you and size F hook, attach E at marker at beg of neck shaping on right front and work 36 [36—38—38] sc evenly across neck edge to shoulder, work 4 sc across back neck shaping; then, marking first and last sc, work 23 [23—23—25] sc across last row of back, 4 sc across back neck shaping and 36 [36—38—38] sc across left front neck edge to corresponding marker (103 [103—107—109] sts). Ch 1, turn. Work short rows as follows for collar shaping. **2nd row:** Sc in each of next 63 [63—65—67] sc, do not work across remaining sc; ch 1, turn. **3rd row:** Sc in each of next 23 [23—23—25] sc (these are the sc between markers); ch 1, turn. **4th row:** Sc in each sc of last row, then sc in each of next 4 sc of first row; ch 1, turn.

Continue to work as for 4th row, working 4 extra sts on each row until all sts of collar are worked (on medium and large sizes only, there will be only 2 extra sts on last 2 rows). Break off.

Border: 1st row: With wrong side of work facing you, using size F hook, attach E to center st on lower edge of back. Sc evenly across lower edge of back and front, work 2 sc in corner st, continue in sc along front edge, then work across last row of collar, other front edge, work 2 sc in corner st, work sc along lower edge to center of back. Do not join; ch 1, turn.

Mark right front for 3 buttonholes. The first one about 8" from lower edge, the third one 1½" below start of neck shaping, the second one centered in between. **2nd row:** Sc in each sc around, making buttonholes at each marker **(for buttonhole,** at each marker ch 2, and skip 2 sts). At end of row, ch 1, turn. **3rd row:** Sc in each sc, working 2 sc in each ch-2 buttonhole; at end of row, ch 1, turn. Work 1 row more in sc. Break off. Sew seam in border. Sew on buttons.

Hat

Note: Hat is reversible. You can use it with either side of brim for right side.

Use F hook for crown and H hook for brim.

CROWN: Starting at top, with R, ch 4. Join with sl st to form ring. **1st rnd:** Work 6 sc in ring. Mark end of rnd but do not join rnds. **2nd rnd:** Work 2 sc in each sc around (12 sc). **3rd rnd:** Work (1 sc in next sc, 2 sc in next sc) 6 times (18 sc). **4th rnd:** Work (1 sc in each of next 2 sc, 2 sc in next sc) 6 times (24 sc). **5th rnd:** Sc in each sc around. **6th rnd:** Sc around, increasing 6 sc evenly spaced.

Repeat 5th and 6th rnds until there are 72 sc (at end of 20th rnd). Work even on 72 sc until hat measures 6½" from center, decreasing 1 st on last row (71 sc).

BRIM: Change to size H hook and work in rows, not rnds, from now on. Work in pattern st as follows: **1st row:** With R, sc in each sc across. Ch 1, turn (do not join). **2nd row:** Sc in each sc across. Drop R, attach E; ch 1, turn.

Starting with 3rd row of pattern, work in pattern as for back of blazer, repeating 3rd through 6th rows for 5", ending with a 5th row of pattern. Break off both R and E. Sew back seam of brim. Turn brim up as shown in photograph.

Distaff Flight Jacket

The feminine version of the lumber jacket in aqua acrylic and mohair yarn worked together for a soft and fluffy look. The shells and single crochet are worked in opposite directions to give the pattern a different slant. Zipper front.

SIZES: 8–10 [(12–14)—(16–18)]. Jacket measures 17" [18½"—20"] across back at underarms; 18" [18¾"—19½"] from back of neck to lower edge.

MATERIALS: Unger Roly-Sport (100% Orlon acrylic) 6 [7—8] (1¾-ounce) balls No. 4001 (white); Unger Lovely (80% acrylic, 20% mohair), 6 [7—8] (40-gram, about 1½-ounce) balls No. 160 (white); aluminum crochet hook size H (or Canadian hook No. 8) *or the size that will give you the correct gauge;* 18" [18"—20"] separating zipper.

GAUGE: 4 sts (sc's and ch-1's) = 1"; 4 rows = 1".

Note: Work with 1 strand each of Roly-Sport and Lovely throughout.

Body of jacket (lower bodice) is made in one piece without side seams. Yoke and sleeves are made in two pieces, with seam at center back.

LOWER BODICE SECTION: Starting at lower edge above waistband, ch 128 [140—152] to measure about 32" [35"—38"]. **1st row:** Sc in 2nd ch from hook, * skip 2 ch, work 5-dc shell in next ch, skip 2 ch, sc in next ch. Repeat from * across (21 [23—25] shells); ch 3, turn. **2nd row:** 2 dc in first sc (half shell made), * sc in center dc of next shell, shell in next sc. Repeat from * across, ending with sc in last shell, 3 dc in last sc (half shell); ch 1, turn. **3rd row:** Sc in first dc, * work shell in next sc, sc in center dc of next shell. Repeat from * across, ending with shell in last sc, sc in top of ch-3; ch 2, turn. **4th row:** Sc in first sc, * (ch 1, skip next dc, sc in next dc) twice; ch 1, sc in next sc. Repeat from * across (64 [70—76] sc); ch 1, turn. **5th row:** Sc in first ch-1 sp, * ch 1, sc in next ch-1 sp. Repeat from * across, ending ch 1, sc in turning ch-2 sp (64 [70—76] sc); ch 2, turn. Repeat 5th row 10 times more. At end of last row, ch 1, turn. **16th row:** Sc in first sc, skip next sp and sc, shell in next sp, * skip next sc and sp, sc in next sc, skip next sp and sc, shell in next sp. Repeat from * across, ending with sc in last sc (21 [23—25] shells); ch 3, turn. Repeat 2nd and 3rd rows twice, then 2nd row once more. **22nd row:** Sc in first dc, ch 1, skip next dc, sc in next dc, * ch 1, sc in next sc, (ch 1, skip next dc, sc in next dc) twice. Repeat from * across, ending with ch 1, sc in last sc, ch 1, sc in next dc, ch 1, sc in top of ch-3 (64 [70—76] sc); ch 2, turn. Repeat 5th row 11 times. Break off. Lower bodice section completed. Set this piece aside.

YOKE AND SLEEVE SECTION: Starting at cuff, ch 39 to measure about 9½". **1st row:**

Sc in 3rd ch from hook, * ch 1, skip next ch, sc in next ch. Repeat from * across (19 sc); ch 2, turn. Repeat 5th row of back 11 times (19 sc on each row). At end of last row, ch 1, turn. Work 16th row of bodice (6 shells). Repeat 2nd and 3rd rows of bodice twice, then repeat 2nd row once more. **19th row:** Repeat 22nd row of back (20 sc). **20th row (inc row):** Sc in first sc, ch 1, in next ch-1 sp work sc, ch 1 and sc (inc made), (ch 1, sc in next sp) 8 times; ch 1, inc in next sp, ch 1, sc in last sc (24 sc); ch 2, turn. Repeat 5th row of back 4 times (24 sc on each row). **25th row (inc row):** Sc in first sc, ch 1, inc in next sp, * ch 1, sc in next sp. Repeat from * to within last sp, ch 1, inc in ch-2 turning sp, ch 1, sc in ch (28 sc); ch 2, turn. Repeat 5th row of bodice 5 times (28 sc on each row). **31st row:** Repeat 16th row of bodice (9 shells). Repeat 2nd and 3rd rows of back twice, then repeat 2nd row once more. Repeat 22nd row of back (29 sc); ch 2, turn.

For size 8–10 only: Work even in sc and ch-1 pattern for 11 more rows (29 sc on each row). **For size 12–14 only:** Work even in sc and ch-1 pattern for 5 more rows (29 sc on each row). Inc in first and last sp of next row (31 sc). Work even for 5 more rows. **For size 16–18 only:** Work even in sc and ch-1 pattern for 2 rows (29 sc on each row). Inc in first and last sp of next row (31 sc). Work 4 rows even. Inc in first and last sp and in center of next row (34 sc). Work even for 3 more rows.

For all sizes: Repeat 16th row of bodice (9 [10—11] shells). Repeat 2nd and 3rd rows of bodice twice, then repeat 2nd row once more. Place marker at end of last row (underarm). Repeat 22nd row of bodice (29 [32—35] sc).

Work even in sc and ch-1 pattern for 11 [13—15] rows. Work 6 rows in shell pattern.

Work even in sc and ch-1 pattern to center of row (side neck); ch 2, turn. Continue in sc and ch-1 pattern over half the shells for 10 more rows. Break off.

Attach yarn at side neck and complete other side to correspond. Make other sleeve in same manner.

FINISHING: Sew sleeve seams from cuff to underarm marker. With right sides facing you, whipstitch last rows of corresponding back yoke sections together to form center back seam, then whipstitch yoke to lower bodice.

Waistband: With right side facing you, attach yarn to lower left corner of lower bodice. Ch 2, sc in same place; working over foundation chain, work in sc and ch-1 pattern, working 46 [50—54] sc evenly spaced across lower edge; ch 2, turn. Continue in pattern for 6 more rows. Break off.

Front Bands: With right side facing you, attach yarn to upper corner of left front. Ch 2, sc in same place; work sc and ch-1 pattern evenly spaced along front edge; ch 2, turn. Continue in pattern for 4 more rows. Break off. Work right front band to correspond.

Collar: 1st row: With right side facing you, attach yarn to upper corner of right front. Ch 2, sc in same place; work in sc and ch-1 pattern, working 28 sc evenly spaced across neck edge; ch 2, turn. Work even in sc and ch-1 pattern for 2 rows. Continuing in pattern, inc in first and last sp of next row, then every other row 6 times more (42 sc). Work 1 row even. Break off.

Insert zipper.

Yellow Jacket

With wittily concocted tiered sleeves in double crochet with a dash of red single crochet in between. White zip-front, pocketed body also worked in double crochet.

SIZES: Small (6–8) [medium (10–12)—large (14–16)]. This snug-fitting garment measures 15" [16"—17"] across from side seam to side seam; length from back of neck to lower edge is 17".

MATERIALS: Bucilla Paradise (78% acetate, 22% nylon), 11 (1-ounce) skeins white No. 401; Bear Brand Spectator (100% Orlon acrylic), 3 (2-ounce) balls chrome yellow No. 15, 1 ball scarlet No. 27; aluminum crochet hook size H (or Canadian hook No. 8) *or the size that will give you the correct gauge;* one 12" white separating zipper.

GAUGE: Using 2 strands of Paradise: 13 dc = 4"; 2 rows = 1".

Note: Use 2 strands of yarn held together throughout, except for sleeves, which are worked with a single strand of yarn.

BACK: (Note: Waistband is worked vertically.) Starting at one end of waistband with white, ch 9. **1st row:** Sc in 2nd ch from hook and in each ch across (8 sc); ch 1, turn. **2nd row:** Working in back lp of each st, sc in each sc across; ch 1, turn.

Repeat 2nd row until piece measures 13" [14"—15"], when slightly stretched; ch 3. Do not turn or break off but work along one long edge (top edge) of waistband as follows: **1st row:** Work 47 [51—55] dc, evenly spaced, across top edge of band (48 [52—56] dc, counting ch-3 as 1 dc); ch 3, turn. **2nd row:** Skip first dc, dc in each dc across, ending with dc in top of turning ch; ch 3, turn. Repeat 2nd row for pattern until piece measures 9½" from beg or desired length to underarm; ch 1, turn.

To Shape Raglan Armholes: 1st row: Sl st across first 2 [3—3] dc, ch 3, skip next dc, dc to within last 2 [3—3] dc; ch 3, turn. **2nd row (dec row):** Skip first dc, * y o hook, insert hook in next dc and draw lp through, y o, draw through 2 lps on hook. Repeat from * once more; y o, draw through all 3 lps on hook (1 dc dec); dc in each dc across to within last 2 sts, dec 1 dc; ch 3, turn. Repeat dec row 12 [13—14] times more, omitting last ch-3 (18 [18—20] dc). Break off.

RIGHT FRONT: Work waistband same as for back until piece measures 7" when slightly stretched; then ch 3 instead of ch 1. Work 24 [26—28] dc evenly spaced across top edge of waistband (25 [27—29] dc); ch 3, turn. Repeat 2nd row of back for pattern until piece measures same as back to underarm; ch 1, turn.

To Shape Raglan Armhole and Neck: 1st row: Sl st in first 2 [3—3] dc, ch 3, skip next dc, dc in each dc across; ch 3, turn. **2nd row (dec row):** Dc across to within last 2 sts, dec 1 dc; ch 3, turn. **3rd row (dec row):** Skip first dc, dec 1 dc in each dc across; ch 3, turn.

Repeat 2nd and 3rd dec rows 3 times more, ending at neck edge; ch 1, turn. **Next row:** Sl st across first 5 [5—6] dc, ch 3, skip next dc, dc in each dc across to within last 2 sts, dec 1 dc; ch 3, turn. Continuing in pattern as established, dec 1 dc at armhole edge every row 4 [5—6] times more and, *at the same time,* dec 1 dc at neck edge every row twice more (3 dc); omit last ch-3. Break off.

LEFT FRONT: Work same as for right front; pieces are reversible.

SLEEVES: (Note: Cuff is worked vertically.) Using 1 strand yellow, work cuff same as waistband for back until cuff measures 8" when slightly stretched; then ch 1. Do not turn but work 32 [32—35] sc across top edge of cuff. Drop yellow, attach scarlet; ch 1, turn.

2nd row (inc row): With scarlet, work 2 sc in first sc, sc in each sc across, work 2 sc in last sc (2 sts inc, 34 [34—37] sc); ch 1, turn. Repeat 2nd inc row once more (36 [36—39] sc). Break off scarlet; pick up yellow. With yellow, ch 3; turn. **4th row (inc row):** With yellow, dc in first sc for small and medium sizes; skip first sc for large size only; then continue for all sizes as follows: * 1 dc in next sc, 2 dc in each of next 2 sc. Repeat from * across to within last 2 sts, ending 1 dc in next dc, 2 dc in last dc (60 [60—64] dc, counting ch-3 as 1 dc); ch 3, turn.

5th row: Skip first dc, dc in each dc across, ending with dc in top of turning ch; ch 3, turn. Repeat 5th row twice more. **8th row (dec row):** Skip first dc, (dec 1 dc) twice; * dc in next dc, (dec 1 dc) twice. Repeat from * across to within 0 [0—4] sts; for large size only, work dc in next dc, dec 1 dc, dc in last dc (36 [36—39] sts). For all sizes, break off yellow; attach scarlet. With scarlet, ch 1, turn. **9th row:** Sc in first st and in each st across; ch 1, turn. **10th row:** Repeat 9th row (36 [36—39] sc). Break off scarlet, ch 1, turn. Repeat 4th through 10th rows for pattern once more, break off.

To Shape Raglan Cap: 1st row: With yellow, make lp on hook, y o hook, dc in 5th sc of last scarlet row. Repeat from * on 4th row (inc row) across to within last 4 sc (46 [46—51] dc); ch 3, turn. **2nd, 3rd, and 4th rows:** Skip first dc, dc in each dc across (46 [46—51] sts); ch 3, turn. **5th row (dec row):** Dc in each dc across, decreasing 18 [18—20] sts evenly spaced (28 [28—31] sts). Break off yellow; attach scarlet; ch 1, turn. **6th row:** Draw up a lp in each of first 2 sts, y o and draw through all 3 lps on hook (1 sc dec); sc in each dc across to within last 2 sts, dec 1 sc; ch 1, turn.

7th row: Sc in each sc across, decreasing 1 sc at beg and end of row (24 [24—27] sts). Break off scarlet; attach yellow; ch 3, turn. **8th row (inc row):** Dc in each sc across, increasing 16 [16—17] sts as evenly spaced as possible (40 [40—44] sts); ch 3, turn. **9th, 10th, and 11th rows:** Work even. **12th row (dec row):** Dc in each dc across, decreasing 16 [16—17] sts as evenly spaced as possible (24 [24—27] sts). Break off yellow; attach scarlet; ch 1, turn. **13th row:** Repeat 6th row. **14th row:** Repeat 7th row (20 [20—23] sts).

Work as for 8th through 14th rows once more, increasing 13 [13—14] sts on inc row and decreasing 13 [13—14] sts on dec row (16 [16—19] sts). Then work as for 8th through 14th rows once more, increasing 11 [11—12] sts on inc row and decreasing 11 [11—12] sts on dec row (12 [12—15] sts). At end of last row do not break off scarlet; ch 1, turn. **Next row:** Sc in each sc across; ch 1, turn. **Next (dec) row:** * Dec 1 sc. Repeat from * across (6 [6—8] sc). Break off.

Edging: With yellow, make lp on hook. With right side of work facing you, sc over side of first red sc above cuff, sc over side of each st to armhole. Sc in same manner along edge of raglan cap and opposite side. Break off.

Cord: These are short cords that stretch from one red band to next on inside of sleeves so that yellow areas will puff. With wrong side of sleeve facing you, mark center of each red band. Attach yellow with sl st to first marked sc, * ch 6, sl st in marked sc on next band. Repeat from * 5 times more. Break off. Work cord on other sleeve in same manner.

COLLAR: Right Half: Starting at neck edge with white, ch 27 [28—29]. **1st row:** Sc in 2nd ch from hook and each ch across (26 [27—28] sc). Mark end of row as front edge; ch 1, turn. **2nd row:** Work 2 sc in first sc, sc in each sc across; ch 1, turn. **3rd row:** Work even. **4th row:** Work 2 sc in first sc, sc in each sc to within last 2 sts (2 sts dec); ch 1, turn. **5th row:** Skip first 2 sc, sc in each sc across; ch 1, turn. Repeat 4th and 5th rows until 4 [5—6] sts remain. Break off.

Left Half: Work same as right half; pieces are reversible.

POCKETS (make 2): Starting at lower edge with white, ch 7. **1st row:** Sc in 2nd ch from hook and each ch across (6 sc); ch 1, turn. **2nd row:** Work 2 sc in first sc, sc in each sc across, work 2 sc in last sc; ch 1, turn. Repeat 2nd row once more (10 sc). Work 7 rows even in sc, omitting ch-1 at end of last row. Do not turn or break off but sc evenly around, working 2 sc in each corner; join. Break off.

FINISHING: Sew sleeves to raglan armholes. Sew side and sleeve seams. Sew center back seam of collar. Sew collar to neck edge.

Collar Edging: With right side of collar facing you, make lp on hook with white and work sc evenly spaced around collar. Break off.

Front Edging: With right side of work facing you, attach white to lower right front edge and work sc along edge to neck. Break off. Work along left front edge to correspond. Sew zipper in place. Following photograph for position, sew pockets in place.

Yellow Smock

Dotted with red and blue popcorn stitches, it has a shirty look with its collar and sleeves gathered at the cuffs. Mostly single crochet.

SIZES: 10–12 [(14–16)—(18–20)]. Cardigan measures 18" [19½"—21"] across at underarms, 28½" [29¼"—30"] from shoulder to lower edge.

MATERIALS: Brunswick Germantown knitting worsted (100% wool) 8 [8—9] (4-ounce) skeins saffron No. 4051 (color Y), 1 skein each thunderstorm (blue) No. 4231 (B) and scarlet No. 421 (S); 12 ball buttons, ¾" in diameter; aluminum crochet hook size G (or Canadian hook No. 9) *or the size that will give you the correct gauge.*

GAUGE: 4 sc = 1"; 4 rows = 1".

BACK: Starting at lower edge with Y, ch 89 [95—101] to measure about 22" [23½"—25"]. **1st row:** Sc in 2nd ch from hook and in each ch across (88 [94—100] sts); ch 1, turn. **2nd row:** Sc in each sc across; ch 1, turn. Repeat 2nd row 3 times more.

6th (S dot) row (right side): Attach S. **(Note:** Hold color not in use along top edge of previous row and crochet over it so that it will be concealed within sts.) With Y, sc in first 1 [4—1] sc; work S dot as follows: (Each dot contains 1 sc and 1 dot.) With Y, draw up lp in next st, drop Y, pick up S, y o, draw through both lps on hook (sc made); y o, insert hook in next st, y o and draw lp through st, y o, draw through 2 lps on hook, y o, insert hook in same st, y o and draw lp through st, (y o, draw through 2 lps on hook) twice; drop S, pick up Y, y o, draw through both lps on hook (dot completed); * with Y, sc in next 10 sts, work S dot. Repeat from * across, ending with 1 [4—1] sc (88 [94—100] sts, 8 [8—9] dots made); break off S; ch 1, turn.

7th row (dec row): With Y, skip first sc (1 sc dec), sc in each st across to within last 2 sts, skip next st (1 sc dec), sc in last st (86 [92—98] sts); ch 1, turn. Repeat 2nd row 4 times more.

12th (B dot) row (right side): Attach B; with Y, sc in first 6 [9—6] sts, work B dot; * sc in next 10 sts, work B dot. Repeat from * across, ending with 6 [9—6] sc (86 [92—98] sts, 7

[7—8] dots); break off B; ch 1, turn. **13th row:** Repeat 7th (dec) row (84 [90—96] sts).

Continue in established pattern, alternating S and B dot rows every 6th row and, *at the same time,* decrease 1 sc at beg and end of row every 1½" until 72 [78—84] sts remain. (Piece should measure about 12" from beg.) Work even in pattern until piece measures 21" [21¼"—21½"] from beg.

To Shape Armholes: Sl st in each of first 3 [4—5] sts, work in pattern to last 3 [4—5] sts; ch 1, turn. Maintaining established pattern, dec 1 st at beg and end of every other row 5 times (56 [60—64] sts). Work even in pattern until armholes measure 7½" [8"—8½"] from beg.

To Shape Shoulders and Neck: 1st short row: Sl st in each of first 5 [6—7] sts, ch 1, work in pattern across next 13 [14—14] sts; ch 1, turn. **2nd short row:** Work in pattern to within last 5 [6—6] sts; ch 1, turn. **3rd short row:** Sl st in each of first 4 sts, ch 1, sc in remaining 4 sts. Break off. Attach yarn to other arm edge and complete to correspond to first shoulder (20 [20—22] sts remain for back neck).

RIGHT FRONT: Starting at lower edge with Y, ch 43 [46—49] to measure about 10½" [11¼"—12"]. Work as for back on 42 [45—48] sts through 5th row. **6th (S dot) row (right side-front edge):** Attach S; with Y, sc in first 8 sc, work S dot, * sc in next 10 sc, work S dot. Repeat from * across, ending 8 [11—2] sc (3 [3—4] dots); break off S; ch 1, turn. **7th row (dec row):** With Y, dec 1 st at beg of row (side edge), sc in each st across (41 [44—47] sts); ch 1, turn. Repeat 2nd row of back 4 times more.

12th (B dot) row: Attach B; with Y, sc in first 2 sc, work B dot, * sc in next 10 sc, work B dot. Repeat from * across, ending 1 [4—7] sc (4 B dots); break off B; ch 1, turn. **13th row:** Repeat last dec row. Continue in established pattern, alternating S and B dot rows every 6th row and, *at the same time,* decrease 1 sc at side edge of front every 1½" until 34 [37—40] sts remain. (Piece should measure about 12" from beg.) Work even in pattern until piece measures same as back to underarm, ending at side edge.

To Shape Armhole: Starting at side edge, sl st in each of first 3 [4—5] sts, work in pattern across; ch 1, turn. Maintaining established pattern, dec 1 st at armhole edge every other row 5 times. Work even on 26 [28—30] sts until armhole measures 1" less than back armhole, ending at neck edge; ch 1, turn.

To Shape Neck and Shoulder: 1st row: Sl st across first 4 [4—5] sts, work in pattern across; ch 1, turn. Maintaining established pattern, dec 1 st at neck edge every row 4 times, ending at arm edge (18 [20—21] sts); ch 1, turn. **Next row:** Sl st across first 5 [6—7] sts, ch 1, work across in pattern; ch 1, turn. **Following row:** Work across to within last 5 [6—6] sts; ch 1, turn. **Next row:** Sl st across first 4 sts, ch 1, work across row; break off.

LEFT FRONT: Work to correspond to right front.

SLEEVES: Cuff: Starting at lower edge with Y, ch 30 to measure about 7". Work as for back on 29 sts through 5th row. **6th row (right side):** Attach B; with Y, sc in first sc, ch 2, skip 2 sc for buttonhole, sc in next 4 sc, work B dot, sc in next 10 sc, work B dot, sc in next 5 sc, skip 2 sc for buttonhole, sc in last sc; break off B; ch 1, turn. **7th row:** Working 2 sc in ch-2 sps, sc in each st across ch 1, turn. Work 4 more rows even.

Next row: Sl st across first 2 sts, ch 1, sc in each st across to within last 2 sts (25 sts); ch1, turn. **Following row (inc row):** Work 2 sc in each of first 4 sc, * 3 sc in next sc, 2 sc in each of next 4 sc. Repeat from * across, ending 3 sc in last sc (55 sts); ch 1, turn.

Body of Sleeve: Work 5 rows even; ch 1, turn. **6th row (right side):** Attach S; with Y, sc in first 8 sc, work S dot, * sc in next 10 sc, work S dot. Repeat from * across, ending 9 sc (4 dots); break off S; ch 1, turn. Work 5 rows even; ch 1, turn. **12th row:** Attach B; with Y, sc in first 2 sts, work B dot, * sc in next 10 sts, work B dot. Repeat from * across, ending 3 sc (5 B dots); break off B; ch 1, turn. Continue alternating S and B dot rows every 6th row until piece measures 16" from beg of sleeve body or desired length to underarm.

To Shape Cap: 1st row: Sl st across first 4 [3—2] sts, ch 1, work in pattern across to within last 4 [3—2] sts; ch 1, turn. **2nd row:** Sl st across first 2 sts, ch 1, work in pattern across to within last 2 sts; ch 1, turn. Maintaining established pattern, dec 1 st at beg and end of every other row 8 [9—10] times; then repeat 2nd row 4 times more (11 sts remain). Break off.

FINISHING: Block to measurements. Sew shoulder and side seams. Sew sleeve seams, leaving 2" open from wrist edge. Sew sleeves in place.

Right Front Border: 1st row: With right side of garment facing you, attach Y at lower edge of right front; work row of sc evenly spaced along front edge to neck; ch 1, turn. **2nd row:** Work even; ch 1, turn. **3rd row:** Starting about 3" from lower edge, mark edge for 7 buttonholes evenly spaced (8th buttonhole will be worked on collar). Work sc in each sc to first marker, * ch 2, skip 2 sc, sc in each sc across to next marker. Repeat from * across, ending sc in remaining sc; ch 1, turn. **4th row:** Sc in each sc across, working 2 sc in each ch-2 sp for buttonholes; ch 1, turn. Work 1 row even. Break off.

Left Border: Work to correspond to right border, omitting buttonholes.

Collar: 1st row: With right side facing you, attach Y at right front edge of neck opening; work 1 row sc evenly spaced around neck edge; ch 1, turn. **2nd row:** Dec 1 sc, work across; ch 1, turn. **3rd row:** Dec 1 sc, ch 2, skip 2 for buttonhole, work across; ch 1, turn. **4th row:** Dec 1 sc, sc across, working 2 sc in ch-2 sp; ch 1, turn. Repeat 2nd row twice more. **7th row (inc row):** Work 2 sc in first sc (inc made), work across, ch 1, turn. **8th row:** Mark collar for 4 S dots evenly spaced; attach S; with Y, dec 1 sc, * sc in each sc to within 2 sts of next marker, work S dot. Repeat from * across, ending with sc in remaining sc; break off S; ch 1, turn. Repeat 7th (inc) row 5 times more.

Maintaining established pattern, repeat 8th row, working B dots. Repeat 7th (inc) row 3 times more. Break off.

Edging: With Y, work 1 row sc evenly spaced around collar and cuffs, working 3 sc in corners. Break off.

Sew buttons in place.

Cufflinks: Crochet 1"-long chain. Attach 1 button to each end.

Dressy Sweaters

How to Block Linen Garments

Follow these blocking instructions for the newly finished garment before it has been worn, as well as for the soiled garment.

Natural linens last longer and look better if washed rather than dry-cleaned. It is best to hand-wash them, using hot or cool water and soap or detergent. Wash colored linens separately as they may not be completely colorfast when new.

If possible, do not wash garments in humid weather as linens should take no longer than twenty-four hours to dry or they may become musty.

Wash even the newly made sweater thoroughly as washing will remove some of the sizing and make a softer garment. Squeeze or wring out as much water as possible (linen is a strong fiber and becomes even stronger when wet). Roll sweater briefly in a towel, if desired.

Do not spread sweater flat to block as it takes too long to dry. Hang it on a wooden or plastic hanger and shape while still wet by pulling downward and smoothing the stitches with the palm of the hand. Make garment look relatively long and skinny; it will pull up and stretch as needed on the body.

Important: Test all pressing on a swatch first to be sure that the temperature of the iron is correct. Linen can stand a hot iron, but you must work quickly to avoid scorching.

When sweater is dry, steam-press over a wet cloth. Then remove cloth and quickly go over garment with iron, pressing hard to flatten stitches and to bring out the natural sheen of the linen. Do not press buttons.

Old-Fashioned Peplum Camisole

Body is worked in rows of double crochet and clusters, with an open flower-motif front panel. Lined in lavender.

SIZES: 6–8 [(10–12)—(14–16)]. Camisole measures about 15" [16½"—18"] across back below underarms, 20" [20½"—21"] from shoulder to lower edge.

MATERIALS: Frederick J. Fawcett 10/2 linen yarn, 1 [1—2] (8-ounce) tubes natural; steel crochet hook No. 00 *or the size that will give you the correct gauge;* tapestry needle; 1 yard voile or other sheer fabric for lining.

GAUGE: (blocked and unblocked): 5 dc = 1"; 2 rows = 1".

Important: In order to insure correct gauge, make a sample swatch as follows: Ch 24. **1st row:** Dc in 4th ch from hook and in each ch across; ch 3, turn. **2nd row:** Skip 1st dc, dc in each of next 2 dc, * in next dc work cl as follows: (y o, insert hook in st and pull up lp, y o and draw through 2 lps on hook) 5 times, y o and draw through all 6 lps on hook (cl completed); dc in each of next 2 dc. Repeat from * across, ending with dc in turning ch; ch 3, turn. **3rd row:** Skip 1st dc, dc in each st across; ch 3, turn. Repeat 2nd and 3rd rows 3 times more. Break off. Block (see directions above) to measure 4" square and check gauge.

BACK: Starting at lower edge above peplum, ch 70 [78—86]. **1st row (right side):** Dc in 4th ch from hook and in each ch across (68 [76—84] dc, counting turning ch-3 as 1 dc); ch 3, turn. **2nd row:** Skip 1st dc, dc in next 1 [2—2] dc; * work cl in next dc, dc in each of next 2 dc. Repeat from * across. **For sizes 6–8 and 14–16 only:** Work last dc of last repeat in top of turning ch. **For size 10–12 only:** Work 1 more dc in turning ch. **For all sizes:** Ch 3, turn. **3rd row:** Skip 1st dc, dc in each remaining dc and in each cl across (68 [76—84] dc); ch 3, turn. Repeat 2nd and 3rd rows 4 times, then repeat 2nd row once more. **Next row (inc row):** Dc in 1st dc, work in pattern up to last dc, work 2 dc in last dc (2 dc inc—70 [78—86] dc); ch 3, turn. Working added sts in pattern, work 3 rows even, then repeat inc row (72 [80—88] dc). Work even in pattern for 4 more rows.

To Shape Armholes: 1st row (wrong side): Sl st in first 7 [9—11] dc, sc in next dc, dc in each of next 2 [1—2] dc, (cl in next dc, dc in each of next 2 dc) 18 [19—20] times; cl in next 0 [1—1] dc, dc in each of next 0 [1—1] dc, sc in next dc; turn. **2nd row:** Sl st in first 3 [4—6] sts, ch 3, dc in next 51 [53—53] sts; turn. **3rd row:** Sl st in first st and in next 0 [1—0] sts, dc in next st, (cl in next st, dc in each of next 2 sts) 16 times; dc in next st (50 sts); ch 3, turn.

Right Strap: 1st row: Skip first 2 dc, dc in each of next 9 sts, sc in next st; ch 3, turn. **2nd row:** Skip first sc, dc in next dc, (cl in next dc, dc in each of next 2 dc) twice; cl in next dc, dc in next dc; ch 3, turn. **3rd row:** Skip first dc, dc in each of next 8 sts; ch 3, turn. **4th row:** Skip 1st dc, (cl in next dc, dc in each of next 2 sts) twice; cl in next dc, dc in next dc; ch 3, turn. Work even in pattern for 5 [6—7] more rows, omitting ch-3 on last row. Break off.

Left Strap: Skip center 26 sts. **1st row (right side):** Sc in next st, dc in each of next 9 sts; ch 3, turn. **2nd row:** Skip 1st dc, (cl in next dc, dc in each of next 2 dc) twice; cl in next dc, dc in next sc; ch 3, turn. Work even in pattern for 7 [8—9] more rows, omitting ch-3 on last row. Break off.

FRONT: Starting at lower edge above peplum ch 72 [80—88]. **1st row (right side):** Dc in 4th ch from hook and in each of next 27 [31—35] ch (29 [33—37] dc, counting turning ch-3 as 1 dc); (ch 3, skip 3 ch, in next ch work sc, ch 3 and sc) twice; ch 3, skip 3 ch; dc in each of next 29 [33—37] dc; ch 3, turn. **2nd row:** Skip first dc, dc in next 1 [2—0] dc, (cl in next dc, dc in each of next 2 dc) 9 [10—12] times; * skip next ch-3 sp, in next ch-3 sp work cl, (ch 3 and cl) twice (3-cl motif made). Repeat from * once more, skip next ch-3 sp; (dc in each of next 2 dc, cl in next dc) 9 [10—12] times; dc in each of next 2 [3—1] dc; ch 3, turn. **3rd row:** Skip first dc, dc in each of next 28 [32—36] dc; ch 3, sc in top of center cl of next 3-cl motif, ch 3, sc in sp between 3-cl motifs, ch 3, sc in top of center cl of next 3-cl motif, ch 3, dc in each of next 29 [33—37] dc; ch 3, turn. **4th row:** Skip first dc, dc in next 1 [2—0] dc, (cl in next dc, dc in each of next 2 dc) 9 [10—12] times; ch 5, skip next ch-3 sp, sc and ch-3 sp; in next sc work 3-cl motif, ch 5, skip next ch-3 sp, sc and ch-3 sp; (dc in each of next 2 dc, cl in next dc) 9 [10—12] times; dc in each of next 2 [3—1] dc; ch 3, turn. **5th row:** Skip first dc, dc in each of next 28 [32—36] dc, ch 3, in 4th ch of next ch-5 sp work sc, ch 3 and sc; ch 3, sc in top of center cl of next 3-cl motif, ch 3; in 2nd ch of next ch-5 sp work sc, ch 3 and sc; ch 3, dc in each of next 29 [33—37] dc; ch 3, turn. **6th row:** Skip first dc, dc in next 1 [2—0] dc, (cl in next dc, dc in each of next 2 dc) 9 [10—12] times; * skip ch-3 sp, in next ch-3 sp work 3-cl motif, skip next ch-3 sp *, skip sc. Repeat from * to * once more; (dc in each of next 2 dc, cl in next dc) 9 [10—12] times; dc in each of next 2 [3—1] dc;

ch 3, turn. Repeat 3rd through 6th rows 3 times more, increasing 1 st at each end of 13th and 17th rows. Then repeat 3rd and 4th rows once.

To Shape Neck and Armholes: 1st row: Skip first dc, dc in each of next 26 [30—34] sts; ch 3, skip next dc, cl and dc; in next dc work sc, ch 3 and sc; ch 3, in 4th ch of next ch-5 sp work sc, ch 3 and sc; ch 3, sc in top of center cl of next 3-cl motif, ch 3, in 2nd ch of next ch-5 sp work sc, ch 3 and sc; ch 3, in next dc work sc, ch 3 and sc; ch 3, skip next dc, cl and dc; dc in each of next 27 [31—35] dc; turn. **2nd row:** Sl st in first 7 [9—11] dc, sc in next st, dc in each of next 2 [1—3] sts, (cl in next dc, dc in each of next 2 dc) 5 [6—7] times; cl in next dc, dc in next dc; (skip next ch-3 sp, 3-cl motif in next ch-3 sp) twice; skip next 2 ch-3 sps, (3-cl motif in next ch-3 sp, skip next ch-3 sp) twice; dc in next dc, (cl in next dc, dc in each of next 2 dc) 6 [6—7] times; cl in next 0 [1—0] dc, dc in each of next 0 [1—1] dc, sc in next dc; turn. **3rd row:** Sl st in first 3 [4—5] sts, ch 3, dc in each of next 15 [16—17] sts; in next st work sc, ch 3 and sc; (ch 3, sc in top of center cl of next 3-cl motif, ch 3, in next sp between 3-cl motifs work sc, ch 3 and sc) 3 times; ch 3, sc in top of center cl of next 3-cl motif, ch 3, in next dc work sc, ch-3 and sc; dc in each of next 16 [17—18] sts; turn.

Right Strap: 1st row: Sl st in first 3 [4—5] sts, ch 3, (cl in next dc, dc in each of next 2 dc) twice; cl in next dc, dc in next dc; ch 3, turn. **2nd row:** Skip first dc, dc in each of next 8 sts; ch 3, turn. Work even in pattern for 8 [9—10] more rows, omitting ch-3 on last row. Break off.

Left Strap: Skip center 5 dc, 13 ch-3 sps and 5 dc. **1st row (wrong side):** Dc in next dc, (cl in next dc, dc in each of next 2 dc) twice; cl in next dc, dc in next dc; ch 3, turn. Starting with 2nd row, complete as for right strap.

FINISHING: Sew right side and shoulder seams. Starting at armhole, sew left side seam, leaving 5" opening (see drawing).

Peplum: Work along opposite edge of starting chain along lower edge of camisole. **1st row:** With right side facing you and starting at back corner of 5" opening (X), in first ch work sc, ch 3 and sc; * ch 3, skip 3 ch, in next ch work sc, ch 3 and sc. Repeat from * 34 [38—42] times more, ending last repeat in last ch in front corner of opening; ch 3, turn. **2nd row:** Work 3-cl motif in first ch-3 sp, * skip next ch-3 sp, work 3-cl motif in next ch-3 sp. Repeat from * across (35 [39—43] motifs); ch 3, turn. **3rd row:** Sc in top of center cl of first cl motif, * ch 3, in next sp between motifs work sc, ch 3 and sc; ch 3, sc in top of center cl of next motif. Repeat from * 33 [37—41] times more; ch 3, in top of last cl of last motif work sc, ch 3 and sc; ch 3, turn. **4th row:** Work 3-cl motif in first ch-3 sp, * skip next ch-3 sp, sc and ch-3 sp, work 3-cl motif in next ch-3 sp. Repeat from * across (33 [37—41] motifs); ch 3, turn. Repeat 3rd and 4th rows once more, then repeat 3rd row once again, omitting last ch-3. Break off.

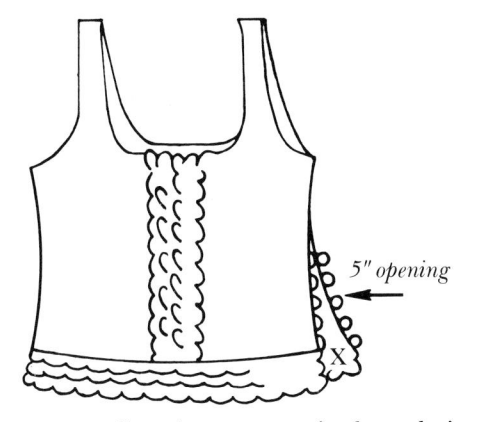

Button Loops: Work along front edge of side opening. With right side facing you, sl st in corner at lower edge above peplum, * ch 5, skip 1 dc, sl st over side of next dc (button loop made). Repeat from * 4 times more. Break off.

Buttons (make 5): Starting at center, ch 4. Join with sl st to form ring. **1st rnd:** Work 8 sc in ring. **2nd rnd:** Sc in each sc around. Repeat 2nd rnd twice more; sl st in next st. Break off, leaving 12" end. With yarn, wind a ball about ½" in diameter. Insert ball in button, leaving 12" end extending. Thread end in needle and sew opening closed. Sew buttons in place after sweater has been blocked.

With wrong side facing you, work 1 row sl st evenly spaced around armhole edges and neck edge, omitting front center panel.

See How to Block Linen Garments (p. 80) for blocking instructions. Sew on buttons.

Lining: (Note: Peplum is not lined.) Cut front and back pieces following outline of blocked crocheted piece and adding ½" all around for seam allowance. Stitch shoulder and side seams, leaving 5" opening at lower edge of left side seam. Turn under raw edges ½" and topstitch. Insert in camisole, wrong sides facing, and blindstitch around neck and armholes. Tack to side seams.

Charming Square-Neck Pullover and Cloche

Worked mostly in single crochet, with yarn doubled, in soft ivory, with mock-cable details. Cloche to match.

SIZES: 6–8 [(10–12)—(14–16)]. Pullover measures about 16" [18"—20"] across back at underarm.

MATERIALS: Bucilla Perlette acrylic yarn, 9 [10—10] (1¾-ounce) balls ivory No. 23 for pullover, 2 balls for cloche; aluminum crochet hook size I (or Canadian hook No. 7) *or the size that will give you the correct gauge.*

GAUGE: For pullover, 7 dc = 2"; for cloche, 3 dc = 1".

Note: Work with yarn held double throughout.

Pullover

BACK: Starting at lower edge, ch 58 [64—72] to measure about 16" [18"—20"]. **1st row (wrong side):** Sc in 2nd ch from hook, * ch 1, skip next ch, sc in next ch. Repeat from * across (29 [32—36] sc); ch 3, turn. **2nd row:** Skip first sc, * dc in next ch-1 sp, dc in next sc. Repeat from * across (57 [63—71] dc, counting turning ch as 1 dc); ch 1, turn. **3rd row:** Sc in first dc, * ch 1, skip next dc, sc in next dc. Repeat from * across, ending last repeat with sc in turning ch; ch 3, turn.

To Establish Mock Cable Pattern: 4th row (right side): Skip first sc, (dc in next sp, dc in next sc) 5 [6—8] times; * y o, insert hook under post of next dc 1 row below, y o and draw up lp so that st lies flat, (y o, draw through 2 lps on hook) twice (post dc made); dc in next sc, skip next 3 dc 1 row below, post dc over next dc 1 row below, working behind last post dc made, dc in next sc; working in front of last post dc made, post dc over 2nd skipped dc 1 row below (cable made), dc in next sc, skip next dc 1 row below, post dc over next dc 1 row below *; (dc in next sc, dc in next sp) 10 [11—11] times; dc in next sc. Repeat from * to * once more, (dc in next sc, dc in next sp) 5 [6—8] times; dc in last sc; ch 1, turn.

5th row: Repeat 3rd row. **6th row (right side):** Skip first sc, (dc in next sp, dc in next sc) 5 [6—8] times; * (post dc over next post dc 1 row below, dc in next sc) 4 times *; (dc in next sp, dc in next sc) 10 [11—11] times. Repeat from * to * once more, (dc in next sp, dc in next sc) 5 [6—8] times; ch 1, turn. **7th row:** Repeat 3rd row. **8th row:** Skip first sc, (dc in next sp, dc in next sc) 5 [6—8] times; * post dc over next post dc, dc in next sc, skip next post dc, post dc over next post dc; working behind last post dc made, dc in next sc, post dc over skipped post dc, dc in next sc, post dc over next post dc * ; (dc in next sc, dc in next sp) 10 [11—11] times; dc in next sc. Repeat from * to * once more, (dc in next sc, dc in next sp) 5 [6—8] times; dc in last sc; ch 1, turn.

Repeat 5th through 8th rows for pattern until piece measures about 16" [17"—17"] from beg, or desired length to underarm, ending with a right-side row. At end of last row, ch 5, turn.

To Shape Cap Sleeves: 1st row (wrong side): Sc in 2nd ch from hook, ch 1, skip next ch, sc in next ch, ch 1, skip next ch, sc in first dc, continue in pattern across; ch 5, turn. **2nd row (right side):** Dc in 3rd ch from hook and in each of next 2 ch, continue in pattern across (65 [71—79] sts); ch 9, turn. **3rd row:** Sc in 2nd ch from hook, (ch 1, skip next ch, sc in next ch) 3 times; ch 1, skip next ch, sc in next dc, continue in pattern across; ch 9, turn. **4th row:** Dc in 3rd ch from hook and in each of next 6 ch, continue in pattern across; ch 1, turn.

5th row: Work even in pattern on 81 [87—95] sts; ch 3, turn. **6th row:** Skip first sc, to establish cable pattern, repeat from * to * of 4th row of back, then work in pattern across to within last 8 sts. Repeat from * to * of 4th row of back, dc in last sc; ch 1, turn. Work in established pattern on 4 cables for 4 rows, ending with a right-side row.

11th row (inc row): Sc in first dc, * ch 1, skip next dc, sc in next dc *. Repeat from * to * twice more, ch 1, skip next dc, in next dc work sc, ch 1 and sc (2 sts inc). Repeat from * to * across to last 10 dc, ch 1, skip next dc, in next dc work sc, ch 1 and sc (2 sts inc), then repeat from * to * 3 times; ch 1, skip next dc, sc in turning ch. Work in established pattern on 85 [91—99] sts until sleeve measures about 6" [6½"—7"] from beg, ending with a wrong-side row.

Mark off center 21 [23—23] sts. Move markers on each row.

To Shape Shoulders: 1st row (right side): Sl st in first 9 sts, ch 3 (counts as first dc), work in established pattern to within first marker, (dc in next sc, post dc over next dc 1 row below) 10 [11—11] times; dc in next sc; work in established pattern to last 8 sts (69 [75—83] sts); ch 1, turn. **2nd row:** Work even in pattern. Repeat last 2 rows once more (53 [59—67] sts). Remove markers.

To Shape Neck: 1st short row: Sl st in first 9 [11—15] sts, ch 3 (counts as first dc), work in established pattern across next 7 sts, dc in next st; ch 1, turn. **2nd short row:** Work even in pattern. Break off.

With right side facing you, skip 19 [21—21] sts at neck edge, with lp on hook dc in next st and work other side of neck to correspond.

FRONT: Work same as for back through 6th row of sleeve shaping.

7th row: Work even in pattern. Mark off center 21 [23—23] sts. **8th row:** Skip first sc, work in established pattern to first marker, (dc in next sc, post dc over post of next dc 1 row below) 10 [11—11] times; dc in next sc, work in established pattern across; ch 1, turn. Work 2 rows in pattern. Remove markers.

11th row (inc row): Repeat 11th (inc) row of back sleeve shaping.

To Shape Neck: Work on one side only from now on. **1st row:** Work in established pattern across first 33 [35—39] sts; ch 1, turn. Work even in pattern until sleeve measures same as back to shoulder, ending with a wrong-side row.

To Shape Shoulder: Next row: Sl st across first 9 sts, ch 3 (counts as first dc), work in established pattern across; ch 1, turn. **Following row:** Work even in pattern. Repeat last 2 rows once more.

Next row: Sl st across first 9 [11—15] sts, ch 3 (counts as first dc), work in pattern across next 7 sts, dc in next st; ch 1, turn. **Following row:** Work even in pattern. Break off.

With right side facing you, skip 19 [21—21] sts at neck edge, with lp on hook, dc in next st and work other side of neck to correspond.

Sew side and shoulder seams. Work 1 rnd in sc and ch-1 pattern around neck edge.

Cloche

CROWN: Starting at center, ch 5; join with sl st to form ring. **1st rnd:** Work 8 sc in ring; join with sl st to first sc. Mark beg of each rnd. **2nd rnd:** Ch 3 (counts as first dc), work 1 more dc in first st, (2 dc in next sc) 7 times (16 dc); join with sl st to top of first ch-3. **3rd rnd:** Ch 3, work 1 more dc in first st, 2 dc in each dc around (32 dc); join.

4th rnd: Ch 3, skip first st, * dc over post of next dc, dc in next dc. Repeat from * 14 times more; dc over post of last dc; join. **5th rnd:** Ch 3, work 1 more dc in first st, * dc over post of next dc, 2 dc in next dc. Repeat from * around, ending dc over post of last dc; join. Piece should measure about 5½" in diameter. **6th rnd:** Ch 3, skip first st, 2 dc in next dc, * dc over post of next dc, dc in next dc, 2 dc in next dc. Repeat from * around, ending dc over post of last dc (64 sts); join.

7th rnd: Ch 3, skip first dc, work even in pattern; join. **8th rnd:** Ch 3, skip first st, dc in each of next 2 dc, * dc over post of next dc, dc in each of next 7 dc. Repeat from * around, ending last repeat with dc in each of last 4 dc; join. Work even in established pattern for 3 more rnds.

Next rnd: Ch 3, skip first st, * dc over post of next dc, dc in next dc. Repeat from * around, ending dc over post of last dc; join.

BRIM: 1st rnd: Ch 3, skip first st, * dc in each of next 2 dc, 2 dc in next dc. Repeat from * around (85 dc); join. **2nd rnd:** Ch 3, skip first st, dc in each dc around; join. **3rd rnd:** Ch 3, skip first st, dc in each dc around, increasing 8 dc as evenly spaced as possible; join. **4th rnd:** Ch 3, skip first st, dc in each dc around, increasing 12 dc as evenly spaced as possible; join. **5th rnd:** Sl st in each st; join. Break off.

INSIDE BAND: With wrong side of last rnd of crown facing you, sc over post of any dc that is not a post dc on last rnd of crown, * ch 1, skip post dc, sc around post of next dc. Repeat from * around; join. Break off.

Crochet a chain to measure about 36". Break off. Weave chain under post dc's on last rnd of crown; tie in bow.

Side-Tie Sweater

Rippling ruffles of chain-loop shells ornament V-neck and wrist edges. In aqua linen.

SIZES: 8–10 [(12–14)—(16–18)]. Sweater measures 17" [19"—21"] across back at underarms, 20" [20½"—21"] from back of neck to lower edge.

MATERIALS: Frederick J. Fawcett 10/2 linen yarn, 2 [3—3] (8-ounce) tubes aqua; steel crochet hook size 00 *or the size that will give you the correct gauge;* tapestry needle.

GAUGE: After washing and blocking, 3 cl = 1"; 5 rows = 2". Unblocked gauge, 3 cl = 1"; 3 rows = 1".

Important: In order to insure correct gauge, make a sample swatch as follows: Ch 25. Follow 1st and 2nd rows of back for pattern, working 10 rows. Block (see How to Block Linen Garments, p. 80) to measure 4" square and check gauge.

BACK: Starting at lower edge above waistband, ch 101 [113—125]. **1st row:** Pull up lp in 2nd ch from hook and in each of next 3 ch, y o and draw through all 5 lps on hook, ch 1 (cl made); * pull up lp in last ch-1 sp made, pull up lp in same foundation ch as last lp of previous cl, pull up lp in each of next 2 ch, y o and draw through all 5 lps on hook, ch 1 (another cl made). Repeat from * across, dc in same ch as last lp of previous cl; ch 2, turn. **2nd row:** Pull up lp in 2nd ch from hook, pull up lp in dc, pull up lp in ch-1 sp above first cl, pull up lp in next st (horizontal lp), y o and draw through all 5 lps on hook, ch 1 (first cl made); * pull up lp in last ch-1 sp made, pull up lp in same st as last lp of previous cl, pull up lp in each of next 2 sts (top of cl and next horizontal lp), y o and draw through all 5 lps on hook, ch 1 (cl made). Repeat from * across, dc in same st as last lp of previous cl (49 [55—61] cl); ch 2, turn. Each cl should be directly over cl on previous row. Repeat 2nd row for pattern 12 [13—14] times more.

Next row (inc row): Pull up lp in 2nd ch from hook, pull up lp in dc, y o and draw through all 3 lps on hook, ch 1 (inc cl made). Repeat from * across on 2nd row through last cl. Pull up lp in last ch-1 sp made, pull up lp in same st as last lp of previous cl, y o and draw through all 3 lps on hook, ch 1 (inc cl made), dc in same st as last lp of previous cl; ch 2, turn. Work even in pattern on 51 [57—63] cl for 13 more rows, omitting dc at end of last row; ch 1, turn.

To Shape Armholes: Next row (dec row): Sl st in ch-1 sp above first cl and in each of next 5 [5—7] sts, pull up lp in each of next 4 sts, y o and draw through all 5 lps on hook, ch 1, work 43 [49—53] more cl; ch 1, turn. **Following row (dec row):** Sl st in ch-1 above first cl and in each of next 1 [5—5] sts, pull up lp in each of next 4 sts, y o and draw through all 5 lps on hook, ch 1, work 40 [42—46] more cl, dc in same st as last lp; ch 2, turn. Work even on 41 [43—47] cl for 15 [17—18] more rows, omitting dc at end of last row; ch 1, turn.

To Shape Shoulders: Next row: Sl st in each of first 10 [12—12] sts, work 29 [29—33] cl, sc in next st, sl st in next st; ch 1, turn. **Following row:** Skip sl st, sc in sc, work 23 [23—25] cl, sc in next st, sl st in next st; ch 1, turn. **Last row:** Skip sl st, sc in sc, work 17 cl, sc in next st, sl st in next st. Break off.

FRONT: Work same as for back to armhole.

To Shape Armhole and V-Neckline: Next row: Sl st in each of first 6 sts, work 22 [25—28] cl, dc in same st as last lp; ch 1, turn. **Following row:** Working on one side only, *to dec 1 cl,* sl st in dc, pull up lp in each of next 4 sts, y o and draw through all 5 lps on hook, ch 1, work 19 [20—22] more cl, dc in same st as last lp; ch 2, turn. Continue working on one side only for 17 [19—19] more rows, decreasing 1 cl *at neck edge only.* End at neck edge with dc in same st as last lp (12 [12—14] cl); ch 1, turn.

To Shape Shoulder: Next row: Dec 1 cl, work 6 [6—5] cl, sc in next st, sl st in next st; ch 1, turn. **Following row:** Sl st in sc and in each of next 6 [6—4] sts, work 2 cl, dc in same st as last lp. Break off.

To work other side, attach yarn at neck edge and work 21 [24—27] cl, dc in same st as last lp; ch 1, turn. Complete to correspond to other side.

SLEEVES: Starting at lower edge above ruffle, ch 43 [47—47]. **1st row:** Pull up lp in 2nd ch from hook and in each of next 3 ch, y o and draw through all 5 lps on hook, ch 1, work 19 [21—21] more cl across, dc in same st as last lp; ch 2, turn. Continue working in pattern, increasing 1 cl each side (same as for back) every 4th row 10 [10—11] times. Work even in pattern on 40 [42—44] cl until sleeve measures 17½" [18"—18½"] or desired length to underarm when blocked. Omit dc at end of last row, ch 1 and turn.

To Shape Cap: Next row: Sl st in each of first 4 sts, work 34 [36—38] cl across; ch 1, turn. **Following row:** Sl st in each of first 2 sts, work 31 [32—33] cl, dc in same st as last lp; ch 2, turn.

Work even in pattern on 31 [32—33] cl for 8 [10—10] rows, then dec 1 cl each side of next 3 [3—4] rows, omitting dc at end of last row (25 [26—25] cl); ch 1, turn. **Next row:** Sl st in each of first 4 sts, work 19 [20—19] cl, sc in next st, sl st in next st; ch 1, turn. **Following row:** Skip sl st, sl st in sc, sl st in each of next 4 sts, work 13 [14—13] cl, sc in next st, sl st in next st. Break off.

ASSEMBLY: Using one strand of yarn, sew shoulder and side seams, lining up rows and leaving 3" open at lower end of left side. Sew sleeve seams. Sew in sleeves, easing in excess fullness at shoulders.

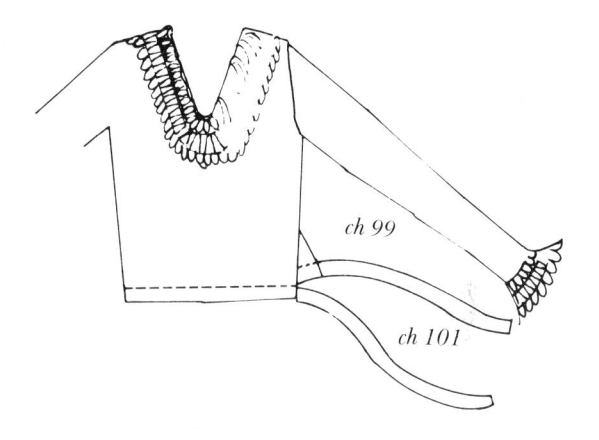

ch 99

ch 101

WAISTBAND AND TIE: Ch 99 (see drawing). With right side of back facing you, turn garment upside down. Join chain to garment with sc in first ch at 3" opening. Work as follows across foundation ch of back and front: * ch 1, skip 1 ch, sc in next ch (between cl). Repeat from * across, ch 1, sc in last ch; ch 101. **Next row:** Starting in 2nd ch from hook, work cl across chain, front, back, and first chain, dc in same ch as last lp; ch 1, turn. Continue working in pattern, decreasing 1 cl at each end of next 3 rows. Work 1 row sl st. Break off.

LACE TRIM: Cuff: With right side facing you, work dc in st next to sleeve seam. **1st rnd:** * Ch 5, dc in st between cl. Repeat from * around, ch 5, sl st in top of 1st dc. **2nd rnd:** Sl st in 1st ch-5 lp, ch 4, work 4 tr in same ch-5 lp, * ch 3, work 5 tr in next ch-5 lp (5-tr cl made). Repeat from * around, ch 3, sl st in top of 1st ch-4. **3rd rnd:** Sl st in each of next 2 tr, ch 6, work dc in same st as last sl st, * ch 3, sc in ch-3 lp, ch 3, in center tr of next 5-tr cl work dc, ch 3 and dc. Repeat from * around, ch 3, sc in ch-3 lp, ch 3, sl st in 3rd ch of ch-6. **4th rnd:** Sl st in 1st ch-3 lp, ch 4, work 2 tr in same ch-3 lp; ch 4, sl st in last tr (picot made); work 2 tr in same ch-3 lp, * ch 3, skip 2 ch-3 lps, in next ch-3 lp work 3 tr, picot and 2 tr. Repeat from * around, ch 3, sl st in top of 1st ch-4. Break off.

Collar: Make lp on hook and, with wrong side facing you, work dc in left shoulder seam.

1st rnd: (Ch 5, dc in st between cl) 17 times across back of neck; ch 5, dc in right shoulder seam. Work as follows along edges of V-neck: Ch 5, dc over next dc (end st of every other row); ch 5, sl st in top of 1st dc made on rnd.

2nd through 4th rnds: Work as for cuff.

See How to Block Linen Garments (p. 80) for blocking instructions.

Extraordinary Sparkle Sweater

In a combination of a beautiful twisted ginger wool and a copper metallic yarn. The sweater is worked in vertical sections which are joined together.

SIZES: Small (8–10) [medium (12–14)—large (16–18)]. Sweater measures 16" [18"—20"] across bust when stretched slightly and about 22" [23"—24"] from shoulder to lower edge.

MATERIALS: Reynolds Classique (100% wool), 7 [8—9] (50 gram—about 1¾-ounce) balls Faisan No. 2591 (ginger—color A) and Reynolds Feu d'Artifice (viscose rayon and Lurex metallic), 2 (20 gram—about ⅔-ounce) balls copper (B); aluminum crochet hook size I (or Canadian hook No. 7) *or the size that will give you the correct gauge;* 1 small button.

GAUGE: 9 sts (ch-1's and sc's) = 2"; 5 rows = 1" when stretched slightly.

Important: You must get the exact stitch and row gauge for this sweater to fit properly. Adjust the size of your crochet hook if necessary.

BACK: Border: Border is worked vertically. Starting at side edge with A, ch 12 [13—14].

1st row: Sc in 2nd ch from hook and in each ch across (11 [12—13] sc); ch 1, turn.

2nd row: Working in back lp of each st, sc in each sc across; ch 1, turn. Repeat 2nd row until border measures 15" [16"—17"] when slightly stretched. Ch 1, do not turn or break off but work along one long edge (top edge) of border and start body of sweater as follows:

1st row: Sc in same place as last sc, (work ch 1 and sc) 36 [41—46] times evenly spaced across top edge of border (73 [83—93] sts); ch 1, turn.

2nd row: Sc in first sc, * ch 1, skip next ch-1, sc in next sc. Repeat from * across; ch 1, turn.

Repeating 2nd row for pattern, work even on 73 [83—93] sts until piece measures 14½" [15½"—16½"] from beg of border; ch 1, turn.

To Shape Armholes: 1st row (dec row): Sl st across first sc and first ch-1 (2 sts dec at beg of row), ch 1, continue across row in pattern as established to within last 2 sts (2 sts dec at end of row—69 [79—89] sts); ch 1, turn.

Dec 2 sts at beg and end of each row 1 [2—3] times more.

Work even in pattern on 65 [71—77] sts until armholes measure 4¾" [5"—5¼"] from beg; ch 1, turn.

To Divide for Back Opening: 1st row: Work in pattern across 31 [35—37] sts to center (do not work remaining sts); ch 1, turn. Work even in pattern for 2", ending at armhole edge.

To Shape Shoulder: 1st row: Sl st across first 5 [7—9] sts, ch 1, work across row. **2nd row:** Work even. **3rd row:** Sl st across first 6 sts, ch 1, work across row. Work even for 1 row, then repeat 3rd row once more. Break off.

For other side, skip center 3 [1—3] sts, attach yarn and work remaining 31 [35—37] sts to correspond.

SLEEVES: Work border as for back until piece fits around wrist (about 7" when stretched), then for first row of pattern work 22 sc with ch-1's between (43 sts); break off A, attach B. Work even in stripe pattern of 5 [5—6] rows B and 4 [5—5] rows A until 3rd B stripe is completed, then continue with A only and, *at the same time,* inc as follows: Work even for 2½". **Next row (inc row):** Work sc, ch 1 and sc in first sc, work in pattern across row, work sc, ch 1 and sc in last sc (2 sts inc at beg and end of row—47 sts).

Repeat inc row every 4" [3"—2"] 2 [3—4] times more.

Work even on 55 [59—63] sts until sleeve measures 18" [18¼"—18½"] from beg of cuff or desired length to underarm.

To Shape Cap: Dec 2 sts at beg and end of next row, then dec 2 sts at beg and end of every 6th row 3 times. Dec 2 sts at beg and end of every row 5 [6—7] times. Break off.

FRONT: Border: Work as for back border, but break off when piece measures 15" [16"—17"] stretched slightly. Put this piece aside.

Lower Half: Starting at right-hand corner with A, ch 8. **1st row (right side):** Sc in 2nd ch from hook, (ch 1, skip next ch, sc in next ch) 3 times (4 sc); ch 1, turn. **2nd row:** Sc in first sc, (ch 1, skip next ch-1, sc in next sc) 3 times; ch 1, turn. Mark last sc for lower edge. **3rd row:** Sc in first sc, (ch 1, skip ch-1, sc in next sc) twice; ch 1, inc as follows: in next sc work sc, ch 1, sc, ch 1 and sc (2 sc inc for corner), ch 1; then, working along short edge of piece, sc in starting ch of first row; ch 1, turn. **4th row:** Sc in first sc, * ch 1, sc in next sc. Repeat from * across last row (7 sc); ch 1, turn. **5th row:** Sc in first sc, (ch 1, sc in next sc) 3 times; ch 1, inc for corner in next sc, then (ch 1, sc in next sc) twice. Break off A, attach B; ch 1, turn.

6th row: With B, repeat 4th row (9 sc); ch 1, turn. **7th row:** Sc in first sc, (ch 1, sc in next sc) 4 times; ch 1, inc for corner in next sc, (ch 1, sc in next sc) 3 times; ch 1, turn.

Continue to work as for last 2 rows, increasing 2 sc in corner st every right-side row (there will be one more ch-1 and sc on each side of corner as you work) until 5 [5—6] rows of B are completed. Continue to inc in same manner, working in stripe pattern of 4 [5—5] rows A and 5 [5—6] rows B until 4th B stripe is completed; break off B. Piece should measure 8" [9"—10"], when stretched slightly, across lower edge.

Sweater is worked vertically and with A only from now on. **Next row:** Starting at lower edge, attach A and work across in pattern to corner st (22 [24—26] sc with ch-1's between). Do not work across top edge; ch 1, turn. **Following row:** Work even in pattern as established; ch 1, turn. Continue to work even on these sts only, until piece measures 8" [9"—10"] from last B row. When stretched slightly, entire piece should measure 16" [18"—20"] across lower edge. Break off. Put this piece aside.

Top Half: Starting at upper left-hand corner with B, ch 16. **1st row:** Sc in 2nd ch from hook, (ch 1, skip next ch, sc in next ch) 7 times (8 sc); ch 1, turn. Work even in pattern for 2 rows more. **4th row:** Work in pattern across to last sc, inc as follows for shoulder: In last sc, work sc, ch 1 and sc (1 sc inc made for shoulder); ch 1, turn. Mark inc edge for shoulder.

5th row (right side): Working across in pattern, inc as follows in last sc for corner: work sc, ch 1, sc, ch 1 and sc in last sc (2 sc inc for corner); ch 1, do not turn; working along short edge of work, skip ¼" of edge sc in next st, ch 1, sc in starting ch of first row. Break off B, attach A; ch 1, turn. **6th row:** Work even in pattern; ch 1, turn. **7th row:** Work in pattern, inc 2 sc in corner st; ch 1, turn.

Repeat last 2 rows once more. **10th row:** Work in pattern, inc 1 sc at shoulder edge as before. Break off A, attach B.

Working in stripe pattern of 5 [5—6] rows B and 4 [5—5] rows A, continue to inc 2 sc for corner in same manner as before and, *at the same time,* inc 1 sc at shoulder edge on 15th row. Work until 19th [21st—23rd] row is completed, ending at side edge. Ch 5 for armhole shaping, turn.

Armhole and Neck Shaping: 1st row: Sc in 2nd ch from hook, ch 1, skip next ch, sc in next ch, ch 1, sc in next sc, work across in pattern to within last 6 sts (3 sc and 3 ch-1's) of shoulder edge for neck shaping; do not work across remaining sts; ch 1, turn.

2nd row: Sl st across first sc and first ch-1; then ch 1, sc in next sc, work to end of row. **3rd row:** Work to within last ch-1 and last sc; ch 1, turn. **4th row:** Repeat 2nd row.

Continue in stripe pattern, working even at neck edge and continuing to inc at corner until 4th B stripe is completed. Break off B. There are 33 [35—38] rows in all. Piece should measure about 8" [9"—10"] along lower edge when stretched slightly.

Sweater is worked vertically and with A only from now on. **Next row:** Starting at neck edge with A, work across in pattern to corner st. Do not work across lower edge; ch 1, turn. Work even in pattern for 9 [9—11] rows more, ending at neck edge. Ch 3, turn at end of last row.

Neck Shaping: 1st row: Sc in 2nd ch from hook, ch 1, sc in next sc, work to end of row. **2nd row:** Work to within last sc, work sc, ch 1 and sc in last sc; ch 3, turn. **3rd row:** Sc in 2nd ch from hook, ch 1, sc in next sc, work to end of row. **4th row:** Work across row; ch 7, turn.

5th row: Sc in 2nd ch from hook, (ch 1, skip next ch, sc in next ch) twice; ch 1, sc in next sc, work to end of row. Mark beg of 5th row for shoulder. Work even in pattern for 3 rows, ending at shoulder edge.

9th row (shoulder dec): Sl st across first sc and first ch-1, work to end of row.

Continue in pattern and repeat shoulder dec every inch twice more; then work even until 19 [21—23] rows have been worked from shoulder marker, ending at lower edge.

Next row: Armhole Shaping: Sc in first sc, (ch 1, sc in next sc) 7 [8—9] times; do not work across remaining sts; ch 1, turn. Work even on these sts only for 1". Break off.

FINISHING: Blocking: When pieces are completed, pin them, matching pieces together, wrong side up on a padded surface. Place a damp cloth over them. Then with warm (not hot) iron, holding the weight of the iron in your hand, pat lightly (do not press) so that the pieces are lightly steamed. Remove when dry. **Assembly:** Sew both halves of top together following photograph. Sew front border to lower edge, easing top section to fit. Sew shoulder and sleeve seams. Sew sleeves in place. With right side facing you, with A, work 1 row sc along edges of back opening. **Neckband:** With B, work 4 rows of sc around neck edge; at end of last row ch 6 for button loop, sc in same st as last st. Break off. Sew button to opposite side of back opening.

Sensational Rust Jacket

Has trumpet sleeves, a lacy openwork yoke, and a flowerette at the belted waist.

SIZES: 8–10 [(12–14)—(16–18)]. Snug-fitting top measures about 15" [17"—18½"] across back at underarms and 20½" [21½"—22½"] from underarm to lower edge.

MATERIALS: Frederick J. Fawcett 10/2 linen yarn, 3 (8-ounce) tubes rust; steel crochet hook size 00 *or the size that will give you the correct gauge;* large hook and eye; tapestry needle.

GAUGE: Main pattern after washing and blocking: 11 dc = 2"; 9 rows = 4".

Important: In order to insure correct gauge, make a sample swatch as follows: Ch 24. **1st row:** Dc in 4th ch from hook and in each remaining ch; ch 3, turn. **2nd row:** Skip first dc (ch-3 counts as first dc), dc in each of next 4 dc, work a front post tr around next dc (see 2nd row of back), * dc in each of next 10 dc, work a front post tr around next dc, dc in each of last

4 dc, dc in top of turning ch; ch 3, turn. **3rd row:** Repeat last row, but work back post tr around each tr (see 3rd row of back).

Repeat last 2 rows until 9 rows are completed. Break off. Block (see How to Block Linen Garments, p. 80) to measure 4" square and check gauge.

BACK: Starting at lower edge ch 103 [113—123]. **1st row:** Dc in 4th ch from hook, dc in each of next 4 [5—6] ch, * tr in next ch, dc in each of next 10 [11—12] ch. Repeat from * to within last 7 [8—9] ch, tr in next ch, dc in each of last 6 [7—8] ch (101 [111—121] sts); ch 3, turn.

2nd row (right side): Skip first dc (ch-3 counts as first dc), dc in each of next 5 [6—7] dc, work a front post tr around next tr as follows: Y o hook twice, insert hook around tr from front to back to front, y o hook and draw lp through, complete tr as before (front post tr completed); * dc in each of next 10 [11—12] dc, work a front post tr around next tr. Repeat from * across, ending with dc in each of last 5 [6—7] dc, dc in top of turning ch (9 front post tr in row); ch 3, turn.

3rd row: Skip first dc, dc in each of next 5 [6—7] dc, work a back post tr around post tr of last row as follows: Y o hook twice, insert hook around next tr from back to front to back, y o hook and draw lp through, complete tr as before (back post tr completed); * dc in each of next 10 [11—12] dc, work a back post tr around next tr. Repeat from * across, ending with dc in each of last 5 [6—7] dc, dc in top of turning ch (9 back post tr in row); ch 3, turn.

Working around post tr of last row, repeat 2nd and 3rd rows 9 times more.

22nd row (dec row): Skip first dc, dc in each of next 4 [5—6] dc, skip next dc (first dec made), work a front post tr around next tr, * skip next dc (another dec made), dc in each of next 8 [9—10] dc, skip next dc (dec made), work a front post tr around next tr. Repeat from * to within last 6 [7–8] sts, skip next dc (last dec), dc in each of last 5 [6—7] sts (18 dc dec); ch 3, turn.

23rd row: Skip first dc, dc in each of next 4 [5—6] dc, work a back post tr around next tr, * dc in each of next 8 [9—10] dc, back post tr around next tr. Repeat from * across, ending with dc in each of last 5 [6—7] sts (83 [93—103] sts); ch 3, turn.

Work even in new pattern as established until 46 [48—50] rows have been completed in all, omitting ch-3 at end of last row.

To Shape Armholes: 1st row: Sl st in each of first 5 [6—7] sts, sc in next tr, * dc in each of next 8 [9—10] dc, post tr around next tr. Repeat from * across to within last post tr, sc in last post tr. Do not work in remaining 5 [6—7] sts. Turn. **2nd row:** Sl st in first sc, ch 3, work across in pattern as established to within last sc; ch 3, turn. Dec 1 st at beg and end of next 0 [1—2] rows.

Work even in pattern as established on 71 [77—83] sts until 15th [16th—17th] row of armhole shaping has been completed, omitting ch-3 at end of last row.

To Shape Shoulders: 1st row: Sl st in each of first 11 [12—13] sts, sc in next st, work in pattern across row to within last 12 [13—14] sts, sc in next st; turn. **2nd row:** Repeat last row. Break off. The 27 [29—31] sts remaining in center are for back neck.

LEFT FRONT: Starting at lower edge, ch 81 [89—97]. Work in pattern on 79 [87—95] sts as for back. There are 7 post tr on each row instead of 9. Work until 22nd row (dec row) is completed. There are 14 dc dec on dec row.

Work even on 65 [73—81] sts until piece measures same as back to underarm, ending with a right-side row. Ch 3, turn.

To Shape Armhole: 1st row (wrong side):

Skip first dc, dc in each of next 3 [4—5] dc, * skip next dc, work a back post tr around next post tr, skip next dc, dc in each of next 6 [7—8] dc. Repeat from * across to within last 7 [8—9] sts, dc in next dc, sc in next tr. Do not work last 5 [6—7] sts (12 dc dec, in addition to sts not worked at armhole edge); ch 3, turn. Work in pattern for 3 rows more, decreasing 1 st at armhole edge only on each row. Work even in pattern for 1 [3—3] rows.

Next row (right side): Dec 1 st at beg and end of row and, *at the same time,* dec 1 dc each side of every post tr as before; ch 3, turn.

Lace Yoke: Change to lace yoke pattern as follows: **1st row (wrong side):** Skip first dc group, dc in top of post tr, * skip next dc group, work 3 dc in sp before next post tr, ch 3, work 3 dc in sp after same post tr (open shell made). Repeat from * 3 [4—4] times more (4 [5—5] open shells), ending as follows: **For small size only:** Skip last dc group, dc in top of post tr; ch 3, turn. **For medium and large sizes:** Dc in top of turning ch; ch 3, turn.

For all sizes: 2nd row: Dc in top of first dc, work a shell of 9 dc in ch-3 sp of each shell across (4 [5—5] shells); dc in turning ch; ch 3, turn. **3rd row:** * Skip first dc of next shell, work 3 dc in next dc, ch 5, skip center 5 dc of same shell, work 3 dc in next dc. Repeat from * across, dc in turning ch; ch 3, turn. **4th row:** Dc in top of first dc, work a shell of 9 dc in ch-5 sp of each shell across; dc in turning ch; ch 3, turn.

Repeat 3rd and 4th rows twice more. Do not ch 3 at end of last row. Break off.

RIGHT FRONT: Work to correspond to left front, reversing all shaping.

SLEEVES: Starting at lower edge, ch 103 [113—123]. Work even in same pattern as for back for 25 rows, then work dec row of back.

Work even on 83 [93—103] sts for 12 rows more, then on next row dec 18 dc again in same manner as before. Work even on 65 [75—85] sts for 1 [2—3] rows more. Do not ch 3 at end of last row.

To Shape Cap: 1st row: Sl st in each of first 4 [5—6] sts, sc in next tr, work across in pattern to within last post tr, sc in last post tr. Do not work in remaining 4 [5—6] sts. Turn. **2nd row:** Sl st in first sc, ch 3, work across in pattern to within last sc; ch 3, turn. Dec 1 st at beg and end of next 3 [4—5] rows. Work even in pattern as established on 49 [55—61] sts for 11 rows more.

On each of the next 2 rows, dec 14 dc in same manner as before. This will pull together top edge of sleeve. **Last row:** Sc in first st, * skip 1 st, sc in next st. Repeat from * across. Break off.

BELT: Crochet a chain 2" longer than waist measurement. **1st row:** Work a tr in 4th ch from hook, tr in each remaining ch; ch 3, turn. **2nd row:** Skip first tr, work a front post tr around each tr across, work last tr in top of turning ch. Do not break off. Sl st loosely around all four edges of belt. Break off.

FLOWER (made in 3 sections): First Section: Ch 6, join with sl st to form ring. **1st rnd:** Ch 3, 2 dc in ring, * ch 3, work 3 dc in ring. Repeat from * 4 times more, ch 3; join with sl st in top of first ch-3. **2nd rnd:** Sl st in first 2 dc, sl st in ch lp, ch 3, work 8 dc in same ch lp (first shell), work a 9-dc shell in each of next 5 ch lps around; join as before. **3rd rnd:** Sl st in next dc, ch 3, work 2 dc in same st as sl st, * ch 5, skip center 5 dc of shell, work 3 dc in next dc, skip last dc of same shell and first dc of next shell, work 3 dc in next dc. Repeat from * around, ending ch 5, skip 5 dc, 3 dc in next dc; join. **4th rnd:** Sl st in first 2 dc, sl st in ch lp, ch 3, work 14 tr in same lp, work 15 tr in each ch lp around. Join and break off.

Second section: Work as for first section to end of 2nd rnd. **3rd rnd:** Sl st across 8 dc of first shell, ch 3, * work 9 dc in sp before next shell. Repeat from *around. Join and break off.

Third section: Ch 5, join as before to form ring. **1st rnd:** Work 12 sc in ring. **2nd rnd:** * Skip next sc, work 9 dc in next sc. Repeat from * around. Join and break off.

Gather center opening of each section until closed. Place all 3 sections together, with 3rd section on top and 1st section on bottom, and sew. Sew flower to belt after blocking.

FINISHING: Sew shoulder seams, tacking center stitch of each shell of last row of front to back shoulder seam. Sew side and sleeve seams. Sew sleeves in place. Sew hook and eye on belt.

See How to Block Linen Garments (p. 80) for blocking instructions. Block flower and sew to one end of belt.

Long Skirts, Dresses, Suits and Wraps

Romantic Wedding Dress

To wear now and to pass on to the next generation as a family heirloom. This one is done in white, but would look equally pretty in a color. Body is worked in single and double crochet, chains, and picots. Front and back of dress are made by crocheting a large pyramid-shaped piece for each, which is then treated (cut and sewed) as "fabric" according to a pattern. Ruffled sleeves and hem are worked separately and then sewn on.

SIZES: Small (6–8) [medium (10–12)—large (14–16)]. Finished dress measures 15" [17"–19"] across bust for a snug-fitting bodice, 18" [20"–22"] across hips (measured 7" below waist), 26" [28"–30"] across lower edge (measured above ruffle). Skirt length is 36" from waistline to lower edge (including 12" ruffle). All measurements can be adjusted in the finishing.

MATERIALS: D.M.C. Cordonnet crochet cotton No. 10, 87 [98—109] (124-yard) balls white; steel crochet hook No. 0 *or the size that will give you the correct gauge;* 2½ yards of 72"-wide nylon net for lining; 22" neckline zipper; 3 sets of hooks and eyes for belt.

TO ENLARGE PATTERN: You will need felt-tipped marker, pencil, ruler, and sheets of brown paper, pieced if necessary, to make a large enough sheet for a pattern. With pencil and ruler mark paper with a grid of 2" squares as follows: First, mark your paper into a true square or rectangle. Then mark dots 2" apart (see diagram, p. 96) around edges, making the same number of spaces between dots as there are squares around edges of pattern diagram. Form a grid by joining the dots across opposite sides of paper. Check to make sure you have the same number of squares as the diagram. With marker, draw in each square the same pattern lines you see in the corresponding square on the diagram. In this way your pattern will be enlarged to full size.

Note: The front and back of dress are made by crocheting a large pyramid shaped piece for each (the back piece has opening for zipper). Both pieces are cut to the correct size and shape, then sewn together. Sleeves, ruffles and collar are worked separately and added later. Any minor adjustments needed in width can be made easily in the finishing.

GAUGE: 1 whole pattern = 2"; 10 rows = 3".

Note: Work with 2 strands of thread held together except where noted otherwise.

FRONT: Starting at lower edge of rectangle, ch 177 [189—201] to measure about 28" [30"—32"].

1st row: Sc in 6th ch from hook, * ch 3, skip next 3 ch sts, work 2 dc, ch 1 and 2 dc in next ch (first shell made), skip next 3 ch sts, work a shell of 2 dc, ch 1 and 2 dc in next ch, ch 3, skip next 3 ch sts, sc in next ch. Repeat from * to within last 3 sts, ch 3, skip next 2 ch sts, dc in last ch (14 [15—16] double-shell groups made); ch 3, turn.

2nd row: Skip first ch-3 lp, sc in next ch-3 lp, * ch 3, work shell in ch-1 sp of each of next 2 shells, (ch 3, sc in next ch-3 lp) twice. Repeat from * across; ch 3, turn.

3rd row: Dc in first ch-3 lp, * ch 3, skip next ch-3 lp, work shell in each of next 2 shells, ch 3, skip next ch-3 lp, sc in next lp. Repeat from * across, ending with ch 3, dc in last sp; ch 3, turn.

4th row: Skip first ch-3 lp, work shell in next lp, * ch 3, skip next shell, sc in sp between shells, ch 3, skip next shell, work shell in each of next 2 ch lps. Repeat from * across, ending last repeat with shell in ch lp, ch 3, sc in last lp (13 [14—15] double-shell groups made, with a 1-shell group at beg and end of row); ch 4, turn.

5th row: Shell in first shell, (ch 3, sc in next ch lp) twice. Repeat from * across on 2nd row, ending with shell in last shell, ch 2, dc in last lp; ch 3, turn.

6th row: Shell in first shell, ch 3, skip next ch-3 lp, sc in next lp. Repeating from * on 3rd row, work across, ending with ch 3, skip next lp, shell in last shell, dc in turning ch; ch 5, turn.

7th row: Sc in first shell, * ch 3, work shell in each of next 2 ch lps, ch 3, skip next shell, sc in sp between shells. Repeat from * across, ending last repeat with shell in each of next 2 ch lps, ch 3, sc in center of last shell, ch 3, dc in last sp; ch 3, turn.

Repeat 2nd through 7th rows for pattern until piece measures about 12" from beg, ending with a 6th row of pattern, then ch 1 (instead of ch-5), turn.

There will be 2 whole patterns decreased on the next row, 1 at beg of row and 1 at end of row. **Next row (dec row):** Sl st in each st across first shell, sl st across next 2 ch lps and next shell, sc in sp between shells, ch 5, sc in next shell, repeat from * across on 7th row, ending with dc in sp between shells of last double-shell group (do not work over next shell, 2 ch lps and last shell); ch 3, turn.

Work even in pattern as established and repeat this 2-pattern decrease every 12" twice more. Work even in pattern on 8 [9—10] patterns until piece measures 42" [43"—44"] from beg. Break off.

BACK: Work as for front until piece measures 19" [20"—21"] from beg. Divide work in half as follows for zipper opening: Put a marker in center of last row. **Next row:** Working in pattern as established, work across to marker (do not work remaining sts); ch 3, turn.

Keeping pattern as established, and decreasing patterns at side edge as for front, work on sts of one side only until piece measures same length as front. Break off.

Attach thread at marker, work other side to correspond.

SLEEVE: Starting at top edge of sleeve cap, holding 3 strands of thread together, ch 24.

Pattern No. 1: 1st row: In 5th ch from hook work an open shell of 1 sc, ch 3 and 1 sc (first open shell made), * ch 10, skip 7 ch sts, work an open shell in next st. Repeat from * once more (ending with an open shell), then skip 2 sts, dc in last st; ch 3, turn.

2nd row: Dc in first dc, ch 2, work an open shell in ch-3 sp of open shell, (ch 10, open shell in next open shell) twice; ch 2, dc in last sp; ch 3, turn.

3rd row: Dc in first dc, ch 3, work open shell in next open shell, (ch 10, open shell in next open shell) twice; ch 3, dc in last sp; ch 3, turn.

Continue as for 3rd row, but instead of ch-3 after the first dc and before the last dc of each row, work 1 st more in chains. For example: On the 4th row you ch 4, on the 5th row you ch 5, etc., until 8th [9th—10th] row is completed. Break off one strand of thread. Pattern No. 1 completed.

Pattern No. 2: Work with 2 strands of thread for the remainder of the sleeve as follows: **1st row:** Ch 4, turn, work 1 tr at base of ch-4, (ch 10, work 5 tr in shell) 3 times; ch 10, work 2 tr in turning ch.

2nd row: Ch 4, turn, work 1 tr in first tr, * ch 10, skip ch lp, tr in first tr of 5-tr group, (ch 1, tr in next tr of same group) 4 times. Repeat from * across, ch 10, skip ch lp, 1 tr in last tr and in top of turning ch.

3rd row: Ch 4, turn, tr in first tr, * ch 9, skip ch lp, tr in next tr, (work ch 1, tr in next tr) 4 times. Repeat from * across, ch 9, tr in last tr and in turning ch.

4th row (inc row): Ch 4, turn, tr in first tr, * ch 9, skip ch lp, tr in next tr, ch 1, tr in next tr, ch 1, in next tr work tr, ch 1, tr, ch 1 and tr, (ch 1, tr in next tr) twice. Repeat from * across, ch 9, tr in last tr and in turning ch.

5th row: Ch 4, turn (mark 4th st of ch), tr in first tr, * ch 8, skip ch lp, tr in first tr of group, work ch 1 and tr in each tr of group. Repeat from * across, ch 8, tr in last tr and in turning ch.

Cap shaping is completed. Sleeve should measure 5¼" [5½"—5¾"] from beg. Continue as follows with Pattern No. 2: Drop lp from hook. With sl st attach 2 strands of thread at marker, ch 8 for underarm. Break off.

6th row (inc row): Pick up dropped lp and ch 10 for other underarm, turn, tr in 6th ch from hook, (ch 1, skip 1 ch st, tr in next st) twice; (ch 1, tr in next tr) twice; * ch 8, tr in first tr of next group, work ch 1 and tr in each tr to within center tr of group, ch 1, in center tr work tr, ch 1, tr, ch 1 and tr (2 tr inc), work ch 1 and tr in each remaining tr of this group. Repeat from * across, ch 8, skip last ch lp, tr in next tr, ch 1, tr in next st; then working across ch, (ch 1, skip 1 st, tr in next st) 4 times.

7th row: Ch 5, turn, skip first tr and ch-1, * tr in next tr, work ch 1 and tr in each tr of this group, ch 7. Repeat from * across, ending tr in next tr, ch 1 and tr in each tr to end (working last tr in top of turning ch).

8th row: Ch 5, turn, tr in first tr (1 tr inc), work ch 1 and tr in each tr of this group, * ch 7, tr in first tr of next group, work ch 1 and tr in each tr to within center tr of group, ch 1, inc 2 tr in center tr as before, work ch 1 and tr in each remaining tr of this group. Repeat from * across, working tr, ch 1 and tr in last st (1 tr inc).

9th and 10th rows: Repeat 7th and 8th rows, but ch 6 (instead of ch 7). **11th and 12th rows:** Repeat 7th and 8th rows, but ch 5 (instead of ch 7). At the end of the 12th row there are 15 tr in each of the three center groups and 9 tr in group at beg and end of row. Sleeve should measure 4" from underarm. Pattern No. 2 completed.

Pattern No. 3: Continue as follows: **1st row:** Ch 4, turn, tr at base of turning ch, ch 4, sc in 4th ch from hook (picot made), work 2 tr in next tr, (work picot, skip 1 tr, work 2 tr in next tr) 3 times; * ch 3, skip last tr of this group, in ch-5 lp work sc, ch 3 and sc (open shell made), ch 3, skip first tr of next group, work 2 tr in next tr, (picot, skip next tr, 2 tr in next tr) 6 times. Repeat from * across, ending last repeat after 4th picot is completed; work last 2 tr in turning ch.

2nd row: Ch 4, turn, 2 tr in first tr, ** ch 5, sc in 4th ch from hook, ch 1 (picot lp made), skip picot below, make joined 2-tr cl as follows: * y o hook twice, insert hook in next tr, y o and draw lp through, (y o and draw through 2 lps on hook) twice. Repeat from * once more, then y o and draw through all lps on hook (joined 2-tr cl made), tr in same tr as last tr of cl was made. Repeat from ** across to open shell, ch 3, in open shell work sc, ch 3 and sc, then ch 3, work cl in first tr of next group, tr in next tr. Continue in this manner across row, ending with picot lp, work 3 tr in turning ch.

3rd row: Ch 4, turn, work joined 2-tr cl in 2nd tr, (make picot lp, skip picot lp below, work joined 3-tr cl in top of next tr) 4 times; * ch 3, work open shell in open shell, ch 3, work joined 3-tr cl in next tr, (picot lp, skip next picot lp, joined 3-tr cl in next tr) 6 times. Repeat from * across, ending last repeat 4 times (instead of 6).

Repeat last row 3 times more, working joined tr cl in top of joined tr cl of previous row. Break off.

BLOCKING: Baste zipper opening closed on back section. With wrong side up, stretch and pin back and front sections to a padded board. Using a warm steam iron (or place a damp cloth over "fabric" and use a dry iron), steam pieces 42" [43"—44"] long and 28" [30"—32"] wide across lower edge. The pieces will taper narrower toward the top. Be careful not to let weight of iron rest on "fabric." Allow to dry thoroughly before removing from board. Steam sleeves in same manner. Now treat front and back pieces of crochet as "fabric."

TO CUT PATTERNS AND "FABRIC": Enlarge dress pattern according to instructions on page 94. Adjust measurements if desired and cut full pattern from folded paper. Patterns are not needed for sleeve or ruffle.

Center pattern on "fabric" with lower edges matching; pin in place. Do not mark or cut along lower edge of pieces. Following lines on diagram for your size (or adjust measurements if desired), pin outline on "fabric." Baste along pinned outlines and remove pins and pattern. Place tissue paper under basted areas and, using a fine stitch, machine stitch through tissue and crochet along basted lines; then stitch once more close to first line. These stitching lines will keep your crochet from raveling after it is cut.

Tear away tissue paper and, leaving ½" seam allowance on all seams, cut away excess crochet.

LINING: Using paper pattern of dress, cut out two pieces of lining (one for front, one for back), adding 1" seam allowance at lower edge and ½" allowance on all other edges. If you wish to add darts at bustline, pin them into lining before you pin pattern in place. Cut

Each square = 2"

Romantic Wedding Dress

opening for zipper in back piece. The sleeves are not lined. Ruffle (to be made) will be lined.

Sew shoulder and side seams of lining.

TO ASSEMBLE: With right sides facing, stitch shoulder and side seams of dress, stitching along previous stitching lines. Insert net lining into dress, with wrong sides facing. Turn in seam allowance of lining around neckline, armhole and lower edge and sew in place. Tack along side seams and waistline. Turn in ¼" along zipper opening and baste.

Stitch sleeve seams, then stitch sleeves in place. If desired, entire lining can be tacked to crocheted dress at 2" intervals.

BACK RUFFLE: Starting at top edge of ruffle, holding 3 strands together, crochet a chain to fit across lower edge of back of dress. This chain must be a multiple of 8 sts.

Pattern No. 1: Starting with first row of sleeve Pattern No. 1, work as for sleeve, repeating pattern as many times as necessary across each row until 6th row is completed. Break off 1 strand of thread and continue with 2 strands for remainder of ruffle.

Pattern No. 2: Continue as follows: **1st row:** Ch 4, turn, work 2 tr at base of ch-4, * ch 10, work 5 tr in open shell. Repeat from * across, ending ch 10, work 3 tr in turning ch.

2nd row: Ch 5, turn, tr in first tr (1 tr inc), (ch 1, tr in next tr) twice; * ch 10, skip ch lp, tr in first tr of 5-tr group, (ch 1, tr in next tr of same group) 4 times. Repeat from * across, ch 10, skip ch lp, tr in next tr, ch 1, tr in next tr, ch 1, 2 tr in top of turning ch (1 tr inc).

3rd row: Ch 5, turn, skip first tr, tr in next tr, (ch 1, tr in next tr) twice; * ch 9, skip ch lp, tr in next tr, (ch 1, tr in next tr) 4 times. Repeat from * across, ending ch 9, tr in next tr, (ch 1, tr in next tr) twice; ch 1, tr in top of turning ch.

4th row (inc row): Ch 5, turn, tr in first tr (inc), (ch 1, tr in next tr) 3 times; * ch 9, skip ch lp, tr in next tr, ch 1, tr in next tr, ch 1, in next tr work (tr, ch 1, tr, ch 1 and tr), (ch 1, tr in next tr) twice. Repeat from * across, ch 9, tr in first tr of next group, (ch 1, tr in next tr) twice; ch 1, in turning ch work tr, ch 1 and tr (inc).

5th row: Ch 5, turn, skip first tr, tr in next tr, (ch 1, tr in next tr) 3 times; * ch 8, tr in first tr of next group, work ch 1 and tr in each tr of group. Repeat from * across, ch 8, tr in next tr, (ch 1, tr in next tr) 3 times; ch 1, tr in top of turning ch.

6th row: Ch 5, turn, tr in first tr, (ch 1, tr in next tr) 4 times; * ch 8, tr in first tr of next group, (ch 1, tr in next tr) twice; ch 1, in next tr work (tr, ch 1, tr, ch 1 and tr), (ch 1, tr in next tr) 3 times. Repeat from * across, ch 8, tr in next tr, (ch 1, tr in next tr) 3 times; ch 1, in turning ch work tr, ch 1 and tr.

Working as for Pattern No. 2 of sleeve, repeat 7th through 12th rows; then continue with Pattern No. 3 from first row to end. Break off. Ruffle should measure about 12" deep.

Make another ruffle in same manner for front.

Finishing for Ruffle: Block in same manner as other crocheted pieces, pinning ruffles out in curved sections.

Using ruffle as a pattern, cut out two pieces of lining (one for front and one for back), still keeping ruffle circular, and add ½" seam allowance on all edges.

Sew side seams of ruffle and lining, then line crocheted ruffle with lining, turning in all seam allowances.

Sew lined ruffle to lower edge of dress.

COLLAR: Working with 2 strands of thread, ch 81 [81—93] to fit around neck edge of dress. Repeat 1st, 2nd, and 3rd rows of Front of Dress, omitting ch-3 at end of 3rd row. Break off.

Block collar and cut lining, adding ½" seam allowance on all sides. Line collar. Sew collar to neck edge.

BELT: Working with 3 strands of thread, ch 150 [162—174]. **1st row:** In 5th ch from hook work open shell of 1 sc, ch 3 and 1 sc, * ch 10, skip 11 ch sts, open shell in next st. Repeat from * across, ending dc in last st. **2nd row:** Ch 3, turn. Work an open shell in ch-3 sp of open shell, * ch 10, open shell in next open shell. Repeat from * across, ending with dc in last sp.

Repeat 2nd row 4 times more. Break off. Block belt, do not line.

Sew hooks and eyes, spaced evenly apart, at each narrow end.

BACK OPENING: Work 2 rows of sc along back opening, then sew in zipper.

Breezy Beach Cover-Ups

Left, hooded cape in loose double crochet stripes edged with shell ruffle.

Cool caftan, right, has exotic medallion decoration on yoke and sleeves. Vertical stripes are in double crochet.

Hooded Cape

SIZE: One size fits all.

MATERIALS: Brunswick Fore-'n-Aft acrylic sport yarn, 4 (2-ounce) skeins each powder blue No. 6011 (color A), white No. 6000 (B), maize No. 60031 (C), and tender green No. 6019 (D); aluminum crochet hook size K (or Canadian hook No. 4) and wooden hook No. 13, *or the sizes that will give you the correct gauge.*

GAUGE: On size K hook: 3 dc = 1"; 3 rnds or rows = 2". On No. 13 wooden hook: 2 dc = 1"; 1 row = 1", not stretched.

Note: Because the stitches are very loose, the rows will stretch out to measure about 1¼" when the cape is worn.

HOOD: Starting at top of crown with size K hook and A, ch 5. Join with sl st to form ring. **1st rnd:** Ch 3, work 10 dc in ring (11 dc, counting ch-3 as 1 dc). Do not join, but work around spiral fashion, marking beg of each rnd. **2nd rnd:** Ch 3, dc in last dc made, * 2 dc in next dc (1 dc inc). Repeat from * around (22 dc). **3rd rnd:** Repeat 2nd rnd (44 dc). **4th rnd:** Ch 3, 2 dc in next dc, * dc in next dc, 2 dc in next dc. Repeat from * around (66 dc.) **5th rnd:** Ch 3, dc in each dc around. Repeat 5th rnd 5 times more, or until piece measures about 7" from center to edge.

NECK SHAPING: 1st row: Ch 3, dc in next 35 dc; ch 3, turn. Unworked dc go across top of head or forehead. **2nd row:** Skip first dc, dc in each dc across, increasing 4 dc as evenly spaced as possible (40 dc); ch 3, turn. **3rd row:** Skip first dc, dc in each dc across (40 dc); ch 3, turn. **4th and 5th rows:** Repeat 2nd row (48 dc). **6th row:** Skip first dc, dc in each dc across, increasing 5 dc as evenly spaced as possible (53 dc); ch 3, turn. **7th row:** Skip first dc, * 2 dc in next dc, dc in next dc. Repeat from * across (79 dc); ch 3, turn. **8th row:** Repeat 7th row (118 dc). **9th row:** Skip first dc, dc in each dc across, increasing 7 dc as evenly spaced as possible (125 dc); ch 3, turn. **10th row:** Work even. **11th row:** Repeat 9th row (132 dc). Break off A, attach C (see note below) and change to No. 13 hook; ch 3, turn.

Note: To change colors, work last dc to point where 2 lps remain on hook, y o hook with new color and draw through 2 lps on hook, ch 3 with new color, turn.

CAPE SECTION: 12th row: With C, dc in

first dc, * 2 dc in next dc. Repeat from * across (264 dc); ch 3, turn. **13th row:** Work even (264 dc). Break off C, attach B. Repeat last row in the following color sequence: 1 row B, 3 D, 2 B, 4 A, 4 D, 2 C, 3 A, 2 C, 4 B, 4 C, 4 D. Break off.

EDGING: With right side facing you, starting at lower left front corner, using No. 13 hook and B, sl st in first dc at lower edge. **1st rnd:** Ch 3, dc in same place, work 8 dc in next dc (shell made), * skip next dc, work shell in next dc. Repeat from * across lower edge to within last 3 dc, skip 2 dc, work 2 dc in last dc; work sc evenly spaced along right front edge, around hood and along left front edge; sl st in first sl st at beg of rnd. **2nd row of shells:** Sl st in each ch to top of ch-3, ch 3, dc between first and 2nd dc, * work shell between 4th and 5th dc of next shell. Repeat from * across, ending with 2 dc before last 2 dc. Break off.

HOOD CASING: With right side facing you, using size K hook and B, sl st in sc worked into last dc of last color A row on hood, ch 4, skip next sc, dc in next sc, * ch 1, skip next sc, dc in next sc. Repeat from * around face edge to other end of last color A row on hood. Break off.

TIE: With B held double and using size K hook, crochet a chain 42" long. Weave chain through ch-1 sps of casing. Tie under chin.

Cool Caftan

SIZES: 8–14 [16—18]. Skirt measures 21" [23"] across.

MATERIALS: Columbia-Minerva Nantuk acrylic sports yarn, 7 [8] (2-ounce) skeins each turquoise No. 6010 (color T) and white No. 6000 (W); Columbia-Minerva Sweater and Afghan yarn, acrylic knitting worsted-weight, 1 (2-ounce) skein each hot pink No. 6328 (H), bright yellow No. 6305 (Y), avocado #1 No. 6320 (A), gold #4 No. 6327 (G), purple No. 6371 (P), tangerine (dark orange) No. 6307 (D), and orange No. 6306 (O); aluminum crochet hooks sizes E and F (or Canadian hooks No. 11 and 10) *or the sizes that will give you the correct gauge.*

GAUGE: With F hook, on body: 13 dc = 3"; 1 stripe = 1".

Note: To change colors, work to within last st of first color group, draw up lp in last st, drop yarn and pick up new color; y o with new color and draw through both lps on hook to complete st. Crochet over ends of yarn as you work to avoid having to weave them in later.

NECK MEDALLION: Note: It is important that the size of the medallion is accurate so that it will fit the body of caftan. If your piece does not correspond to our measurements, change your hook size.

Starting at center with size E hook and color O, ch 6. **1st rnd (right side):** Work 3 sc in 2nd ch from hook (shell made), 1 sc in each of next 3 ch, 3 sc in next ch (shell made); working along opposite side of foundation chain, work h dc in next ch, 3 dc in next ch, h dc in next ch. Break off O; attach H.

2nd rnd: With H, sc in next sc, 3-sc shell in center sc of next shell, sc in each of next 5 sc, 3-sc shell in next sc (center of shell), sc in each of next six O sts, sc in each of next 2 H sts, 3-h dc shell in next sc (center of shell), dc in each of next 7 sc, 3-h dc shell in next sc (center of shell), sc in each of next 2 sts. Break off H; attach P. **3rd rnd:** With P, work sc in each of next 2 sts, 2 sc in next st, sc in each of next 5 sts, 5 sc in next h dc (center of shell); mark 4th sc. Sc in each of next 9 sts, 5 sc in next h dc (center of shell), sc in each of next 3 sts, sc in each of next 3 P sts, ch 3, work 1 sc in each of next 9 sts; ch 3 (ch-3 counts as 1 dc), turn. **1st short row (wrong side):** Skip first sc, dc in each of next 8 sts, 5 dc in ch-3 sp (shell made), dc in each of next 9 sts; ch 1, turn. **2nd short row (right side):** Sc in first dc (mark this st), sc in each of next 10 sts, 3 sc in next dc (center dc of 5-dc shell), sc in each of next 11 dc. Break off.

4th rnd (right side): Attach W with sc in first marked sc on 3rd rnd, sc in each of next 5 sc, 3 sc in next sc, sc in each of next 6 sc; break off. (Mark these sts for upper edge.) With right side facing you, attach W with sc to 2nd marked st on 3rd rnd, sc in each of next 11 sc, 3 sc in next sc (center of shell), sc in each of next 12 sc; break off. (Mark these sts for lower edge.) Piece should measure 3¼" from upper to lower edge, 3¾" across at widest point. **5th row (right side):** Attach T with sc to side of last P sc directly below last W st worked; working along upper edge, work 2 sc over post of next ch-3, sc in each of next 15 W sc, 2 sc over post of next P dc, sc in side of next P sc. Break off T, attach A; ch 3, turn. **6th rnd (wrong side):** Working along upper edge, skip first sc, work dc in each of next 2 sts, h dc in next st, sc in each of next 6 sts, ch 3, skip 1 st, sc in each of next 6 sts, h dc in next st, dc in each of next 3 sts, ch 3. Working along lower edge, sc in first W sc and in each of next 11 sts, ch 3, skip 1 sc, sc in next sc (center of 3-sc shell), ch 3, skip 1 sc, sc in each of next 12 sts (45 sts, 5 ch-3 sps); ch 3, join with sl st to top of starting ch-3. Break off A, attach Y; ch 3, turn. **7th rnd (right side):** Work 3 dc in next ch-3 sp, dc in each of next 3 sc, h dc in each of next 2 sc, sc in next sc, ch 7, skip 6 sc, 3 dc in next ch-3 sp, ch 3, skip 1 sc, 3 dc in next ch-3 sp, ch 7, skip 6 sc, sc in next sc, h dc in each of next 2 sc, dc in each of next 3 sc, 3 dc in ch-3 sp, dc in each of next 4 sts, ch 7, skip next 6 sts, 5 dc in ch-3 sp, ch 7, skip 6 sc, dc in each of next 3 sts; join to top of ch-3. Break off Y, attach A; ch 1, turn.

8th row (wrong side): With A, work sc in first st and in each of next 2 dc; working in front of the Y ch-7 lp and leaving lp free, work 1 tr in each of next 6 A sc 1 row below, sc in each of next 5 Y dc; working in front of next Y ch-7, work 1 tr in each of next 6 A sts 1 row below, sc in each of the next 4 Y dc. Break off A; attach T. **9th rnd (wrong side):** With T, work sc in each of next 9 Y sts; leaving the next Y ch-7 free on right side as on 8th row, work dc in each of next 6 A sc 1 row below, ch 3, skip 3 Y dc, 3 sc in next Y ch-3 sp, ch 3, skip next 3 Y dc; leaving next Y ch-7 free as before, work 1 dc in each of next 6 A sc 1 row below, sc in each of next 9 sts, sc in each of next 4 A sc, 9 dc in next Y ch-7 lp, sc in each of next 5 A sc, 9 dc in ch-7 lp, sc in each of last 4 A sts (64 T sts, 2 ch-3 lps). Break off T; attach D. Piece should measure 5" long by 5½" wide. **10th row (wrong side):** With D, sc in each of next 3 T sc, ch 3, skip next sc, sc in each of next 5 sc, 8 dc in next Y ch-7 lp, 3 sc in next T ch-3 sp, sc in next sc, 2 sc in next sc, sc in next sc, 3 sc in next ch-3 sp, 8 dc in next ch-7 lp, sc in each of next 5 T sc, ch 3, skip 1 sc, sc in each of next 3 sc. Break off D, attach W; ch 1, turn. **11th rnd (right side):** With W sc in each of first 2 sc, h dc in next st, 5 dc in next ch-3 sp, dc in each of next 6 sts, h dc in each of next 2 sts, sc in each of next 2 sts, h dc in each of next 2 sts, dc in each of next 5 sts, 5 dc in next sc, skip next sc (center shell made), dc in each of next 4 sc, dc in next dc, h dc in each of next 2 dc, sc in each of next 2 dc, h dc in each of next 2 dc, dc in each of next 6 sts, 5 dc in next ch-3 sp, h dc in next sc, sc in each of last 2 D sc, sc in each of next 13 T sts, skip 2 sc, 5 dc in next sc, skip 2 sc, sc in each of next 13 sts (86 sts); join to first sc. **12th rnd:** Ch 3, work h dc in each of next 2 sts, sc in each of next 10 sts, ch 3, skip 3 sts (mark these skipped sts), 3 sc in next st, ch 3, skip 3 sts, sc in each of next 6 dc, ch 3, skip center 3 dc of 5-dc shell, sc in each of next 6 dc, ch 3, skip 3 sts, 3 sc in next st, ch 3, skip 3 sts, sc in each of next 10 sts, h dc in each of next 2 sts, dc in next st. Break off W; attach G. **13th row:** With G, work dc in each of next 4 sts, h dc in next st, sc in each of next 21 sts, h dc in next st, dc in each of next 4 sts; ch 1, turn. **Short row (wrong side):** Work sc in each G st across. Break off G; attach P.

14th row: With P, sc in each of next 13 W sts, work 3 sc in ch-3 sp, sc in each of next 3 sc, 3 sc in ch-3 sp, sc in each of next 5 sc (mark these 5 sc), skip 1 sc; keeping ch-3 free and to right side of work, work dc in each of next 3 W dc 1 row below, skip next sc, sc in each of next 5 sc (mark these 5 sc), 3 sc in ch-3 sp, sc in each of next 3 sc, 3 sc in ch-3 sp, sc in each of next 13 sts. Break off P; attach T. **Neck Opening: 15th row (wrong side):** With T work * sc in each of next 15 sts *; ch 1, turn. **Short row:** Repeat from * to * once; break off; turn. With wrong side facing you, skip next free G st on upper edge; with T, sc in next st, work to correspond to 15th row and short row. Break off T; attach D (neck edge); ch 1, turn.

16th row (wrong side): With D, work sc in each of next 6 sc, h dc in each of next 3 sts, dc in each of next 3 sc, h dc in each of next 3 sts, dc in each of next 5 P sts. Break off D; skip 1 st, attach A with sl st to next st. **17th row:** With A, ch 3, work dc in each of next 12 sts. Break off; turn. **18th row (right side):** Attach H to first of 3 marked skipped sts on 12th rnd, ch 4, tr in each of next 2 sts, ch 3, work tr in each of next 3 skipped sts on 12th rnd, work sc in each of next 5 marked P sts, 3 dc in W ch-3 sp, sc in each of next 5 marked P sts, tr in each of next 3 skipped sts on 12th rnd, ch 3, tr in each of next 3 skipped sts. Break off H; turn. **19th row (wrong side):** With A, work other side of lower edge to correspond to 17th (A) row. Break off A, skip 1 st, attach D. **20th row:** With D, work to correspond to 16th row, ending at neck opening. Break off; turn. **21st row (right side):** Counting from neck edge, skip first 10 D sts, attach O in next st, ch 4, dc in each of next 2 sts, ch 3, skip 2 sts, h dc in next st, sc in each of next 4 sts, ch 5 over skipped P st, dc in each of next 10 A sts; working over H ch-3, sc in each of last 3 A sts, sc in each of next 19 H sts; working over H ch-3, work sc in each of first 3 A sts, dc in each of next 10 A sts, ch 5 over skipped P st, sc in each of next 4 D sts, h dc in next st, ch 3, skip 2 sts, dc in each of next 2 sts, tr in next st. Break off O. **22nd row (right side):** Attach P with sc to first D st at neck edge, work sc in each of next 5 sc, h dc in each of next 2 sts, skip 1 st, 5 dc in next st, 3 dc over post of next tr (mark last dc). Break off. With right side facing you, using P, work other side of neck opening to correspond, omitting marker. Break off. **23rd row (right side):** Attach Y with sc to post of marked st; work 1 sc over post of same st, sc in each of next 2 sts, 5 sc in ch-3 sp, sc in each of next 5 sts, work 5 tr over ch-5 sp into skipped P st, sc in next st (mark this st), h dc in next st, dc in each of next 6 sts, h dc in next st, sc in each of next 3 sts. Break off Y; skip 21 sts, attach Y in next st and work other side to correspond, omitting marker. Break off Y. **24th row (right side):** Attach T with sc to marked st on last row, sc in each of next 2 sts, skip 3 sts, work 11 tr in next st (to form corner), skip 3 sts, sc in each of next 2 sts, 3 dc in next O st, h dc in next st, sc in each of next 2 sts. Break off T; skip 13 sts, attach T to next st and work other side to correspond. Break off T.

RIGHT FRONT NECK: Note: Work with right side facing you, starting each row at front neck opening. After completing each row for right neck, work left neck to correspond. **1st row:** Attach W with sc to first P st, h dc in next st, dc in next st, skip 1 st, 3 dc in next st, skip 1 st, dc in next st, skip 3 sts, 5 dc in next st (center of P shell), skip 2 sts, tr in each of next 3 sts and into side of next Y sc. Break off W. **2nd row:** Skip first 3 sts at neck edge, attach A with sc in next st, sc in each of next 12 sts across. Break off A. **3rd row:** Attach H with sc to first W st at beg of first row, sc in each of next 2 W sts and next 7 A sts, h dc in next st, dc in remaining 5 sts. Break off H. **4th row:** Skip first 6 H sts, attach T with sc in next st, sc in each of next 2 sts, h dc in each of next 3 sts, dc in each of last 4 sts. Break off. **5th row:** Skip first 2 T sts of last row, attach G with sc in next st, sc in each of next 2 sts, h dc in each of next 3 sts, dc in each of last 2 sts. Do not break off; ch 1, work 2 sc over post of last dc worked, then work 1 row sc evenly spaced around medallion, completing last row of left neck edge to correspond to right. Break off. Medallion should measure 9" along side edges by 9½" wide.

SLEEVE MEDALLION (make 2): Work same as for neck medallion through 10th row. Break off D; attach W. **11th row (wrong side):** With W, sc in next T st, h dc in each of next 2 sts, dc in next st, 3 dc in next st, dc in next st, h dc in each of next 3 sts, sc in each of next 2 sts, h dc in next st, dc in next st, skip 2 sts, 3 dc in next st (shell made); skip 2 sts, dc in next st, h dc in next st, sc in each of next 2 sts, h dc in each of next 3 sts, dc in next st, 3 dc in next st (shell made); dc in next st, h dc in each of next 2 sts, sc in next st. Break off W, attach O; turn. **12th rnd (right side):** With O, ch 3, skip first st, dc in each of next 4 sts, 5 tr in next st (corner shell), dc in each of next 2 sts, h dc in next st, sc in each of next 15 sts, h dc in next st, dc in each of next 2 sts, 5 tr in next st (corner shell). Work dc in each of next 6 sts (mark first dc); h dc in each of next 2 sts, 3 dc in next ch-3 sp, h dc in next st, dc in each of the next 3 sts, 3 dc in next st, dc in each of next 3 sts, 5 tr in next st (corner shell made); dc in each of next 3 sts, h dc in next st, 2 sc in next st, sc in each of next 8 sts, 2 sc in next st, h dc in next st, dc in each of next 3 sts, 5 tr in next st (corner shell made); dc in each of next 3 sts, 3 dc in next st, dc in each of next 3 sts, h dc in next st, 3 dc in ch-3 sp, h dc in each of next 2 sts, dc in next st; join with sl st to first st. Break off O. **13th row (right side):** Attach Y with sc to marked dc on last rnd, sc in each of next 7 sts; break off. Skip 3 dc, attach W to next st, ch 2 (counts as 1 h dc), h dc in next st, dc in each of next 8 sts; break off. Skip 5-tr shell, attach W with sc to next st, * sc in each of next 7 sts; break off * . Skip 4 sts, attach W to next st, repeat from * to * once. Skip 5-tr shell, attach W to next st, ch 3, dc in each of next 7 sts, h dc in each of next 2 sts; break off. Skip 3 sts, attach Y to next st; repeat from * to * once. **14th rnd:** With T, dc in each of next 2 sts, 5 dc in next st, dc in each of next 9 sts, h dc in each of next 2 sts, sc in each of next

3 sts, h dc in each of next 2 sts, dc in each of next 9 sts, 5 dc in next st, dc in each of next 2 sts, sc in each of next 8 sts, ch 1, skip 1 st, 3 sc in next st, ch 1, skip 1 st, sc in each of next 7 sts, h dc in each of next 3 sts, dc in each of next 2 sts, 5 dc in next st, 1 dc in each of next 2 sts, 2 h dc in next W st, 1 sc in each of next 7 sts, 1 dc in each of next 4 sts, 1 sc in each of next 7 sts, 2 h dc in next st, 1 dc in each of next 2 sts, 5 dc in next st, 1 dc in each of next 2 sts, h dc in each of next 3 sts, sc in each of next 7 sts, ch 1, skip 1 st, 3 sc in next st, ch 1, skip 1 st, sc in each of next 8 sc (121 sts, not counting ch-1's). Break off; skip next 7 sts, attach Y to next st. **15th rnd (right side): 1st short row:** With Y, ch 3 and dc in each of next 4 sts, skip 1 st, (3 dc in next st, skip 1 st, dc in each of next 3 sts, skip 1 st) twice; 3 dc in next st, skip 1 st, dc in each of next 5 sts. Break off. **2nd short row:** Skip next 5 sts (5-dc shell), attach G in next st, ch 3, dc in each of next 9 sts, ch 4, skip next 3 sc, dc in next sc and in each of next 11 sts. Break off. **3rd short row:** Skip 5 sts (5-dc shell), attach Y to next st, ch 3, 2 dc in next st, dc in each of next 3 sts, skip 1 st, 3 dc in next st, skip 1 st, dc in each of next 3 sts, skip 1 st, 2 dc in each of next 2 sts; skip 1 st, dc in each of next 3 sts, skip 1 st, 3 dc in next st, skip 1 st, dc in each of next 3 sts, 2 dc in next st, dc in next st. Break off. **4th short row:** Skip next 5 sts (5-dc shell), attach G to next st, ch 3, dc in each of next 11 sts, ch 4, skip next 3 sc, dc in next sc and in each of next 9 sts; break off. **16th rnd:** Attach W to next st, ch 4 (counts as 1 tr), tr in next st, 5 tr in next st, tr in each of next 2 sts, sc in each of next 25 Y sts, tr in each of next 2 sts, 5 tr in next st, tr in each of next 2 sts, sc in each of next 10 G sts: working over ch-4, work tr in each of next 3 T sc on row below, sc in each of next 12 G sc, tr in each of next 2 sts, 5 tr in next st, tr in each of next 2 sts, sc in each of next 28 Y sts, tr in each of next 2 sts, 5 tr in next st, tr in each of next 2 sts, sc in each of next 12 sts; working over ch-4, tr in each of next 3 T sc on row below, sc in each of next 10 sc; join to first tr. Break off W. **17th rnd (right side):** Attach G to st where last sl st was made, ch 3, dc in each of next 3 sts, 5 dc in next st, dc in each of next 33 sts, 5 dc in next st, dc in each of next 12 sts, h dc in each of next 2 sts, sc in each of next 3 sts, h dc in each of next 2 sts, dc in each of next 14 sts, 5 dc in next st, dc in each of next 4 sts, 2 dc in next st, dc in each of next 26 sts, 2 dc in next st, dc in each of next 4 sts, 5 dc in next st, dc in each of next 14 sts, h dc in each of next 2 sts, sc in each of next 3 sts, h dc in each of next 2 sts, dc in each of next 8 sts; join. Break off. **18th rnd:** With H, work * 5 dc in center dc of corner shell, work dc in each st across to within next corner dc. Repeat from * around; join to first st. Break off. **19th rnd:** With H, work * 3 sc in center dc of any corner shell, sc in each dc across to within next corner dc. Repeat from * around; join. Break off. **20th rnd:** With H, work * 3 dc in center of corner shell, dc in each dc across to within next corner sc. Repeat from * around; join. Break off. Medallion should measure 12" along lower edge and 11" along remaining edges.

BODY: Sleeve and Yoke Section: Back: Starting along sleeve seam with size F hook and T, ch 217 to measure about 50". **1st row:** Work dc in 4th ch from hook and in each ch across (215 sts, counting turning ch as 1 dc); ch 1, turn. **2nd row:** Work sc in each dc across; ch 3, turn. **3rd row:** Skip first sc, work dc in next sc and in each sc across (T stripe completed). Break off T, attach W; ch 3, turn. **4th row:** Skip first dc, work dc in next dc and in each dc across; ch 1, turn. **5th row:** Work sc in each dc across; ch 3, turn. **6th row:** Skip first sc, work dc in each sc across (W stripe completed). Break off W, attach T; ch 3, turn. With T, repeat 4th through 6th rows once (T stripe completed). Break off.

To Shape First Sleeve and Medallion Opening: Work short rows as follows: **10th row:** Skip first 46 sts, attach W in next st, ch 3, work dc in next st and in each st across to within last 46 sts; ch 1, turn. Continuing in pattern as established, complete W stripe, then work 1 T, 1 W, and 1 T stripe. Break off T, attach H; ch 3, turn. **Next row:** With H, repeat 4th row. Do not break off H. Piece should measure 7½" from beg.

Front: To Shape Right Neck Medallion Opening: Work short rows as follows: **1st row:** Work sc in each of next 46 sts; ch 3, turn. **2nd row:** Repeat 6th row. Break off H. Maintaining established pattern, work (1 T, 1 W stripe) twice. Break off.

Joining for Right Sleeve Medallion: With right side of one sleeve medallion facing you, attach T to wrist edge corner of medallion. **Next row:** Ch 3 and, working along side of medallion, skip first st, work dc in each of next 45 sts (46 sts), then on sleeve, work dc in each st across last row; ch 1, turn. Continuing in established pattern, complete T stripe, then work 1 W and 1 T stripe. Break off.

With right sides tog, using T, join top edge of medallion to sleeve with row of sc through corresponding sts, working 2 sc over posts of dc's and 1 sc over posts of sc's on sleeve; continue along remaining side edge, working 1 row sc through matching sts.

Left Sleeve: Skip center 45 sts on H row for back neck edge, attach H in next st and complete left sleeve to correspond to right. Break off.

Starting at wrist edge with right sides tog, using T, crochet underarm seams to within last 23 [28] sts of front yoke opening. Break off.

SKIRT: Try on yoke and sleeve section. To determine length of skirt, measure distance from underarm of garment to ankle. **Note:** Skirt is worked vertically.

Front: Starting at side edge of skirt with T [W], crochet a chain to measure desired length. **1st row:** Work dc in 4th ch from hook and in each ch across; ch 1, turn. **2nd row:** Work sc in each dc across; ch 3, turn. **3rd row:** Skip first sc, work dc in each sc across; change colors; ch 3, turn. **For size 16–18 only:** Continuing in stripe pattern as for yoke, work 1 T stripe. **For both sizes:** Work (1 W, 1 T stripe) twice, then 1 W stripe. Break off.

Medallion Opening: Next row: Skip first 4 sts (upper edge), attach T in next st, ch 3, dc in next st and in each st across. Complete T stripe, then work (1 W, 1 T stripe) 4 times, ending at lower edge. Break off T, attach W; ch 3, turn. **Next row:** With W work dc in each st across; ch 5, turn. **Following row:** Work sc in 2nd ch from hook and in each of next 3 ch, sc in each dc across; ch 3, turn. Complete W stripe, then work (1 T, 1 W stripe) twice, 1 T stripe. Break off T. **For size 16–18 only:** Work 1 more W stripe.

BACK: For both sizes: Starting at underarm with W [T], work same as for front through 3rd row. Continuing in stripe pattern, work stripes to correspond to front, omitting medallion opening.

FINISHING: With right sides together, pin side seams, leaving seams open from lower edge to knee or hip as desired. With T, crochet seams, working 1 row of sc through corresponding sts. With right sides tog, using T, matching underarm and side seams, join yoke and sleeve section to body with row of sc through matching sts, working 2 sc over posts of dc's and 1 sc over posts of sc's.

With right sides tog, pin medallion in neck opening. With T, work 1 row sc through corresponding sts around. **Neck Edging:** With right side facing you, attach H to first st at neck opening on medallion. **1st row:** Work 1 row dc evenly spaced around neck edge; ch 1, turn. **2nd row:** Work 1 sc in each st around; break off. **Ties:** With H, crochet four 15" chains. With sl st, attach 1 chain to beg and end of last 2 rows.

Spiraling Swirl Skirt

You make it in one piece (with a side seam) in double crochet and chain-one pattern. Orange and cyclamen swirls are worked over it later. Ties at waist with drawstring. Lined with long A-line slip.

SIZES: Small (6–8) [medium (10–12)—large (14–16)]. Skirt measures about 36" [39"—43"] around hips (measured 7" below waist), waistline is adjustable, length is about 37".

MATERIALS: Bear Brand Winsom Orlon acrylic yarn, 9 [10—11] (2-ounce) skeins rosy pink No. 342 (color A), 1 skein each orange No. 91 (B) and cyclamen No. 363 (C); aluminum crochet hook size G (or Canadian hook No. 9) *or the size that will give you the correct gauge.*

GAUGE: 9 sts (dc's and ch-1's) = 2"; 2 rows = 1".

Note: Skirt is worked in one piece with one side seam. It is important that your stitch and row gauges are accurate.

Starting at waist, ch 130 [146—162] to measure about 29" [32"—36"]. **1st row:** Dc in 6th ch from hook (1 sp made), * ch 1, skip 1 ch, dc in next ch (another sp made). Repeat from * across (64 [72—80] dc, counting turning ch as 1 dc; 63 [71—79] sps); ch 4, turn. **2nd row (inc row):** Skip first dc and ch-1, dc in next dc, (ch 1, dc in next dc) 5 [6—7] times; ch 1, work inc as follows: Dc in next dc, ch 1, dc in same dc (inc made); * (ch 1, dc in next dc) 7 [8—9] times, ch 1, inc in next dc. Repeat from * 6 times more, working last inc in 2nd ch of ch-4 (72 [80—88] dc); ch 4, turn. **3rd row:** Skip first dc and ch-1, dc in next dc, * ch 1, dc in next dc. Repeat from * across, ending ch 1, dc in 2nd ch of ch-4; ch 4, turn. Repeat 3rd row 6 times more. **10th row (inc row):** Skip first dc and ch-1, dc in next dc, ch 1, inc in next dc, * (ch 1, dc in next dc) 8 [9—10] times; ch 1, inc in next dc. Repeat from * 6 times more; (ch 1, dc in next dc) 6 [7—8] times, working last dc in 2nd ch of ch-4 (80 [88—96] dc); ch 4, turn. Repeat 3rd row 5 times more. **16th row (inc row):** Skip first dc and ch-1, dc in next dc, (ch 1, dc in next dc) 5 times; ch 1, inc in next dc, * (ch 1, dc in next dc) 9 [10—11] times; ch 1, inc in next dc. Repeat from * 6 times more; (ch 1, dc in next dc) 2 [3—4] times, working last dc in 2nd ch of ch-4 (88 [96—104] dc); ch 4, turn. Repeat 3rd row 3 times more. **20th row (inc row):** Skip first dc and ch-1, inc in next dc, * (ch 1, dc in next dc) 10 [11—12] times; ch 1, inc in next dc. Repeat from * 6 times more; (ch 1, dc in next dc) 9 [10—11] times, working last dc in 2nd ch of ch-4 (96 [104—112] dc); ch 4, turn. Repeat 3rd row 3 times more. Skirt should measure about 11½" from beg.

Continue to work in pattern as established, increasing 8 times evenly spaced as before on all inc rows, being sure that increases do not fall over previous increases. The following rows are inc rows: 24th row, 28th, 34th, 38th, 44th, 48th, 54th, 58th, 62nd, 66th and 67th. Work even as for 3rd row on the rows between.

68th row: Work even on 184 [192—200] dc. Skirt should measure 34" from beg. Break off. Turn.

FIRST SCALLOP: With A, form lp on hook. **1st row:** Dc in first dc of last row, * ch 1, dc in next dc. Repeat from * 21 [22—23] times more, increasing twice, as evenly spaced as possible (25 [26—27] dc); ch 4, turn. **2nd row:** Work even; ch 4, turn. **3rd row (dec row):** Skip first sp and dec 1 dc (to dec 1 dc, work dc in next dc to point where 2 lps remain on hook, y o hook, draw up lp in next dc, y o, draw through all 3 lps on hook). Continue across without decreasing to within last 2 dc, dec 1 dc; ch 4, turn. **4th and 5th rows:** Repeat 3rd row. Break off.

NEXT SCALLOP: With A, form lp on hook. **1st row:** Dc in next free dc on 68th row, * ch 1, dc in next dc. Repeat from * 21 [22—23] times more, increasing twice, as evenly spaced as possible (25 [26—27] dc); ch 4, turn. Complete as for first scallop. Make 6 more scallops in same manner.

TRIM: To divide waistline into 8 sections, skip first 7 [8—9] dc, place marker in next dc, * skip next 7 [8—9] dc, place marker in next dc. Repeat from * 6 times more (8 marked dc). **1st Swirl:** Spread skirt on flat surface with right side facing you. With sewing needle and contrasting color thread, starting at lower edge of skirt in dip between 2 scallops and following photograph, baste a diagonal line up to a marked dc at waist edge.

Then, using basting line as guideline, with crochet hook and B, sl st over post of marked dc, * ch 4, sc in 3rd ch from hook, ch 1 (picot made), sl st over post of next dc 1 row below. Repeat from * to within dip of scallop; continue in pattern around edge of scallop, working sl st directly in dc rather than over post, ending with picot in dc before next dip. Break off.

Work 7 more swirls in same manner, alternating colors B and C. Sew side seam.

DRAWSTRING: With 2 strands of A, crochet 66" chain. Weave through sps of first row, adjust to fit and tie in bow.

SKIRT LINING: We recommend a long A-line slip for lining. If you can't get one in the right color, purchase a white one and tint it. Insert slip in skirt and tack around waist edge.

Tank Top and Plaid Skirt

A versatile two-piece outfit to be seen in anywhere. Top is worked in simple chain-one and single crochet pattern, and could, of course, be worn over a blouse. The long skirt is worked on the bias for a soft, swingy effect.

Tank Top

SIZES: Petite (5–6) [small (8–10)—medium (12–14)]. Garment measures 14" [15"—16"] across bust from side seam to side seam.

MATERIALS: Brunswick Germantown knitting worsted, 2 (4-ounce) skeins saffron No. 4051, aluminum crochet hook size H (or Canadian hook No. 8) *or the size that will give you the correct gauge.*

GAUGE: In pattern stitch: 4 stitches (ch 1, sc, ch 1, and sc) = 1"; 4 rows = 1".

BACK: Starting at lower edge, ch 58 [62—66] to measure about 14" [15"—16"]. **1st row:** Sc in 2nd ch from hook, * ch 1, skip next ch, sc in next ch. Repeat from * across (57 [61—65] sts); ch 1, turn. **2nd row:** Sc in first sc, * ch 1, skip next ch-1, sc in next sc. Repeat from * across; ch 1, turn. Repeat last row until piece measures 11" from beg, or desired length to underarms.

To Shape Armholes: 1st row (dec row): Sl st across first 4 sts; ch 1, work across to last 4 sts;

ch 1, turn. **2nd row:** Dec 2 sts, ch 1, work across to last 2 sts (45 [49—53] sts); ch 1, turn. Work even until armholes measure 5¼" [5½"—5¾"].

To Shape Neck and Shoulders: First Shoulder: Work in pattern across 15 [17—19] sts (neck edge); ch 1, turn. Dec 2 sts at neck edge every row 3 times. Work even on 9 [11—13] sts until armhole measures 7½" [7¾"—8"]. Break off. **2nd Shoulder:** Skip center 15 sts at back neck, attach yarn at neck edge and work 15 [17—19] sts to armhole edge. Work to correspond to other side.

FRONT: Work same as for back until armholes measure 4¼" [4½"—4¾"]. Work neck and shoulder shaping same as for back.

FINISHING: Sew side and shoulder seams. **Edging:** Work one row of ch-1 and sc pattern around armhole and neck edge.

Long Plaid A-line Skirt

SIZES: One size will fit 10 through 14. Waistline will stretch to fit 24" to 28". Finished skirt length is 38" from waistline to lower edge and can be adjusted by depth of hem. Skirt measures 36" across lower edge from side seam to side seam.

MATERIALS: Brunswick Germantown knitting worsted, 5 (4-ounce) skeins bright navy No. 4131 (color N), 3 skeins shamrock green No. 443 (G), and 2 skeins saffron yellow No. 4051 (Y); aluminum crochet hook size H (or Canadian hook No. 8) *or the size that will give you the correct gauge;* 1 yard ½"-wide elastic.

GAUGE: 7 sts = 2"; 9 average rows = 4½".

Note: Skirt is crocheted on the bias, so be sure to have the correct row and stitch gauge for proper fit.

See Blazer (p. 130) for how to work with 2 colors within a row and how to change colors. Work with 3 colors in one row in same manner, working over 2 strands of unused colors.

BACK: Starting at lower right-hand corner, with N, ch 4. **1st row:** Work 3 dc in 4th ch from hook (always count turning ch as one st—4 sts). **2nd row (right side):** Ch 3, turn; work 2 dc in first dc (2 sts inc), 1 dc in each of next 2 dc, work 3 dc in top st of turning ch (another 2 st inc—there are now 8 sts in row). Drop N loop from hook. Do not turn.

Note: All sc rows (like next row) are worked with Y only, with right side of work facing you, working 2 sc in first and last st except where stated otherwise. **3rd row (right side):** Make loop on hook with Y. Starting at beg of last row, work 2 sc in top st of turning ch, work 1 sc in each dc across, working 2 sc in last st (2 sts inc in row—10 sts). Break off Y. Turn. **4th row:** Insert hook in dropped N loop and ch 3; attach G and, working with N (over G), dc in first st (1 st inc), work 1 N dc in each of next 4 sc (changing to G on last dc), with G work 1 dc in next sc (changing to N), with N work 1 dc in each of next 3 sc, work 3 dc in last sc (2 sts inc at end of row—13 sts). **5th row:** Ch 3, turn; with N (working over G) work 2 dc in first dc (2 sts inc), with N work 1 dc in each of next 5 dc (changing to G on last dc), work 1 G dc over G dc below (changing to N); with N, dc in each dc across, working 3 dc in top of turning ch (17 sts in row). **6th row:** With G, ch 3, turn; in first dc work 1 G dc; attach Y and work 1 Y dc in same st (2 st inc), with G (working over N and Y), dc in each dc across, in last st work 1 Y dc and 2 G dc (first green stripe completed—21 sts).

7th row: With N, ch 3, turn; (working over Y and G) work 2 dc in first st, 1 N dc in next st, 1 Y dc in next Y dc, working over Y and G work 7 N, 1 G, 7 N, 1 Y in next Y dc, 1 N dc, then 2 N dc in last st (3 st inc in row—24 sts). **8th row:** Ch 3, turn; work 1 Y and 1 N dc in first st, working over unused colors and matching colors of last row, dc across to within last 2 sts, then work 1 N dc, in last st work 1 Y and 2 N dc (4 st inc in row—28 sts). Drop N loop from hook. Turn. **9th row (right side):** With a separate strand of Y, make loop on hook, work in sc across, inc 1 st in first and last sts (30 sts). Break off Y. Do not turn. Check row gauge. Piece should measure 4½" from beg. **10th row:** Insert hook in dropped N loop, ch 3, work 2 dc in first st, work across row, working colors as for 8th row, working 3 dc in last st (34 sts). **11th row:** Ch 3, turn; 1 N dc in first st, work across row, matching colors of last row, working 3 N dc in last st (37 sts). Drop N loop from hook. Turn.

12th row (right side): With new strand of Y, work 2 sc in first st, sc in each st across, work 3 sc in last st (40 sts). Break off. **13th row (right side):** Insert hook in N loop, ch 3, work 1 N dc and 1 G dc in first st, starting with N, work across row, matching colors of 11th row, in last st work 1 N and 1 G (43 sts). **14th row:** With N, ch 3, turn; in first G st work 1 N dc and 1 G dc, work across row, matching colors of last row, working 3 N dc in last st (47 sts). **15th row:** With G (over Y and N), ch 3, turn; work 2 dc in first st, * with G, dc in each dc to Y dc below, work 1 Y dc, 3 G dc, and 1 Y dc. Repeat from * once more; with G, dc in each dc to last st, working 2 dc in last st (2nd green stripe completed—50 sts).

16th row: With N, ch 3, turn; work 2 dc in first st, 1 N dc in each of next 2 sts, * 1 G dc, 7 N dc, 1 Y dc, 3 N dc, 1 Y dc, 7 N dc. Repeat from * once more; work 1 G and 5 N dc, work 3 N dc in last st (54 sts). **17th row:** With N, ch 3, turn; in first st work 1 N and 1 Y dc, working in dc across row, work 7 N, 1 G, continue across matching colors of last row, working 2 N dc in last st (57 sts). Drop N, do not turn. **18th row:** Repeat 12th row (60 sts). **19th row (wrong side):** Insert hook in N loop, ch 3, turn; in first st work 1 N dc and 1 Y dc, work across row, matching colors of 17th row, working 1 N, 1 Y, and 1 N dc all in last st (64 sts). **20th row:** With N, ch 3, turn; work 2 N dc in first st, 1 Y dc in next st, work across row, matching colors of last row, working 2 N dc in last st (67 sts). Drop N, do not turn. **21st row:** Repeat 12th row (70 sts). **22nd row:** With N, ch 3, turn; working in dc, work 1 N in first st, 1 Y, 3 N, 1 Y, continue in pattern as established on row before last, working 3 N in last st (73 sts). **23rd row:** With G, ch 3, turn; work 2 N dc in first st, work across row in pattern, working 3 N dc in last st (77 sts). **24th row (wrong side):** With G, ch 3, turn; work 1 G dc in first st, * with G dc in each dc to Y dc, work 1 Y dc. Repeat from * across, working 3 dc in last st (3rd green stripe completed—80 sts). Mark beg of this row for lower edge and end of row for side edge of skirt.

Working in color pattern as for last 9 rows, and keeping increased sts in new patterns, continue to increase as before: **At side edge:** Inc 2 sts every dc row and inc 1 st every sc row, *and at the same time* **At lower edge:** Inc 2 sts one row, then 1 st the next row alternately, until 6th green stripe is completed (170 sts). Put a marker at end of this stripe at side edge for start of decrease for waistline, put a marker at lower edge of same stripe for start of decrease for other side edge.

Keeping pattern as established, dec as follows: **1st row (dc row):** Starting at waistline edge, ch 1, turn; sl st across first 3 sts, ch 3 (as ch-3 counts as 1 st, this is a 2-st dec), work across to within last 7 sts. Do not work over these last 7 sts (7 sts dec). **2nd row (dc row):** Starting at lower edge, ch 1, turn; sl st across 8 sts, ch 3 (this is a 7-st dec as ch-3 counts as 1 st), work across to within last 2 sts (2 sts dec). **3rd row (sc row):** Make lp on hook and, starting at waistline edge, skip first 2 sts, sc in next st and in each st across to within last 7 sts. Break off.

Continue in pattern as established, dec 2 sts at waistline edge every row and 7 sts at side edge every row until 18th dec row is completed. Break off.

FRONT: Work as for back until 3rd row is completed. **4th row (wrong side):** Ch 3, turn; with N work 2 dc in first dc (mark this edge for side edge), work 3 N dc, 1 G dc, with N dc across, working 2 dc in last st (mark this edge for lower edge).

Work as for back, reversing shaping as follows: **At side edge:** Inc 2 sts every dc row and inc 1 st every sc row *and at the same time* **At lower edge:** Inc 2 sts one row and 1 st next row alternately as for back. Complete to correspond to back, reversing all shaping.

FINISHING: Taking in about ½" side seams, sew front and back together. Cut elastic to fit waistline and sew ends, forming a circle. Turn top edge of skirt to wrong side over elastic, making a casing about 1" deep, and sew in place.

Turn up a hem about 1½" or desired depth and sew in place. Block lightly.

One-Piece-Look Dress

Is really a skirt and matching pullover that are brought together by repeating the skirt's patterned band along the bottom of the pullover. Solid areas are worked in single and double crochet, bands in shell stitch and single crochet.

SIZES: Small (8–10) [medium (12–14)—large (16–18)]. Top measures 16" [18"—20"] across back from side seam to side seam and 21" [21½"—22"] from back neck to lower edge when finished. Skirt measures 17" [19"—21"] across from side seam to side seam, measured 7" below waist, and 26" in length from waist to lower edge when finished. Skirt length is adjustable.

MATERIALS: Brunswick Germantown knitting worsted, 7 [8—9] (4-ounce) skeins curry heather No. 490 (color A), 1 skein each of dark turquoise No. 4412 (B), copper No. 432 (C), medium cherry No. 4562 (D), medium lime No. 4272 (E), and salmon No. 437 (F); aluminum crochet hook size H (or Canadian hook No. 8) *or the size that will give you the correct gauge;* one ¾"-diameter button; 1 yard ⅜"-wide elastic; tapestry needle.

GAUGE: 4 sts (sc, dc, sc, and dc) = 1".

Skirt

BACK: Starting above color band with A, ch 89 [97—105] to measure 22" [24"—26"]. **1st row:** Sc in 2nd ch from hook, dc in next ch, * sc in next ch, dc in next ch. Repeat from * across (88 [96—104] sts); ch 1, turn. **2nd row:** Sc in each dc and dc in each sc across; ch 1, turn. Repeat 2nd row for pattern throughout and work decreases as follows: **Next row (dec row):** Draw up a lp in each of first 2 sts, y o and draw through all 3 lps on hook (1 st dec made), work across in pattern to last 2 sts, draw up a lp in each of last 2 sts, y o and draw through all 3 lps on hook (another 1 st dec made—86 [94—102] sts). Work even in pattern for 3½". **Next row (dec row):** Place 3 safety pins as markers in work evenly spaced across row. Dec 1 st at beg as before, * work to next pin, draw up a lp in each of next 3 sts, y o and draw through all 3 lps on hook (2 st dec made). Repeat from *

twice more; work to last 2 sts, dec 1 st at end as before (8 sts dec across row). Work decreases as for last row every 3½" 3 times more, decreasing 1 st at beg and end of row and 2 sts before each marker (54 [62—70] sts). Work even until piece measures 18" or 7½" less than desired finished length. Break off.

Border: 1st row: With A, sc in first st of starting chain at lower edge, working across unworked loops of starting chain, * ch 1, skip next ch, sc in next ch. Repeat from * across (45 [49—53] sc). Drop A; attach B; ch 1, turn. **2nd row (right side):** With B, sc in first sc, * work 3 dc in next sc (shell made), sc in next sc. Repeat from * across (22 [24—26] shells). Break off B; attach D; ch 1, turn. **3rd row:** With D, sc in first sc, ch 1, * sc in center dc of next shell, ch 3. Repeat from * across ending with sc in center dc of last shell, ch 1, sc in last sc. Break off D; pick up A; ch 1, turn. **4th row:** With A, insert hook in first B sc *2 rows below* and work sc (long sc made), * sc in next D sc, work long sc in next B sc. Repeat from * across. Drop A; attach C; ch 1, turn. **5th row:** With C, sc in first long sc, * ch 3, sc in next long sc. Repeat from * across. Break off C; do not turn work but pick up A at right-hand edge, ch 1. **6th row:** With A, sc in first sc, * ch 1, work long sc in next A sc *2 rows below*, ch 1, sc in next sc. Repeat from * across. Break off A; attach E; ch 1, turn. **7th row:** With E, sc in first sc, * ch 1, sc in next long sc, ch 1, sc in next sc. Repeat from * across. Break off E; attach B; ch 1, turn. **8th row:** With B, sc in first sc, * ch 1, sc in next sc. Repeat from * across. Break off B; attach F; ch 1, turn. **9th row:** With F, repeat 2nd row. Drop F; attach D; ch 3, turn. **10th row:** With D, dc in first sc, * sc in center dc of next shell, work 3-dc shell in next sc. Repeat from * across, ending with dc in last sc. Break off D; do not turn work but pick up F at right-hand edge; ch 1. **11th row:** With F, sc in first dc, * work 3-dc shell in center dc of shell *2 rows below* (this is same place as D sc was worked), sc in center dc of next D shell. Repeat from * across, ending with sc in last dc. Break off F; attach E; ch 1, turn. **12th row:** With E, sc in first sc, * ch 1, sc in center dc of next shell, ch 1, sc in next sc. Repeat from * across. Break off E; attach A; ch 1, turn. **13th row:** With A, repeat 8th row. Drop A; attach B; ch 1, turn. Repeat 2nd through 13th rows for border pattern until border measures 8" or until skirt measures desired finished length.

FRONT: Work same as for back.

FINISHING: Block to measurements. Sew side seams. **Waistband:** With A threaded in tapestry needle, sew in a row of ½"-high herringbone stitches around wrong side of waist edge. Cut elastic to fit your waist measurement; thread elastic through herringbone-stitch casing; sew elastic ends securely together.

Herringbone Stitch

Top

BACK: Starting above color band with A, ch 65 [73—81]. Work in pattern st on 64 [72—80] sts same as for skirt until piece measures 7" from beg or 7½" less than desired finished length to underarms.

To Shape Armholes: Sl st in each of first 3 [4—5] sts, ch 1, work in pattern to last 3 [4—5] sts (58 [64—70] sts); ch 1, turn. Dec 1 st at beg and end of next 3 [4—5] rows (52 [56—60] sts).

To Divide for Neck Opening: Next row: Work in pattern across first 26 [28—30] sts. Work even on one side only until armhole measures 7" [7¼"—7½"], ending at arm edge.

To Shape Shoulder: 1st row: Starting at arm edge, sl st in each of first 5 sts, ch 1, work in pattern to end; ch 1, turn. **2nd row:** Work in pattern to last 5 sts, ch 1, turn. **3rd row:** Sl st in each of first 4 [5—6] sts, ch 1, work in pattern to end. Break off. Attach yarn at base of slit and complete other side to correspond to first side.

Border: Work border same as for skirt (33 [37—41] sc at end of first row).

FRONT: Work same as back, omitting neck opening, until armholes measure 4½" [4¾"—5"] (52 [56—60] sts).

To Shape Neck: 1st row: Work across 20 [22—24] sts, ch 1, turn. Work on one side only. **2nd row:** Starting at neck edge, sl st in each of first 3 sts, ch 1, work in pattern to end; ch 1, turn. **3rd row:** Work in pattern to last 3 sts (14 [16—18] sts); ch 1, turn. Work even in pattern until piece measures same as back to shoulder.

To Shape Shoulder: Work same as shoulder shaping for back until 2nd row is completed. Break off. Skip center 12 sts, attach yarn and complete other side to correspond.

Border: Work border same as for back.

SLEEVES: Note: To inc, work 2 sts in one st. Starting at lower edge with A, ch 31. Work in pattern and inc 1 st at beg and end of row every 1½" 8 [9—10] times (46 [48—50] sts). Work even in pattern until sleeve measures 17½" or length desired to underarm.

To Shape Cap: 1st row: Sl st in each of first 2 [3—4] sts, ch 1, work in pattern to last 2 [3—4] sts; ch 1, turn. Dec 1 st at beg and end of every other row 6 [7—8] times, then every row 6 times. Dec 2 sts at beg and end of next 2 rows (10 [8—6] sts remain). Break off.

FINISHING: Block to measurements. Sew shoulder, side, and sleeve seams. Sew sleeves in place.

Neck Edge: 1st row: With right side facing you, attach F to left corner of back neck edge; spacing sc about ½" apart, work a row of ch 1 and sc around neck edge. Break off F. **2nd row:** With right side facing you, with D, work sc in first sc made on last row. Working from

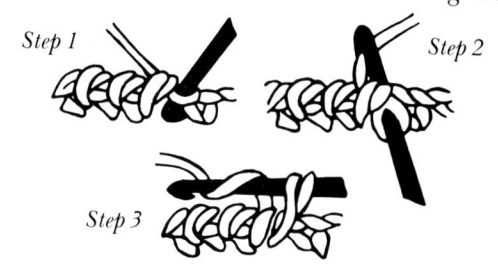

Step 1 *Step 2*

Step 3

Reverse Single Crochet

left to right, work reverse sc (see diagram) in each st across. Break off.

Neck Opening: With right side of work facing you, attach A to right corner of neck opening; ch 5 for button loop, sc at base of last F sc, then spacing sc about ½" apart, work row of ch-1 and sc around neck opening. Break off. Sew button in place.

Sweater Dress

Has a solid-color short-sleeved top with stripe and collar details, worked in double crochet. The A-line skirt is striped in rows of single and treble crochet.

SIZES: 10 [12—14—16—18]. Finished dress measures 16½" [17"—17½"—18½"—19"] across bust for a snug-fitting bodice, 17½" [18½"—19"—19½"—20"] across hips (measured 7" below waist), 22½" [23"—23½"—24½"—25"] across hemline. Skirt length is 21" and is adjustable.

MATERIALS: Bear Brand Win-Knit (100% acrylic fiber, knitting worsted-weight), 3 [3—3—3—4] (4-ounce) skeins medium turquoise No. 412 (color T), 1 [1—2—2—2] skeins spearmint No. 448 (S), and 1 skein copper No. 445 (C); aluminum crochet hook size K (or Canadian hook No. 4) *or the size that will give you the correct gauge;* seam binding if desired.

Note: The top section of this dress is crocheted from the waistline up to the shoulders; then the skirt is added, starting at the waistline and working down to hemline so that any adjustment needed in length can be easily made.

GAUGE: Top and sleeves: 3 sc = 1"; 3 rows = 1". Skirt: 3 sts = 1"; 11 rows average 5".

Bodice

BACK: Starting at waist with T, ch 40 [42—44—46—48] to measure about 13½" [14"—14½"—15½"—16"]. **1st row:** Sc in 2nd ch from hook and in each ch across (39 [41—43—45—47] sc); ch 1, turn.

2nd row (wrong side): Sc in front lp of each sc across; ch 1, turn. **3rd row (right side):** Sc in both lps of each sc across; ch 1, turn. Repeating 2nd and 3rd rows for pattern, inc 1 st each side every 1" 5 times. Work even on 49 [51—53—55—57] sts until piece measures 7" [7"—7¼"—7¼"—7½"] from beg, omitting ch-1 at end of last row.

To Shape Armholes: 1st row: Sl st across first 2 [3—3—4—4] sts, ch 1, work across row to last 2 [3—3—4—4] sts; ch 1, turn. **2nd row:** Work even. **3rd row:** Draw up a lp in each of next 2 sts, y o hook and draw through 3 lps (dec made), work across row to last 2 sts, dec 1 st; ch 1, turn (2 sts dec). Repeat last 2 rows twice more. Work even on 39 [39—41—41—43] sts until armholes measure 6¾" [7"—7"—7¼"—7¼"]. **To Shape Shoulders:** Sl st across 9 [9—10—10—11] sts, ch 1, work across row to last 9 [9—10—10—11] sts. Break off. The 21 sts in center are for neck.

FRONT: Work same as for back until first row of armhole shaping is completed and there are 45 [45—47—47—49] sts.

To Shape Neck: 1st short row: Work across 20 [20—21—21—22] sts. Do not work over remaining sts. Ch 1, turn. Working on one side only, dec 1 st at beg and end of every other row 3 times (armhole dec completed); then continue to dec 1 st every other row at neck edge only, 5 times more.

Work even on 9 [9—10—10—11] sts until armhole measures same as back armhole to shoulder. Break off.

For other side, skip 5 sts at center of neck; with T work the 20 [20—21—21—22] sts of other side to correspond.

Skirt

BACK: All rows for skirt are worked with right side of work facing you. Start each row at beg of previous row, with lp of new color on hook. Break off at end of each row, do not turn work.

Turn back bodice upside down and with right side of work facing you, work as follows: **1st row:** This row is worked over sc's of first row of bodice. With T, insert hook in sp between sc's, and sc across, increasing 4 sts evenly spaced (43 [45—47—49—51] sts). Break off.

2nd row: With C, sc in each sc across. **3rd row:** With T, sc in each sc across. **4th row:** With S, work 2 tr in each of first 2 sc (double inc made), tr in each sc across to last 2 sc, work 2 tr in each of next 2 sc (4 sts inc). **5th row:** With T, sc in each tr across.

6th row: With C, sc across. **7th row:** With T, sc across. **8th row:** With S, work 2 tr in first sc, tr in each sc across, work 2 tr in last sc (2 sts inc). **9th row:** With T, sc in each tr across.

Repeat 2nd through 9th rows once more; then repeat 6th through 9th rows 6 times more.

Work even in pattern as established on 67 [69—71—73—75] sts for 6 rows more; ending with a 7th row of pattern. Skirt should measure 21". If desired, work more or fewer rows, ending with a 7th row of pattern.

FRONT: Working along front bodice, work same as for back.

SLEEVES: Starting at lower edge with T, ch 33 [34—35—36—37] to measure about 10¾" [11"—11¼"—11½"—11¾"]. Work even in pattern as for back of bodice on 32 [33—34—35—36] sc for 2" [2"—2½"—2½"—2½"], omitting ch-1 at end of last row.

To Shape Cap: 1st row: Sl st across first 3 sts, ch 1, work across row to last 3 sts; ch 1, turn. Work even for 2 rows, then dec 1 st at beg and end of next row. Repeat last 3 rows twice more. Work even for 1 [2—2—3—3] rows. **Next row:** Sl st across first 2 sts, work across row to last 2 sts. Repeat last row twice more. Break off.

FINISHING: Machine stitch or hand sew shoulder, side, and sleeve seams, placing seam binding in shoulder and side seams if desired. Sew sleeves in place. **Sleeve edging:** With wrong side of sleeve facing you, with C, work 1 rnd of sc around lower edge of sleeve; join with sl st and break off. Turn. With right side of sleeve facing you, with T, work 1 rnd of sc; join and turn. With T, sl st in each st around. Join and break off. **Neck edging:** With right side of dress facing you, with T, work 68 [68—68—70—70] sc evenly spaced around; join and break off. Turn. From wrong side, with C, work 1 rnd of sc. Join and break off. Turn. From right side, with T, repeat last rnd. Mark center front st of last rnd.

Collar: 1st row: With wrong side facing you and starting in 12th st from marked st, with T, work sc across neck edging to within 11 sts of same marked st. Do not work over center 23 sts. Ch 1, turn. **2nd row:** Sc in each sc across; ch 1, turn. **3rd and 4th rows:** Working in sc, dec 1 st at beg and end of row; ch 1, turn. Work even in sc for 4 rows more. Break off. Tack corners of collar to right side of neck edging.

With T, and wrong side of lower edge of skirt facing you, sl st around. Break off.

Two delicate ruffled and flounced dresses in pale pastels with that distinctive hand-crocheted look. Skirts are worked from the waist down to go to any length you choose.

V-Neck Ruffle Dress

In ecru with spice trim.

SIZES: Small (6–8) [medium (10–12)—large (14–16)]. Finished dress measures 14" [16½"—19"] across bust for a snug-fitting bodice, 24¾" [27"—29¼"] across hips (measured 7" below waist), 37" [43½"—50"] across hemline (measured above ruffle). Skirt length is 22" (including ruffle) and is adjustable.

MATERIALS: J. & P. Coats Knit-Cro-Sheen, 16 [18—20] (250-yard) balls ecru No. 61 (color A), 2 [2—2] (175-yard) balls spice No. 51 (B) for trim; aluminum crochet hook size G (or Canadian No. 9) *or the size that will give you the correct gauge;* ecru lining fabric, if desired.

Note: The dress is made without side seams. The bodice of dress is crocheted around in one piece and is worked from the waistline up to the shoulders; then the skirt is added, starting at the waistline and working around to the hemline so that any adjustment needed in length can easily be made.

GAUGE: 19 average sts (dc's and ch-1's) = 3"; 2 rows = 1".

Note: Work with 2 strands of same color throughout.

Bodice

Starting at waistline with A, ch 132 [144—156] to measure about 26" [29"—32"]. Being careful not to twist chain, join with sl st to first ch to form a ring.

1st rnd (right side): Ch 3, work 2 dc in same st as sl st (first shell made), * skip next ch, dc in next ch, ch 1, skip next ch, dc in next ch, skip next ch, work a shell of 3 dc in next ch. Repeat from * around to last 5 ch sts, skip next ch, dc in next ch, ch 1, skip next ch, dc in next ch, skip next ch, sl st in top of ch-3 (22 [24—26] shells).

2nd rnd: Ch 3, * skip shell, dc in sp before next dc, ch 1, dc in next ch-1 sp, work shell of 3 dc in sp before next shell. Repeat from * around, ending with skip last shell, dc in sp before next dc, ch 1, dc in next sp, 2 dc in last sp, sl st in top of ch-3.

3rd rnd: Ch 4, dc in next ch-1 sp, shell in sp before next shell. Repeat from * on 2nd rnd, ending ch 1, sl st in ch-4 sp.

4th rnd (inc rnd): Ch 4, shell in sp before next shell, * (ch 1, dc in next sp) twice; ch 1, shell in sp before next shell. Repeat from * around, ending ch 1, dc in last sp, ch 1, sl st in ch-4 sp.

5th rnd: Ch 3, work 2 dc in same sp as sl st, * (ch 1, dc in next dc) twice; ch 1, shell in next sp. Repeat from * around, ending (ch 1, dc in next sp) twice; ch 1, sl st in top of ch-3.

Continue working in pattern as established (as for 2nd through 5th rnds, with extra ch-1's on 2nd and 3rd rnds) until piece measures 7" [7½"—7½"] from beg or desired length to armhole. Do not break off.

To Divide Work in Half for Back and Front: With a pin, mark last sl st worked for one side seam (first marker), then for back of dress skip next 88 [96—104] sts, mark last st for other side seam (2nd marker). Remaining 88 [96—104] sts will be used for front of dress. Work in rows from now on.

To Shape Back Armholes: 1st row: Sl st across first 6 sts of back, ch 4 (ch replaces one st of dec; 5 sts dec at beg of row), work in pattern to within 5 sts of 2nd marker, turn. **2nd row:** Sl st over first 4 sts, ch 4, work in pattern across, turn (3 sts dec at beg of row). Repeat last row 3 times more; then work even until armholes measure 6½" [7"—7"] from beg.

To Shape Neck and Shoulders: Work across first 15 [16—20] sts for 1 row. Break off. Attach thread at other armhole and work across first 15 [16—20] sts for 1 row. Break off. Remaining sts in center are for back of neck.

To Shape Front Armhole and Divide for V-Neck: On front of dress, count first 44 [48—52] sts from marker and place pin in work to mark center front. Work as follows for first half of front armhole and neck shaping: **1st row:** Attach thread at marker at side seam, then sl st across first 6 sts of front, ch 4 (5 st dec), work in pattern across to within 3 sts of pin at center front, turn. Do not work across remaining sts. **2nd row:** Sl st across first 4 sts, ch 4, work in pattern across, turn (3 st dec at beg of row).

Repeat last row 4 times more, ending at armhole edge; ch 4, turn at end of 6th row. Work even for 1 row.

Keeping armhole edge even, continue to dec 3 sts at neck edge every other row 3 [4—4] times more. Work even on 15 [16—20] sts if necessary until armhole measures same as back armhole. Break off.

Second Half of Front: Attach thread at other side seam and work to correspond to first half. After second half is completed there are 6 sts left free at center front.

Skirt

Work around lower edge of bodice. With right side of work facing, join A with sl st in first sp to left of first shell worked at side seam on first row. (**Note:** If you want a shorter skirt, omit some of the even rows. Shell pattern slants in opposite direction on skirt.) **1st rnd:** Ch 3, work 2 dc in same sp, * (ch 1, dc in next sp) twice; ch 1, skip shell, work shell in next sp. Repeat from * around, ending (ch 1, dc in next sp) twice; ch 1, sl st in top of ch-3 (22 [24—26] shells).

2nd rnd (inc rnd): Ch 4, shell in next sp, * (ch 1, dc in next sp) twice; ch 1, shell in next sp, ch 1, dc in next sp, ch 1, in next sp work dc, ch 1 and dc (inc made), ch 1, shell in next sp.

Repeat from * around, omitting last dc on last repeat, join with sl st in ch-4 lp (11 [12—13] inc made).

3rd rnd (inc rnd): Ch 4, shell in next sp, * ch 1, dc in next sp, ch 1, in next sp work dc, ch 1 and dc, shell in next shell, (ch 1, dc in next sp) 3 times; ch 1, shell in next sp. Repeat from * around, end as for last rnd (11 [12—13] inc made).

4th and 5th rnds: Work even in pattern as established with 3 ch-1 and dc groups between shells.

6th and 7th rnds: Increase in alternate panels as for 2nd and 3rd rnds.

8th and 9th rnds: Work even in pattern with 4 ch-1 and dc groups between shells.

***10th and 11th rnds:** Inc in alternate panels as for 2nd and 3rd rnds. Work even in pattern with 5 ch-1 and dc groups between shells for 5 rnds.

Repeat from * at beg of 10th rnd twice more; working 6 and then 7 ch-1 and dc groups.

31st rnd: Work even in pattern. Skirt should measure about 16"; border and ruffle will add about 6". If you want your skirt longer, work more rows.

Border Ruffle: 1st rnd: Working in sc, work 2 sc in each ch-1 sp and 2 sc over each shell around.

Work even in sc for 2 rnds. **4th rnd (side shells):** * Sc in next sc, ch 4, work 4 dc in last sc worked, skip next 3 sc. Repeat from * around, sl st in first sc. **5th rnd:** Sl st in first 2 ch of ch-4, sc in ch-4 sp, * ch 5, sc in same sp, ch 5, skip one side shell, sc in next ch-4 sp. Repeat from * around, ending sl st in first sc. **6th rnd:** Sl st to center of next sp, sc in same sp, * ch 5, sc in next sp. Repeat from * around, ending sl st in first sc. **7th rnd:** Sl st to center of next sp, ch 8, * dc in next sp, ch 5. Repeat from * around, ending sl st in 3rd ch of ch-8. Repeat 7th rnd twice more. **10th rnd:** Repeat 6th rnd. Break off. **11th rnd (picot rnd):** With B, make lp on hook. With right side facing, sc in any sp, ch 4, sc in 3rd ch from hook (picot made), ch 2, sc in same sp, ch 2, * sc in next sp, ch 4, picot, ch 2, sc in same sp, ch 2. Repeat from * around, ending sl st in first sc. Break off.

FINISHING: Sew shoulder seams.

Neck Border Ruffle: 1st rnd: With right side facing, using A, work 81 [87—87] sc evenly spaced around neck edge. **2nd rnd:** Sc in each sc around. **3rd rnd:** Sl st in each sc around. **4th rnd:** * Sl st in next sl st, ch 3, work 2 dc in last sl st worked, skip next 2 sl sts. Repeat from * around, sl st in first sl st worked. **5th rnd:** * Sc in next ch-3 sp, (ch 5, sc in same sp) twice; ch 5. Repeat from * around, sl st in first sc. **6th rnd:** Sl st to center of next sp, * ch 5, sc in next sp. Repeat from * around, ch 5, sl st in center of first sp. Repeat 7th rnd of skirt ruffle twice. Repeat 6th rnd (above) twice. Break off.

With B make lp on hook. Work 11th rnd (picot rnd) of skirt ruffle. With right side facing, with B, make lp on hook and sc in any lp on 8th rnd. Work picot rnd over lps on 8th rnd. Break off.

Armhole Border Ruffle: With right side facing, with A, work 48 [54—54] sc evenly spaced around armhole edge. Work 2nd through 6th rnds as for neck. Repeat 7th rnd of skirt ruffle 3 times. Repeat 6th rnd of neck ruffle but work ch-8 (instead of ch-5) 3 times. With B, work 13th rnd as for picot rnd of skirt ruffle and work picot rnd over 10th rnd.

BELT: Using 6 strands of A, make chain 64" long. **Flowers:** With A, ch 6, join with sl st to form first ring, then ch 6, join with sl st in same st as first sl st was worked to form 2nd ring. **1st rnd:** Ch 1, working over both rings, work 20 h dc, join. **2nd rnd:** (Ch 4, sc in each of next 4 sts) 5 times; join. Break off.

Weave belt through sts of first bodice rnd. Sew one flower to each end. Line dress if desired.

Lining a Dress: Make patterns from crocheted pieces after they have been blocked. Lay the pieces on clean paper (brown wrapping paper is fine) on a flat surface. Carefully draw around the pieces, using a hard pencil (a soft one might smudge). Cut paper patterns ½" outside the outline (seam allowance).

Cut back pattern from center neck to lower edge. Pin the 2 halves 1" apart to another strip of paper (center pleat allowance). Slash pattern for dress front from side toward center 2" down from armhole, so that front can be spread to measure 1" longer along side seam than back, from armhole to waist.

Arrange patterns on lining fabric with vertical center front and back lines on the lengthwise grain; pin in place. Cut out around edge of pattern pieces.

Stitch bustline darts on dress front lining 2" down from armholes, ½" deep at side seams and tapering to nothing about 3" toward front.

Form ½" center back pleat; tack at neck and waistline.

With right sides facing, stitch all main seams. Turn in seam allowances around neckline and armholes; baste.

Assemble crocheted garment. Insert lining, wrong sides facing, and slip-stitch in place around neckline and armholes. Loosely tack side-seam allowances of lining to corresponding allowances of garment from underarm to not more than 14" below waistline. Hem dress lining separately from dress.

Yoked Dress

Sleeveless yoked dress in cream on pink.

SIZES: Small (6–8) [medium (10–12)—large (14–16)]. Finished dress measures 14" [16"—18½"] across bust for a snug-fitting bodice, 17½" [19½"—21½"] across hips (measured 7" below waist), 34" [37"—40"] across hemline. Skirt length is 22" and is adjustable.

MATERIALS: J. & P. Coats Knit-Cro-Sheen (175-yard balls), 15 [17—19] balls beauty pink No. 65 (color A) and 4 balls cream No. 42 (B); aluminum crochet hook size G (or Canadian hook No. 9) *or the size that will give you the correct gauge;* ecru lining fabric, if desired.

Note: The dress is made without side seams. The bodice is crocheted around in one piece and is worked from the waistline up to the shoulders; then the skirt is added, starting at the waistline and working around to the hemline so that any adjustment needed in length can easily be made.

GAUGE: 13 average sts (dc's and ch-1's) = 3"; 7 rows = 3".

Note: Work with 2 strands of same color throughout.

Bodice

Starting at waistline with 2 strands of A, ch 120 [130—140] to measure about 28" [32"—37"]. Being careful not to twist ch, join with sl st in first ch to form ring. **1st rnd:** ch 3, skip these 3 ch sts, dc in each of next 3 ch sts, * ch 1, skip next ch st, dc in each of next 4 ch sts. Repeat from * around, ending ch 1, skip last ch st; join with sl st to top of ch-3 (24 [26—28] groups made). Always count ch-3 as one dc.

For all dc's throughout dress, always insert hook as follows: y o hook, insert hook into next dc from front to back, *under top 3 strands of st*

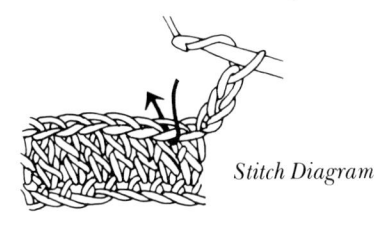

Stitch Diagram

(instead of the usual 2 strands—see diagram, above), complete dc as usual.

2nd rnd: Ch 3, work 1 dc in each of next 3 dc, * ch 1, skip ch-1, dc in each of next 4 dc. Repeat from * around, ending ch 1, skip ch-1; join with sl st to ch-3.

Repeat 2nd rnd for pattern until piece measures 9" [9½"—9½"] from beg or desired length to underarm. Break off A.

To Divide Work in Half for Back and Front: With a pin, mark last sl st worked for one side seam (first marker), then for front of dress skip 12 [13—14] groups, mark last dc of the 12th [13th—14th] group for other side seam (second marker). Remaining sts will be used for back of dress.

Note: The side of work that has been facing you will now become wrong side of dress. Work in rows from now on.

To Shape Front Armholes: 1st row: Loop row: Counting from first marker, skip first group of 4 dc, skip ch-1 and next dc, join 2 strands of B with 1 sc in next dc, ch 8, sl st in last sc (first loop made), working across sts between first and second markers for front of dress, sc in each of next 2 dc, then working into dc's or ch-1's of last rnd, work as follows: * Ch 8, sl st in last sc, sc in each of next 2 sts. Repeat from * across until 22 [25—27] loops are made, then ch 8, sl st in last sc, sc in next st (23 [26—28] loops). Do not work remaining sts to second marker; ch 3, turn.

2nd row (right side): Hold loops down on side of work facing you as you work (or skip) sc's of last row. Skip first sc, dc in each of next 2 sc, (ch 1, skip next sc, dc in each of next 4 sc) 8 [9—10] times; ch 1, skip next sc, dc in each of next 3 sc (10 [11—12] groups with 3 sts in first and last group); ch 1, turn.

3rd row: Loop row: Sc in first st, * ch 8, sl st in last sc, working into dc's or ch-1's, sc in each of next 2 sts. Repeat from * across (23 [26—28] loops). Ch 3, turn.

4th row: Repeat 2nd row. At end of row ch 3 (instead of ch 1), turn.

Work even in pattern as established on last row until piece measures about 5½" [5½"—6"] from first B row, ending with a right-side row; ch 3, turn.

To Shape Neck: 1st row (wrong side): Work across until 13th [14th—15th] dc is completed (counting ch-3 as one dc); ch 3, turn. **2nd row:** Work across in pattern; ch 1, turn. **3rd row: Loop row:** Work in loop pattern as for 3rd row of armhole shaping; ch 3, turn. **4th row (right side):** Holding down loops as before, skip first st, dc in each sc across; ch 1, turn. **5th row:** Repeat 3rd row, but ch 1 (instead of ch 3) at end of row. **6th row:** Holding down loops as before, sc in each sc of last row. Break off.

With wrong side of work facing you, skip center 12 [14—16] dc (and ch-1's) for neck, using 2 strands of B, sl st in next dc, ch 3, work in pattern to end of row (13 [14—15] dc, counting ch-3 as one dc); ch 3, turn. Starting with 2nd row of neck shaping, complete as for first side.

To Shape Back Armholes: 1st row: Using 2 strands of A and starting at 2nd marker, sl st across first 4-dc group, then ch 4, skip ch-1, dc in each of next 4 dc, ch 1, continue in pattern across until there are 10 [11—12] groups of 4 dc, ch 4, skip ch-1, dc in next dc. Do not work remaining sts; ch 4, turn.

2nd row: Skip first dc and ch-1, * dc in each of next 4 dc, ch 1. Repeat from * across, ending with dc in 3rd st of ch-4; ch 4, turn. Repeat 2nd row 3 [4—4] times more.

First Half of Back: Place a marker in center of last row. **1st row:** Work in pattern across to marker, ending with 4th [2nd—4th] dc of last group. Do not work remaining sts; ch 3, turn. **2nd row:** Work across in pattern. Work even on these sts until armhole measures 6¾" [7"—7¼"] from beg. Break off.

Second Half of Back: Join yarn at back opening and work as for first half.

Skirt

Entire skirt is worked with wrong side of bodice facing you. Working around lower edge of bodice (with wrong side of bodice facing you), using 2 strands of A, join with sl st in first dc of 4-dc group at point where side seam would be, ch 3, dc in each of next 3 dc, * ch 1, dc in each of next 4 dc. Repeat from * around entire bodice, then ch 1, join with sl st to ch-3 (24 [26—28] groups made). Work even in pattern as established for 4 more rnds.

6th rnd (inc rnd): Ch 3, work 1 dc in next dc, 2 dc in next dc, 1 dc in next dc, * ch 1, work 1 dc in each of next 2 dc, 2 dc in next dc, 1 dc in next dc. Repeat from * around; join. Work even in new pattern (with 5 dc in each group) for 6 more rnds.

Next rnd (inc rnd): Inc 1 dc in center dc of each 5-dc group. Work even in new pattern (with 6 dc in each group) for 6 more rnds.

Continue to inc 1 dc in each group of dc's every 7th rnd 3 times more (9 dc in each group). Work even in new pattern until skirt measures 21" or until skirt is 1" less than desired length. Break off A.

Border: 1st rnd (loop rnd): With 2 strands of B, work as for 3rd row (loop row) of front armhole shaping; join with sl st. Ch 3, turn work (reversing direction) so that right side of skirt is facing you.

2nd rnd: Holding down loops as before, work 1 dc in each sc of last rnd; join. Ch 3 and turn work (reversing directions again).

Work 1 more loop rnd, join. Break off.

BELT: With 4 strands of A, make a chain 68" long. Break off.

FINISHING: Loop Edging: Work with B around front neck and front of armholes only. Work first row with right side of work facing you. **1st row:** For left armhole, join B at first marker, work in sc evenly along armhole edge to shoulder. Ch 1, turn. Repeat 3rd through 6th rows of front neck edging. Break off. Starting at shoulder edge, work loop edging across right armhole edge. Break off. Starting at left shoulder, work loop edging around front of neck. Break off.

Sew shoulder seams, matching groups of dc where possible, leaving sts free at each center back for neck. **Armhole Border:** With A, work 2 rnds of sc all around both armholes.

Border for Back Opening: With A, work in rows of sc evenly spaced across edge of left side for ¾". Break off. Mark border for 3 buttons spaced evenly apart. Work as for left border along right side edge for ¾", then work buttonholes opposite markers on next row. Sc to pin, (ch 4, skip about ½" of work, sc to next pin) twice; ch 4, skip about ½" of work, sc to end of row. **Last row:** Sc in each sc and work 4 sc over each ch loop across. Break off.

Buttons: Make 3 buttons with A and 2 with B. **For one button:** Ch 4, join with sl st to form first ring, then ch 6, join with sl st in same st as first sl st to form a larger ring. Ch 1, working over both rings and working into center of first ring, work h dc's until ring is filled up very closely. Join with sl st to first h dc. Break off. Button should measure about ¾" in diameter.

Sew 3 color-A buttons along back opening. Weave belt through sts around waistline. Sew one B button to each end.

Line dress if desired. (See instructions for lining, p. 114.)

Layered-Look One-Piece Dress

Skirt in red shell pattern connects with vertically striped vest, also in a combination of shell stitch and single crochet, over double-crochet sleeves and turtleneck.

SIZES: Small (8–10) [medium (12–14)—large (16)]. Dress measures 15" [16"—17"] across back at bustline from side seam to side seam for snug-fitting bodice, 18" [19"—20"] across at hipline 7" below waistline.

MATERIALS: Brunswick Germantown knitting worsted, 6 [7—8] (4-ounce) skeins cherry smash No. 420 (color A), 4 [5—5] skeins light orchid No. 408 (B), 1 skein each tornado No. 4232 (C) and saffron No. 4051 (D); aluminum crochet hook size G [H—I] (or Canadian hook No. 9 [8—7]) *or the size that will give you the correct gauge*; hooks and eyes.

GAUGE: On size G hook: For bodice, 9 sts = 2". For sleeves and yoke, 4 dc = 2". For skirt, 1 sc, 1 shell, and 1 sc = 1".

On size H hook: For bodice, 4 sts = 1". For

sleeves and yoke, 7 dc = 2". For skirt, 1 shell and 1 sc = 1".

On size I hook: For bodice, 7 sts = 2". For sleeves and yoke, 3 dc = 1". For skirt, 1 sc, 1 shell, 1 sc, 1 shell, and 1 sc = 3".

Note: Bodice is worked vertically and skirt is worked horizontally.

BODICE BACK: Starting at underarm seam with color A, ch 52. **1st row:** Sc in 2nd ch from hook, * ch 1, skip 1 ch, sc in next ch. Repeat from * across (26 sc). Drop A; attach C; ch 1, turn. **2nd row:** With C, sc in first sc, * ch 3, skip 1 sc, sc in next sc. Repeat from * across, ending with sc in next to last sc, ch 1, sc in last sc (14 sc). Break off C; do not turn work but pick up A; ch 1. **3rd row:** With A, sc in first sc, * ch 1, insert hook in next skipped sc *2 rows below* and work sc (long sc made), ch 1, sc in next sc. Repeat from * across, ending with long sc in last sc 2 rows below. Drop A; attach B; ch 1, turn. **4th row:** With B, sc in first long sc, * work 3 dc in next sc (shell made), sc in next long sc. Repeat from * across, ending with 2 dc in last sc (half shell made). Break off B; do not turn work but pick up A; ch 1. **5th row:** With A, work long sc in first long sc 2 rows below, * ch 1, sc in center dc of next shell, ch 1, work long sc in next long sc 2 rows below. Repeat from * across, ending with ch 1, sc in last dc; ch 25 for armhole edge; turn. **6th row:** With A, sc in 2nd ch from hook, (ch 1, skip 1 ch, sc in next ch) 11 times; ch 1, skip last ch, * sc in next sc, ch 1, sc in next long sc, ch 1. Repeat from * across, ending with sc in last long sc (38 sc). Drop A; attach D; ch 1, turn. **7th row:** With D, sc in first sc, * ch 1, sc in next sc. Repeat from * across. Break off D; do not turn work but attach C to beg of row just worked; ch 1. **8th row:** With C, repeat 7th row. Break off C; do not turn work but pick up A; ch 1. **9th row:** With A, sc in next sc, * ch 1, work long sc in next sc 2 rows below (this is same place as C sc was worked), ch 1, sc in next sc. Repeat from * across, ending with long sc; ch 1, turn. **10th row:** With A, * sc in first long sc, ch 1, sc in next sc, ch 1. Repeat from * across; ch 1, turn. **11th row:** With A, repeat 7th row. Drop A; attach C; ch 1, turn. **12th row:** With C, sc in first sc, * ch 3, skip 1 sc, sc in next sc. Repeat from * across, ending with sc in next to last sc, ch 1, sc in last sc. Break off C; do not turn work but pick up A; ch 1. **13th row:** With A, work long sc in next skipped sc 2 rows below, ch 1, work sc in first sc (1 sc inc at shoulder), * ch 1, long sc in first sc 2 rows below, ch 1, sc in next sc. Repeat from * across, ending with long sc in last sc 2 rows below (39 sc and long sc). Drop A; attach B; ch 1, turn. **14th row:** With B, repeat 4th row, ending with sc instead of half shell (19 shells). **15th row:** With A, work as for 5th row, ending with long sc (20 long sc). Break off A (shoulder edge), turn.

To Shape Neck: Attach A to 4th long sc from shoulder edge (the skipped sts are at side neck edge); ch 1. **Next row:** Sc in same place as A was attached, work ch-1 and sc in each sc and long sc across (33 sc). Drop A; attach D; ch 1, turn. Work in pattern as for 7th through 10th rows, starting and ending rows in pattern sequence. With A, ch 1, turn. **21st row:** With A, repeat 7th row. Break off A; attach C; ch 1, turn. **22nd row:** With C, sc in first sc, ch 1, * sc in next sc, ch 3, skip 1 sc. Repeat from * across, ending with sc in next to last sc, ch 1, sc in last sc. Break off C; do not turn work but attach A at beg of row; ch 1. **23rd row:** With A, work long sc in first sc 2 rows below, * ch 1, sc in next sc, ch 1, work long sc in next skipped sc 2 rows below. Repeat from * across, ending with ch 1, work long sc in last sc 2 rows below. Drop A; attach B; ch 1, turn. **24th row:** With B, sc in first long sc, * work 3-dc shell in next sc, sc in next long sc. Repeat from * across. Break off B; do not turn work but pick up A; ch 1. **25th row:** With A, work long sc in first long sc 2 rows below, * ch 1, sc in center dc of next shell, ch 1, work long sc in next long sc 2 rows below. Repeat from * across; ch 1, turn. **26th row:** With A, sc in first long sc, * ch 1, sc in next sc, ch 1, sc in next long sc. Repeat from * across. Drop A; attach D; ch 1, turn. **27th through 30th rows:** Work in pattern as for 7th through 10th rows, starting and ending rows in pattern sequence. Repeat 21st through 30th rows once more. **41st row:** With A, repeat 7th row across, do not break off but ch 14. Drop A; attach C; turn. **42nd row:** Sc in 2nd ch from hook, (ch 3, skip 3 ch, sc in next ch) 3 times, * ch 3, skip 1 sc, sc in next sc. Repeat from * across, ending with sc in next to last sc, ch 1, sc in last sc (21 sc). Break off C; do not turn work but pick up A; ch 1. **43rd row:** Skip first sc, (work long sc over next lp into chain, ch 1, sc in next sc, ch 1) 3 times; * ch 1, long sc in skipped sc 2 rows below, ch 1, sc in next sc, ch 1. Repeat from * across, ending with long sc in last sc 2 rows below (20 long sc). Drop A; attach B, ch 1, turn. **44th row:** Repeat 4th row, ending with sc in last long sc (19 shells). **45th row:** Work same as for 5th row but end with long sc in last sc (dec made at shoulder); ch 1, turn. **46th row:** Repeat 26th row. **47th row:** Repeat 7th row to within last 2 sc, ch 1, draw up lp in each of last 2 sc, y o, draw through all 3 lps on hook. Break off; pick up A, ch 1. Now repeat 8th through 11th rows. Break off A; attach C to 13th sc from shoulder edge; ch 1. Repeat 2nd row. Break off C; do not turn work but attach A to beg of row just completed; ch 1. Repeat 3rd, 4th, and 5th rows once. After last sc on last row, ch 1, turn. **Next row:** With A, sc in first sc, * ch 1, sc in next long sc, ch 1, sc in next sc. Repeat from * across. Break off.

SKIRT BACK: Attach A to lower right corner of bodice. With right side of work facing you, work a row of 52 sc evenly spaced across lower edge of bodice; ch 1, turn. **2nd row:** Working in front lp of sc only, * (sc in next sc, ch 1) 3 times; skip next sc. Repeat from * across, ending with sc in last sc (39 sc); ch 1, turn. **3rd row:** Sc in first sc, * work 3 dc in next sc (shell made), sc in next sc. Repeat from * across (19 shells); ch 1, turn. **4th row:** Sc in first sc, * ch 1, sc in center dc of next shell, ch 1, sc in next sc. Repeat from * across; ch 3, turn. **5th row:** Work dc in first sc, * sc in next sc, work 3-dc shell in next sc. Repeat from * across, ending with 2 dc in last sc (half shell made); ch 1, turn. **6th row:** Sc in first dc, * ch 1, sc in next sc, ch 1, sc in center dc of next shell. Repeat from * across, ending with sc in top of ch-3; ch 1, turn. Repeat 3rd through 6th rows for pattern. Work even until skirt measures about 8″ from beg, ending with a 6th row of pattern. Ch 3, turn. **Next row (1st inc row):** Dc and sc in first sc, * work shell in next sc, sc in next sc. Repeat from * across, ending with sc and 2 dc in last sc (half shell increased at each end); ch 1, turn. Starting with a 6th row of pattern (41 sc on row), work even until piece measures about 12″ from beg, ending with a 6th row of pattern. Ch 3, turn. **Next row (2nd inc row):** Dc and sc in first sc, (work shell in next sc, sc in next sc) 3 times; (work shell and sc in next sc) twice; * work shell in next sc, sc in next sc. Repeat from * across, ending with shell in 10th sc from end, (work sc and shell in next sc) twice; (sc in next sc, work shell in next sc) 3 times, work sc and 2 dc in last sc (2 shells and 2 half shells increased); ch 1, turn. Starting with a 6th row of pattern, work even until piece measures about 15″ from beg, ending with a 6th row of pattern. Ch 3, turn. **Next row (3rd inc row):** Sc in first sc, (work shell in next sc, sc in next sc) 7 times; (work shell and sc in next sc) twice; shell in next sc, (sc in next sc, work shell in next sc) 6 times; (work sc and shell in next sc) twice; (sc in next sc, work shell in next sc) 7 times; sc in last sc (2 shells inc—25 shells); ch 1, turn. Starting with a 6th row of pattern, work even until skirt measures 21″ from beg or desired length. Break off.

FRONT BODICE AND SKIRT: Work same as for back bodice and skirt.

SLEEVES: With B, ch 28. **1st row:** Dc in 4th ch from hook and in each remaining ch across (26 dc, counting ch-3 as first dc); ch 3, turn. **2nd row:** Skip first dc, dc in each dc across; ch 3, turn. **3rd row (inc row):** Work dc in first dc (1 inc made), dc in each dc across, ending with 2 dc in last dc (another inc made); ch 3, turn. Repeat 2nd row for pattern and work inc row every 3rd row 7 times more (42 dc). Work even until sleeve measures 17½″ or desired length to underarm.

To Shape Cap: Next row: Sl st across first 3 dc, ch 3, dc across to within 2 dc of end (2 dc dec at each end); ch 3, turn. Repeat last row once more. Work 1 row even. Dec 1 dc at beg and end of every row 3 times, then dec 3 dc at beg and end of every row twice. Break off.

FINISHING: Sew shoulder seams. **Yoke:** Attach A to center back neck edge. **1st row:** With right side facing you, work 22 sc around neck edge to shoulder, 48 sc around front to opposite shoulder and 22 sc around to center back. Break off A; attach B to beg of row just completed; ch 3. **2nd row:** Dc in each sc around; ch 3, turn. **3rd row:** Work in dc, decreasing 12 sts as evenly spaced as possible; ch 3, turn. Repeat last row twice more (56 dc). Work even in dc for 8 rows more. Break off. With A, crochet a row of sc around back opening of yoke. Sew hooks and eyes at back opening.

Reverse Single Crochet
Step 1   Step 2   Step 3

Sew side and sleeve seams. Sew sleeves in place. **Hipline Trim:** Attach B to seam edge at top of skirt. Working into free loop of 2nd skirt row, work a row of reverse sc (work from *left to right*—see diagram) all around top skirt edge. Break off.

Capelet

Keep the heat down and your shoulders warm with this shell-patterned capelet made of knitting worsted.

SIZE: Cape measures about 22" from front neck to lower edge.

MATERIALS: Knitting worsted, 3 (4-ounce) skeins cranberry (color A), 1 skein each orange (B), scarlet (C), magenta (D), and pink (E); aluminum crochet hook size I (or Canadian hook No. 7) *or the size that will give you the correct gauge.*

GAUGE: 4½ shells = 4"; 3 rows = 2".

Starting at neck edge with A, ch 52 to measure about 18". **1st row:** Sc in 2nd ch from hook and in each ch across (51 sc); ch 3, turn. **2nd row:** Skip first 2 sc, 3-dc shell in next dc, * (skip 2 sc, 3-dc shell in next sc) 3 times; skip 2 sc, in next sc work shell, ch 2 and shell (double shell made). Repeat from * twice more; (skip 2 sc, shell in next sc) 4 times; ch 3, turn. **3rd row:** Skip first 2 dc, shell in next dc, (skip 2 dc, shell in next dc) 3 times; * work double shell in ch-2 sp of next double shell, (skip 2 dc, shell in next dc) 4 times. Repeat from * twice more; skip last shell, work shell in top of turning ch; ch 3, turn. **4th row:** Skip first 2 dc, shell in next dc, (skip 2 dc, shell in next dc) 4 times; work double shell in next double shell, (skip 2 dc, shell in next dc) 5 times. Repeat from * once more; double shell in next double shell, (skip 2 dc, shell in next dc) 4 times; skip last shell, shell in turning ch; ch 3, turn. **5th row:** Work with 2 colors on this row. Hold color not in use along top edge of previous row and crochet over it so that it will be concealed within sts. Skip first 2 dc, work 2 dc in next dc, y o, draw up lp in same dc, y o, draw through 2 lps on hook, drop A, attach B, y o and draw through remaining 2 lps on hook. **(Note:** Always change colors in this manner.) (Skip 2 dc, with B work shell in next dc, skip 2 dc, A shell in next dc) twice; * double shell in next double shell, working first half with B and second half with A, (skip 2 dc, B shell in next dc, skip 2 dc, A shell in next dc) 3 times. Repeat from * once more; double shell in next double shell as before, (skip 2 dc, B shell in next dc, skip 2 dc, A shell in next dc) twice; skip 2 dc, B shell in next dc, break off B, skip last shell, A shell in turning ch; ch 3, turn. **6th row:** With A only, skip first 2 dc, shell in next dc, (skip 2 dc, shell in next dc) 5 times; * double shell in next double shell, (skip 2 dc, shell in next dc) 7 times. Repeat from * once more; double shell in next double shell, (skip 2 dc, shell in next dc) 5 times; skip last shell, shell in turning ch; ch 3, turn.

7th row: Skip first 2 dc, A shell in next dc, drop A, attach C and, alternating colors, work in shell pattern across, working double shells in double shells and ending with A shell in turning ch; break off C; ch 3, turn. **8th row:** With A only, skip first 2 dc, shell in next dc, work across in shell pattern, working double shells in double shells and ending with shell in turning ch; ch 3, turn.

Repeat last 2 rows for pattern, working even-numbered rows with A only and odd-numbered rows with A alternated with D, E, B, C, and D, ending with an odd-numbered row (17 rows in all). Do not break off A.

LEFT FRONT: To Form Arm Slits: 1st short row: With A only, skip first 2 dc, shell in next dc, work across in shell pattern to within first double shell (mark ch-2 sp), work shell in double shell (13 shells); drop A, turn. **2nd short row:** With E make lp on hook, y o and work shell in first dc, skip 1 dc, A shell in next dc, then work alternating colors across, ending with A shell in turning ch; break off E (7 A, 7 E shells); ch 3, turn. **3rd short row:** With A only, skip first 2 dc, shell in next dc, work in shell pattern across; ch 3, turn. **4th short row:** With A work 2 dc in first dc, skip 1 dc, B shell in next dc, then work alternating colors across, ending with A shell in turning ch; break off B; ch 3, turn. **5th short row:** Repeat 3rd short row, omitting ch-3 at end; turn. **6th short row:** Alternating C and A, repeat 2nd short row. **7th short row:** Repeat 3rd short row. **8th short row:** Alternating A and D, repeat 4th short row, omitting ch-3 at end (9 A, 8 D shells). Break off.

BACK: Attach A in ch-2 sp at slit marker. **1st short row:** Ch 3, 2 dc in same sp, skip 2 dc, shell in next dc; continue in shell pattern across, working double shell in double shell at center back, to within second double shell (mark ch-2 sp), shell in double shell (40 shells, 1 double shell); drop A, turn. Work 2nd through 8th short rows as for left front, working double shell in center back double shell.

RIGHT FRONT: Attach A in ch-2 sp at last slit marker and work to correspond to left front. Do not break off A; ch 3, turn.

To Join at Base of Slits: 1st row: Work in shell pattern across right front, ch 2, shell in first dc on back, skip 1 dc, shell in next dc, continue in pattern across back, ch 2, shell in first dc on left front, skip 1 dc, shell in next dc, continue in pattern across left front (90 shells, 1 double shell); ch 3, turn. Work in pattern for 8 rows more, working double shell in the 3 ch-2 sps. Break off.

Closing Ties (make 6): With A, crochet a chain about 9" long. **1st row:** Sc in 2nd ch from hook and in each ch across. Break off. Attach 3 ties to each side of front edge, the first at neck edge, the 2nd 6" below first, and the 3rd 6" below 2nd. Tie in bows.

The unusual combination of crochet and weaving results in this luxurious look of hand-woven tweed. Both the coat and the suit (see p. 124) are executed in a simple double crochet pattern that creates an openwork of stitches through which strands of yarn are woven with a tapestry needle.

Casual Coat

In fuzzy purple mohair and green and turquoise knitting worsted. Its casual style and simple lines make for easy elegance. It wraps around and belts with its own belt.

SIZES: Small (6–8) [medium (10–12)—large (14–16)]. Measures 16″ [18″—20″] across back from side seam to side seam at underarms, 32″ long from underarm to lower edge (can be adjusted).

MATERIALS: Bucilla DeLuxe knitting worsted (100% wool), 5 (4-ounce) skeins green No. 80 (color A), 3 skeins turquoise No. 313 (B); and Bucilla or Bear Brand Supra-Mohair (40-gram ball, about 1½ ounces), 11 [12—12] balls purple No. 24 (C); aluminum crochet hook size G (or Canadian hook No. 9) *or the size that will give you the correct gauge;* seam binding; lining if desired.

GAUGE: 2 spaces = 1″; 2 rows = 1″.

BACK: See General Directions, p. 124, for mesh. Starting at lower edge with A, ch 112 [120—128] to measure about 27″ [29″—31″]. Work mesh on 54 [58—62] sps, working striped pattern as follows: 6 rows A, * 2 rows C, 2 rows B, 2 rows C, 4 rows A. Repeat from * for striped pattern, decreasing 1 sp at beg and end of row when piece measures 6″ for a coat 32″ from underarm to lower edge when completed. Work fewer rows for a shorter coat, or more rows for a longer coat, before starting to dec. Then dec 1 sp at beg and end of row every 2″ 10 times more. Work even on 32 [36—40] sps until piece measures 33″ (this includes 1″ for hem), or 1″ more than desired length to underarm.

To Shape Armholes: Do not ch 4 at end of last row; turn. **1st row:** Sl st across first 2 sps, ending in 2nd dc, ch 4, dc in next dc, continue in pattern to within last 2 sps; turn. Dec 1 sp at beg and end of next 1 [2—2] rows. Work even on 26 [28—32] sps until armholes measure about 7½" [7½"—8"].

To Shape Shoulders: Do not ch 4 at end of last row; turn. **1st row:** Dec 3 sps at beg of row, work across 5 [6—7] sps; ch 4, turn. **2nd row:** Work 2 [3—4] sps; break off. Attach yarn at other armhole and work shoulder in same manner. Break off (10 [10—12] sps remain free at center for back neck).

LEFT FRONT: Starting at lower edge with A, ch 60 [64—68] to measure about 14" [15"—16"]. Work mesh on 28 [30—32] sps for 2 rows. At end of last row ch 31, turn. **3rd row:** Dc in 6th ch from hook (mark this first sp made), make 12 more sps on chain, ch 1, dc in first dc of mesh (14 sps added, 7 for front facing and 7 for front edge), continue across in pattern to end of row (42 [44—46] sps). Work even in striped pattern as for back until piece measures 6", ending at side edge.

Continue in pattern and dec 1 sp at beg (side edge) of next row, then dec 1 sp at same edge every 2" 8 times more, ending at front edge (33 [35—37] sps). Piece should measure 22" from beg.

To Shape Front Facing and Armhole: Inc 1 sp at beg of next row (front edge), then inc at same edge every 2" 6 times more and, *at the same time,* continue to dec at side edge every 2" twice more (38 [40—42] sps); then keep side edge even until piece measures same as back to underarm. Shape armholes as follows: at armhole edge dec 2 sps once, then dec 1 sp at same edge on each of the next 1 [2—2] rows. Work until armhole measures 6" and there are 35 [36—38] sps, ending at front edge.

To Shape Neck: 1st row: Sl st across first 23 [23—24] sps, ending with sl st in dc, ch 4, continue in pattern across row (12 [13—14] sps); ch 4, turn. Dec 1 sp at neck edge every row 3 times (9 [10—11] sps—front shoulder has 1 more sp than back shoulder). Work even, if necessary, until armhole measures same as back armhole to shoulder, ending at armhole edge.

To Shape Shoulder: Do not ch 4 at end of last row; turn. **1st row:** Dec 4 sps at beg of row, work across row (5 [6—7] sps); ch 4, turn. **2nd row:** Work 2 [3—4] sps. Break off.

RIGHT FRONT: Work as for left front (pieces are reversible).

SLEEVES: Starting at lower edge with A, ch 48 to measure about 11". Work mesh on 22 sps for 6 rows with A. Starting with 2 rows C, work in striped pattern as for back of coat and, *at the same time,* when sleeve measures 7" from beg, inc 1 sp at beg and end of next row, then every 5" [4"—3"] 1 [2—3] times more (26 [28—30] sps). Work even until sleeve measures 18" [18½"—19"] from beg (including 1" for hem), or 1" longer than desired length to underarm.

To Shape Cap: Dec 2 sps at beg and end of next row. Dec 1 sp at beg and end of every other row 3 times. Dec 1 sp at beg and end of each of next 5 [6—7] rows (6 sps). Break off.

COLLAR: Starting at neck edge with A, ch 72 to measure about 17". Work mesh on 34 sps for 1 row. **2nd row:** With A, inc 1 sp at beg and end of row. Repeating last row, work 2 rows C, 2 rows B, 2 rows C, and 2 rows A (52 sps). **11th row:** With A, dec 4 sps at beg and end of row. **Last row:** Work even with A on 44 sps. Break off.

BELT: With A, ch 20. Work mesh on 8 sps, starting with 4 rows A, then work even in striped pattern as for back for 62". Break off.

WEAVING: Back: Find and mark with pins or thread the st between the 2 center sps at lower edge of back. Cut 3 strands of A and weave through the next 2 vertical rows to the right of center st. Following chart, * weave 2 rows C, 2 rows B, 2 rows C, 4 rows A. Repeat

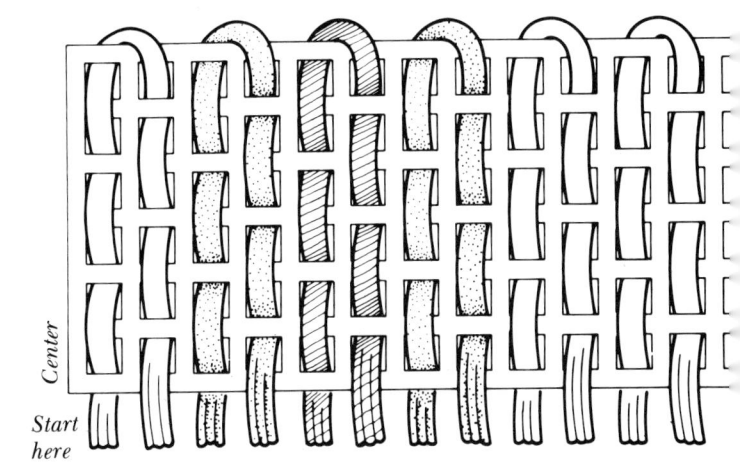

Lower Edge

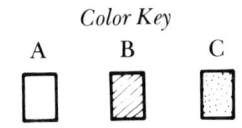

Color Key

A B C

from * to side edge. Weave pattern across other half of back.

Left Front: Starting at marked sp at lower edge and working to side edge, weave the first 2 vertical rows along front edge with B, * 2 rows C, 4 rows A, 2 rows C, 2 rows B. Repeat from * across to side edge; weave short rows for facing to correspond.

Right Front: Starting at marked sp at lower edge, weave as follows: * 2 rows B, 2 rows C, 4 rows A, 2 rows C. Repeat from * across to side edge; weave short rows for facing to correspond.

Sleeves: Find and mark the center st at lower edge of sleeves. Cut 3 strands of A and weave through the next 2 vertical rows to the right of center st. Weave 2 rows C, 2 rows B, 2 rows C, 3 rows A. Finish in pattern along shaped edges. Weave pattern across other half of sleeve.

Collar: Find and mark the st between the 2 center sps at neck edge of collar. Cut 3 strands A and weave through the next 2 vertical rows to the right of center st. * Weave 2 rows C, 2 rows B, 2 rows C, 4 rows A. Repeat from * to front edge. Weave pattern across other half of collar.

Belt: Weaving lengthwise, weave 2 rows C, 2 rows B, 2 rows C, 2 rows A.

FINISHING: Make lining if desired (see p. 125). Seam sides, shoulders, and sleeves. Sew sleeves in place. Turn up 2-row hems along lower edge of coat and sleeves and sew in place.

Turn in facings along front edges and sew in place. Sew top edge of lapel. On collar, turn up 2-row hem along outer edge and side edges. Center collar and sew to neck edge, leaving 4" of coat free at each end. Sew seam binding along shoulder and neck seams, holding in to desired size.

Fold belt in half lengthwise and sew.

Classic Wraparound Suit

In a soft blend of lavender, rose, and copper.

GENERAL DIRECTIONS: MESH BACKGROUND: Crochet a chain the number of stitches for the length specified. **1st row:** Dc in 6th ch from hook, * ch 1, skip next ch, dc in next ch. Repeat from * across; ch 4, turn. **2nd row:** Skip first dc and first ch-1, dc in next dc, * ch 1, dc in next dc. Repeat from * across, ending with ch 1, dc in 2nd st of turning ch; ch 4, turn. Repeat last row for pattern.

To Change Colors: Do not ch 4 or turn at end of last row. Make lp on hook with new color, draw it through the lp of last color and tighten lp of last color. Then with new color, ch 4 and turn.

To Dec 1 Space at Beg of Row: At end of last row, ch 2; turn. **Dec row:** Skip first dc, dc in next dc (the ch-2 and dc form a point instead of the usual lp, decreasing 1 sp at beg of row), ch 1, dc in next dc, continue in pattern across.

To Dec 1 Space at End of Row: Work in pattern to within last 2 sps, ch 1, holding back on hook the last lp of each dc, work dc in next dc and in turning ch, y o, draw through all 3 lps on hook (1 sp dec at end of row); ch 4, turn.

To Inc 1 Space at Beg of Row: At end of last row ch 6 (instead of ch 4), turn. Dc in 6th ch from hook, ch 1, dc in next dc, work across in pattern.

To Inc 1 Space at End of Row: Work across in pattern, ending with last sp in turning ch as usual. Then ch 1 and work another dc in same st as last dc; ch 4, turn.

WEAVING VERTICAL STRIPES: Cut 3 strands of yarn about 12" longer than *twice* the length of mesh. Hold strands together, ends even. Fold in half and tie strands together at fold with a bit of thread to mark center, then unfold strands. Thread the 3 strands in tapestry needle. Starting at specified edge of mesh, weave down through 1 sp and up through next sp to opposite edge of mesh, pulling strands through so that center marking thread is at top edge of mesh (half the length has been woven through the sps). Then, pass same length of yarn over top bar of mesh and start weaving through the next row of spaces, working down to starting edge, being careful to alternate weaving pattern. Remove needle and leave ends until all weaving has been completed. Follow chart, if specified, for color sequence. (Note that charts show only the color pattern of the weaving, and do not show the full length or color pattern of the mesh.) At shaped side edges you will find that the last few weaving rows will be short as you will not be able to weave all the way up.

When weaving has been completed, fold ends over to wrong side at line of mesh. Then run 2 or 3 rows of machine stitching or backstitch by hand along edge of mesh, catching folded ends of woven strands so they will not pull out. Cut all lengths to about 1". When turning up hem, ends will be inside hem.

LININGS: We recommend lining your woven garments to help them keep their shape properly.

Lining a Skirt: If the skirt has been made in two or more shaped pieces, lay the pieces on the lining fabric on a flat surface; pin in place. Be sure the vertical center line of the skirt is on the lengthwise grain of the fabric. Cut fabric ½" outside the skirt pieces (seam allowance).

Join the side seams, leaving slits at lower edges for walking ease. If the skirt is to have a zipper opening at the top, leave a similar opening in the lining. Assemble skirt, sewing lining to top of skirt. Turn under seam allowance around top opening; if skirt has zipper, stitch lining to zipper tape. Hem lining separately from and slightly shorter than skirt.

Lining a Jacket or Coat: Make paper patterns from crocheted pieces after they have been blocked. Lay the pieces on clean paper (brown wrapping paper is fine) on a flat surface. Carefully draw around the pieces, using a hard pencil (a soft one might smudge). Cut paper patterns ½" outside the outline (seam allowance), allowing an additional ½" in length for sleeves and 3" for hem.

Cut back pattern in half from neckline to lower edge; pin halves 1½" apart on a strip of paper (center pleat allowance). Slash shoulders on back pattern so they can be spread 1" wider than garment shoulders (dart allowance). Slash shoulders on front pattern so they can be spread 2" wider than garment shoulders.

Arrange patterns on lining fabric with vertical center front and back lines on the lengthwise grain; pin in place. Cut out along edge of pattern pieces.

Sew darts on shoulders, tapering back darts from ½" at seam to nothing about 4" down, and front darts from 1" at seam to nothing about 5" down.

Form ¾" center back pleat; tack at neck and waistline. Baste ¼" pleat across sleeve below elbow (to be released after lining is set into garment).

With right sides facing, stitch shoulder, side, and sleeve seams. Set in sleeves.

Assemble main pieces of crocheted garment. With wrong sides facing, pin lining into garment at neckline and along shoulder and side seam allowances. Do not pin lower than 14" below waistline. Tack loosely where pinned. Pin sleeve lining edges in place ½" from edges; stitch in place.

If garment has front facings or turnback,

tack along turn line; press lightly. Sew in side edge of facing through lining to garment.

Hem garment and lining separately.

If collars and cuffs are to be lined, you should do so (using pieces as patterns) before they are attached.

If the garment is especially heavy, or has appreciable "stretch," catch-stitch it invisibly to the lining at intervals.

SIZES: Small (6–8) [medium (10–12)—large (14–16)]. *Skirt measurements:* 17" [19"—21"] across hips 7" from side seam to side seam (directions allow for 8" front overlap), 25" [27"—29"] across lower edge, 24" long (can be adjusted). *Jacket measurements:* 16" [18"—20"] across back from side seam to side seam at underarms, 24" long from back neck to lower edge.

MATERIALS: Bucilla DeLuxe knitting worsted (100% wool), 7 (4-ounce) skeins copper No. 330 (color A), 4 skeins each dusty pink No. 336 (B) and purple No. 64 (C); aluminum crochet hook size G (or Canadian hook No. 9) *or the size that will give you the correct gauge;* 1 yard ½"-wide ribbon to tie inside jacket at waist; 1 button for skirt; small square of Velcro or 1 snap fastener for jacket; lining fabric (optional), see p. 125.

GAUGE: 2 spaces = 1"; 2 rows = 1".

Skirt

BACK: See General Directions for mesh. Starting at lower edge with color C, ch 104 [112—120] to measure about 25" [27"—29"]. Work mesh on 50 [54—58] sps, working striped pattern as follows: * 2 rows C, 2 rows A, 2 rows B, 2 rows A. Repeat from * for striped pattern, decreasing 1 sp at beg and end of row when piece measures about 5" for a 24"-long skirt when completed. Work fewer rows for a shorter skirt or more rows for a longer skirt, before starting to dec. Then dec 1 sp at beg and end of row every 2" 9 times more (30 [34—38] sps). Work even until piece measures 25" (including 1" for hem), or 1" more than desired length. Break off. Hem skirt and work waistband after weaving has been completed.

RIGHT FRONT: Starting at lower edge with C, ch 60 [64—68] to measure about 14" [15"—16"]. Work mesh on 28 [30—32] sps for 2 rows. At end of last row, break off C, attach A and ch 15; turn. **3rd row:** Dc in 6th ch from hook (mark this first sp with pin for start of weaving), make 4 more sps on chain, ch 1, dc in first dc of mesh (6 sps added, 3 for front hem and 3 for front edge); continue in pattern to end of row (34 [36—38] sps). Work even in striped pattern as for back until piece measures 5" from beg, or same length as back to first dec. Keeping front edge straight, dec 1 sp at side edge on next row, then every 2" 9 times more (24 [26—28] sps). Work even until front measures same as back. Break off.

LEFT FRONT: Starting at lower edge with C, ch 72 [76—80] to measure about 17" [18"—19"]. Facing is not necessary on left front. Keep one edge (front edge) even and dec at other edge (side edge) same as for right front, working throughout in striped pattern. Break off.

WEAVING: See General Directions.

Back: Find and mark with pins or thread the 2 center sps at lower edge of back. Cut 3 strands A and weave through 2 center vertical rows. Following chart, weave 2 rows C, 2 rows

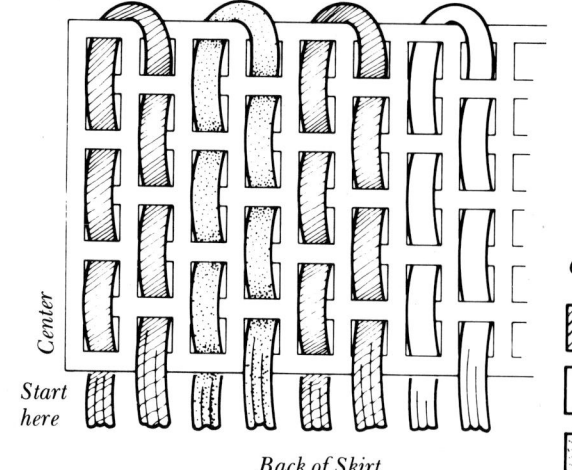

Color Key
⟋ A
☐ B
▦ C

Center *Start here* *Back of Skirt*

A, and 2 rows B. Then repeat the 8-row pattern across. Weave pattern across other half of back.

Right Front: Starting at lower edge in marked sp, weave first 2 rows along front edge with A, 2 rows B, 2 rows A, 2 rows C. Continue in pattern to side edge.

Left Front: Weave to match right front.

FINISHING: Cut lining if desired (see General Directions). Seam sides by machine or hand sew, allowing ¼" seam allowance on wrong side of each seam. Turn up 2-row hem at lower edge. Turn in 3-row hem along right front edge.

Waistband: 1st row: With A and right side of work facing you, work 112 [118—124] sc, evenly spaced, across waist edge; ch 1, turn. **2nd row:** Sc in each sc across; ch 1, turn. **3rd row:** Sc in each sc, decreasing 28 sc as evenly spaced as possible (84 [90—96] sc); ch 1, turn. **4th row (wrong side):** Sc in each sc to within 4 sc of right front edge, ch 2, skip next 2 sc for buttonhole, sc in each of next 2 sc; ch 1, turn. Working 2 sc over ch-2 lp on 4th row, work even for 2 more rows. Break off.

Jacket

BACK: Starting at lower edge with A, ch 68 [76—84] to measure about 16" [18"—20"]. Work even on 32 [36—40] sps in striped pattern of 2 rows A, 2 rows C, 2 rows A, 2 rows B, until piece measures 17" (including 1" for hem), or 1" longer than desired length to underarms.

To Shape Armholes: Do not ch 4 at end of last row; turn. **1st row:** Sl st across first 2 sps, ending in 2nd dc, ch 4, dc in next dc, continue across in pattern to within last 2 sps (28 [32—36] sps); turn. Dec 1 sp at beg and end of next 2 rows (24 [28—32] sps). Work even until armholes measure about 7½" [7½"—8"].

To Shape Shoulders: Do not ch 4 at end of last row; turn. **1st row:** Dec 3 sps at beg of row, work 5 [6—7] sps; ch 4, turn. **2nd row:** Work 2 [3—4] sps; break off. attach yarn at other armhole and work shoulder in same manner. Break off (8 [10—12] sps remain free at center for back neck).

LEFT FRONT: Starting at lower edge with A, ch 52 [56—60] to measure about 12" [13"—14"]. Work mesh on 24 [26—28] sps for 2 rows. At end of last row, break off A, attach C and ch 15; turn. **3rd row:** Dc in 6th ch from hook (mark this first sp made), make 4 more sps on chain, ch 1, dc in first dc of mesh (6 sps added, 3 for front facing and 3 for front edge); continue in pattern to end of row (30 [32—34] sps). Work even in striped pattern as for back until piece measures 11", ending at side edge.

To Shape Front Facing and Armhole: Continue in pattern and inc 1 sp at end (front edge) of next row, then at same edge every other row 10 times more, and *at the same time,* when piece measures same as back to underarm, shape armhole as follows: At armhole edge, dec 2 sps once, then dec 1 sp on each of next 2 rows. Keep armhole edge even while continuing to inc at facing edge until there are 37 [39—41] sps, ending at front edge.

To Shape Neck: Do not ch 4 at end of last row; turn. **1st row:** Sl st across first 25 [26—27] sps, ending with sl st in dc, ch 4, continue in pattern across row (12 [13—14] sps); ch 4, turn. Dec 1 sp at neck edge every row 4 times (8 [9—10] sps). Work even, if necessary, until armhole measures same as back armhole, ending at armhole edge.

To Shape Shoulder: Do not ch 4 at end of last row; turn. Shape shoulder same as for back shoulder. Break off.

RIGHT FRONT: Work as for left front (pieces are reversible).

SLEEVES: Starting at lower edge with A, ch 44 to measure about 9½". Work mesh on 20 sps for 4 rows with A. Starting with 2 rows C, work in striped pattern as for back of jacket and inc 1 sp at beg and end of next row, then every 4" 2 [2—3] times more (26 [26—28] sps). Work even until sleeve measures 18" [18½"—19"] from beg (including 1" for hem), or 1" longer than desired length to underarm.

To Shape Cap: Dec 1 sp at beg and end of each of next 2 rows. Work 2 rows even. Dec 1 sp at beg and end of next row. Work 1 [1—2] rows even. Dec 1 sp at beg and end of each of next 2 rows. Work 1 row even. Dec 2 [2—3] sps at beg and end of next row (12 sps). Break off.

COLLAR: Starting at outer edge, with A, ch 100 to measure about 24". Working 2 rows A, 2 rows C, 2 rows A, 2 rows B, 1 row A, work mesh on 48 sps for 6 rows. **7th row:** Dec 1 sp at beg and end of row (46 sps). Work 2 rows even. Break off.

WEAVING: Back: Find and mark with pins or thread the 2 center sps at lower edge of back. Cut 3 strands B and weave through 2 center vertical rows. * Weave 2 rows A, 2 rows C, 2 rows A, 2 rows B. Repeat from * to side edge. Weave pattern across other half of back.

Left Front: Starting at marked sp at lower

edge and working to side edge, weave the first 2 vertical rows along front edge with C, * 2 rows A, 2 rows B, 2 rows A, 2 rows C. Repeat from * across to side edge; weave short rows for facing to correspond.

Right Front: Weave to match left front.

Sleeves: Find and mark the center 2 sps at lower edge of sleeves. Cut 3 strands C and weave through 2 center vertical rows, weave 2 rows A, 2 rows B, 2 rows A, 2 rows C, 1 row A. Finish in pattern along shaped edges. Weave pattern across other half of sleeve.

Collar: Find and mark the 2 center sps at outer edge of collar. Cut 3 strands C and weave through 2 center vertical rows. * Weave 2 rows A, 2 rows B, 2 rows A, 2 rows C. Repeat from * to front edge. Weave pattern across other half of collar.

FINISHING: See finishing for skirt. Seam sides, shoulders, and sleeves. Sew sleeves in place. Turn up 2-row hems at lower edge of jacket and sleeves and sew in place. Turn in facings along front edges and sew in place.

On collar, turn in short ends on a slant, turning in more at neck edge. Turn up 2-row hem along outer edge of collar. Center collar and sew to neck edge, leaving 3″ of jacket free at each end.

Cut two 14″ lengths ribbon. Sew end of one length to left front edge 6″ up from lower edge. Try on jacket. Sew end of 2nd length to inside of right front where it touches first length. Tie ends together.

Sew Velcro or snap fastener to right front facing and to matching section of left front.

Belt: With A, ch 190. Work mesh on 93 sps for 2 rows. Break off. With 3 strands B, weave one horizontal row. With 3 strands C, weave another horizontal row. Fold narrow ends at angle and sew in place.

Mix-and-Match Blazer Suit

A classic three-piece suit in knitting worsted. Plaid tailored blazer, tweedy striped V-neck vest, and an ingenious pleated skirt that has a flat hip section to eliminate bulkiness.

Vest

SIZES: Small (6–8) [medium (10–12)—large (14–16)]. Snug-fitting vest measures 14″ [15″—16″] across bust from side seam to side seam.

MATERIALS: Brunswick Germantown knitting worsted, 2 (4-ounce) skeins Monhegan-Aran No. 4301 (color M,) 1 skein each dark lime No. 4273 (L) and cardinal red No. 424 (R); aluminum crochet hook size H (or Canadian hook No. 8) *or the size that will give you the correct gauge.*

GAUGE: 4 sts (ch 1, sc, ch 1 and sc) = 1″; 4 rows = 1″.

BACK: Starting at lower edge with R, ch 58 [62—66] to measure about 14″ [15″—16″]. **1st row:** Sc in 2nd ch from hook and in each ch

For Women

Double-Strap Backpack, page 146

Espadrilles, page 155

Classic Cloche, page 139

Fluffy Seven-Footer, page 154

Shawl-Collared Pullover, page 55

Extraordinary Sparkle Sweater, page 88

Contemporary Sweater Duo, page 58

Casual Coat, page 122

Boldly Striped Sweater Set, page 67

Scalloped Sweater Set, page 65

Mosaic Vest, page 29

Cap-Sleeved Shrink Top, page 42

For Children

Scarlet Bib Jumper, page 178

Toddler's Jumper, page 181

Girl's Sweater Set, page 185, and Boy's Sweater Set, page 186

Four Soft Foam-Filled Blocks, page 195

Zoo Animals to Cuddle, page 197

For Men

Vest in Basket-Weave Stitch, *page 219*

Right, Zip-Front Battle Jacket, *page 217*

Decorating with Crochet

Rug in the Round, page 244
Candy Pockets, page 246

Four Fruits Tablecloth, page 237

Pink Scallops, page 232

Bedspread, page 227

Filet Café Curtain, page 241

across to within last st, change to L as follows: draw up lp in last st, break off; make lp on hook with L and draw it through last lp of R (always change colors in this manner); with L, ch 1, turn. **2nd row:** Sc in each sc across, change to M; ch 1, turn. **3rd row:** Sc in first sc, * ch 1, skip next sc, sc in next sc. Repeat from * across (57 [61—65] sts); ch 1, turn. **4th row:** Sc in first sc, * ch 1, skip ch-1, sc in next sc. Repeat from * across; ch 1, turn. Repeat 4th row 4 [6—8] times more but do not ch 1 at end of last row. Attach L to M and, working with double yarn, ch 1, turn.

Work stripe pattern as follows: **1st row:** Work across in pattern with double yarn; break off L; with M, ch 1, turn. **2nd row:** With M, work across in pattern; attach R and with double yarn ch 1, turn. **3rd row:** Work across in pattern with double yarn; break off R; with M, ch 1, turn. Work pattern of 6 rows M with single yarn and 3 rows stripe pattern until piece measures 13½" from beg, or desired length to underarms; ch 1, turn.

To Shape Armholes: 1st row (dec row): Keeping in pattern as established, sl st across 4 sts, ch 1, continue across row in pattern to within last 4 sts (4 sts dec at beg and end of row); ch 1, turn. Dec 2 sts at beg and end of each row 2 [3—3] times. Work even in pattern across 41 [41—45] sts until armholes measure 7¼" [7½"—7¾"] from beg; ch 1, turn.

To Shape Shoulders: Dec 4 sts at beg and end of next 3 rows (17 [17—21] sts remain for back neck). Break off.

FRONT: Work as for back until piece measures 2" less than back to underarms.

To Shape Neck and Armholes: 1st row: Work in pattern to 15th [16th—17th] sc (center front); do not work across remaining sts; ch 1, turn. **2nd row (dec row):** Dec 2 sts, ch 1, work across in pattern; ch 1, turn. Work even in pattern for 7 rows. **Next row:** Dec 2 sts at neck edge, continue in pattern to within last 4 sts; ch 1, turn (4 sts dec at armhole edge). Dec 2 sts at armhole edge every row 2 [2—3] times, and *at the same time*, continue to dec at neck edge every 8th row 3 times more. Work even on 11 [13—13] sts until armhole measures same as back armholes.

To Shape Shoulder: Dec 4 sts at armhole edge of next 2 rows. Break off.

Second Side of Front: Attach yarn to center st and work across to armhole edge; ch 1, turn. Work to correspond to other side, reversing shaping.

FINISHING: Sew side and shoulder seams.

Armhole Edging 1st rnd: With right side of work facing you, make lp on hook with L and work sc at side seam, * skip about ¼" of edge and work sc in edge. Repeat from * around, spacing sc's evenly; sl st in first sc. Break off. **2nd rnd:** Attach R and work sc in each sc around; sl st in first sc. Break off.

Neck Edging: Attach L at shoulder seam and work as for armhole edging.

Skirt

SIZES: Small (6–8) [medium (10–12)—large (14–16)]. Skirt measures 17" [18"—19"] across hips (measured 5" below waistline) and 28" [30"—32"] across hemline when stretched. Skirt length is 23", but can be adjusted.

MATERIALS: Brunswick Germantown knitting worsted, 6 (4-ounce) skeins dark lime No. 4273; aluminum crochet hook size H (or Canadian hook No. 8) *or the size that will give you the correct gauge;* 1 yard ½"-wide elastic.

GAUGE: 4 sts (ch-1's and sc's) = 1"; 4 rows = 1".

Note: Skirt is worked vertically. To make skirt longer, add 2 sts to starting chain for each extra ½" desired; for a shorter skirt, subtract 2 sts for each ½".

Lower Section: Starting at side edge, ch 84 to measure 21" or ch desired length (see note, above). **1st row:** Sc in 2nd ch from hook, * ch 1, skip 1 st, sc in next st. Repeat from * across (42 sc with ch-1's between); ch 1, turn.

2nd row: Sc in first sc, * ch 1, skip ch-1, sc in next sc. Repeat from * across; ch 1, turn. Repeat last row 5 times more. **8th row:** On this row continue in pattern but work only in back lps of sc's to form ridge for pleats; ch 1, turn. **9th and 10th rows:** Repeat 2nd row. **11th row:** Repeat 8th row (this row forms ridge on reverse side for pleats); ch 1, turn.

Repeat 2nd through 11th rows 23 [25—27] times more. Break off.

FINISHING: For top edge, fold pleats and sew them down for about 3". **Top Section: 1st**

row: Attach yarn and working along top edge, work in pattern as for 2nd row, working 68 [72—76] sc across; ch 1, turn. **2nd row:** Working in pattern, dec evenly across row to 60 [64—68] sc. Work even in pattern for 1 row. Dec 6 sc evenly spaced every other row 3 times. Break off.

Sew side seam. Work 1 rnd of pattern across lower edge. Block lightly.

Casing: With yarn, work herringbone st (see diagram) along waistband edge on wrong side

Herringbone Stitch

of skirt. Cut elastic to waist measurement and insert it behind herringbone st. Sew ends of elastic together.

Blazer

SIZES: Small (6–8) [medium (10–12)—large (14–16)]. Blazer measures 15″ [17″—19″] across bust for a snug-fitting jacket and 18″ from underarm to lower edge.

MATERIALS: Brunswick Germantown knitting worsted, 3 (4-ounce) skeins cardinal red No. 424 (color R), 2 skeins Monhegan-Aran No. 4301 (M) and 1 skein each Danish blue No. 484 (B) and dark lime, No. 4273 (L); aluminum crochet hook size H (or Canadian hook No. 8) *or the size that will give you the correct gauge;* 2 silver buttons ¾″ in diameter.

GAUGE: 7 sts = 2″; 6 rows average 3″.

Working with 2 Colors: Always change colors within a row as follows: Work to within last st of old color, work last st until there are 2 loops of old color on hook, pick up new color and draw loop of new color through both loops on hook. Continue with new color, holding color not in use across top of piece and crocheting over it, concealing it within sts of new color.

When changing colors at end of row, break off old color, leaving a 3″ end. Tie on new color and work over ends as before.

BACK: Starting at lower edge with R, ch 55 [61—67] loosely to measure about 15″ [17″—19″]. **1st row:** With R, dc in 4th ch from hook and in each of next 0 [1—2] ch (changing to M on last dc); * with M, dc in next ch (changing to R); with R, dc in each of next 3 ch (changing to M on last dc); work 1 M dc, 6 [7—8] R dc. Repeat from * across, ending with 1 M dc, 3 R dc, 1 M dc, 2 [3—4] R dc (53 [59—65] sts; ch 3, turn). **2nd row:** Skip first dc (turning ch counts as first dc), work 1 [2—3] R dc, 1 M dc, continue across row matching colors of last row, working last R dc in top st of turning ch. Break off R. With M, ch 1, turn. **3rd row:** With M, sc in each dc across, sc in top of turning ch (53 [59—65] sc). Attach R; with R, ch 3, turn. **4th row (dc row):** Skip first st, work 1 [2—3] R, * 1 M, 3 R, 1 M, 6 [7—8] R. Repeat from * across, ending with 1 M, 3 R, 1 M and 2 [3—4] R; ch 3, turn. **5th row:** Repeat last row until last R dc is made; then break off R, attach B. With B, ch 3, turn. **6th row:** Work as for 4th row, using B instead of R. Do not ch 3 at end of row. Break off B. With M, ch 1, turn. **7th row:** With M, sc in each st across. Attach L and ch 3, turn. **8th and 9th rows:** Using L instead of R, work as for 4th row. Break off L at end of 9th row. With M, ch 1, turn. **10th row:** With M, sc in each st across, Attach B, ch 3, turn. **11th row:** Using B instead of R, work as for 4th row. At end of row break off B; attach R, ch 3, turn. **12th row:** Repeat 4th row.

Repeat 2nd through 12th rows twice more, then repeat 2nd row of pattern once again. Piece should measure 18″ from beg. Ch 1, turn.

To Shape Armholes: 1st row: Being careful to keep pattern as established, sl st across first 3 [4—5] sts, work across to within last 3 [4—5] sts (do not work across these sts); ch 1, turn. **2nd and 3rd rows:** Sl st in first st, work across to within last st; ch 1, turn.

Work even in pattern on 43 [47—51] sts until armholes measure 7¼″ [7½″—7¾″].

To Shape Shoulders: 1st row: Sl st across first 5 [6—6] sts, work in pattern across to within last 5 [6—6] sts. **2nd and 3rd rows:** Sl st across first 5 [5—6] sts, work across row to last 5 [5—6] sts. Break off (13 [15—15] sts remain for neck).

RIGHT FRONT: Starting at lower edge with R, ch 29 [32—35] loosely to measure about 8″ [9″—10″]. **1st row (dc row):** With R, dc in 4th ch from hook, work 1 M, (6 [7—8] R, 1

M, 3 R, 1 M) twice; then work 2 [3—4] R (27 [30—33] sts); ch 3, turn. Mark beg of this row for front edge. All increases will be made at marked edge.

Working in pattern as for back, inc 1 st at marked edge every row 5 times. Work even in pattern on 32 [35—38] sts until piece measures 10" from beg. Being careful to keep increased sts in pattern, for lapels inc 1 st at marked edge on next row, then repeat this inc every 2" 4 times more. On 5th inc row for lapel, work across row to side edge for start of armhole shaping. Piece should measure same as back to armholes and must end on 2nd row of pattern. Ch 1, turn (37 [40—43] sts).

To Shape Armhole: Sl st across 3 [4—5] sts, work across row. Dec 1 st at end of next row and at beg of following row. Work even on 32 [34—36] sts for 1" more, ending at front edge. Inc 1 st at front edge at beg of next row. Work even on 33 [35—37] sts until armhole measures about 6" [6¼"—6½"], ending at arm edge.

To Shape Lapel and Shoulder: 1st short row: Work across in pattern to within last 10 [11—11] sts; ch 1, turn. **2nd short row:** Sl st across first 4 sts, then work to end; turn. **3rd short row:** Work across to last 5 sts, then work next 2 sts tog for dec; turn. **4th short row:** Work across to within last 5 [6—6] sts for first shoulder shaping; ch 1, turn. **5th short row:** Sl st across first 5 [5—6] sts, work across remaining 5 [5—6] sts. Break off.

LEFT FRONT: Starting at lower edge, ch as for right front. To reverse pattern, work first row as follows: With R, dc in 4th ch from hook and in each of next 0 [1—2] ch, working in dc (work 1 M, 3 R, 1 M, 6 [7—8] R) twice; then 1 M, 2 R (27 [30—33] sts); ch 3, turn. Mark end of this row for front edge. All increases will be made at this edge.

Complete as for right front, reversing all shaping.

Note: The sleeve is planned to measure 18" from wrist to underarm, ending with a 2nd row of pattern, so that the plaid patterns will match across shoulders. If you have to adjust the sleeve length, change the color sequence at lower edge of sleeve, at start of pattern.

SLEEVE: Starting at lower edge, with R ch 30 [33—34]. **1st row:** With R, dc in 4th ch from hook and in each of next 4 [5—5] ch, work 1 M, 3 R, 1 M, 6 [7—8] R, then 1 M, 3 R, 1 M, and 6 [7—7] R (28 [31—32] sts); ch 3, turn.

Working in plaid pattern as for back and keeping added sts in pattern, inc 1 st at beg and end of row every 2½" [2½"—2"] 6 [6—7] times. Work even on 40 [43—46] sts until sleeve measures 18" from beg, ending with a 2nd row of pattern.

To Shape Cap: Repeat first row of back armhole shaping. Work even for 1½", then dec 1 st at beg and end of row. Work even for 1". Sl st across first 2 sts, work across to within last 2 sts. Repeat last row until 12 [13—10] sts are left. Break off.

COLLAR: Starting at neck edge, with M ch 44 to measure 12½". **1st row:** Sc in 2nd ch from hook and in each ch across (43 sc). **2nd row:** In first sc work 1 R, 1 M and 1 R (2 sts inc); working 1 dc in each sc work as follows: work 6 R, (1 M, 3 R, 1 M, 7 R) twice; 1 M, 3 R, 1 M, 6 R; in last sc work 1 R, 1 M and 1 R (2 sts inc). **3rd row:** Working in pattern, work 3 dc in first and last sts. **4th row:** With B and M, working in pattern, inc 1 st at beg and end of row. **5th row:** With M, work 1 sc in each dc (53 sc). With L and M, work even in pattern for 2 rows, then work 1 row sc with M. Break off.

FINISHING: Sew shoulder, side, and sleeve seams. Sew sleeves in place. Fold collar in half, center on neck edge to within first row of lapel shaping and sew in place. There are no buttonholes. Sew buttons to left front, one 6", the other 9" from lower edge, and button through spaces in crochet.

Trim: With R, ch 6. Work first and 2nd rows of pleated skirt. Repeat 2nd row of skirt pattern until trim fits around lapels, front and lower edge of blazer. Break off.

Make another piece to fit around collar and one to fit around lower edge of each sleeve.

Fold trim in half lengthwise, place over edges of blazer and sew in place. Block lightly.

Romantic Coatdress

Crochet the Irish way this exquisitely romantic coatdress. Rose-patterned squares are joined at the edges and worked in fine fingering yarn on a background of picot loops. Solid picot loops are used for the sleeves. You may want to line the sleeves if you wish to wear it as a coat. Of course, you may select any color-over-color scheme you like. White-on-white would be dressy enough for a wedding.

SIZES: 8–18.

MATERIALS: Coats and Clark's Red Heart Super Fingering yarn (100% wool), 24 (1-ounce) skeins white for sizes 8–14, 28 skeins for sizes 16 and 18; steel crochet hook No. 1 (or Canadian hook No. 0), *or the size that will give you the correct gauge;* sixteen ½" button molds; long-sleeved basic A-line dress pattern with jewel neckline in size required; turquoise polyester knit fabric for lining (see pattern for yardage).

GAUGE: 1 square motif = 8" square, blocked.

GENERAL DIRECTIONS: The dress pattern is used as lining pattern and the joined crocheted squares are treated as fabric. The crochet for front and back consists of 8" squares, which are joined as you work to form rectangles of "fabric." The sleeves are worked in picot netting. The diagram shows the number of motifs needed for an average pattern up to size 12, and how they are assembled. You may have to add extra motifs to obtain wider or longer "fabric" for sizes 14, 16, and 18.

Back measures 40" long and 25" wide across lower edge. Crochet "fabric" measures 4 squares (32") by 5 squares (40"). **Each front** measures 40" long and 12½" wide across lower edge. Crochet "fabric" measures 2 squares (16") by 5 squares (40"). **Sleeves** measure 25" to shoulder and 14" wide at underarm. Crocheted picot netting measures 14" by 25".

CROCHETED MOTIFS: BACK: First Square: Starting at center of rose, ch 8. Join with sl st to form ring. **1st rnd:** Ch 6, (dc in ring and mark the dc with pin, ch 4) 5 times; join with sl st to 2nd ch of ch-6 (6 lps made). Piece should measure 1" in diameter. **2nd rnd:** In each lp work 1 sc, 1 h dc, 3 dc, 1 h dc and 1 sc (6 petals made); join with sl st to first sc. Piece should measure 1⅝" in diameter. **3rd rnd:** * Ch 5, sl st in back of work in next marked dc of first rnd. Repeat from * around (6 lps made across back of petals). **4th rnd:** In each lp work 1 sc, 1 h dc, 5 dc, 1 h dc and 1 sc (6 petals made behind first layer of petals); sl st in first sc. **5th rnd:** * Ch 8, sl st in back of work in last sc of next petal. Repeat from * around (6 lps made across back of petals). **6th rnd:** In each lp work 1 sc, 1 h dc, 7 dc, 1 h dc and 1 sc (6 petals made behind 2nd layer of petals); sl st in first sc (completed rose should measure 2⅞" in diameter). **7th rnd:** * Make p lp as follows: Ch 5, sc in 4th ch from hook (p made), ch 5, make p, ch 1 (p lp completed), sc in center dc of next petal, make p lp, sc in first sc of next petal. Repeat from * around, ending with sl st in first sl st (12 p lps made). **8th rnd:** Sl st in first ch st and in first p of first lp, sc in next ch st, * ch 8, sc over next lp between the 2 p's (mark this sc with pin), ch 3, turn; over ch-8 lp just made work 9 dc for shell, dc in next sc, ch 4, turn; skip first 2 dc of shell, dc in next dc, (ch 1, skip next dc, dc in next dc) 3 times; ch 1, skip last dc, dc in top of ch-3 (5 spaces—shell completed); ch 5, p, ch 1, sc over lp with marked sc, remove marker; (make p lp, sc over next lp between p's) twice. Repeat from * 3 times more, joining last p lp with sl st to base of first shell (4 shells, each separated by 2 p lps). **9th rnd:** Make 2 sl sts on post of first dc on shell, sl st in top of same dc, sl st in each of next 2 ch sts of first ch-4 on shell, sc in next ch st, * make p lp, sc in center sp on shell, make p lp, skip next 2 sps, sc in last dc of shell, (make p lp, sc over next lp between p's) twice; make p lp, sc in first sp on next shell. Repeat from * 3 times more, joining last p lp with sl st to beg of first lp (20 lps made). **10th rnd:** Sl st in first ch st and in p of first lp, sc in next ch st, * ch 8, sc over next lp between p's (mark this sc), ch 3, turn; work 9 dc over lp just made for shell, dc in next sc, ch 4, turn; complete shell as in 8th rnd, ch 5, p, ch 1, sc over same lp with marked sc, remove marker, (make p lp, sc over next lp between p's) 4 times. Repeat from * 3 times more, joining last p lp with sl st to top of dc on first shell (4 shells, each separated by 4 p lps). **11th rnd:** Sl st in each of next 2 ch sts of first ch-4 on shell, sc in next ch st, * make p lp, sc in center sp on shell, make p lp, skip next 2 sps, sc over next lp, (make p lp, sc over next lp between p's) 4 times; make p lp, sc in first sp on next shell. Repeat from * 3 times more, joining last p lp with sl st to beg of first p lp (28 p lps made). Place pin as marker in 2nd p lp made on rnd. Break off. Piece should measure 6½" unblocked.

Second Square: Work as for first square through 10th rnd. **11th rnd (joining):** Work as for first square until 14 lps have been completed, ending with sc in first sp of 3rd shell. Work joining ch as follows: Ch 5, p, join with sl st between p's on marked lp on first square, ch 5, p, ch 1 (joining ch made—2 corner lps joined), sc in center sp of shell on 2nd square; following direction of arrow on 2nd square on diagram, make joining ch over next lp on first square, skip next 2 sps on 2nd square, sc over next lp, * make joining ch over next lp on first square, sc over next lp on 2nd square. Repeat from * 3 times more; make joining ch over next lp on first square, sc in first sp of next shell on 2nd square, make joining ch over next lp on first square, sc in center sp on shell on 2nd square, make joining ch over next lp on first square, skip next 2 sps on 2nd square, sc over next lp (1 side joined). Work last side of 2nd square in pattern. Break off.

Work squares 3 and 4, joining each to the previous one as shown on the diagram.

Fifth Square: Work as for first square through 10th rnd. Then work as for 2nd square through 11th rnd, joining to first square as shown on diagram.

Sixth Square: Work as for first square through 10th rnd. **11th rnd (joining):** Work as for first square until 7 lps have been completed, join to 5th square as before, working in direction of arrow, ending with joining ch over joined corner lps, skip next 2 sps on 6th square, sc over next lp. Now join 6th square to 2nd square as before, working in direction of arrow. Complete square in pattern. Break off.

Following sequence on diagram, continue making and joining squares through 20th square. Piece may be made longer or wider by adding squares to fit your pattern.

FRONT (make 2): Following sequence on diagram, work and join 10 squares as before.

SLEEVES: Note: Sleeves are written for a piece measuring 14" by 25". If your sleeve pattern is wider than 14", you must make a wider piece with a longer foundation chain than the one given. The chain is a multiple of 5 sts and each lp measures a little more than 1". **1st row:** Ch 90 for foundation ch to measure 14"; sc in 4th ch from hook (p made), ch 5, p, ch 1, skip next 5 ch, sc in next ch (first lp made), * make p ch, skip next 4 ch, sc in next ch (another lp made). Repeat from * 15 times more (17 lps made); turn. **2nd row:** Ch 8, p, ch 5, p, ch 1, sc over first lp between p's, * make p lp, sc over next lp between p's. Repeat from * 15 times more (17 lps made); turn. Repeat 2nd row until piece measures 25", stretched as though blocked, or desired length to fit pattern. Break off.

FINISHING: Blocking: Pin crochet "fabric," wrong side up, to a padded board, stretching it so that each motif measures 8" square for front and back pieces and so that sleeve pieces will fit pattern. Steam through a damp cloth with a fairly hot iron. Allow to dry thoroughly before removing from board.

LINING PATTERN: Following pattern directions, cut back and front. Cut front in half lengthwise. Stitch darts. Cut sleeves if lining for sleeves is desired.

DRESS PATTERN: On tracing paper, trace back and sleeves from *pattern*, indicating seam and cutting lines. Trace both fronts from cutout fabric *lining*, indicating seam and cutting lines. This will eliminate bust darts on coat as crochet "fabric" will be molded over lining. Diagrams show outline of pattern (broken lines) on "fabric." Your pattern may not fit in quite the same manner (you may have extra "fabric" at sides and top) but be sure in all cases to *match lower and center front edges of pattern with picot edges of crochet.* Pin tissue patterns on crochet "fabric," omitting hem allowance. (A detail of netting pattern is shown on sleeve diagram.) Baste along seam lines. Using a fine stitch, machine stitch through tissue and crochet along basted seam lines. Stitch once more close to first line. These stitching lines will keep crochet from raveling after it is cut. Cut out pattern along cutting lines, leaving 5/8" for seams, 1/4" along neck and front edges. Tear away tissue.

ASSEMBLING: Coat: Stitch shoulder and side seams along stitching lines; stitch sleeves in place. **Lining:** Stitch shoulder and side seams. Stitch sleeve seams (if there are sleeves) and stitch in place.

Left Front Border: 1st row: Attach yarn at left front neck edge, work sc evenly spaced along front edge to lower corner; ch 1, turn. **2nd row through 5th row:** Sc in each sc across; ch 1, turn. **6th row:** * Sc in each of next 3 sc, ch 3, sc in 3rd ch from hook (p made). Repeat from * across, ending with sc in each remaining sc. Break off. Mark edge with pins for 16 buttons, evenly spaced.

Right Front Border: Work as for left front border through 3rd row. Mark edge with pins for buttonholes. **4th row:** * Sc in each sc to next pin, ch 3, skip next 3 sc. Repeat from * across, ending with sc in each remaining sc; ch 1, turn. **5th row:** * Sc in each sc to next lp, work 3 sc over lp. Repeat from * across, ending with sc in each sc to end; ch 1, turn. Complete as for left front.

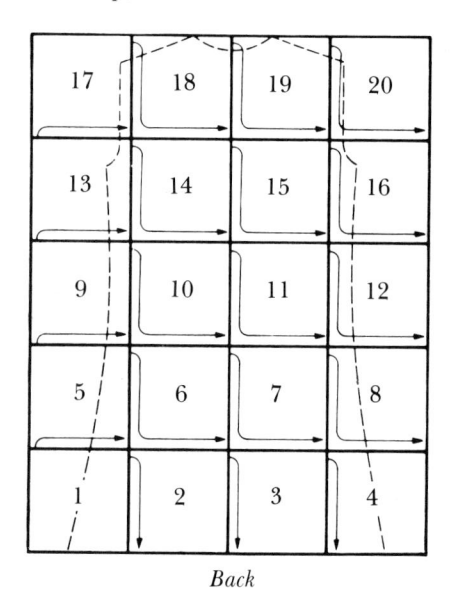

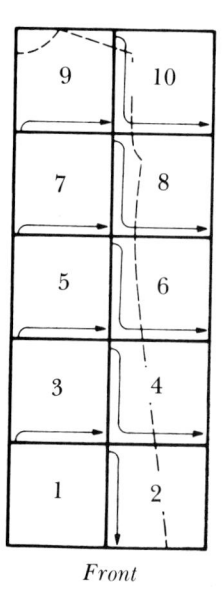

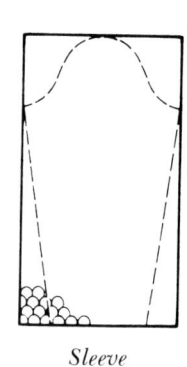

Back

Front

Sleeve

Border for Neck, Lower Edge, and Sleeves: Work as for left front border.

To Insert Lining: With wrong side of lining facing wrong side of coat, insert lining into coat. Turn in ½" around neck and sew in place at inside edge of border, leaving border free. For sleeveless lining, turn in allowance around armholes and sew in place. Pin side seams of crochet to lining and tack. Turn in lining ½" along front and lower edges and slip-stitch in place, leaving 4 rows of borders free. If there are sleeve linings, tack along seams, and turn in allowance at lower edge as for fronts.

BUTTON COVERS: Starting at center, ch 4. Join with sl st to form ring. **1st rnd:** Work 8 sc in ring. **2nd rnd:** Work 2 sc in each sc around (16 sc). **3rd rnd:** Sc in each sc around. Place button mold in crocheted cup. **4th rnd:** Sc in every other sc around. Break off, leaving 10" end. Thread end in needle and draw through back lp of each sc on last rnd. Draw up tightly and fasten. Make 15 more button covers and sew buttons in place.

Belt: Make 53"-long braid with 21 strands of yarn. Make and attach a tassel on each end of braid.

Turtleneck Poncho and Matching Beret

Turtleneck, sleeved poncho is worked in squares that are alternately sewn together horizontally and vertically for a checkerboard effect. Chevron details on beret and cuffs. Worked with double strands of knitting worsted, in single crochet.

SIZE: Medium.

Note: Poncho measures 38" across lower edge from side seam to side seam.

MATERIALS: Knitting worsted (used double throughout), 48 ounces rust (color R), 4 ounces each of brown (B) and dark green (G); aluminum crochet hook size K (or Canadian hook No. 4), *or the size that will give you the correct gauge.*

GAUGE: 3 sc = 1"; 5 rows = 2". Each finished square = 5½".

Poncho

SQUARE (make 70): With R, ch 16 to measure about 5". **1st row:** Sc in 2nd ch from hook and in each ch across (15 sc). Ch 1, turn. **2nd**

row: Working in back lps only, sc in each sc across. Ch 1, turn. Repeat 2nd row 11 times more. Piece should measure about 5" from beg.

EDGING: Sc in back lp of each sc of last row, working 3 sc in last st for corner; then work 13 sc along side edge, working 3 sc in corner; continue along opposite edge of starting ch and work 1 sc in each st, working 3 sc in last st; work 13 sc along other side edge, work 3 sc in last st. Join with sl st to first sc. Break off. Square should now measure 5½". Mark side of work facing you for right side of work.

Using 35 squares for each, form 2 large rectangles for front and back. Each one is 7 squares wide by 5 squares in length; alternate placement of squares (one vertical, the next one horizontal) to form checkerboard effect. With R and right side of squares facing, sew squares together through back lps of sts only. Beginning at neck edges, sew shoulder seams about 14½" in from each edge, leaving 9½" open at center for neck. Beginning at lower edge, sew about 20½" side seams, leaving 7" open for each armhole.

COLLAR: With wrong side facing and R, work 57 sc evenly spaced around neck opening, join. Work even in rnds of sc, through front lps only, until collar measures 2" from beg. Then, working in back lps only, continue in rnds of sc until collar measures 6" from beg.

ARMHOLE FINISHING: With right side facing and G, beginning at underarm seam, work 36 sc around armhole, join. **2nd rnd:** (Skip next 2 sc, sc in next 3 sc, 3 sc in next sc, sc in next 3 sc) 5 times. Repeat last rnd for pattern, working 4 more rnds G, 4 rnds B, and 5 rnds R. Break off. Work other side in same manner.

Beret

Starting at center with B, ch 4, join to form ring. **1st rnd:** Ch 3, work 13 dc in ring, join with sl st to ch-3 (14 dc, counting ch-3 as 1 dc). (**Note:** Work sc's in back lp only for remainder of hat.) **2nd rnd:** (Ch 1, 2 sc in next dc, 5 sc in next dc) 7 times, ending 5 sc in sl st, join. **3rd rnd:** (Skip ch-1 and next 2 sc, sc in next 2 sc, work 5 sc in next sc, sc in next 2 sc) 7 times (63 sts). **4th rnd:** Skip next sc, sc in next 3 sc, (work 5 sc in next sc, sc in next 3 sc, skip next 2 sc, sc in next 3 sc) 7 times. Do not work in last sc (77 sts). Break off B, attach G. **5th rnd:** (Skip next sc, sc in next 4 sc, work 5 sc in next sc, sc in next 4 sc, skip next 2 sc) 7 times, ending last repeat with skip 1 sc instead of skip 2 sc (91 sts). **6th through 11th rnds:** Continue in same manner, increasing 2 sc on each point (14 sc inc each rnd). Break off G at end of 9th rnd and attach R. **12th rnd:** * Skip next sc, draw up a lp in each of next 2 sc, y o hook and draw through 3 lps on hook (dec made), sc in next 9 sc, work 3 sc in next sc, sc in next 9 sc, dec 1 sc, skip 1 sc. Repeat from * 6 times more. **13th rnd:** (Skip next sc, dec 1 sc, sc in next 17 sc, dec 1 sc, skip 1 sc) 7 times. **14th rnd:** (Skip next sc, dec 1 sc, sc in next 13 sc, dec 1 sc, skip 1 sc) 7 times. **15th rnd:** (Skip next sc, dec 1 sc, sc in next 9 sc, dec 1 sc, skip 1 sc) 7 times. **16th rnd:** (Skip next sc, dec 1 sc, sc in next 5 sc, dec 1 sc, skip 1 sc) 7 times. **17th rnd:** Sc in each sc around. Break off.

FINISHING: With R, make a chain about 50" long. Weave in and out between sc's on last row. Make knots on ends. Adjust to fit and tie in bow.

Accessories

Head-Warmers Supreme

The copper beret, on the left, has a halo of rosy-pink hazelnut stitches (a variation of the popcorn stitch). You start at the crown and single-crochet down. The hazelnut round is bordered by a round of treble crochet.

The cap on the right keeps its shape close to the head. It is also worked in single crochet. Three colorful rows of hazelnuts make a wide textured band around the edge.

Blithe Beret

SIZE: One size fits all.

MATERIALS: Bear Brand Winsom Orlon acrylic yarn, 1 (2-ounce) skein copper No. 382 (color A); Bucilla Soufflé acrylic and Vinyon yarn, 1 (1¾-ounce) skein strawberry No. 430 (B); aluminum crochet hooks sizes J and G (or Canadian hooks No. 6 and No. 9) *or the sizes that will give you the correct gauge.*

GAUGE: With size J hook: 4 sc = 1"; 4 sc rnds = 1".

Starting at center top with size J hook and A, ch 4; join with sl st to form ring. **1st rnd (right side):** Work 10 sc in ring. Do not join unless otherwise specified, but mark beg of each rnd. **2nd rnd:** Work 2 sc in each sc around (20 sc). **3rd rnd:** * Sc in next sc, 2 sc in next sc (1 sc inc). Repeat from * around (30 sc). **4th rnd:** Work 1 sc in each sc around. **5th rnd:** * Sc in each of next 2 sc, 2 sc in next sc. Repeat from * around (40 sc). **6th rnd:** Sc in each sc around.

Continue in this manner for 9 rnds more, increasing 10 sc every other rnd and working 1 more sc between incs on each inc rnd. **16th rnd:** Work 1 rnd even on 90 sc. Piece should measure about 8" in diameter. Join with sl st in next sc. **17th rnd:** Ch 4, tr in each sc around (90 tr, counting ch-4 as 1 tr); join with sl st in top of ch-4. Break off A. **18th rnd (hazelnuts):** With wrong side facing you, make lp on size J hook with B, sc in first tr; * to make hazelnut, y o hook and draw up lp in next tr, y o and draw through 2 lps on hook, (y o and draw up lp in same st, y o and draw through 2 lps on hook) 4 times; y o and draw through all 6 lps on hook (hazelnut completed); sc in each of next 2 tr. Repeat from * around, ending last repeat with sc in last tr (30 hazelnuts); join. Break off B. **19th rnd:** With right side facing you, make lp on size G hook with A, y o twice and insert hook in any st of last rnd, complete tr and work 1 tr in each remaining st around (90 tr); join.

HEADBAND: 20th and 21st rnds: Sc in each st around. **22nd rnd (dec rnd):** Sc in each sc around, decreasing 12 sc as evenly spaced as possible (to dec 1 sc, draw up lp in each of 2 sc, y o and draw through all 3 lps on hook). Repeat dec rnd once more (66 sc); join. Break off.

Darling Cloche

SIZE: One size fits all.

MATERIALS: Bear Brand Winsom Orlon acrylic yarn, 1 (2-ounce) skein Persian blue No. 321 (color A), violite No. 366 (B), and rosy pink No. 342 (C); aluminum crochet hooks sizes J and F (or Canadian hooks No. 6 and No. 10) *or the sizes that will give you the correct gauge.*

GAUGE: With size J hook: 4 sc = 1"; 4 sc rnds = 1".

Starting at center top with A and size J hook, work 1st through 9th rnds as for beret. Then work even on 60 sc until crown measures 6" from center. Break off A. **First hazelnut rnd (see Blithe Beret):** With wrong side facing you, make lp on size J hook with B, sc in first sc, * work hazelnut in next sc, sc in each of next 2 sc. Repeat from * around, ending last repeat with sc in last sc (20 hazelnuts); join. Break off B. **2nd hazelnut rnd (wrong side):** Make lp on hook with C, sc in first sc, * work hazelnut in next hazelnut, sc in each of next 2 sc. Repeat from * around, ending last repeat with sc in last sc; join. Break off C. **3rd hazelnut rnd (wrong side):** Make lp on hook with B, repeat last rnd. Break off B.

HEADBAND: Following rnd (wrong side): Make lp on hook with size F hook and A, work sc in each st around (60 sc). Work even in sc for 4 rnds more. Join. Break off.

Sporty Fedora

With lots of style and wear. The crown is worked with three strands of yarn for a tweedy look. The edge of the brim is solid green.

SIZE: One size fits 21½"–23" head.

MATERIALS: Bear Brand Winsom Orlon acrylic yarn, 2 (2-ounce) skeins emerald No. 297 (color A), 1 skein each aqua green No. 329 (B) and spearmint (lime green) No. 367 (C); aluminum crochet hooks sizes G and H (or Canadian hooks No. 9 and No. 8) *or the sizes that will give you the correct gauge;* 1 yard 1"-wide grosgrain ribbon.

GAUGE: With size G hook, 3 sc = 1".

Note: Work with 3 strands yarn held together throughout.

CROWN: Starting at center with size H hook and 1 strand each A, B, and C, ch 5; join with sl st to form ring. **1st rnd:** Work 10 sc in ring. Do not join, but mark beg of each rnd. **2nd rnd:** Work 2 sc in each sc around (20sc). **3rd rnd:** * Sc in next sc, 2 sc in next sc (1 sc inc). Repeat from * around (30 sc). **4th rnd:** Sc in each sc around. **5th rnd:** * Sc in each of next 2 sc, 2 sc in next sc. Repeat from * around (40 sc). Piece should measure 3½" in diameter.

Continue in this manner for 6 rnds more, increasing 10 sc evenly spaced every other rnd (70 sc). Work 3 rnds even in sc. Change to size G hook and work even until crown measures about 8½" from center.

BRIM: (Note: Work 1st and 2nd rnds in front lp only of each st.) **1st rnd (inc rnd):** Sc in each sc around, increasing 6 sc as evenly spaced as possible. **2nd rnd:** Repeat inc rnd (82 sc). Work through both lps of each st from now on. **3rd rnd:** Work even. **4th rnd:** Repeat inc rnd. **5th rnd:** Work even. Break off strands B and C; attach 2 more strands A and work with 3 strands A from now on. **6th rnd:** Repeat inc rnd. **7th rnd:** Work even. Repeat inc rnd twice more (106 sc). Work one rnd even, sl st in next sc. Break off.

Cut ribbon to fit head size. Sew around inside of 1st and 2nd rnds worked on brim, drawing in hat slightly, if necessary, to fit.

Classic Cloche for Summer

The brim is worked in single crochet, crown in double-crochet chain pattern in ecru with deep rose and orange accents. A packable hat, quick and easy to make.

SIZE: One size fits all.

MATERIALS: Kentucky All Purpose yarn (rayon), 2 (100-yard) skeins ecru No. 703 (color A), 1 skein each deep rose No. 734 (B) and orange No. 708 (C); aluminum crochet hooks sizes E and F (or Canadian hooks No. 11 and No. 10) *or the sizes that will give you the correct gauge.*

GAUGE: On size F hook: 5 sts (dc's and ch-1's) = 1"; 2 rows = 1". On size E hook: 5 sc = 1"; 11 rnds = 2".

CROWN: Starting at center with F hook and color A, ch 6. Join with sl st to form ring. **1st rnd:** Ch 4, (dc in ring, ch 1) 9 times (10 dc, counting turning ch as 1 dc); join with sl st to 3rd ch of ch-4. **2nd rnd:** Sl st in first ch-1 sp, ch 4, dc in same sp, ch 1, * in next sp work dc, ch 1 and dc (inc made), ch 1. Repeat from * 8 times more (20 dc); join. **3rd rnd:** Sl st in first ch-1 sp, ch 4, dc in next sp, ch 1, inc in next sp, ch 1 * (dc in next sp, ch 1) twice; inc in next sp, ch 1. Repeat from * to within last 2 sps, (dc in next sp, ch 1) twice (26 dc); join. **4th rnd:** Sl st in next sp, ch 4; continuing in pattern of dc and ch 1, inc 8 dc around as evenly spaced as possible (34 dc). **5th rnd:** Work even in pattern. **6th rnd:** Continuing in pattern, inc 6 dc around (40 dc). **7th rnd:** Inc 8 dc around (48 dc). Work even in pattern until piece measures about 6" from center of crown, or for desired depth. Break off.

BAND: 1st rnd: With B and size F hook, sc in any ch-1 sp, ch 1, * sc in next ch-1 sp, ch 1. Repeat from * around (48 sc); join with sl st in first sc. **2nd rnd:** * Ch 1, sc in next ch-1 sp. Repeat from * around. Break off. **3rd rnd:** With C, work dc in back lp of any sc until 2 lps remain on hook, drop C, y o with B and draw through both lps on hook (always change colors in this manner and hold yarn not in use at back of work); * with B dc in back lp of next st, with C dc in back lp of next st. Repeat from * around (96 dc); join with sl st in first dc. Break off C only. **4th rnd:** With B, ch 2, skip next dc, sc in next dc, * ch 1, skip next dc, sc in next dc. Repeat from * around (48 sc); join. Break off.

BRIM: (**Note:** Be sure to get the correct gauge so that brim will have body and will not ripple.) **1st rnd:** With E hook and color A, sc in front lp of each st around, increasing 4 sc evenly spaced (100 sc). (To inc, work 2 sc in 1 sc.) **2nd rnd:** Ch 1, sc in same place as sl st, * sc in each sc around, increasing 20 sc evenly spaced (120 sc); join. **3rd rnd:** Work even. **4th rnd:** Ch 1, sc in each st around, increasing 12 sc (132 sc); join. **5th and 6th rnds:** Work even. **7th rnd:** Inc 12 sc (144 sc). **8th and 9th rnds:** Work even. **10th rnd:** Inc 10 sc (154 sc). **11th and 12th rnds:** Work even. **13th rnd:** Inc 10 sc (164 sc). **14th and 15th rnds:** Work even. **16th rnd:** Inc 10 sc (174 sc). Brim should measure about 3". If necessary, work even until brim is correct width. Break off.

BORDER: With B, sc in each of next 5 sc, insert hook 1 row below next sc and draw up lp, y o and draw through both lps on hook (long sc made), * sc in each of next 5 sc, work long sc. Repeat from * around; join. Break off.

Three Winter Hats

Three supershapely head-warmers are done with needlepoint and crewel wool in magnificent colors. The beret is in single crochet with popcorns to top it off. The romantic cloche, also in single crochet, is embroidered with silver lazy daisies. And a cozy hood, in double crochet and popcorn stitches, ties under the chin with a heavy cord.

GENERAL DIRECTIONS: Crewel yarn: This type of yarn, sometimes called Persian yarn, can be divided into 3 separate strands. Crochet with all 3 strands held together throughout. The yarn is sold in 10-yard lengths on cards and in 10- or 40-yard lengths in skeins. We have specified the yardage you will need for each color.

To Increase 1 sc: Work 2 sc in same st.

To Decrease 1 sc: Draw up lp in 1 st, then draw up lp in next st, y o and draw through all 3 lps on hook.

Working with Two Colors: When changing colors at end of rnd, break off old color, leaving 3" end. Tie on new color. Conceal yarn ends in work by holding them along top edge of previous rnd and crocheting over them.

To change colors in middle of rnd, work to within last st of first color group. With first color, draw up lp in next st, pick up new color, y o with new color and complete st. Continue with new color.

To carry unused color, hold it along top edge of previous rnd and crochet over it so that it is concealed within sts.

Note: Carefully check to make sure your gauges are accurate. However, if you wish your hat to fit snugly, pull the carried yarn a bit on each rnd.

Beret

SIZE: One size fits all.

MATERIALS: Bucilla needlepoint and crewel wool (see General Directions above), 50 yards each medium peacock No. 83 (color A) and red No. 36 (B), 40 yards medium red No. 35 (C), 30 yards each apricot No. 78 (D), royal blue No. 33 (E), sun yellow No. 98 (F), lavender No. 71 (G), and dark emerald No. 69 (H), 20 yards chartreuse No. 73 (I), 10 yards each dark rose No. 11 (J) and henna No. 51 (K); aluminum crochet hook size F (or Canadian hook No. 10) *or the size that will give you the correct gauge.*

GAUGE: 6 sc = 1".

Note: See General Directions.

Starting at center of crown with color A, ch 4. Join with sl st to form ring. **1st rnd:** Ch 1, work 12 sc in ring. Do not join.

2nd rnd (inc rnd): Work 2 sc in first sc; with D, work 2 sc in next sc, (2 A sc in next sc, 2 D sc in next sc) 5 times (24 sc).

3rd rnd (inc rnd): D sc in next sc, (2 A sc in each of next 2 sc, D sc in each of next 2 sc) 5 times; 2 A sc in each of next 2 sc, D sc in next sc (36 sc). **4th rnd:** (A sc in each of next 2 sc, D sc in each of next 4 sc) 6 times.

5th rnd (inc rnd): D sc in next sc, (2 A sc in each of next 2 sc, D sc in each of next 4 sc) 5 times; 2 A sc in each of next 2 sc, D sc in each of next 3 sc (48 sc). **6th rnd:** A sc in each of next 2 sc, (D sc in each of next 4 sc, A sc in each of next 4 sc) 5 times; D sc in each of next 4 sc, A sc in each of next 2 sc.

7th rnd (inc rnd): A sc in each of next 3 sc, (2 D sc in next sc, D sc in each of next 3 sc, 2 A sc in next sc, A sc in each of next 3 sc) 5 times; 2 D sc in next sc, D sc in each of next 3 sc, 2 A sc in next sc (60 sc). **8th rnd:** D sc in each of next 4 sc, (A sc in each of next 5 sc, D sc in each of next 5 sc) 5 times; A sc in each of next 5 sc, D sc in next sc.

9th rnd (inc rnd): (2 D sc in next sc, D sc in each of next 4 sc, 2 A sc in next sc, A sc in each of next 4 sc) 6 times (72 sc). Break off. Piece should measure about 4½" in diameter.

10th rnd (popcorns): Turn piece with wrong side facing you. With E work sc in first D sc of a D group, E sc in each of next 2 sc, work E popcorn in next sc as follows: Y o, insert hook in next sc, y o and draw lp through st to ½", y o and draw through 2 lps on hook, (y o, insert hook in same sc, y o and draw lp through st to ½", y o and draw through 2 lps on hook) 5 times; y o and draw through all 7 lps on hook, ch 1 (popcorn completed; make sure it "bubbles" out on right side); E sc in each of next 2 sc. Work C sc in each of next 3 sc (first 3 sc of next A group), C popcorn in next sc, C sc in each of next 2 sc. Continue around in pattern

(12 popcorns—84 sts in all, counting ch-1 over each popcorn). Break off. Tie yarn ends tog at beg and end of rnd, with knot on wrong side. Always tie ends in this manner after yarns have been cut.

11th rnd: Turn piece with right side facing you. With H work sc in each C st and J st in each E st (84 sc). **12th rnd:** J sc in next sc, (H sc in next 7 sc, J sc in next 7 sc) 5 times; H sc in next 7 sc, J sc in next 6 sc. Break off. **13th rnd:** With F work sc in each H sc and G sc in each J sc. Break off.

14th rnd (inc rnd): With K work sc in any sc of last rnd, * with I work 2 sc in next sc, K sc in next sc. Repeat from * around, ending with 2 I sc in last sc (126 sc).

15th rnd (inc rnd): I sc in next sc, * (2 K sc in next sc, I sc in each of next 2 sc) 4 times; K sc in next sc, I sc in each of next 2 sc. Repeat from * 7 times more, 2 K sc in next sc, I sc in each of next 2 sc, 2 K sc in next sc, I sc in last sc (160 sc). Break off.

16th rnd (wrong side): E sc in each of 2 K sc, * F sc in each of next 2 sc, E sc in each of next 2 sc. Repeat from * around, ending with 2 F sc. Beret edge will ripple a bit at this point. **17th rnd:** F sc in first sc, * E sc in each of next 2 sc, F sc in each of next 2 sc. Repeat from * around, ending with 1 F sc. Break off.

18th rnd (right side): Work B sc in each of 2 E sc, * G sc in each of next 2 sc, B sc in each of next 2 sc. Repeat from * around, ending with 2 G sc. **19th rnd:** G sc in first sc, * B sc in each of next 2 sc, G sc in each of next 2 sc. Repeat from * around, ending with 1 G sc. Break off.

20th rnd (wrong side): Work A sc in each of 2 B sc, * D sc in each of next 2 sc, A sc in each of next 2 sc. Repeat from * around, ending with 2 D sc. **21st rnd:** D sc in first sc, * A sc in each of next 2 sc, D sc in each of next 2 sc. Repeat from * around, ending with 1 D sc. Break off.

22nd rnd (right side): * Work C sc in each of 2 A sc, E sc in each of next 2 sc. Repeat from * around. **23rd rnd:** Work C sc in each C sc and E sc in each E sc around. Break off.

24th rnd (wrong side): Work G sc in each C sc and work F sc in each E sc around. **25th rnd:** Work G sc in each G sc and F sc in each F sc around. Break off.

26th rnd (right side): Work C sc in each G sc and A sc in each F sc around. **27th rnd:** Work A sc in each A sc and C sc in each C sc around. Break off.

28th rnd (dec rnd—wrong side): Work B sc in each of 2 A sc, dec as follows: Draw up H lp in each of next 2 sc, y o with B and draw through all 3 lps on hook (dec completed), * work 2 B sc, 2 H sc. Repeat from * around, decreasing 7 more sc as evenly spaced as possible (152 sc). **29th rnd:** Work B sc in each B sc and H sc in each H sc around. Break off.

Band: (Note: On each of the remaining rnds, always work with right side facing you and, on all but the last rnd, pull the carried yarn every few sts to tighten band for correct fit.)

30th rnd (dec rnd): Starting in any st, * work 1 K sc, dec 1 K sc in next 2 sc, work 1 K sc, work 1 I sc, dec 1 I sc in next 2 sc, work 1 I sc. Repeat from * around (114 sc). **31st rnd:** I sc in next I sc, * K sc in each of next 3 sc, I sc in each of next 3 sc. Repeat from * around, ending with 3 K sc, 2 I sc. **32nd rnd:** I sc in each of next 2 sc, * K sc in each of next 3 sc, I sc in each of next 3 sc. Repeat from * around, ending with 3 K sc, 1 I sc. Break off.

From now on you will be working with 3 colors on all but the last rnd. Carry the 2 colors not in use and work over them while working with the 3rd color so as to give band body. Try on beret after each rnd, drawing in carried yarns if necessary, to adjust size of band.

33rd rnd: Work 28 C sc, 22 D sc, 64 B sc.

34th rnd (dec rnd): Work 1 B sc, with C work sc across next 28 sts, decreasing 5 sc as evenly spaced as possible; work D sc across next 22 sc, decreasing 4 sc; work B sc across remaining 63 sc, decreasing 8 sc (97 sc).

35th rnd (dec rnd): Work B sc in each of next 2 sc; work C sc across next 22 sc, decreasing 3 sc; work D sc across next 18 sc, decreasing 2 sc; work B sc across remaining 55 sc, decreasing 8 sc (84 sc). **36th rnd:** Work B sc in each of next 3 sc, C sc in next 18 sc, D sc in next 16 sc, B sc in remaining 47 sc.

If band is not as deep as desired, continue to work 1 or more rnds on 84 sc in same color pattern. Break off.

Next rnd (edging): With A work reverse sc (see diagram, p. 144), working from *left to right* around; sl st in first sc. Break off.

Romantic Cloche

SIZE: One size fits all.

MATERIALS: Bucilla needlepoint and crewel wool, 150 yards scarlet No. 92 (color S), 120 yards medium peacock No. 83 (M), 10 yards each dark yellow No. 3 (Y), tangerine No. 95 (T), dark red No. 36 (R), and plum No. 87 (P); Bucilla Spotlight yarn, 1 (20-gram) ball silver; aluminum crochet hook size F (or Canadian hook No. 10) *or the size that will give you the correct gauge;* tapestry needle.

GAUGE: 5 sc = 1"; 9 rnds = 2".

Note: See General Directions for hats, p. 141.

Do not join rnds but work around and around, spiral fashion, marking beg of each rnd.

CROWN: 1st rnd: With M, ch 4. Sl st in 4th ch from hook to form ring. Work 12 sc in ring, attach S. Continue to sc with M only, carrying S and working over it. **2nd rnd:** Work 1 sc in each sc around. **3rd rnd:** Work 2 sc in each sc around (24 sc). **4th rnd:** * Sc in each of next 3 sc, 2 sc in each of next 3 sc. Repeat from * around (36 sc). **5th rnd:** Work 2 sc in each sc around (72 sc). **6th and 7th rnds:** Work even. **8th rnd:** Inc 6 sc evenly spaced around (78 sc). **9th rnd:** Inc 6 sc evenly spaced around, being careful not to work incs over incs of previous rnd (84 sc). **10th rnd:** Work even. **11th rnd:** Inc 10 sc evenly spaced around (94 sc). **12th rnd:** Work even. **13th rnd:** Inc 6 sc evenly spaced around (100 sc). **14th through 16th rnds:** Work even. **17th rnd (dec rnd):** Dec 6 sts evenly spaced around (94 sc). Do not break off M, but start working with S. Work over color not in use.

BRIM: 18th rnd: Work 2 S sc, 9 M, 2 S, 9 M, 2 S, 22 M, 2 S, 9 M, 2 S, 12 M, 2 S, 10 M, 2 S, 9 M. Piece should measure about 4" from center to edge.

19th rnd: Work 3 S, 8 M, 3 S, 8 M, 3 S, 10 M, 2 S, 9 M, 3 S, 8 M, 3 S, 7 M, 2 S, 2 M, 3 S, 9 M, 3 S, 8 M. **20th rnd:** 4 S, 4 M, 2 S, 1 M, 4 S, 7 M, 4 S, 9 M, 3 S, 4 M, 2 S, 2 M, 4 S, 7 M, 4 S, 3 M, 2 S, 1 M, 3 S, 1 M, 4 S, 8 M, 4 S, 7 M. **21st rnd:** 5 S, 3 M, 8 S, 6 M, 5 S, 8 M, 4 S, 3 M, 3 S, 1 M, 5 S, 6 M, 5 S, 2 M, 3 S, 1 M sc and 1 S sc in next sc, 8 S, 7 M, 5 S, 6 M (95 sc). **22nd rnd:** 6 S, 2 M, 9 S, 5 M, 6 S, 7 M, 5 S, 1 M, 2 M sc in next sc, 4 S, 1 M sc and 1 S sc in next sc, 5 S, 5 M, 6 S, 1 M, 14 S, 6 M, 6 S, 5 M (97 sc).

23rd rnd: 7 S, 2 M sc in next sc, 10 S, 2 M, 2 M sc in next sc, 1 M, 7 S, 4 M, 2 M sc in next sc, 1 M, 6 S, 2 M, 12 S, 3 M, 2 M sc in next sc, 22 S, 2 M, 2 M sc in next sc, 2 M, 7 S, 2 M, 2 M sc in next sc, 1 M (103 sc). **24th rnd:** 8 S, 1 M, 11 S, 4 M, 8 S, 1 M, 2 M sc in next sc, 4 M, 7 S, 1 M, 13 S, 3 M, 2 M sc in next sc, 12 S, dec 1 S sc, 9 S, 5 M, 8 S, 2 M sc in next sc, 2 M, 2 M sc in last sc (106 sc). **25th rnd:** 9 S, 1 M, 11 S, 2 M, 2 M sc in next sc, 9 S, 6 M, 22 S, 2 M sc in next sc, 3 M, 23 S, 3 M, 2 M sc in next sc, 9 S, 4 M, 2 M sc in last sc (110 sc). **26th rnd:** 22 S, 2 M sc in next sc, 1 M, 2 M sc in next sc, 10 S, 2 M, 2 M sc in next sc, 1 M, 2 M sc in next sc, 9 S, dec 1 S sc, 12 S, 2 M sc in next sc, 2 M, 2 M sc in next sc, 24 S, 2 M sc in next sc, 3 M, 10 S, 2 M sc in next sc, 4 M (117 sc).

27th rnd: 12 S, 2 S sc in each of next 2 sc, 9 S, 4 M, 2 S sc in next sc, 6 S, 6 M, 11 S, 2 S sc in each of next 2 sc, 10 S, 5 M, 10 S, 2 S sc in each of next 2 sc, 13 S, 4 M, 5 S, 2 S sc in each of next 2 sc, 4 S, 5 M (126 sc). **28th rnd:** 26 S, 3 M, 13 S, 5 M, 26 S, 4 M, 28 S, 3 M, 14 S and 4 M (126 sc). **29th rnd:** 5 S, 2 S sc in each of next 2 sc, 20 S, 2 M, 14 S, 4 M, 4 S, 2 S sc in each of next 2 sc, 13 S, 2 S sc in each of next 2 sc, 6 S, 3 M, 29 S, 2 M, 15 S, 3 M (132 sc).

30th rnd: 23 S, 2 S sc in each of next 2 sc, 5 S, 1 M, 15 S, 3 M, 32 S, 2 M, 6 S, 2 S sc in each of next 2 sc, 13 S, 2 S sc in each of next 2 sc, 7 S, 1 M, 3 S, 2 S sc in each of next 2 sc, 11 S, 2 M (140 sc). **31st rnd:** 26 S, dec 1 S sc, 21 S, 2 M, 33 S, 1 M, 27 S, dec 1 S sc, 25 S, 1 M (138 sts). Break off M.

32nd rnd: With S only, sc in each sc around, increasing 16 sc as evenly spaced as possible (154 sc). **33rd rnd:** Work even. **34th rnd:** Inc 20 sc around (174 sc). **35th and 36th rnds:** Work even. **37th rnd:** Inc 12 sc around (186 sc). **38th and 39th rnds:** Work even. Break off S; attach Y. **40th rnd:** With Y, sc around, increasing 2 sc evenly spaced (188 sc). Break off Y; attach T. **41st rnd:** With T, work even. Break off T; attach R. **42nd rnd:** With R, work even. Break off R; attach P. **43rd rnd:** With P, work even. Break off P; attach A. **44th rnd:** With A, working from *left to right*, work reverse sc in each sc around (see diagram). Break off.

EMBROIDERY: With tapestry needle and

S, following photograph and stitch diagram, work lazy daisy stitches at random on right side of crown. **Note:** Work stitches neatly, using short lengths of yarn. Weave in ends. With silver, work embroidery on under side of brim in same manner.

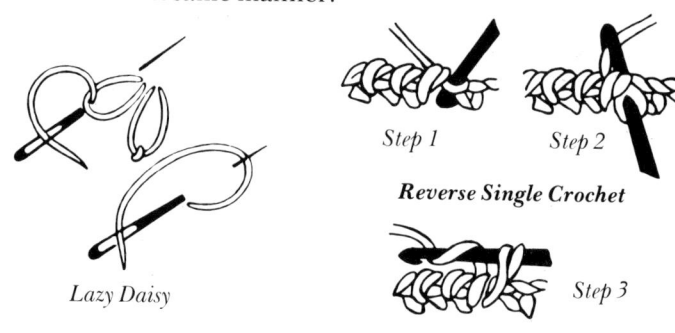

Lazy Daisy

Reverse Single Crochet
Step 1 *Step 2* *Step 3*

Cozy Hood

SIZE: One size fits all.
MATERIALS: Bucilla needlepoint and crewel wool (see General Directions for hats, p. 141), 180 yards tan No. 16 (color A), 150 yards dark rose No. 11 (B), 50 yards light antique gold No. 20 (C), 40 yards each bright blue No. 32 (D) and medium peacock No. 83 (E), 30 yards each dark peacock No. 84 (F), scarlet No. 92 (G), and dark chartreuse No. 110 (H), 20 yards each sage green No. 46 (I), fuchsia No. 86 (J), henna No. 51 (K), and light aqua No. 22 (L), 10 yards lavender No. 71 (M); small amount light-blue mohair (N); aluminum crochet hook sizes E and F (or Canadian hooks No. 11 and 10) *or the sizes that will give you the correct gauge.*
GAUGE: Because of the variety of sts and change of hook size, we cannot give stitch gauge for this hood. After 5th rnd is completed, working popcorn and shell pattern, 5 average rnds should measure 2" on wrong side of hat.
Note: See General Directions for hats.
Starting at top of crown with size F hook and color E, ch 8. Join with sl st to form ring.
1st rnd (right side): (Work 1 sc, 3 dc and 1 sc in ring) 5 times (5 shells made); join with sl st to first sc. Break off. **2nd rnd:** With right side facing you, attach A to center dc of any shell and work ch 3 (counts as 1 dc), 6 dc in same st, * skip next 4 sts, work 7-dc shell in center dc of next shell. Repeat from * 3 times more, ending with skip next 4 sts; join with sl st to top of first ch-3 (35 sts). Break off. **3rd rnd:** With right side facing you, attach D in last sl st made, sc in same place, sc in each of next 2 dc, work 5 dc in next dc, * skip next dc, sc in each of next 4 dc, skip next dc, work 5 dc in next dc. Repeat from * 3 times more, ending with skip next dc, sc in each of next 2 dc; join to first sc. **4th rnd:** Sc in each st around, decreasing 6 sc as evenly spaced as possible (40 sts); join to first sc. Break off.

5th rnd: With wrong side facing you, attach G to first sc of last rnd, ch 2, in same st work a popcorn as follows: (y o hook, draw up lp in same st, y o, draw through 2 lps on hook) 6 times, y o, draw through all 7 lps on hook, ch 1 (popcorn made), insert hook in next st, y o, draw lp through st, drop G, attach C, with C, y o hook, draw lp through 2 lps on hook (sc begun with old color and completed with new color). (**Note:** On popcorn rnds, always change colors in this manner.) * With C, work popcorn in next st, begin sc in next st, drop C, pick up G, with G complete sc, work popcorn in next st, begin sc in next st, drop G, pick up C, with C complete sc. Repeat from * around 8 times more, ending with a C popcorn and sc (20 popcorns, 20 sc). Break off. Piece should measure about 4½" in diameter.

6th rnd: With wrong side facing you, attach A to ch-1 sp of any G popcorn, ch 2, in same st work a popcorn, sc in next sc, * with F work popcorn in next ch-1 sp of next popcorn, sc in next sc, with A work popcorn in next ch-1 sp of next popcorn, sc in next sc. Repeat from * around 8 times more, ending with an F popcorn in last popcorn, sc in last sc; join to first popcorn. Break off F.

7th rnd: With right side facing you, using A, work 5-dc shell in same place as last sl st made, (skip next sc, draw up lp in ch-1 sp of next popcorn and in next sc, y o and draw through all 3 lps on hook—1 sc dec; work a 5-dc shell in ch-1 sp of next popcorn) 3 times; * sc in next sc, work shell in ch-1 sp of next popcorn. Repeat from * around 12 times more, ending with sc in last sc (17 shells); join to first dc of first shell. Break off. **8th rnd:** With right side facing you, using D, sc in center dc of any 5-dc shell, * work a 5-dc shell in next sc, sc in center dc of next shell. Repeat from * around 15 times more, ending with a 5-dc shell in last sc; join to first sc. Break off.

9th rnd: With wrong side facing you, * (with K, work popcorn in first dc of any 5-dc shell, skip next dc, sc in next dc, skip next dc, pick up H, work popcorn in last dc of shell, sc in next sc) 3 times; work popcorn in center dc of next shell, sc in next sc. Repeat from * 3 times more, ending with popcorn in first dc of last shell, skip next dc, sc in next dc, work popcorn in last dc of shell, sc in last sc; join to first popcorn (30 popcorns and 30 sc). Break off.

10th rnd: With right side facing you, using A, sc in ch-1 sp of any popcorn, work a 4-dc shell in next sc, skip next popcorn, sc in next sc, work shell in next popcorn, skip next sc, * sc in next popcorn, work a 4-dc shell in next sc, skip next popcorn, sc in next sc, shell in next popcorn, skip next sc. Repeat from * 8 times more (20 shells, 20 sc). Do not join. Break off.

11th rnd: With wrong side facing you, using C, * (work C popcorn in center of next 4-dc shell, sc in next sc, with E, work popcorn in center of next 4-dc shell, sc in next sc) twice; work C popcorn in first dc of next shell, skip next dc, sc in next dc, work E popcorn in next dc, sc in next sc. Repeat from * 3 times more (24 popcorns, 24 sc). Do not join. Break off.
12th rnd: With right side facing you, using A, work a 4-dc shell in each sc around (24 shells); join to first dc of first shell.

13th rnd: With wrong side facing you, alternating L and B every 2 sts, * (sc in first dc of next shell, skip next dc, popcorn in next dc, skip next dc) 3 times; sc in next dc, popcorn in next dc, sc in next dc, popcorn in next dc. Repeat from * 5 times more (30 popcorns, 30 sc); join to first sc. Break off. **14th rnd:** With right side facing you, using A, work a 3-dc shell in each sc around; join to first dc of first shell. Break off.

15th rnd: With wrong side facing you, alternating G and I every 2 sts, * work popcorn in center dc of next shell, sc in next dc. Repeat from * around (30 popcorns, 30 sc); join to first popcorn. Break off. **(Note:** Remainder of hat is worked with size E hook.)

16th rnd: Repeat 14th rnd. **17th rnd:** With F and J repeat 15th rnd.

Earflaps: Mark off 12 popcorns for front of hat, mark off next 5 popcorns for one earflap, mark off next 8 popcorns for back and last 5 popcorns for other earflap.

With wrong side facing you, starting at first sc of an earflap, work as follows; **1st row:** Alternating every 2 sts with D and A (work popcorn in next sc, sc in next popcorn) 4 times. Break off. **2nd row:** With I and B, repeat first row. **3rd row:** Alternating every 2 sts with E and C, (work popcorn in next sc, sc in next popcorn) 3 times. Break off. **4th row:** With M and C, repeat 3rd row. Work other earflap to correspond.

FINISHING: Next rnd: With right side facing you, using A, work a 3-dc shell in each space between popcorns around lower edge of hat; join with sl st. Break off. At lower edge of each earflap, mark first dc of center shell. **Following rnd:** Starting at a marked dc, with right side facing you, using A, work 5 dc in same st, ch 3, skip 3 dc, 5 dc in next st, work sc in each st around to within next marked dc, work 5 dc in next st, ch 3, skip 3 dc, work 5 dc in next st, sc in each remaining st around; join.

Edging: With right side facing you, using N, work a rnd of reverse sc, working from *left to right* around lower edge of hat (see stitch diagram p. 144); join. Break off.

Cord: With size F hook and B, ch 6. Join with sl st to form ring. **1st rnd:** Work 6 sc in ring. **2nd rnd:** Sc in each sc around. Repeat 2nd rnd until cord measures about 27". Break off.

Petal Pompons: Petal: With size F hook and B, ch 4. Join with sl st to form ring. **1st rnd:** Work 6 sc in ring; join with sl st to first sc. **2nd rnd:** Ch 3, work dc in same place as last sl st; work 2 dc in each remaining sc around (12 dc, counting ch-3 as 1 dc); join to ch-3. **3rd rnd:** Ch 1, work 3 sc in sl st, work 3 sc in each remaining dc around (36 sc); join. **4th rnd:** Ch 1, work 3 sc in sl st, work 3 sc in each remaining sc around (108 sc). Break off. Work 2 petals each E and C and 1 D.

Following photograph, sew D and B petals together at center (pompon completed). Make 2 E and C pompons in same manner.

Pull cord through ch-3 lp on each earflap. Sew 1 D and C pompon to each end of cord. Sew other pompon to top of crown.

Double-Strap Backpack

With an individualized look all its own. Make it with leftover knitting worsted and cotton, the more colors the merrier. Single crochet all the way, drawstring to close the top.

SIZE: About 27" around and 17" deep.

MATERIALS: Knitting worsted, 20 ounces in assorted colors; Coats and Clark's Speed-Cro-Sheen, 8 (100-yard) balls in assorted colors; aluminum crochet hook size H (or Canadian hook No. 8) *or the size that will give you the correct gauge;* tapestry needle.

GAUGE: 7 sc = 2"; 7 rnds = 2".

Note: Work with 1 strand each knitting worsted and Speed-Cro-Sheen held together throughout. Work stripes in desired colors. Your gauge must be accurate or the backpack will not be the size specified.

BACKPACK: Starting at center of bottom, ch 4; join with sl st to form ring. **1st rnd:** Work 6 sc in ring. Do not join rnds, but mark beg of each rnd. **2nd rnd:** Work 2 sc in each sc around (12 sc). **3rd through 16th rnds:** Sc in each sc around, increasing 6 sc evenly spaced on each rnd. Piece should measure about 9½" in diameter. Work even on 96 sc until piece measures 16" from last inc rnd.

Next rnd (beading): Sl st in next sc, ch 3, dc in each of next 5 sc, ch 2, skip 2 sc, * dc in each of next 6 sc, ch 2, skip 2 sc. Repeat from * around, ending with sl st in top of ch-3. **Following rnd:** Sc in same place as sl st, sc in each of next 5 dc, 2 sc in next sp, * sc in each of next 6 dc, 2 sc in next sp. Repeat from * around; join and break off.

STRAPS: With right side of top edge of backpack facing you, mark off any 14 sc (7 sc for each strap) on 6th row down from top edge. With 2 strands knitting worsted and 1 strand Speed-Cro-Sheen, work as follows: **1st row:** Work sc over each of first 7 marked sts; ch 1, turn. **2nd row:** Sc in each sc of strap; ch 1, turn. Repeat 2nd row until strap measures 17". Break off. Work sc into remaining 7 marked sc and complete other strap in same manner.

With tapestry needle and yarn, sew free ends of straps, about 10" apart, to lower edge of backpack on 17th rnd.

DRAWSTRING: The backpack is shown with twisted cord drawstring (directions follow), but you can braid or crochet a chain with several strands of yarn if you prefer.

To make twisted cord, cut eight 66" lengths of one color of yarn and two 66" lengths of another color. Hold together, and knot one end. Have friend hold knotted end (or loop it over a door knob or close it firmly in a drawer).

Holding opposite end, stand far enough back so that yarn is taut. Twist yarn tightly in one direction until kinks form when tension is slightly released. Keeping yarn taut, hold center of cord with one hand and bring end in other hand to knotted end. Starting from folded center, pinch cord at about 3" intervals, releasing it as you go. It will twist neatly around itself. Make knot about 2" from each end; trim and straighten strands to form tassels. Weave cord through beading and tie in bow.

Stretchy Tote

Rug yarn in earth and sky colors, worked in single and double crochet, stretches deep to carry all.

SIZE: About 21" deep without handle.

MATERIALS: Aunt Lydia's heavy rug yarn (75% rayon, 25% cotton), 1 (70-yard) skein each phantom red No. 140 (color A), national blue No. 715 (B), turquoise icing No. 735 (C), bongo tangerine No. 315 (D), mint green No. 645 (E), beige No. 405 (F), medium blue No. 710 (G), 3 skeins of burnt orange No. 320 (H); aluminum crochet hook size J (or Canadian hook No. 6) *or the size that will give you the correct gauge.*

GAUGE: 2 dc = 1".

Note on Colors: You can work more or fewer rounds of any color, or even change color in the middle of any round.

BAG: Starting at bottom of bag, with A, ch 22. **1st rnd:** In 4th ch from hook work 4 dc (mark 2nd dc with pin), dc in each of next 17 sts, work 5 dc in last st (mark 3rd dc of group); working along opposite edge of foundation chain, dc in each of next 17 sts; join with sl st in top of ch-3 (44 dc, counting ch-3 as 1 dc). Break off. **2nd rnd:** Make lp on hook with B, and working in back lp of sts, sc in each dc around, working 3 sc in st above marked st at each end; join with sl st in back lp of first sc. Break off.

Note: For all following dc rnds, draw up first lp of dc ¾" long. **3rd rnd:** Make lp on hook with H, and dc in back lp of each st around, working 3 dc in st above marked st at each end; join as before. **4th rnd:** With H, ch 4, and, working through both lps, dc in each st around, working 3 dc above each marked st; join. **5th rnd:** Repeat 4th rnd; break off. Piece should measure 4½" from starting chain.

With C, repeat 3rd rnd once; then with D, continue in same manner for 2 rnds more (72 dc at end of 8th rnd). Break off. **9th rnd:** With A, sc in first dc, * ch 4, skip 1 dc, sc in next dc.

Repeat from * around (36 lps). **10th rnd:** Ch 4, sc in next lp. Repeat from * around; do not join rnds from now on.

Working as for 10th rnd, work 1 rnd more with A, 2 rnds E, 3 rnds F, 3 rnds H, 2 rnds G, 1 rnd B, 2 rnds A, and 2 rnds H.

TOP BORDER: 1st rnd: With H, work 2 sc in each lp around (72 sc). **2nd rnd:** Sc around, decreasing 10 sts evenly spaced. Continue in sc around on 62 sts until border is 2″. Sl st in next 2 sts. Break off.

HANDLE: With H, crochet 34″ chain. Sc in 2nd ch from hook and in each ch across, working 3 sc in last ch. Working along opposite edge of foundation chain, work 1 sc in each st. Break off.

FINISHING: Sew each end of handle securely to inside edge of top border.

Musette Shoulder Pouch

This marvelous bag may look complicated, but it is all done in the basic single crochet stitch. You start at the bottom with a circle, using two strands of yarn as one for sturdiness. Then you work up and up. There are four real pockets that button and two straps. Line it in a pretty fabric for a finishing touch.

SIZE: 10″ in diameter and 12″ deep.

MATERIALS: Bear Brand Winsom (acrylic), 4 (2-ounce) skeins parchment No. 370 (color A), 2 skeins tobacco gold No. 340 (B), 2 skeins camel No. 368 (C); aluminum crochet hook size G (or Canadian hook No. 9) *or the size that will give you the correct gauge;* ½ yard 36″-wide cotton twill; 4 buttons ¾″ in diameter.

GAUGE: 4 sts = 1″; 7 rnds = 2″.

Note: Work with 2 strands yarn throughout in colors specified.

Starting at center of bottom with 2 strands A, ch 6. Join with sl st to form ring. **1st rnd:** Work 8 sc in ring. Do not join, but work around spiral fashion and mark beg of rnds. **2nd rnd:** Work 2 sc in each sc around (16 sc). **3rd rnd:** * Sc in next sc, 2 sc in next sc. Repeat from * around (24 sc). **4th rnd:** Sc in each of next 2 sc, 2 sc in next sc. Repeat from * around (32 sc). Continue in this manner, increasing 8 sts on each round, working 1 more st between incs until 15th round has been completed (120 sts). Piece should measure about 4″ from center to outer edge. Work 1 rnd even. **16th rnd:** Sc in each sc around, decreasing 8 sc as evenly spaced as possible. (To dec 1 sc: draw up lp in each of next 2 sc, y o hook and draw through all 3 lps on hook.) Repeat 16th rnd twice more. Work even on 96 sts until piece measures 8" from center. **Next rnd:** Sc in each of next 28 sc, ch 20, skip next 20 sc (first pocket opening), sc in each of remaining 48 sc. **Following rnd:** Sc in each sc and in each ch st around (96 sc). Break off A, attach 1 strand each of B and C. Work even for 3½". **Next rnd:** Sc in each of next 4 sc, ch 20, skip next 20 sc (2nd pocket opening), sc in each of next 28 sc, ch 20, skip next 20 sc (3rd pocket opening), sc in each of remaining 24 sc. **Following rnd:** Sc in each sc and in each ch st around. Drop B and C, attach 2 strands A. Work in stripe pattern for 3½", alternating 1 rnd A, then 1 rnd B and C held together. **Next rnd:** Continuing in stripe pattern, sc in each of next 74 sc, ch 20, skip next 20 sc, sc in last 2 sc (4th pocket opening). **Following rnd:** Sc in each sc and in each ch st around (96 sc).

FIRST STRAP: Continue in stripe pattern as established. Sc in each of next 7 sc; ch 1, turn. **Next row:** Sc in each sc across; ch 1, turn. Repeat last row until piece measures 22". Break off.

SECOND STRAP: Skip next 17 sts along last round on pouch edge. With corresponding color, form lp on hook and sc in each of next 7 sc. Complete as for first strap.

POCKET FLAP FOR FIRST POCKET OPENING: 1st row: With right side facing you, using 2 strands A, sc in each st along upper edge of pocket opening (20 sc); ch 1, turn. **2nd row:** Sc in each sc across; ch 1, turn. Repeat 2nd row once more. **4th row:** Dec 1 sc, sc in each of next 7 sc, ch 2, skip 2 sc (buttonhole), sc in next 7 sc, dec 1 sc; ch 1, turn. **5th row:** Dec 1 sc, sc in each st across to within last 2 sc, dec 1 sc (16 sc); ch 1, turn. Repeat 5th row once more (14 sc). Break off. With right side facing you, using A, work 1 row sc evenly spaced along free edges of flap. Break off. Sew button in place underneath buttonhole on flap.

Working in color patterns as established, work remaining pocket flaps as for first flap.

With right side facing you, using A, work 1 row sc around each side of straps and along top edge of pouch.

LINING: From twill, cut one circle 10" in diameter, one rectangle 13" x 26", and eight 5½"-squares. Allowing ½" for seam allowances and with right sides together, sew two squares together along 3 sides for pocket, leaving 1 side open and curving seams at corners. Insert pocket in first pocket opening and sew in place, turning raw edges under.

Make 3 more pockets in same manner.

With right sides together, seam short ends of large rectangle to form cylinder. With right sides together, sew circle to one end of cylinder. Insert lining in bag and sew in place, turning raw edges under.

Following photograph, sew ends of straps in place.

Four Fluffy Bags

To go with any outfit from sporty to dressy. In rug yarn mixed with mohair for a sturdy bag with a furry feel to it. The stitches are quick and easy. The bags all have gussets to guarantee plenty of room inside.

Gray Saddlebag

SIZE: Approximately 12" x 13".
MATERIALS: Aunt Lydia's heavy rug yarn (75% rayon, 25% cotton), 2 (70-yard) skeins steel gray No. 260; 2 (50-gram) balls gray mohair; aluminum crochet hook size (letter) I (or Canadian hook No. 7) *or the size that will give you the correct gauge;* two 2" plastic or metal rings.

GAUGE: 11 sc = 4"; 6 rows = 2½".

Note: Always work in back loop only of each stitch.

Entire bag is worked with 1 strand each of rug yarn and mohair held together.

FRONT: Starting at top edge, ch 25 to measure 8½". **1st row (right side):** Sc in 2nd ch from hook and in each ch across (24 sc); ch 1, turn. **2nd row:** Sc in each sc across; ch 1, turn. Repeat 2nd row until piece measures 3" from beg.

To Shape Bottom: Next row: Work 2 sc in first sc, sc in each st across, working 2 sc in last sc (1 sc inc at beg and end of row—26 sts); ch 1, turn. Inc 1 sc at beg and end of row every 2" twice more (30 sc). Piece should measure 7". Work 2 rows even. **Next row:** Draw up a lp in each of first 2 sc, y o hook, draw through all 3 lps on hook (1 sc dec), work sc in each st across to within last 2 sc, dec 1 sc (28 sc). Dec 1 sc at beg and end of row every 1" 3 times more (22 sc). Piece should measure about 10" from beg.

BACK: Work as for front.

GUSSET: Ch 6. **1st row:** Sc in 2nd ch from hook and in each ch across (5 sc). Work as for 2nd row of bag front for 4" for an extension that will slide through ring at top of bag. **Next row:** Sc across, increasing 1 sc at beg and end of row. Mark this row with pin. Continue to inc 1 sc at beg and end of row every 4 rows 3 times more (13 sts). Work even on 13 sc until piece measures 13 rows less than measurement around 2 sides and bottom of a bag piece. Dec 1 sc at beg and end of next row, then every 4th row 3 times more (5 sc). Mark last row with pin. Work even for 4" for ring extension. Break off.

With wrong sides of bag front and gusset facing, sl st pieces together, working in each st around from gusset marker to gusset marker. Break off.

Sl st bag back to opposite edge of gusset in same manner. Break off.

FLAP: With right side of bag back facing you, work sc in each st across top edge of back (24 sc); ch 1, turn. Work even until flap measures 7" from beg. Dec 1 st at beg and end of next 5 rows (14 sc). Break off.

With right side of flap facing you, attach yarns at beg of flap and work a row of reverse sc (work from *left to right*—see diagram, p. 144) around entire edge of flap. Break off.

Slip gusset extension through each ring and sew ends of gussets to inside of bag.

STRAP: Ch 4. **1st row:** Sc in 2nd ch from hook and in each of next 2 ch; ch 1, turn. **2nd row:** Sc in each of 3 sc; ch 1, turn. Repeat last row until strap measures approximately 41" or desired length. Break off.

FINISHING: Slide one end of strap through ring, fold over 1" of strap and sew in place. Attach other end of strap to other ring in same manner.

Line bag (see note below) and sew snap on flap if desired.

Note on Lining Bags: The four bags shown are not lined, but linings can be added very easily if desired. You will need ⅜ yard of 45"-wide fabric for each bag. Cut fabric pieces the size and shape of bag front, back (including flap if desired), and gusset, adding ½" for seams. Stitch pieces together, wrong side out. Insert in bag and turn in lining seam around top of bag and around flap; blindstitch to bag.

sures 7½". Do not break off. Place markers at beg and end of last row.

FLAP: Continue to work even until back and flap together measure 15" from beg. Break off.

COMBINATION STRAP-GUSSET: Crochet chain to measure 50". **1st rnd:** Sc in 2nd ch from hook and in each ch across one side of chain, working 3 sc in last ch; then work sc in each st along opposite side of ch, working 3 sc in last st; join with sl st to first sc. **2nd rnd:** Ch 1, sc in each sc to first 3-sc group, work 2 sc in next sc, sc in next sc, 2 sc in next sc, work sc in each sc to next 3-sc group, work 2 sc in next sc, sc in next sc, 2 sc in last sc; join. Break off.

BUCKLE STRAP: Crochet chain to measure 29". Complete as for strap-gusset.

FINISHING: Sew ends of strap-gusset together to form ring. With wrong sides facing, place strap-gusset seam at center of lower edge of front. Pin lower edge and sides of front to one edge of strap-gusset. Join pieces with a row of sl st along pinned edge. Break off. Join other edge of strap-gusset to back, between markers, in same manner, leaving flap free.

Place one end of buckle strap at top edge of front and pin in place down center of front, across bottom of gusset and up center of back and flap, leaving about 5" of strap extending beyond flap. Sew strap in place. Sew buckle on strap on bag front and slip 5" extension at other end through it as shown in photograph.

Line bag if desired (see note on page 150).

Black Buckle-Strap Bag

SIZE: Approximately 8½" x 12".

MATERIALS: Aunt Lydia's heavy rug yarn (75% rayon, 25% cotton), 2 (70-yard) skeins black; 2 (50-gram) balls black mohair; aluminum crochet hook size (letter) I (or Canadian hook No. 7) *or the size that will give you the correct gauge;* brass buckle with 1½"-wide opening.

GAUGE: 5 sc = 2"; 2 rows = 1".

Note: Use 1 strand each of rug yarn and mohair held together.

FRONT: Starting at top edge, ch 31 to measure 12". **1st row:** Sc in 2nd ch from hook and in each ch across (30 sc); ch 1, turn. **2nd row:** Sc in each sc across; ch 1, turn. Repeat 2nd row until piece measures 7½". Break off.

BACK: Work as for front until piece mea-

Brown Granny-Square Bag

SIZE: Approximately 11" square.

MATERIALS: Aunt Lydia's heavy rug yarn (75% rayon, 25% cotton), 2 (70-yard) skeins wood brown No. 242; 2 (50-gram) balls dark brown mohair; aluminum crochet hook size (letter) I (or Canadian hook No. 7) *or the size that will give you the correct gauge;* two 2" plastic or metal rings.

GAUGE: One granny square measures about 10".

GRANNY SQUARE: Using 1 strand each of mohair and rug yarn held together, ch 6. Join with sl st to form ring. **1st rnd:** Ch 3, work 2 dc in ring, (ch 1, 3 dc in ring) 3 times (12 dc, counting ch-3 as 1 dc); ch 1, join with sl st to top of ch-3. **2nd rnd:** Sl st in each of next 2 dc and in next ch-1 sp; ch 3, in same sp work 2 dc, ch 1 and 3 dc (first corner made); * ch 1, skip 3 dc, in next sp work 3 dc, ch 1 and 3 dc (another corner made). Repeat from * twice more; ch 1, join to top of ch-3. **3rd rnd:** Sl st in each of next 2 dc and in next ch-1 sp; work a first corner in same sp, * ch 1, skip 3 dc, work 3 dc in next ch-1 sp (shell made), ch 1, work corner in next corner sp. Repeat from * twice more; skip 3 dc, ch 1, work shell in next sp, ch 1; join. **4th rnd:** Sl st in each of next 2 dc and in ch-1 sp, work first corner in same sp, * (ch 1, skip 3 dc, work shell in next sp) twice; ch 1, work corner in next corner sp. Repeat from * twice more; (ch 1, shell in next sp) twice; ch 1; join. **5th rnd:** Sl st in each of next 2 dc and in ch-1 sp, work first corner in same sp, * (ch 1, shell in next sp) 3 times; ch 1, work corner in next corner sp. Repeat from * twice more; (ch 1, shell in next sp) 3 times; ch 1; join. **6th rnd:** Sl st in each of next 2 dc and in ch-1 sp, work first corner in same sp, * (ch 1, shell in next sp) 4 times; ch 1, work corner in next corner sp. Repeat from * twice more; (ch 1, shell in next sp) 4 times; ch 1; join. Break off. **7th rnd:** With right side facing you, using rug yarn only, sl st in any corner sp of square. Sl st in back lp only of each st around; turn. **8th rnd:** Sl st in top lp of each st around 3 sides of square only. Break off. Unfinished side is top edge of bag. Piece should measure about 10" across top edge.

Work a second piece in same manner.

GUSSET: Using mohair and rug yarn, crochet a chain to measure along 2 sides and lower edge of a bag piece, plus 4". **1st rnd:** Sc in 2nd ch from hook and in each ch across to within last ch, work 3 sc in last ch, work sc in each st along opposite side of chain, working 3 sc in last st; join. Break off. Center gusset along both sides and bottom of a bag piece. About 3" of each end of gusset should extend above top edge of bag. These extensions will be folded over rings later. Mark with pins the start of each extension.

With wrong sides of bag piece and gusset together, working with mohair and yarn from marked st to marked st and working in back lp only of each st, sl st gusset to bag piece along sides and bottom. Break off. Sl st other bag piece to other edge of gusset in same manner. Break off. Fold extension on each side over ring and sew end on inside of bag.

STRAP: Using mohair and rug yarn, crochet 35" chain or desired length. Work as for first rnd of gusset. Break off. Slide one end of strap through a ring; fold over 2" of strap to wrong side and sew in place. Attach other end of strap to other ring in same manner.

BUTTON: Starting at center with rug yarn only, ch 4. Join with sl st to form ring. **1st rnd:** Work 8 sc in ring. **2nd rnd:** Work 2 sc in each sc around. **3rd rnd:** Sl st in each sc around. Do not break off. Stuff button with small amount yarn. **4th rnd:** * Sc in next sc, skip next sc. Repeat from * around. Repeat 4th rnd until button opening is closed. Break off.

FINISHING: With right side facing you, using rug yarn only and working in back lp of each st, work a row of reverse sc (work from *left to right*—see diagram, p. 144) along top edge of one side of bag. Break off. Sew button to center of row. Then, with right side facing you, work row of reverse sc along top edge to center of other side of bag, ch 10 for button loop, work reverse sc in each st along remainder of top edge. Break off. Line bag if desired (see note on page 150).

White Shell-Stitch Bag

SIZE: Approximately 9" x 11".

MATERIALS: Aunt Lydia's heavy rug yarn (75% rayon, 25% cotton), 2 (70-yard) skeins natural No. 24; 2 (50-gram) balls natural-color mohair; aluminum crochet hook size (letter) I (or Canadian hook No. 7) *or the size that will give you the correct gauge;* 3" gold frog for clasp.

GAUGE: 1 shell = 1"; 2 rows = 1".

Note: Use 1 strand each of rug yarn and mohair held together.

FRONT: Starting at lower edge, ch 29 to measure 10". **1st row:** Work 3 sc in 2nd ch from hook (shell made), * skip 2 ch, 3 sc in next ch. Repeat from * across (10 shells); ch 1, turn. **2nd row:** * 3 sc in center sc of next shell. Repeat from * across (10 shells). Repeat 2nd row until piece measures 8". Do not break off. **Edging: 1st row:** Sl st evenly along one side, lower edge, and other side of front; ch 1, turn. **2nd row:** Sl st in each sl st around. Break off.

BACK: Work as for front until piece measures 8". Do not break off. Place markers at beg and end of last row.

FLAP: Continue in pattern until back and flap together measure 13½" from beg. Break off. **Back Edging:** Attach yarns at one marker. **1st row:** Sl st evenly along one side, lower edge and other side to 2nd marker (do not work around flap); ch 1, turn. **2nd row:** Sl st in each sl st around. Break off. **Flap Edging:** With right side facing, work row of reverse sc (work from *left to right*—see diagram, p. 144) around flap edges. Break off.

COMBINATION STRAP-GUSSET: Crochet a chain to measure 58". Sc in 2nd ch from hook and in each ch across, working 3 sc in last ch; then work sc in each st along other side of ch, working 3 sc in last st; join with sl st to first sc. Break off.

FINISHING: Sew ends of strap together to form ring. With wrong sides facing, place strap-gusset seam at center of lower edge of front. Pin lower edge and sides of front to one edge of strap-gusset. Join pieces with a row of sl st along pinned edge, working through back lp only on strap-gusset. Break off. Join other edge of strap-gusset to back, between markers, in same manner; leave flap free.

Sew frog to center of flap and bag front. Line bag if desired (see note on p. 150).

Carry-All Shopping Net

Worked in half double crochet. Scrunches up to almost nothing when not in use.

SIZE: 13" deep x 13" wide at base, without stretching.

MATERIALS: J. & P. Coats Knit-Cro-Sheen, 1 (250-yard) ball ecru No. 61; steel crochet hook No. 6 (or Canadian hook No. 3) *or the size that will give you the correct gauge.*

GAUGE: 10 ch sts on lps = 1".

FRONT: Starting at upper edge, ch 28 loosely to measure about 3½". **1st row:** H dc in 4th ch from hook and in each ch across (26 h dc, counting turning ch as 1 h dc); ch 3, turn. **2nd row:** Skip first h dc, h dc in each h dc across; ch 8, turn. **3rd row:** Skip first h dc, sc in next h dc, * ch 8, sc in next h dc. Repeat from * across (25 lps); ch 8, turn. **4th row:** Sc in first lp, * ch 8, sc in next lp. Repeat from * across (25 lps); ch 8, turn. Repeat 4th row until piece measures 13" from beg. Break off.

BACK: Work as for front.

TO JOIN: Attach thread with sl st on side edge of front 7" from top. Ch 4, sc in corresponding lp on back; working toward bottom of bag, * ch 4, sc in next lp on front, ch 4, sc in corresponding lp on back. Repeat from * across side, bottom, and opposite side to within 7″ of upper edge. Break off.

HANDLES: Attach thread in 3rd st from one corner of upper edge of front; crochet 18″ chain, sl st in 3rd st from other corner of upper edge of front, skip 1 st, sl st in corner st; turn. **1st row:** H dc in each ch across, sl st in opposite corner st; turn. **2nd row:** Sc in each h dc across, sl st evenly along side opening to upper edge of back. Work other handle and edging along other side opening in same manner. Break off.

Fluffy Seven-Footer

Scarf, worked in rich tones of copper, burgundy, brass, green, and autumn mist Orlon acrylic, has generous fringe of mohair-blend yarn.

SIZE: About 7′ long without fringe.
MATERIALS: Bear Brand Winsom acrylic yarn, 1 (2-ounce) skein each copper No. 382 (color A), burgundy No. 8 (B), brass No. 384 (C), Scotch green No. 90 (D), and autumn mist (tan) No. 315 (E); Bucilla Melody, 50% mohair/50% acrylic yarn, 1 (100-yard) ball champagne No. 4 (F); aluminum crochet hook size H (or Canadian hook No. 8) *or the size that will give you the correct gauge.*
GAUGE: 7 sc = 2″.

Starting along center with A, ch 279 to measure about 80″. **1st row:** Sc in 2nd ch from hook and in each ch across (278 sc); ch 4, turn. **2nd row:** Skip first sc, tr in next sc, * ch 2, skip 2 sc, tr in each of next 2 sc. Repeat from * across (70 pairs of tr, counting turning ch as 1 tr); ch 1, turn. **3rd row:** Sc in each tr and in each ch across. Break off. Center unit completed.

Mark beg of each rnd, moving marker on each rnd. **4th rnd:** With right side facing you, with B, work sc, ch 1 and sc in first sc (corner made), ch 2, sc in next sc, * ch 2, skip 1 st, sc in next st *. Repeat from * to * across to within last 2 sc, ch 2, skip 1 sc, corner in next sc; continuing around, ch 2, sc into end of center unit, ch 2, corner in next st, ch 2, sc in next st. Repeat from * to * to within last 2 sts, ch 2, skip 1 st, corner in next st, ch 2, sc into end of unit, ch 2; join with sl st in first sc. **5th rnd:** ** Sc in next corner ch-1 sp, ch 5, sc in next ch-2 sp (corner lp made), * ch 5, skip next ch-2 sp, sc in next ch-2 sp *. Repeat from * to * up to next corner, ch 5, sc in corner ch-1 sp (corner lp), ch 4, skip next ch-2 sp, sc in next sc, ch 4, skip next ch-2 sp **. Repeat from ** to ** once more; join.

6th rnd: Work 3 sl sts and 1 sc in first ch-5 corner lp, ch 3, sc in same lp for first corner lp, * ch 3, sc in next lp *. Repeat from * to * across, ending in next corner lp; work 2nd corner lp. Repeat from * to * across end, ending next corner lp; work 3rd corner lp. Repeat from * to * across, ending in next corner lp; work 4th corner lp, (ch 3, sc in next lp) twice, ch 3; join with sl st in first sc. Break off. Piece should measure about 2¾" wide. **7th rnd:** Make lp on hook with C, y o, * work 4-dc shell in corner lp, work shell in each lp across up to next corner lp, work shell in corner lp, 4 sc in each of next 3 lps. Repeat from * once more; join. Break off. Mark 2nd dc of each corner shell. **8th rnd:** With D work 1 sc in each st around; join. Break off. **9th rnd:** Make lp on hook with A, y o, work 3 dc in sc above a marked st, 3 dc in next sc (2-shell corner made), work 1 dc in each sc around, working 2-shell corner in each corner as before; join. Break off. **10th rnd:** Make lp on hook with D, y o, ** work h dc in sp between 2 corner shells, ch 1, h dc in next sp between 2 dc, * ch 1, skip 2 dc, h dc in next sp between 2 dc *. Repeat from * to * to within sp between next 2 corner shells **. Repeat from ** to ** three times more, ch 1; join. **11th rnd:** Sl st in next ch-1 sp, ch 2 (counts as 1 h dc), h dc in same sp, work 2 h dc in each sp around; join. Break off.

EDGING: With one strand each of E and F held together, work sc evenly around entire piece; join. Break off.

FRINGE: Cut three 20" strands each of E and F. Hold together and fold in half to form lp at one end. Working across end of scarf, pull lp through 1 sc on last rnd, draw ends through lp and pull to form knot. Make fringe in this manner in each sc across both ends of scarf.

Espadrilles

Did you ever think of making your own? Now you can. These fashionable sandals have triple-thick soles crocheted of jute twine and colorful rug-yarn uppers.

SIZE: Width is medium; length is adjustable.
MATERIALS: Polished jute twine (available at variety stores), 6 (110-foot) balls for each pair of sandal soles; Aunt Lydia's heavy rug yarn (75% rayon, 25% cotton), 1 (70-yard) skein in each of the following colors for sandal uppers: *red-and-blue sandals,* national blue No. 715 (color A), phantom red No. 140 (B); *orange sandals,* burnt orange No. 320 (color A), sunset No. 550 (B); *candy-striped sandals,* chartreuse No. 296 (color A), lavender No. 249 (B), cerise No. 247 (C), and turquoise icing No. 218 (D); aluminum crochet hook size F (or Canadian hook No. 10) *or the size that will give you the correct gauge;* tapestry needle.

GAUGE: 4 sc = 1" for jute and rug yarn.
TO DETERMINE SOLE SIZE: For the number of stitches in starting chain, measure exact length of foot (not shoe) in inches and multiply by 3. After multiplying, drop any fraction of ½ or less; add 1 for any fraction over ½. This is the number of stitches you will need for starting chain. For example: If your foot measures 8½", 8½ x 3 = 25½. Since the fraction is ½, drop it; then chain 25 for 8½".

SOLE: With jute, crochet chain of desired length. Place a marker in center of chain. **1st rnd:** Work 3 sc in 2nd ch from hook, sc in each ch to marker, work dc in each remaining ch to within last ch, work 5 dc in last ch (toe); dc in each ch st along opposite side of chain to marker (do not remove marker as it will be needed later), work sc in each remaining st, ending with sc in base of ch st where the first 3 sc on rnd were worked (heel). **2nd rnd:** Ch 1, work 2 sc in each of next 2 sc, sc in each st to within group of 5 dc at tip of toe, work sc in next dc and mark st just made, sc in same dc, 2 sc in each of next 4 dc, sc in each st back to heel. **3rd rnd:** Ch 1, work 2 sc in first sc, sc in next sc, 2 sc in next sc, sc in each sc to within marked sc, (2 sc in next sc, sc in next sc) 5 times; sc in each sc back to heel. **4th rnd:** Ch 1, sc in each sc to within marker on first rnd, dc in each sc to within 5 sc of tip of toe, (2 sc in next sc, sc in next sc) 5 times; dc in each sc to marker on first rnd, sc in each sc back to heel; sl st in first sc. Break off.

Work second sole; do not break off.

TO JOIN SOLES: Hold soles tog, with second sole on top. Sl st tog around outside edge, working into both loops of each st of top sole, and into front loop of each st of bottom sole. Break off.

HEEL INSERT: Ch half of starting chain of sole. **1st row:** Sc in 2nd ch from hook and in each ch across to within last ch, work 3 sc in last ch and mark last sc made, work sc in base of each ch along opposite side of chain; ch 1, turn. **2nd row:** Work sc in each sc to marker, work 2 sc in marked st, sc in next st, 2 sc in next st and mark last sc made, sc in each sc along opposite side of heel; ch 1, turn. **3rd row:** Sc in each sc to marker, 2 sc in marked st, (sc in next st, 2 sc in next st) twice, and mark last sc made, sc along opposite side of heel; ch 1, turn. **4th row:** Sc across to marker, 2 sc in marked st, (sc in next st, 2 sc in next st) 3 times; sc across to heel. Break off.

Make second heel in same manner but do not break off. Sl st heels together as for soles, then sl st heel to top sole.

Make a third sole; do not break off. Sl st to top sole and heel insert. Break off.

Red-and-Blue Sandals

HEEL STRAP: With A, ch 50 to measure 13″. **1st row (right side):** Dc in 4th ch from hook and in each ch across (48 dc, counting ch-3 as 1 dc); ch 3, turn. **2nd row:** Skip first dc, dc in each dc across. Break off A; attach B; ch 1, turn. **3rd row:** Sc in each dc across. Break off. **4th row:** With right side facing you, attach B to base of last A st of foundation chain, sc in each st along foundation chain. Break off.

CROSS-STRAPS: With A, ch 9. **1st row:** Dc in 4th ch from hook and in each ch across (7 dc, counting ch-3 as 1 dc); ch 3, turn. **2nd row:** Skip first dc, working in back loop only of each st work dc in each dc across; ch 3, turn. **3rd row:** Skip first dc, working in top loop only of each st work dc in each dc across; ch 3, turn. Repeat 2nd and 3rd rows until strap measures 6". Break off. Using A, work a row of sc, evenly spaced, along both long edges as for heel strap. Make another cross-strap.

Sew end of one cross-strap to edge of sole about 1½" from tip of toe. Sew end of other cross-strap to opposite edge of sole. Place foot on sole, cross straps over instep and mark edges of sole for placement of loose ends of straps. Sew ends in place. Sew heel strap to cross-straps.

Orange Sandals

FRONT UPPER: Starting at toe with A, ch 7. **1st row (right side):** Sc in 2nd ch from hook and in each ch across (6 sc); ch 1, turn. **2nd row (inc row):** Work 2 sc in first sc, sc in each sc to last sc, work 2 sc in last sc (8 sc). Break off A; attach B; ch 1, turn. **3rd row:** Working in back loop only of each st, sc in each sc across; ch 1, turn. **4th row:** Repeat 2nd row (10 sc). Repeat 3rd and 2nd rows 4 times more (18 sts), alternating A and B every 2 rows. **13th row:** Repeat 3rd row, placing a marker in 9th and 10th sc of this row. Break off.

Tab: 14th row: With A, sc in each marked sc of last row; ch 1, turn. **15th and 16th rows:** Sc in each sc; ch 1, turn. Break off.

HEEL SECTION: Starting at lower edge with A, ch 41 to measure 11". **1st row (right side):** Sc in 2nd ch from hook and in each ch across (40 sc); ch 1, turn. **2nd row (dec row):** Draw up a loop in each of first 2 sc, y o, draw through all 3 loops on hook (1 sc dec), sc in each sc across to within last 2 sc, dec 1 sc (38 sc). Break off A; attach B; ch 1, turn. **3rd row:** Working in back loop only of each st, sc in each sc across; ch 1, turn. **4th row:** Repeat 2nd row. Break off B; attach A; ch 1, turn. Repeat 3rd and 2nd rows twice more (32 sts), alternating A and B every 2 rows. Do not break off at end of last row but ch 21 for strap to go around front of ankle. Turn. Sc in 2nd ch from hook and in each ch across. Break off B; attach A and sl st last sc to first sc of row so that piece forms circle. Place marker in center of foundation chain of strap. **9th rnd:** Sc in each sc around. Break off.

With right sides of heel section and front upper facing, sew tab to marked center on ankle strap.

Place upper on top of sole. With jute, sc upper to sole, working in both loops around upper and 1 loop around sole. With A, sc around side openings.

Candy-Striped Sandals

FRONT UPPER: Starting at toe, with A, ch 9. **1st row:** Sc in 2nd ch from hook and in each ch across (8 sc); ch 1, turn. **2nd row (inc row):** Work 2 sc in first sc, sc in each sc to last sc, work 2 sc in last sc (10 sc). Break off A; attach B; ch 1, turn. **3rd row:** Working in back loop only of each st, sc in each sc across; ch 1, turn. **4th row:** Repeat 2nd row. Break off B; attach C; ch 1, turn. Repeat 3rd and 2nd rows 5 times (22 sc), working 2 rows each of C, D, A, B, and C (instep edge). Break off.

HEEL SECTION: Starting at lower edge with B, ch 43 to measure 12½". **1st row:** Sc in 2nd ch from hook and in each ch across (42 sc); ch 1, turn. **2nd row (inc row):** 2 sc in first sc, sc in each sc across to last sc, 2 sc in last sc (44 sc). Break off B; attach A; ch 1, turn. **3rd row:** Working in back loop only of each st, sc in each sc across; ch 1, turn. **4th row:** Repeat 2nd row (46 sc); break off A; attach D; ch 1, turn. **5th and 6th rows:** Repeat 3rd and 2nd rows (48 sc). Break off.

Sew shaped ends of heel section to instep edge of front upper as shown.

Place completed upper on sole about ½" from tip of toe. With jute, sc upper to sole, working through both loops around upper and one loop around sole.

Lacy Cobweb Shawl

What a lovely way to use up leftover yarn in different colors and weights. Go around and around to make an airy wheel of color. Fold in half to wear.

SIZE: Circular shawl measures approximately 62" in diameter.

MATERIALS: 16 ounces of yarn in various weights, such as fingering, sports, knitting worsted, and mohair. You can use your leftover yarns to make this shawl. The colors in our shawl are lavender, gold, dusty pink, olive, aqua, forest green, gray-blue, salmon, blue-green heather, purple heather, rich purple, baby blue, green heather, yellow, skipper blue, and orange; aluminum crochet hook size K (or Canadian hook No. 4).

Note: It is important to alternate the different weights of yarn on each round as you work so that the shawl will hang properly. Occasionally two fine yarns of different colors were used together to achieve a heather effect and a heavier weight.

If you run out of a color before completing a round, just finish the round in another color of the same weight yarn.

GAUGE: Work very loosely for a cobwebby effect.

Starting at center, ch 5. Join with sl st to form ring. **1st rnd:** Work 8 sc in ring; sl st in first sc. **2nd rnd:** Ch 3, work dc in same place as sl st, work 2 dc in each sc around (16 dc, counting ch-3 as 1 dc); join with sl st to top of ch-3. (**Note:** Always count ch-3 at beg of rnds as 1 dc).

3rd rnd: Ch 3, work dc in same place as sl st, work 2 dc in each dc around (32 dc); join. **4th rnd:** Ch 3, dc in each dc around, increasing 16 dc as evenly spaced as possible (48 dc); join. Piece should measure about 7" in diameter.

5th through 8th rnds: Continue to dc in each dc around, increasing 16 dc as evenly spaced as possible on each rnd; join (112 dc at end of 8th rnd). **9th rnd:** Ch 3, dc in each dc around, increasing 8 dc as evenly spaced as possible (120 dc); join.

10th through 13th rnds: Ch 3, dc in each dc around; join. **14th rnd:** Ch 4, tr in each dc around; join to top of ch-4. **15th rnd:** Ch 3, dc in each tr around; join. **16th and 17th rnds:** Dc in each dc around; join.

18th rnd: Ch 3, dc in same place as sl st, ch 1, 2 dc in same place (shell made), * skip next dc, in next dc work 2 dc, ch 1 and 2 dc (another shell). Repeat from * around, skip last dc (60 shells); join. Break off. **19th rnd:** Attach new color with sl st to ch-1 of first shell, ch 3, work shell of 6 dc in same place, * work shell of 7 dc in ch-1 sp of next shell. Repeat from * around; join. Break off. **20th rnd:** Attach new color to 4th dc of first shell, ch 3, work shell of 5 dc, ch 1 and 6 dc in same place, * work shell of 6 dc, ch 1 and 6 dc in 4th dc of next shell. Repeat from * around; join. Break off. **21st rnd:** Attach new color to ch-1 of first shell, ch 3, work shell of 6 dc, ch 1 and 7 dc in same place, * work shell of 7 dc, ch 1 and 7 dc in ch-1 sp of next shell. Repeat from * around; join. Break off. Work 4 more rnds of shells in this manner, working shells of 8 dc, ch 1 and 8 dc on first rnd, shells of 9 dc, ch 1 and 9 dc on 2nd rnd, shells of 10 dc, ch 1 and 10 dc on 3rd rnd and shells of 11 dc, ch 1 and 11 dc on 4th rnd.

Gold and Silver Circular Shawl

Precious gold and silver circular shawl, deeply fringed, is folded in half here, worked in luxurious metallic yarns.

SIZE: About 52" in diameter without fringe.
MATERIALS: Columbia-Minerva Camelot, 12 (1-ounce) balls each gold and silver for shawl, 8 balls each gold and silver for fringe; aluminum crochet hook size H (or Canadian hook No. 8) *or the size that will give you the correct gauge.*
GAUGE: 2 sps = 1"; 2 rnds = 1".

Starting at center with gold, ch 8. Join with sl st to form ring. **1st rnd:** Ch 4, (dc in ring, ch 1) 11 times. Join with sl st in 3rd ch of ch-4 (12 sps). Drop gold; attach silver. **2nd rnd:** Ch 4, dc in next dc, inc 1 sp over next sp as follows: * ch 1, dc in next sp, ch 1, dc in next dc (1 sp inc), inc over next sp, ch 1, dc in next dc. Repeat from * twice more; inc over next sp, ch 1, dc in next sp, ch 1; join (20 sps). Drop silver; pick up gold. **3rd rnd:** Ch 4, * dc in next dc, ch 1. Repeat from * around, increasing 8 sps as evenly spaced as possible; join (28 sps). Alternating colors on every rnd, repeat 3rd rnd 3 times more (52 sps). Continue in pattern, increasing 9 sps on each rnd until 40 rnds have been completed in all (358 sps), then repeat

3rd rnd 12 times more (454 sps). Break off.

FRINGE: For tassel, cut twelve 16" strands of silver. Hold together and fold in half to form lp at one end. Pull lp through one sp on last rnd of shawl, draw ends through lp and pull to form knot. * Skip next sp on last rnd, make gold tassel in next sp, skip next sp, make silver tassel in next sp. Repeat from * around.

Delicate Triangular Shawl

Light and lacy in chain loops and treble crochet, worked loosely with a size K hook. Fringe consists of naturally twisting loops. Three strands of turquoise and one strand of ecru are held together throughout.

SIZE: About 52" x 52" x 68" without fringe.
MATERIALS: J. & P. Coats Knit-Cro-Sheen, 12 (175-yard) balls parakeet No. 132-A; Clark's Big Ball mercerized crochet cotton size 30, 2 (350-yard) balls ecru No. 61; aluminum crochet hook size K (or Canadian hook No. 4) *or the size that will give you the correct gauge.*
GAUGE: 4 tr = 3"; 2 rows = 3".
Note: Work with 3 strands Knit-Cro-Sheen and 1 strand crochet cotton held together throughout.
SHAWL: Starting at center back neck edge, ch 12 loosely to measure about 6½". **1st row:** Work tr in 6th ch from hook as follows: Enlarge lp on hook to 1"; with 2 fingers of right hand, pinch lp just below hook to keep it in place; y o twice, insert hook in st and draw up 1" lp, (y o, draw through 2 lps on hook) twice. You now have approximately 1" strand between lp at end of hook and lp you are holding; y o and draw through both lps on hook. This makes an elongated st between tr posts. (Make all tr's in this manner.) Make 2 more tr in same ch st, 1 tr in next ch, 2 tr in next ch, ch 1, 2 tr in next ch, 1 tr in next ch, 3 tr in next ch, 1 tr in last ch (14 tr, counting turning ch as 1 tr); ch 4, turn. **2nd row:** Skip first tr (first long st), 2 tr in each of next 2 tr (work over 2 lps of the long sts), 1 tr in each of next 3 tr, 2 tr in next tr, ch 2, skip next ch-1, 2 tr in next tr, 1 tr in each of next 3 tr, 2 tr in each of next 2 tr, 1 tr in top of turning ch (20 tr); ch 4, turn. **3rd row:** Work 2 tr in first tr and in each of next 2 tr, 1 tr in each of next 7 tr, work a shell of 2 tr, ch 1 and 2 tr in next ch-2 sp (shell made), 1 tr in each of next 7 tr, 2 tr in each of next 2 tr, 3 tr in top of turning ch (32 tr); ch 4, turn. **4th row:** Work 2 tr in first tr and in each of next 2 tr, 1 tr in each of next 13 tr, work shell in ch-1 sp, 1 tr in each of next 13 tr, 2 tr in each of next 2 tr, 3 tr in top of turning ch (44 tr); ch 4, turn. **5th**

row: Skip first tr, 1 tr in next tr, 2 tr in each of next 2 tr, 1 tr in each tr to ch-1 sp, work shell in sp, 1 tr in each tr to within last 4 tr, 2 tr in each of next 2 tr, 1 tr in next tr, tr in turning ch (52 tr); ch 4, turn. Piece should measure about 7½" from beg. Repeat 5th row 5 times more (8 tr increased on each row—92 tr on 10th row). End last row with ch-5, turn.

11th row: Skip first 2 tr, sc in next tr, * ch 5, skip next tr, sc in next tr *. Repeat from * to * to within 1 tr of center ch-1 sp, skip next tr, (ch 5, sc in ch-1 sp) twice; then repeat from * to * across remaining tr's (47 lps); ch 5, turn. **12th row:** Sc in first ch-5 lp, ch 5, sc in same lp, * ch 5, sc in next lp. Repeat from * across to within last lp, (ch 5, sc in last lp) twice; ch 5, turn. **13th row:** Sc in first lp, * ch 5, sc in next lp. Repeat from * across; ch 5, turn. Repeat 12th and 13th rows once more (51 lps), ending last row with ch 1, turn. **16th row:** * Work 2 sc in next lp, ch 1. Repeat from * across, ending with 1 sc in last lp; ch 4, turn. **17th row:** Skip first sc, tr in next ch st and in each sc and ch st across (151 tr); ch 4, turn. **18th row:** Skip first tr, tr in next tr and in each tr across; ch 4, turn. Repeat last row once more, omitting turning ch at end. Do not break off or turn.

PICOT EDGING: Working along side edge of piece, * ch 3, sl st in 2nd ch from hook, ch 2, skip about 1¼" along edge, sc in edge. Repeat from * along edge to first row of shawl, along starting chain of shawl (back neck), and along other side edge to beg of last tr row completed. Do not break off or turn.

TWISTED CHAIN FRINGE: Sl st in first tr at lower edge; * leaving lp on hook and holding onto chain to prevent it from twisting, turn crochet hook once, counterclockwise, so that lp twists; (ch 4, twist hook) 5 times; sc in next tr. Help lp to twist by wrapping it around index finger. Repeat from * across lower edge. Break off.

Baby Doll Bikini

For lazy summer days, a Betsey Johnson original, complete with pink ribbon drawstrings and picot edging all around. Top buttons in back.

SIZES: 6 [8—10—12—14]. Top measures 32" [33"—34"—35"—36"] around bust. Pants measure 33" [34"—35"—36"—37"].

MATERIALS: Coats & Clark's Speed-Cro-Sheen, 7 [7—7—8—8] (100-yard) balls Nu Ecru; steel crochet hook size 0 *or the size that will give you the correct gauge;* 9 yards ⅜"-wide ribbon; 2 buttons ⅝" in diameter.

GAUGE: 5 sts = 1"; 6 rows = 1".

Top

CUP: Starting at center, ch 4. Join with sl st to form ring. **1st rnd:** Work 6 sc in ring. Work around and around, spiral fashion, marking beg of rnds. **2nd rnd:** 2 sc in each sc around. **3rd rnd:** (Sc in next sc, 2 sc in next sc) 6 times. **4th rnd:** (Sc in each of next 2 sc, 2 sc in next sc) 6 times. **5th rnd:** Sc in each sc around, increasing 6 sc as evenly spaced as possible (30 sc). Repeat 5th rnd 4 times more (54 sc). **10th rnd:** Sc in each sc around. **11th rnd:** Sc in each sc around, increasing 4 sc as evenly spaced as possible. Repeat 10th rnd twice more. **(Note:** work more or fewer rows for a larger or smaller cup, increasing as necessary to fit.) Break off. Make another cup in same manner.

CENTER FRONT SECTION: Starting at lower edge, ch 19. **1st row:** Sc in 2nd ch from hook and in each ch across (18 sts); ch 1, turn. **2nd row:** (Insert hook in next st, y o hook and draw lp through) twice, y o hook and draw through all 3 lps on hook (1 sc dec), sc in each sc to within last 2 sts, dec 1 sc over last 2 sc; ch 1, turn. **3rd row:** Sc in each sc across; ch 1, turn. Repeat 2nd and 3rd rows twice more (12 sts), then repeat 3rd row 7 times more. **15th row:** Work 2 sc in first sc, sc in each sc to within last sc, 2 sc in last sc; ch 1, turn. **16th row:** Repeat 3rd row. Repeat 15th and 3rd rows once more, then 15th row once again (18 sts). Break off.

LEFT SIDE AND BACK SECTION: Starting at lower edge, ch 47 [51—56—60—65]. **1st row:** Sc in 2nd ch from hook and in each ch across (46 [50—55—59—64] sts). **2nd row:** Dec 1 sc, sc in each sc across; ch 1, turn. **3rd row:** Sc in each sc to within last 2 sc, dec 1 sc; ch 1, turn. Repeat 2nd and 3rd rows once more (42 [46—51—55—60] sts). **6th row:** Sc in each sc across; ch 1, turn. Repeat 6th row 3 times more. **10th row:** 2 sc in first sc, sc in each sc across; ch 1, turn. Repeat 6th row once. **12th row:** Sc in first sc and in each of next 12 sc; turn. **13th row:** Sl st in first sc, sc in each sc to within last sc, 2 sc in last sc; ch 1, turn. **14th row:** Sc in first sc and in each of next 10 sc; turn. **15th row:** Sl st in first sc, sc in each sc across; ch 1, turn. **16th row:** Sc in first sc and in each of next 8 sc; turn. **17th row:** Repeat 13th row. **18th row:** Sc in first sc and in each of next 6 sc; turn. **19th row:** Repeat 15th row. Break off.

RIGHT SIDE AND BACK SECTION: Work to correspond to left side and back section.

STRAPS: Starting at front end, ch 12. **1st row:** Sc in 2nd ch from hook and in each ch across (11 sc); ch 1, turn. **2nd row:** Dec 1 sc, sc in each sc to within last 2 sc, dec 1 sc; ch 1, turn. **3rd row:** Sc in each sc across; ch 1, turn. Repeat 2nd and 3rd rows twice more (5 sc). Repeat 3rd row until piece measures 15" or desired length. Break off. Make another strap in same manner.

FINISHING: Pin center front section, side and back sections and straps to cups. Try on piece and adjust arrangement of sections if necessary. Sew in place. (Do not sew straps to back section.) **Lower edge:** Starting on wrong side, work 2 rows sc along entire lower edge. Do not break off, but continue around piece as follows:

EDGING: 1st row: With right side facing, * sc in next st, ch 4, sc in 4th ch from hook (picot made), skip about ⅜" along edge. Repeat from * around entire outer edge; join. Break off. Weave ribbon through chain loops of edging along lower edge and along upper edge of each back and side section, continuing along outer edge of each strap. Beginning at center front and leaving 9" ends for bow, weave ribbon through each side of upper edge, continuing along inner edge of each strap. Sew straps to back. Tie bow at center front. Sew buttons 1" in from left back edge. Button through corresponding chain loops on right back edge.

Pants

BACK: Starting at crotch, ch 11 [11—12—12—11]. **1st row:** Sc in 2nd ch from hook and in each ch across (10 [10—11—11—10] sc); ch 1, turn. **2nd row:** Work 2 sc in first sc, sc in each sc to within last sc, 2 sc in last sc; ch 1, turn. Repeat last row 39 [40—41—42—44] times more (90 [92—95—97—100] sc). Piece should measure about 6¾" [7"—7¼"—7½"—7¾"] from beg. **Next row:** Sc in each sc across; ch 1, turn. Repeat last row 14 times more, decreasing 1 sc at beg and end of row every ⅔". Break off.

FRONT: Starting at crotch, ch 11 [11—12—12—11]. **1st row:** Sc in 2nd ch from hook and in each ch across (10 [10—11—11—10] sc); ch 1, turn. **2nd row:** Sc in each sc across; ch 1, turn. **3rd row:** Work even. **4th row:** Work 2 sc in first sc, sc in each sc to within last sc, 2 sc in last sc; ch 1, turn. Repeat 2nd row 3 times more. **8th row:** Repeat 4th row. Work even for 9 rows. * Repeat 4th row once. Repeat 2nd row twice. Repeat from * twice more. Then repeat 4th row 16 [17—18—19—21] times (52 [54—57—59—62] sts). Piece should measure about 7" [7¼"—7½"—7¾"—8"] from beg. **Next row:** With a 2nd ball of yarn, ch 15, sl st to ch-1 at beg of row just worked; break off. With first ball of yarn, ch 16. Sc in 2nd ch from hook and in each of next 14 ch, sc in each of next 52 [54—57—59—62] sc, sc in each of next 15 ch (82 [84—87—89—92] sc); ch 1, turn. **Following row:** Sc in each sc across; ch 1, turn. Repeat last row 13 times more, decreasing 1 sc at beg and end of row every ⅔". Break off.

FINISHING: Sew side and crotch seams. Work 1 row of sc around each leg opening. Work edging around upper edge and around each leg opening. Weave ribbon in and out chain loops of edging, leaving 9" ends on each side of leg openings and 9" ends at center front of upper edge. Tie bows.

For Children

Clothes

Baby Helmet

Worked around and around in simple stitches in a lovely starlike pattern. In baby or fingering yarn.

SIZE: Infant to 6 months.

MATERIALS: Fingering or baby yarn (wool or Orlon acrylic), 1 ounce blue; aluminum crochet hook size F (or Canadian hook No. 10), *or the size that will give you the correct gauge;* 2 buttons ½" in diameter.

GAUGE: 11 sc rnds = 2".

SIDE SECTION: Starting at center, ch 3. Join with sl st to form ring. Right side of work is always facing you. **1st rnd:** Ch 3, work 11 dc in ring; join with sl st to top of ch-3 (12 sts, counting ch-3 as one st). **2nd rnd:** Ch 1, y o hook and insert hook from front to back in sp before starting ch and bring hook to front of work through sp on other side of starting ch, y o hook and draw lp through (3 lps now on hook), (y o and draw through 2 lps) twice (post dc made—hereafter worked around dc of previous rnds); * sc in each of next 2 dc, work a post dc around same dc as last sc was worked. Repeat from * around, ending last repeat with sc in next sc, sc in first ch-1 (6 post dc). **3rd rnd:** * Post dc over post dc below, work 1 sc in each of next 2 sc, work 1 sc in top of post dc. Repeat from * around (6 post dc). Do not join rnds. Mark beg of rnds. **4th rnd:** * Post dc around post dc, sc in each of next 3 sc, sc in next post dc. Repeat from * around.

Continue to work as for last rnd, having 1 more sc between post dcs every rnd until 13th rnd is completed and there are 13 sc and 1 post dc in each section. Piece should measure 4½" in diameter. Break off. With pins, mark first and third post dcs on last rnd. Put this piece aside.

Make another side section in same manner but do not break off; continue as follows for center section. Mark first and third post dcs on last rnd.

CENTER SECTION: 1st row: Ch 1, turn, sc in each post dc and in each sc across four sides of side section (between markers), then ch 11 for cuff. Do not work over remaining two sides. **2nd row:** Turn, sc in 2nd ch from hook and in each remaining ch, sc in each sc across last row (67 sc). Ch 1, turn. **3rd row:** Sc in each sc across. Ch 1, turn. Repeat last row until center section measures 3½". Break off.

FINISHING: With right sides together, pin free edge of center section to four sides of first section (between markers), leaving 10 sts of center section free for cuff, and sl st both pieces together. Break off.

Work 1 rnd of sc around all outer edges, taking in back edge of center section slightly. To form ridge, fold helmet on first row of center section and work 1 row of sc along this row, then turn work and sl st in each sc. Repeat ridge along last row of center section. Fold cuff to right side and sew a button on each corner of cuff, taking sts through both thicknesses. Make two twisted cords 12" in length and sew one to each side. Make a knot about ½" from free end of each cord.

Baby Jacket

In double crochet, made of synthetic knitting worsted for easy care. Ties with drawstring at the neck.

SIZE: Infant to 6 months. Sweater measures 9" across back to underarms, 9" from back of neck to lower edge.

MATERIALS: Synthetic knitting worsted, 2 ounces white (color A), 1 ounce each yellow (B) and orange (C); aluminum crochet hook size J (or Canadian hook No. 6) *or the size that will give you the correct gauge.*

GAUGE: 7 dc = 2"; 5 rows = 3".

Starting at center of white stripe around body with A, ch 48 to measure about 13". **1st rnd:** Dc in 4th ch from hook, dc in each of next 43 ch, 8 dc in last ch; working along opposite side of chain, dc in each of next 44 ch, 8 dc in base of turning ch-3, marking sp between 6th and 7th dc of 8-dc group; join with sl st to top of ch-3 (104 dc). Break off A; attach B in marked sp. **2nd rnd:** Ch 3, 3 dc in same sp (first 4-dc corner made), dc in each of next 48 dc, 4 dc in sp before next dc (corner), dc in each of next 4 dc, 4 dc in sp before next dc (corner), dc in each of next 48 dc, 4 dc in sp before next dc (corner), dc in each of remaining 4 dc; join. **3rd rnd:** Sl st in sp between 2 center dc of next dc corner, work a first 4-dc corner in same center sp, (dc in each dc to center sp of next corner, work 4-dc corner in center sp) 3 times; dc in each st to complete rnd; join. Break off B. Attach C and repeat 3rd rnd twice more (168 dc). Break off. This rectangle forms front and back body of sweater.

SLEEVES: Starting at lower edge with A, ch

Clothes 169

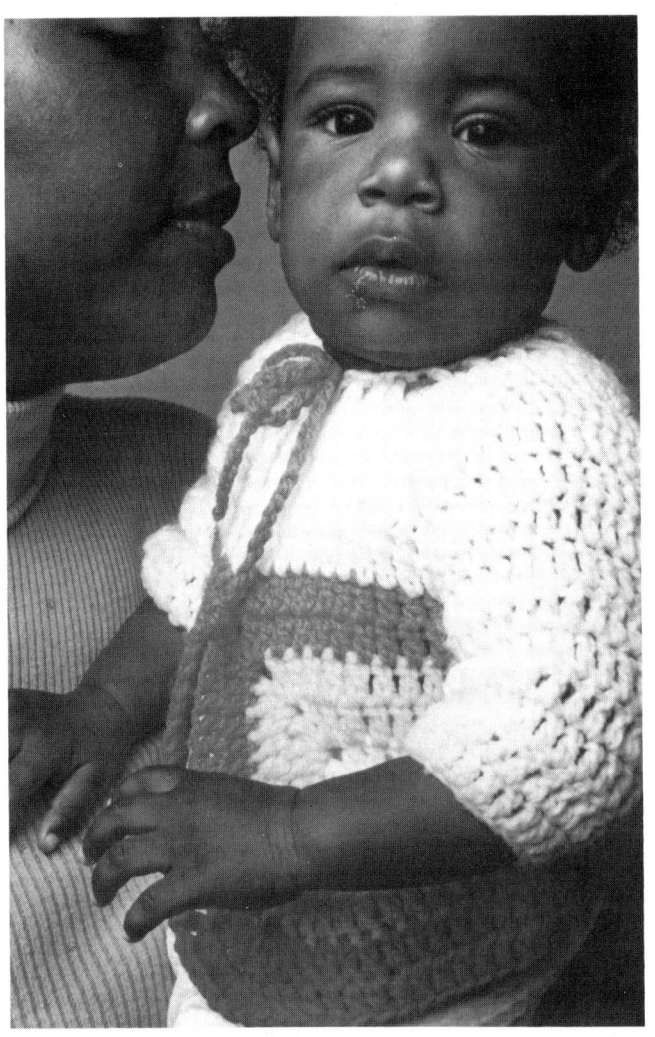

YOKE: Starting at top right front edge, with right side facing you, attach A with sl st to first dc at corner of rectangle. **1st row:** Ch 3, dc in each of next 15 dc (right front), dc in each of 22 sts on last sleeve row of one sleeve (right sleeve), dc in each of next 32 dc on rectangle (back), dc in each of 22 sts on last sleeve row of other sleeve (left sleeve), dc in each of remaining 16 dc on rectangle (left front); ch 3, turn. **2nd row:** Skip first dc, dc in each of next 13 dc; leaving last lp of each st on hook, dc in each of next 4 dc, y o hook and draw through all 5 lps on hook (dec made); dc in each of next 18 dc, make dec, dc in each of next 28 dc, make dec, dc in each of next 18 dc, make dec, dc in remaining 14 dc; ch 3, turn. **3rd row:** Skip first dc, dc in each of next 11 dc; leaving last lp of each st on hook, dc in each of next 2 dc, skip next st (top of dec) and dc in next 2 dc, y o hook, and draw through all 5 lps on hook (dec made); dc in each of next 14 dc, make dec, dc in each of next 24 dc, make dec, dc in each of next 14 dc, make dec, dc in each of remaining 12 dc; ch 3, turn. **4th row:** Skip first dc, dc in each of next 9 dc, make dec as for 3rd row, dc in each of next 10 dc, make dec, dc in each of next 20 dc, make dec, dc in each of next 10 dc, make dec, dc in each of last 10 dc; ch 3, turn. **5th row:** Skip first dc, dc in each of next 7 dc, make dec as for 3rd row, dc in each of next 6 dc, make dec, dc in each of next 16 dc, make dec, dc in each of next 6 dc, make dec, dc in each of last 8 dc. Break off.

DRAWSTRING: With C, crochet chain 28" long. Thread chain through 5th yoke row. Tie in bow.

22. Join with sl st to form ring. **1st rnd:** Ch 3, dc in each ch around (22 dc, counting ch-3 as 1 dc); join. **2nd rnd:** Ch 3, dc in each dc around; join. Repeat last rnd 6 times more. Break off.

Baby Bonnet

This dainty bonnet is crocheted flat, like a doily, then gathered with a drawstring.

SIZE: 6 months to 1 year.

MATERIALS: Acrylic sport yarn, 2 ounces pink, 1 ounce white; aluminum crochet hook size F (or Canadian hook No. 10) *or the size that will give you the correct gauge.*

GAUGE: 5 dc = 1".

Note: Hat will be a slightly ruffled "doily" 14" in diameter until cord is inserted to draw it into shape.

Starting at center with pink, ch 4. Join with sl

st to form ring. **1st rnd:** Ch 3 (counts as 1 dc), work 2 dc in ring, ch 1, (work 3 dc in ring, ch 1) 3 times; sl st in top of ch-3. **2nd rnd:** Sl st in next 2 dc and in ch-1 sp, ch 3, work 2 dc, ch 2 and 3 dc in same sp, ch 2, * work 3 dc, ch 2 and 3 dc in next ch-1 sp, ch 2. Repeat from * twice more; sl st in top of ch-3. Break off pink. **3rd rnd:** With white, form lp on hook, * work 2 h dc in next ch-2 sp, skip next dc, h dc in each of next 2 dc. Repeat from * around (32 h dc); sl st in first h dc. **4th rnd:** Ch 3, dc in each of next 2 h dc, 2 dc in next h dc, * dc in each of next 3 h dc, 2 dc in next h dc. Repeat from * around (40 dc); sl st in top of ch-3. Break off white; attach pink. **5th rnd:** With pink ch 3, dc in each of next 3 dc, 2 dc in next dc, * dc in each of next 4 dc, 2 dc in next dc. Repeat from * around (48 dc); sl st in top of ch-3. Piece should measure 4" in diameter. **6th rnd:** Ch 3, 2 dc in same place as sl st (first shell made), ch 1, skip 2 dc, * 3 dc in next dc (shell made), ch 1, skip 2 dc. Repeat from * around (16 shells); sl st in top of ch-3. **7th rnd:** Sl st in next 2 dc and in ch-1 sp, ch 3, 2 dc in same sp, ch 2, * 3 dc in next ch-1 sp, ch 2. Repeat from * around; join. **8th rnd:** Ch 3, 2 dc in next dc, dc in next dc, 2 dc in next ch-2 sp, * dc in next dc, 2 dc in next dc, dc in next dc, 2 dc in next ch-2 sp. Repeat from * around (96 dc); join. Break off pink; attach white. **9th rnd:** Ch 2 (counts as 1 h dc), h dc in each dc around; join. Piece should measure 7" in diameter. **10th rnd:** Ch 3, 2 dc in same place as sl st, ch 1, skip 2 h dc, * 3 dc in next h dc, ch 1, skip 2 h dc. Repeat from * around (32 shells); join. Break off white; attach pink. **11th rnd:** Ch 3, dc in each dc and ch-1 sp around (128 dc); join. **12th rnd:** Ch 3, 2 dc in same place as sl st, ch 1, skip 3 dc, 3 dc in next dc, ch 1, skip 3 dc, * 3 dc in next dc, ch 1, skip 2 dc. Repeat from * around (42 shells); join. **13th rnd:** Repeat 7th rnd. **14th rnd:** Ch 3, dc in each of next 2 dc, 2 dc in next sp, * dc in each of next 3 dc, 2 dc in next sp. Repeat from * around (210 dc). **15th rnd:** Repeat 5th rnd (252 dc). **16th rnd:** Ch 3, dc in each dc around; join. Break off pink; attach white. **17th rnd:** Ch 2, sc in same place as sl st, skip next dc; * in next dc work sc, ch 3 and sc, skip next dc. Repeat from * around; sl st in first ch. Break off.

DRAWSTRING: With white, crochet 38" chain. Weave through sts of 14th rnd. With white, make 2 pompons ¾" in diameter. Sew pompon to each end of drawstring, pull up to fit and tie in bow.

Infanta Bonnet

A little ruffled bonnet keeps head and ears warm. Rainbow ombré yarn is used for ruffle. Knitting worsted worked in double crochet, and half double crochet for earflaps.

SIZE: 6 months to 1 year.

MATERIALS: Knitting worsted, 2 ounces royal blue, 1 ounce rainbow ombré; aluminum crochet hook size G (or Canadian hook No. 9) *or the size that will give you the correct gauge.*

GAUGE: 4 dc = 1"; 2 rnds = 1".

CROWN: Starting at top with blue, ch 4. Join with sl st to form ring. **1st rnd:** Ch 3, work 11 dc in ring (12 dc, counting ch-3 as 1 dc); join with sl st to top of ch-3. **2nd rnd:** Ch 3, dc in same place as sl st, * 2 dc in next dc. Repeat from * around (24 dc); join. **3rd rnd:** Ch 3, 2 dc in next dc, * dc in next dc, 2 dc in next dc. Repeat from * around (36 dc); join. **4th rnd:** Ch 3, dc in next dc, 2 dc in next dc, * dc in each of next 2 dc, 2 dc in next dc. Repeat from * around (48 dc); join. **5th rnd:** Ch 3, dc in each of next 2 dc, 2 dc in next dc, * dc in each of next 3 dc, 2 dc in next dc. Repeat from * around (60 dc); join. Piece should measure 5" in diameter. **6th rnd:** Ch 3, dc in next dc and each dc around; join. Repeat 6th rnd 4 times more. Do not break off but continue with first earflap as follows:

EARFLAPS: 1st row: Ch 2, h dc in each of next 12 dc on last rnd of crown (13 h dc, counting ch-2 as 1 h dc); ch 2, turn. **2nd row:** Skip first h dc, h dc in each h dc across (13 h dc); ch 2, turn. **3rd row:** Skip first h dc, dec 1 h dc as follows: y o and draw up lp in each of next 2 h dc, y o and draw through all 5 lps on hook; h dc in each h dc to last 2 h dc, dec 1 h dc (11 h dc); ch 2, turn. Repeat 3rd row 3 times more (4 h dc). **7th row:** (Dec 1 h dc) twice. Do not break off but attach ombré yarn and, with both strands, crochet 9" chain for tie. Break off.

Skip next 21 dc along lower edge of crown (face edge). Attach blue to next dc, work other earflap and tie to correspond to first.

RUFFLE: With right side facing you, attach ombré to any dc on edge of crown. Work along last row of crown and over first row of earflaps as follows: **1st rnd:** Ch 3, work 5 dc in same st, * work 6 dc in next st (shell made). Repeat from * around; join. **2nd rnd:** Sl st in each of next 5 dc and in sp between shells, ch 3, work 5 dc in same sp, * work shell in sp between next 2 shells. Repeat from * around; join. Break off.

Summer-Cool Baby Romper and Hat

Two-tone romper has straps that cross and button in back. Worked in double crochet and chain-loop pattern. The flower trim is repeated on the hat.

SIZES: 6 [12—18] months. Suit measures about 20" [21"—22"] around middle when slightly stretched. Hat fits 21" head.

MATERIALS: For set: Kentucky All Purpose Yarn (rayon), 2 (100-yard) skeins orange No. 708, 2 [3—3] skeins gold No. 711. For romper only: 2 skeins orange and 1 gold. For hat only: 1 [2—2] skeins gold and small amount orange. Aluminum crochet hook size E (or Canadian hook No. 11) *or the size that will give you the correct gauge;* 1 yard ⅛"-wide elastic or round hat elastic; 2 buttons ½" in diameter.

GAUGE: On bloomers: 4 dc = 1".

Romper

BLOOMERS: Note: Bloomers are made in one piece with center back seam.

Starting at waist edge with orange, ch 77 [81—85] to measure about 19" [20"—21"]. **1st row:** Work dc in 4th ch from hook and in each ch across (75 [79—83] dc, counting turning ch as 1 dc); ch 3, turn. **2nd row:** Skip first dc, dc in next dc and in each dc across (75 [79—83] dc); ch 3, turn. **3rd row:** Skip first 2 dc, sl st in next dc, * ch 3, skip next dc, sl st in next dc. Repeat from * across (37 [39—41] ch-3 lps); ch 3, turn. **4th row:** Work 2 dc in first ch-3 lp and in each ch-3 lp across (75 [79—83] dc); ch 3, turn.

Repeat 2nd through 4th rows for pattern until piece measures about 7" [7½"—8"] from beg, ending with a 2nd or 4th pattern row and omitting ch-3 on last row. Break off and turn. Mark center 5 dc on last row worked.

Crotch: Attach orange with sl st in first of 5 marked sts. **1st row:** Ch 3 (counts as 1 dc), work 1 dc in each of next 4 marked dc; ch 3, turn. **2nd row:** Skip first dc, dc in each of next

4 dc; ch 3, turn. Repeat 2nd row twice more, omitting ch-3 on last row. Break off.

Sew center back seam. Sew free end of crotch to corresponding sts at center back.

Leg Edging: Attach orange to leg opening. **1st rnd:** With right side facing you, work 1 row sc evenly spaced around entire leg opening; join with sl st in first sc. Break off orange; attach gold. **2nd rnd:** Ch 3, skip first sc, work dc in next sc and in each sc around; join with sl st in top of starting ch-3. **3rd rnd:** * Ch 3, skip next dc, sl st in next dc. Repeat from * around. Break off. Work edging for other leg opening in same manner.

BIB: Starting at waist edge with right side facing you, skip first 24 [25—26] sts from center back seam; attach gold in sp between last dc and next dc. **1st row:** * Ch 3, skip next 2 dc, sl st in next sp between 2 dc. Repeat from * 12 [13—14] times more (13 [14—15] lps); ch 3, turn. **2nd row:** Sl st in first ch-3 lp, * ch 3, sl st in next lp. Repeat from * across (13 [14—15] lps); ch 3, turn. Repeat 2nd row until bib measures 2" [2½"—3"]. Do not break off.

Shoulder Straps: Next row: Sl st in first lp, * ch 3, sl st in next lp. Repeat from * 1 [2—2] times more (3 [4—4] lps); ch 3, turn. Repeat 2nd row of bib until strap measures 9½" [10"—10½"] or long enough to fit over shoulder and diagonally across back to top of bloomers. Omit ch-3 at end of last row. Break off. Attach gold to opposite end of bib, ch 3 and work to correspond to first strap. Break off.

FINISHING: Flowerette (make 2): Starting at center with gold, ch 5, join with sl st to form ring. **1st rnd:** Ch 3, work 11 dc in ring (12 dc, counting ch-3 as 1 dc); join with sl st in top of ch-3. **2nd rnd:** * Ch 2, sl st in next dc. Repeat from * around, ending ch 2, sl st in sl st. Break off. Following photograph, sew flowerette to front of bloomers.

Insert elastic through first sc rnd of leg edging. Adjust to fit, cut, overlap ends, and sew together. Repeat for other leg opening. Insert elastic in first dc row along back edge and sides of waist (omit bib area); adjust to fit, cut, and sew ends at sides.

Sew buttons to back waist edge. Cross straps and button through center lp of last row on straps.

Hat

CROWN: Starting at top with gold, ch 6; join with sl st to form ring. **1st rnd:** Ch 4, (dc in ring, ch 1) 7 times; join with sl st in 3rd ch of starting ch-4 (8 dc and 8 ch-1 sps); sl st in next ch-1 sp. **(Note:** Work around and around in spiral fashion from now on, marking beg of rnds.) **2nd rnd:** * Ch 4, sl st in next ch-1 sp. Repeat from * around, ending with sl st in first sl st (8 ch-4 lps). **3rd rnd:** * (Ch 4, sl st in next lp) twice; ch 4, sl st in same lp. Repeat from * 3 times more (12 lps). **4th rnd:** * Ch 4, sl st in next lp. Repeat from * around (12 lps). **5th rnd:** * (Ch 4, sl st in next lp) 3 times; ch 4, sl st in same lp. Repeat from * 3 times more (16 lps). **6th rnd:** Repeat 4th rnd (16 lps). Piece should measure about 2" from center to edge.

Continue in lp pattern for 8 more rnds, increasing 4 lps as evenly spaced as possible on every other rnd (32 lps). Piece should measure about 4¼" from center. Work even in lp pattern on 32 lps until crown measures 6" [6½"—7"] from beg.

BRIM: 1st rnd: Work 2 sc in each lp around (64 sc). **2nd rnd:** * Work sc in each of next 2 sc, 3 sc in next sc. Repeat from * around, ending with sc in last sc (106 sc). **3rd rnd:** * Work sc in each of next 4 sc, 2 sc in next sc. Repeat from * around, ending with sc in last sc (127 sc). **4th rnd:** Work sc in each sc around. **5th rnd:** * Ch 2, skip next sc, sl st in next sc. Repeat from * around. Break off.

FLOWERETTE: With gold, work 2 flowers as for flowerettes on romper. With orange, crochet a 10" chain. Slide chain halfway through a st at top of crown. Sew flowerette to each end.

Three granny squares, each with a different center motif, work into a jumper, vest, and pinafore. Instructions for each variation are given on the following pages. They are worked in machine-washable acrylic yarns and take little time and yarn to make. You can even use leftovers.

Jumper

SIZES: Toddler's 1 [2—3]. Jumper measures 20" [20½"—21"] around waistline. Length from shoulder to lower edge is 15" [16"—17"] and can be adjusted as you work, if desired.

MATERIALS: Bucilla Wonder Knit Creslan acrylic, knitting worsted-weight, 1 (4-ounce) ball each lavender No. 22 (color L), rose No. 11 (R), and orange No. 8 (O); aluminum crochet hook size H (or Canadian hook No. 8) *or the size that will give you the correct gauge.*

Note: Bucilla Wonder Knit is sold only in 4-ounce balls. If you are using your leftover yarns, you will need only 1 ounce of rose and 2 ounces of orange.

GAUGE: After 4th rnd of front, piece should measure 4" in diameter.

SQUARE FOR FRONT: Starting at center of square with O, ch 2. **1st rnd:** Work 8 sc in 2nd ch from hook. Join with sl st in first sc. **2nd rnd (right side):** Ch 5, y o hook, draw up lp in same sc as sl st, y o, draw through 2 lps on hook (2 lps remain on hook), y o, draw up lp in next sc, y o, draw through 2 lps on hook, y o, draw through remaining 3 lps on hook (2-joined dc made), * ch 2, work a 2-joined dc in last sc used and in the following sc. Repeat from * 5 times more; ch 2, dc in last sc. Join with sl st in 3rd ch of first ch-5. Break off O. There are 8 sp on rnd. **3rd rnd:** Turn work over so that wrong side faces you. Make lp on hook with R and work 3 dc in any ch-2 sp, * ch 2, work 3 dc in next ch-2 sp. Repeat from * around; join with dc in top of first dc. **4th rnd:** Ch 3, turn work over so that right side of work faces you. Holding back on hook the last lp of each dc, work 1 dc in each of next 3 dc, y o and draw through all 4 lps on hook (3-joined dc made), * ch 5, skip ch-2, work a 3-joined dc over next 3 dc. Repeat from * around, ending ch 5; join with sl st to top of ch-3. Break off. Piece should now measure 4" in diameter. **5th rnd:** Make lp on hook with O and work a corner of 3 dc, ch 1 and 3 dc in any ch-5 sp, * ch 2, work 3 dc in next ch-5 sp, ch 2, work a corner in next sp. Repeat from * around, ending with ch 2, work 3 dc in last sp, ch 2; join to top of first dc. Break off. **(Note:** Work will cup slightly, but will lie flat after blocking if correct gauge is maintained.)

6th rnd: Make lp on hook with L and work a corner of 3 dc, ch 1 and 3 dc in any corner sp, * (ch 1, work 3 dc in next sp) twice; ch 1, work corner in next corner. Repeat from * around, ending (ch 1, 3 dc in next sp) twice; ch 1, join to top of first dc. **7th rnd:** Sl st in each of next 2 dc, sl st in next sp (this is a corner sp), ch 3, in same sp work 2 dc, ch 1 and 3 dc, * work ch 1 and 3 dc in each sp to next corner, ch 1, work corner in next corner. Repeat from * around, ending ch 1 and 3 dc in each sp to corner, ch 1, join to top of ch-3. **8th rnd:** Repeat last rnd, then break off. Mark the first and 4th corners for belt.

Make another square in same manner for back.

SIDE BELT: 1st row: With O, sl st in ch-1 sp of first corner of front square, ch 3, work 1 dc in each of next 3 dc, next ch-1 and each of next 3 dc (8 sts, counting ch-3 as 1 dc). **2nd row:** Ch 3, turn, skip first dc, dc in each dc, dc in top of ch-3.

Repeat last row until 7th [8th—9th] row is completed, then pick up back square and join to corresponding sts by holding both pieces with wrong sides together, then sc through both thicknesses of belt and square. Break off.

Join O at other marked corner on front square; work and join another belt in same manner.

SKIRT: Work across lower edge of top sections as follows: **1st rnd:** With O sl st in corner sp of top square, ch 3, work 2 dc in same sp; * working along lower edge of square, (ch 1, work a shell of 3 dc in next sp) 5 times; ch 1, 3-dc shell in corner sp; then working along lower edge of belt continue as follows: (ch 1, work 3 dc over end st of next dc row, ch 1, 3 dc over end st of next dc row, skip next dc row) twice; (ch 1, 3 dc over next dc row) 1 [2—3] times (5 [6—7] shells worked over belt); ch 1, 3 dc in corner sp. Repeat from * once, ending ch 1; join to top of ch-3. Break off.

2nd rnd: With L work a shell of 3 dc in any sp, * ch 1, work a 3-dc shell in next sp. Repeat from * around, ending with ch 1, sl st in top of first dc (24 [26—28] shells in rnd). **3rd rnd:** Ch 4, skip first shell, work a shell of 3 dc in next sp, * ch 1, shell in next sp. Repeat from * around, ending with ch 1, 2 dc in last sp, sl st in 3rd ch of ch-4. **4th rnd:** Sl st in ch-1 sp, ch 3, work 2 dc in same sp, * ch 1, shell in next sp. Repeat from * around, ending ch 1, sl st in top of ch-3. Repeat 3rd and 4th rnds until skirt measures 5½″ [6½″—7½″] from first color O rnd (or desired length).

PICOT TRIM: Ch 1, * sc in ch-1 sp, sc in each of next 2 dc, ch 3, sc in 3rd ch from hook (picot made), sc in same dc as last sc, sc in next dc. Repeat from * around; join and break off.

SHOULDER STRAPS: Work across top edge of front square as follows: **1st row:** With O, sl st in ch-1 sp of corner, ch 3, work 1 dc in each of next 3 dc, in next ch-1 and in next dc (6 sts, counting ch-3 as 1 dc). **2nd row:** Ch 3, turn, skip first dc, dc in each dc and in top of ch-3. Repeat last row until 12th row is completed, then join to corresponding sts of back square, as for belt. With wrong side of work facing you, join O at opposite corner and work another strap in same manner.

FINISHING: Picot Edging: Work with O around all edges of top as follows: **For Armhole:** Join O with sl st in corner sp at top edge of front square at beg of strap and work along edge of strap, as follows: * work 1 sc over end st of each of next 2 rows, ch 3, sc in 3rd ch from hook for picot, work 1 sc over end st of row where last sc was worked. Repeat from * across strap; then, working across back square, work (1 sc in each of next 2 dc, picot, sc in same dc, sc in next dc, skip ch-1) 4 times; complete edging in same manner across top edge of belt and side edge of front square. Join and break off.

Work same edging around neck edge and other armhole edge. Block front and back squares.

Vest

SIZES: Toddler's 1 [2—3]. Completed square measures 7". Will fit chest sizes 20" [20½"—21"].

MATERIALS: Bear Brand Winsom Orlon acrylic, sports yarn weight, 1 (2-ounce) skein each rosy pink No. 342 (color P), green turquoise No. 331 (T) and spearmint green No. 367 (G); aluminum crochet hook size H (or Canadian hook No. 8) *or the size that will give you the correct gauge.*

GAUGE: After 4th rnd, square should measure 4" across.

SQUARE FOR FRONT: Starting at center with P, ch 4. Join with sl st in first st to form ring. **1st rnd:** Ch 3, work 11 dc into ring; join with sl st to top of ch-3. **2nd rnd:** Ch 5, skip 2 dc, sc in next dc, (ch 4, skip 2 dc, sc in next dc) twice; ch 4, skip last 2 dc; join with sl st in first st of ch-5. **3rd rnd:** Ch 3, in first sp work 4 dc; then ch 3, sc in 3rd ch from hook for picot and mark this picot for corner, then in same sp work 5 more dc and another picot; in each of next 3 sps work 5 dc, picot, 5 dc and picot; join with sl st to top of ch-3. Break off. **4th rnd:** Make lp on hook with T and work a corner in marked picot as follows: Work 3 dc, ch 1 and 3 dc in this picot for corner, * ch 1, work a 3-dc shell in next picot, ch 1, work a corner in next picot. Repeat from * around, ending with ch 1, 3-dc shell in last picot, ch 1; join with sl st to top of first dc. Square should now measure 4". **5th rnd:** Sl st in each of next 2 dc, sl st in next sp (this is corner sp), ch 3, in same sp work 2 dc, ch 1 and 3 dc, * work ch 1 and a shell in each sp to corner, ch 1, work corner in next corner. Repeat from * around, ending ch 1 and a shell in each sp to corner, ch 1, join to top of ch-3. Break off. **6th rnd:** With G, sl st in any corner sp, and starting with ch 3, work as for 5th rnd but do not break off. **7th and 8th rnds:** Repeat 5th rnd, breaking off only at end of 8th rnd. Mark the 2nd and 3rd corners for straps.

Make another square in same manner for back.

SHOULDER STRAPS: Work across top edge of front square between markers as follows: **1st row:** With G, sl st in ch-1 sp of 2nd marked corner of front, ch 3, work 1 dc in each of next 3 dc, in next ch-1 and in each of next 3 dc (8 sts, counting ch-3 as 1 dc). **2nd row:** Ch 3, turn, skip first dc, dc in each dc, dc in top of ch-3.

Repeat last row until 7th [7th—8th] row is completed, then pick up back square and join to corresponding sts by holding both pieces with wrong sides together, then sc through both thicknesses of strap and square. Break off.

Join G at third corner on front square, and working across top edge, work and join another strap in same manner.

SIDE STRAPS: Counting along side edge of front square and starting at ch-1 sp of corner at lower edge, skip three 3 dc and ch-1 groups, join G with sl st in next dc, ch 3, work 1 dc in each of next 2 dc, in next ch-1 and in next 3 dc, (7 sts, counting ch-3 as 1 dc). Repeat 2nd row of shoulder strap until 5th [6th—7th] row is completed; then join to corresponding sts on back square in same manner. Join G to corresponding st on other side edge and work and join another strap in same manner.

Pinafore

SIZES: Toddler's 1 [2—3]. Pinafore measures 20" [20½"—21"] around waistline. Length from shoulder to lower edge is 15" [16"—17"] and can be adjusted.

MATERIALS: Bear Brand Winsom Orlon acrylic, sports yarn weight, 1 (2-ounce) skein each cyclamen (pink) No. 363 (color P), electric blue No. 14 (B), and copper No. 382 (C); aluminum crochet hooks sizes H, I and J for all sizes (or Canadian hooks Nos. 8, 7 and 6) *or the sizes that will give you the correct gauge;* 2 snap fasteners.

GAUGE: Using size H hook: 4 dc or 4 sc = 1" on waistband.

FRONT: Top Section: Use size H hook for front. For heart, starting at center of top with P, ch 16. Join with sl st in first st to form ring. **1st rnd:** In ring work the following: 1 sc, 1 h dc, 1 dc, 7 tr (mark 3rd and 6th trs), 6 dc, then ch 4, sc in 3rd ch from hook for picot, work 6 dc, 7 tr (mark 3rd and 6th trs), 1 dc, 1 h dc and 1 sc; join with sl st to first sc. **2nd rnd:** Sc in each sc around, working 2 sc (for inc) in each of the four marked trs and 3 sc in picot; join with sl st to first sc. Break off.

Mark first sc increased, mark sc's before and after the 3 sc worked over picot, then mark last sc increased.

3rd rnd: Make lp on hook with C, in first sc marked work 3 dc, ch 1 and 3 dc (corner made), ch 8, work corner in next marked sc, ch 4, skip picot, work corner in next marked sc, ch 8, work corner in next marked sc, ch 10, join with sl st to top of first dc. **4th rnd:** Sl st in each of next 2 dc, sl st in next sp (this is a corner sp), ch 3, in same sp work 2 dc, ch 1 and 3 dc, * (ch 2, skip 2 sts of ch-8, work 3 dc in next st) twice; ch 2, work a corner in ch-1 sp of next corner, * (ch 2, skip 1 st of ch-4, work 3 dc in next st) twice; ch 2, work a corner in next corner. Repeat from first * to second * once; ch 2, skip 1 ch st, 3 dc in next st, (ch 2, skip 2 ch sts, 3 dc in next st) twice; ch 2; join with sl st to top of ch-3. **5th rnd:** Sl st in each of next 2 dc, sl st in corner sp, ch 3, in same sp work 2 dc, ch 1 and 3 dc, * (ch 1, skip 3 dc, work 3 dc in next sp) 3 times; ch 1, corner in next corner. Repeat from * around, ending with (ch 1, 3 dc in next sp) 4 times; ch 1; join to top of ch-3. Break off.

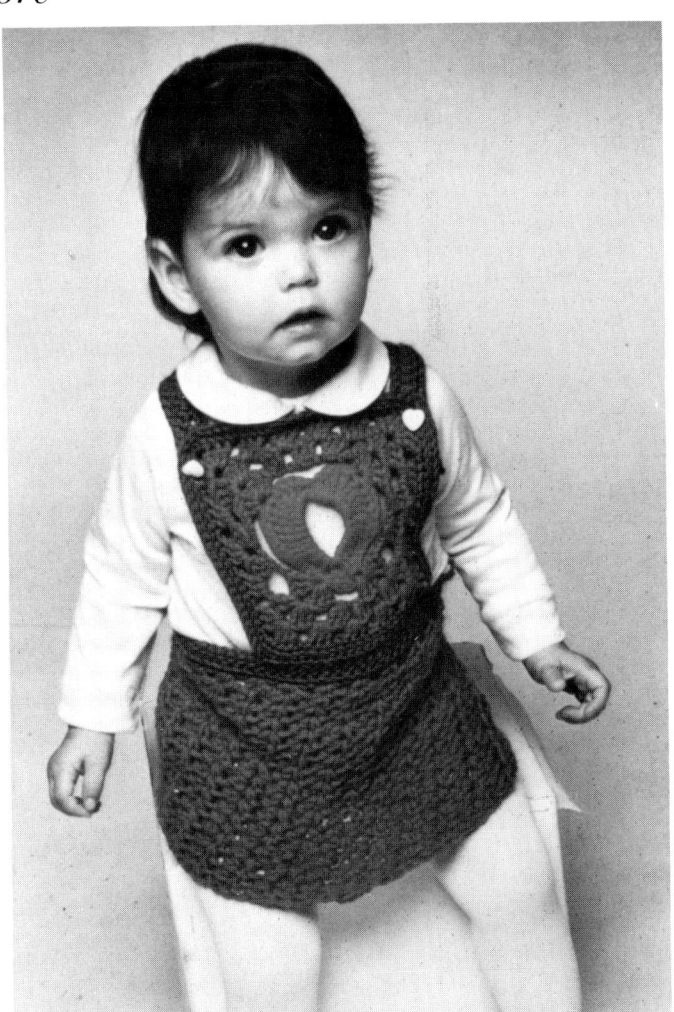

6th rnd: With B, work 1 sc in each dc and in

each ch-1 sp around, working 3 sc in each of the four corner spaces; join with sl st in first sc. **7th rnd:** Working in back lp only, work 1 sc in each sc around; join and break off.

Piece should measure 5½" wide across center and about 6½" high.

SKIRT: Starting at top edge of waistband, with size H hook and B, ch 80 [82—84] loosely to measure about 20" [20½"—21"]. Being careful not to twist chain, join with sl st in first st to form ring. **1st rnd:** Ch 3, work 1 dc in each st of chain; join with sl st to top of ch-3 (80 [82—84] sts, counting ch-3 as 1 st). **2nd rnd:** Ch 1, working in back lp only, work 1 sc in each dc around; join and break off.

Work as follows for skirt pattern: **1st rnd:** Make lp on hook with C, sc in any sc, ch 1, y o hook, insert hook in same sc, y o and draw up lp ½" long, y o and draw through all 3 lps on hook (long h dc made), * skip next sc, in next sc work 1 sc, ch 1 and 1 long h dc (one group made). Repeat from * around; join with sl st to ch-1 of first group (40 [41—42] groups).

2nd rnd: Ch 2, work long h dc in same sp as sl st, * sc in ch-1 sp of next group, ch 1, work long h dc in same sp. Repeat from * around; join with sl st in ch-2 of first group.

Change to size I hook and repeat 2nd rnd until color C section measures 3"; then change to size J hook and work until color C section measures 6½" [7½"—8½"] or desired length. Break off.

FINISHING: Pin lower edge of top section to top edge of waistband with right sides together and sew in place.

STRAPS: Make 2. With size H hook and B, make a chain 15" [16"—17"] long. **1st row:** Dc in 4th ch from hook and in each st of chain. **2nd row:** Ch 3, turn; skip first dc, dc in each dc across, dc in top of ch-3. Break off, leaving a 10" length of yarn for sewing.

Mark off 2" at center back of top edge of waistband; sew one strap to waistband on each side of this 2" space.

Sew half of one fastener to free end of each strap, the other half to wrong side of each corner of top section. Cross straps in back to wear pinafore.

Scarlet Bib Jumper

With ruffled edge and a dash of royal blue and cotton-candy pink, the jumper has the easy fit for a toddler's straight figure. Skirt is worked vertically.

SIZE: Toddler's 2. Jumper fits 18" waist. Skirt is 9" long.

MATERIALS: Brunswick Pomfret sport yarn, 3 (2-ounce) skeins scarlet No. 521 (color A), 1 skein each royal No. 512 (B) and cotton candy No. 5581 (C); aluminum crochet hook size G (or Canadian hook No. 9) *or the size that will give you the correct gauge.*

GAUGE: 7 dc = 2"; 5 rows = 2".

Note: Skirt is worked vertically.

SKIRT: Starting at side edge with A, ch 24 to measure 5½". **1st row:** Dc in 3rd ch from hook and in each ch across (23 dc, counting turning ch as 1 dc); ch 3, turn. **2nd row:** Skip first dc, dc in each dc across, dc in turning ch; ch 3, turn. Repeat 2nd row until 57 rows have been completed. Break off. Sew last row to first row to form tube.

WAISTBAND: Work around 1 edge of tube as follows: **1st rnd (right side):** With C, form a lp on hook; starting at skirt seam (center back), * work dc over post of dc at end of each of next 2 rows, 2 dc over post of dc at end of next row. Repeat from * around (76 dc); join. Break off C. **2nd rnd:** With B form a lp on hook, dc in each dc around, decreasing 6 dc evenly spaced (70 dc), (to dec: leaving last lp on hook, work dc in each of next 2 dc, y o hook, pull through all 3 lps on hook); join. Break off. **3rd rnd:** With A, form a lp on hook, dc in each dc around, decreasing 10 dc evenly spaced (60 dc); join. Break off.

BIB: Count 18 sts from back seam along 3rd rnd of waistline. **1st row:** Attach A to next st, ch 3, dc in next 4 sc, (skip next sc, dc in next 5 sc) 3 times (20 dc); ch 1, turn. **2nd row:** Sl st in first 3 dc, ch 3, dc in each st to last 2 sts (16 dc, counting turning ch as 1 dc); ch 3, turn. **3rd row:** Dec 1 dc, dc across to last 2 dc, dec 1 dc (14 dc); ch 3, turn. **4th row:** Skip first dc, dc in each dc across, dc in turning ch; ch 3, turn. Repeat 4th row 5 times more. Do not break off.

FINISHING: Straps and Top Edging: At end of last row ch 55 as base for first strap. Break off. Attach A at beg of last row worked and ch 57 as base for second strap. **1st row:** With wrong side facing you, dc in 3rd ch from hook and in each ch across, work dc evenly spaced along one side of bib, work 30 dc across back, work dc evenly spaced up the other side of bib, then dc in each ch of first strap base. Break off. **2nd row:** With right side facing you, attach B at center back of last row worked; sc in each dc along half of back, side of bib, and around one strap; work along top of bib as follows: (ch 4, skip next dc, dc in next dc) 6 times; continue working sc in each sc around other strap, along other side of bib, and across back to center; join. **Lower Edge: 1st rnd:** With C, form a lp on hook; starting at center back, work 90 dc evenly spaced around lower edge of skirt; join. Break off C. **2nd rnd:** With B, work dc in each dc around. Break off B. **3rd rnd:** Attach A to first dc of last row, ch 4, sc in same dc, * sc in next dc, ch 4, sc in same dc. Repeat from * around; join. Break off.

Pretty Poncho

In rosy colors to keep your little one warm. Simple shell pattern and single crochet, worked in knitting worsted.

SIZE: About 20" square.

MATERIALS: Knitting worsted, 2 ounces dark rose (color R), 1 ounce each light pink (L), bright pink (B), and purple (P); aluminum crochet hook size G (or Canadian hook No. 9), *or the size that will give you the correct gauge.*

GAUGE: 7 sc = 2"; 4 rows = 1".

Starting at neck edge with B, ch 61 to measure 18". Join with sl st to form ring. **1st rnd:**

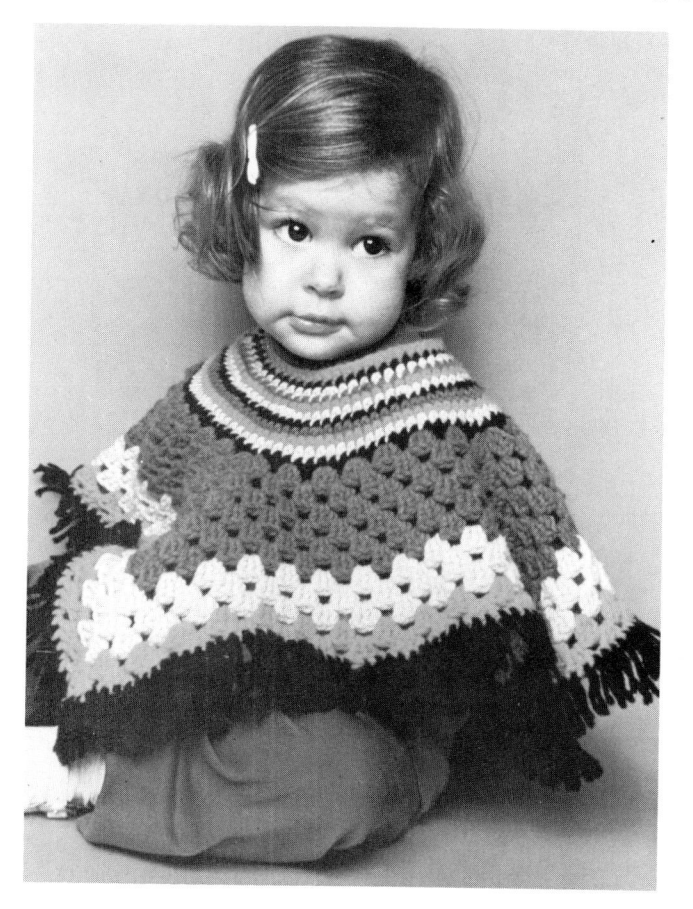

Ch 1, sc in each ch around (60 sc); join with sl st to first sc. Break off B; attach P. **2nd rnd:** Ch 1, sc in each sc around, increasing 3 sts evenly spaced (to inc, work 2 sc in 1 sc); join. Break off P; attach L. Repeat 2nd rnd 7 times more, working stripes of 1 rnd each of L, R, B, L, P, R, B. Work 1 more stripe each of L and P, increasing 6 sc on each rnd (96 sc). Break off. **12th rnd:** With R, form lp on hook, * (work 3 dc in next sc [shell made], ch 1, skip next 2 sc) 7 times; 3 dc in next sc, ch 1, 3 dc in same sc (corner made), ch 1, skip next 2 sc. Repeat from * 3 times more; skip last 2 sc; join. **13th rnd:** Ch 3, 2 dc in base of ch-3, ch 1, (3 dc in next sp, ch 1) 7 times; work corner in next corner sp, * ch 1, (3 dc in next sp, ch 1) 8 times; work corner in next corner sp. Repeat from * twice more; join. Continuing in this manner, working 1 more shell on each rnd between corners, work 4 more rnds with R, 3 rnds L, 2 rnds B (17 shells between corners on last rnd). Break off.

FRINGE: Cut P into 3" strips. Work 1 tassel in each st around last rnd as follows: Fold 1 strip in half; pull lp through st from front to back, then pull ends through lp and tighten.

Toddler's Shorts

Four small granny squares top off these colorful shorts.

SIZES: Toddler's 1 [2—3].

MATERIALS: Brunswick Windrush Orlon acrylic yarn (knitting worsted-weight), 1 (4-ounce) skein each maroon No. 9024 (color A), burnt orange No. 90611 (B), persimmon (yellow) No. 9004 (C), and bright scarlet No. 9025 (D); aluminum crochet hook size I (or Canadian hook No. 7) *or the size that will give you the correct gauge;* 1 yard round elastic; 2 buttons ½" in diameter.

GAUGE: 3 dc = 1"; 2 rows = 1".

Note: The colors specified can be purchased only in 4-ounce skeins. If you wish to substitute other colors or use any knitting worsted-weight yarns you might have on hand, you will need about 2 ounces each maroon and orange and 1 ounce each persimmon and scarlet.

SHORTS: Starting at waist edge with A, ch 56 [58—60] loosely to measure about 18" [18½"—19"]. **1st row (right side):** Dc in 4th ch from hook and in each ch across (54 [56—58] dc, counting turning ch as 1 dc). Break off. Always work with right side of work facing you. Do not turn work at end of row. Start next row in top of first st of last row. **2nd row:** With B, make lp on hook, y o, dc in first st, dc in each dc across. Break off. Repeat 2nd row 3 times more, working 1 row each with C, B, and D. Repeat the 5 rows for stripe pattern twice more, then repeat 0 [1—2] rows of stripe pattern again (15 [16—17] stripe rows in all), or work for desired length from waist to crotch.

To Shape Leg Openings: Mark center 2 dc on last row worked. **Crotch:** Sl st with next color in first marked st. **1st row:** Ch 3, dc in next marked st. **2nd and 3rd rows:** Ch 3, turn, skip first dc, dc in next st. Break off, leaving long enough end to sew back seam. Matching stripes, whipstitch seam. Sew free end of crotch to corresponding sts at center back.

Leg Borders: With next color, work 2 rnds sc around each leg opening, working in each st around.

BIB: Granny Square: Make 4 squares, working through 2nd rnd as for granny square for bib skirt on p. 182. Work through first rnd of each square with C, work 2nd rnd of 2 squares with B and 2 squares with D.

Holding a C-border and a D-border square together, wrong sides facing, whipstitch together across one edge through top lps only. Join other 2 squares in same manner. Join strips to form large square for bib. Treating wrong side of joined squares as right side of bib, whipstitch bib to front of pants.

With A, work 1 row sc around 3 free edges of bib. Break off.

STRAPS: With A, sl st in a top corner st of bib, ch 12½" [13½"—14½"] for strap. **1st row:** Dc in 4th ch from hook and in each ch across, sl st in top of bib, sl st in next st on top edge of bib, turn. **2nd row:** Dc in each st across strap. Break off. Make other strap in same manner.

FINISHING: Cut elastic to fit waist and weave through sts along upper edge of shorts. Sew ends securely. Cross straps on back and sew buttons to strap ends. Button through spaces on shorts.

Toddler's Jumper

Two granny squares made a bib for this little girl's jumper.

SIZES: Toddler's 1 [2—3].
MATERIALS: Brunswick Windrush Orlon acrylic yarn (knitting worsted-weight), 1 (4-ounce) skein each shamrock (Kelly green) No. 9043 (color A), Jamaica heather (peacock blue) No. 9078 (B), dark aqua No. 90393 (C), tender green (apple green) No. 90710 (D), maroon No. 9024 (E), and lilac No. 90143 (F); aluminum crochet hook size H (or Canadian hook size 8) *or the size that will give you the correct gauge;* 1 yard round elastic; 2 buttons ½" in diameter.

Note: The colors specified can be purchased only in 4-ounce skeins. If you wish to substitute other colors or use any knitting worsted-weight yarns you might have on hand, you will need approximately 1 ounce of each color.

GAUGE: 7 dc = 2"; 2 rows = 1".

SKIRT: Note: Skirt is worked in one piece with side seam. All rows are worked with right side facing you.

Starting at waist edge with A, ch 58 [58—60] loosely to measure about 18" [18"—18½"]. **1st row (right side):** Dc in 4th ch from hook and in each ch across (56 [56—58] dc, counting turning ch as 1 dc). Break off. **2nd row (inc row):** With B, make lp on hook, y o, dc in first st, dc in each dc across, increasing 8 dc as evenly spaced as possible (to inc, work 2 dc in 1 st). Break off. **3rd row:** With C, dc in each st across. Break off. Repeat 2nd and 3rd rows 5 times more, working in the following color sequence: 1 row each D, A, E, F, A, B, C, D, E, and F (104 [104—106] dc). Skirt should measure about 6½" from beg. If longer skirt is required, continue in desired colors, increasing every other row.

BIB: Granny Squares: Starting at center with F, ch 4, sl st in 4th ch from hook to form ring. **1st rnd (right side):** Ch 4 (work dc in ring, ch 1) 7 times; join with sl st to 3rd ch of ch-4. Break off. **2nd rnd:** With C, * work 2 dc in next ch-1 sp, ch 1, 2 dc in same sp (corner made); ch 1, 2 dc in next ch-1 sp (shell made), ch 1. Repeat from * 3 times more; join. Break off. **3rd rnd:** With B, * work a corner in next ch-1 corner sp, ch 1, (work 2-dc shell in next ch-1 sp, ch 1) twice. Repeat from * 3 times more; join. Break off.

Work another square in same manner, working 1 rnd each F, D, and A.

STRAPS: First Strap: With B, ch 37 to measure about 12". **1st row (right side):** Dc in 4th ch from hook and in each ch across (35 dc, counting ch-3 as 1 dc); ch 3, turn. **2nd row:** Skip first dc, dc in each dc across. Break off; turn. **3rd row:** With C, sl st in first dc, * ch 3, skip next dc, sc in next dc. Repeat from * across. Break off; turn. **4th row:** With F, sc in first ch-3 lp, * ch 3, sc in next ch-3 lp. Repeat from * across; ch 3, turn. **5th row:** Sc in first ch-3 lp, * ch 3, sc in next ch-3 lp. Repeat from * across, ch 3, sc in beg of last row. Break off.

2nd Strap: Work as for first strap, working 3 rows A, 1 row D, 2 rows F. Break off.

FINISHING: Sew side seam of skirt. Holding granny squares with wrong sides facing, whipstitch squares together across one edge through top lps only. Break off.

Whipstitch granny-square strip to waist edge of skirt. Sew each strap to matching colored granny square. Cut elastic to fit waist and weave through sts of skirt. Sew ends. Cross straps on back and sew buttons to skirt waist. Use spaces between sts for buttonholes.

Tyrolean Smock

Laced-up and ruffled, this colorful smock top has a band of set-in granny squares around the midriff.

SIZE: One size fits 4—6. Smock measures 12½" across back at underarms.

MATERIALS: Bernat Berella "4" Orlon acrylic yarn (knitting worsted-weight), 1 (4-ounce) ball each scarlet No. 8933 (color A), purple No. 8992 (B), myrtle (light) green No. 8985 (C), tapestry (dark) green No. 8981 (D), orange No. 8954 (E), light orange No. 8958 (F), and royal blue No. 8950 (G); aluminum crochet hook size H (or Canadian hook No. 8) *or the size that will give you the correct gauge*; tapestry needle.

Note: The colors specified can be purchased only in 4-ounce balls. If you wish to substitute other colors or use any yarns of knitting worsted weight you might have on hand, you will need the following amounts: 2 ounces each A, B, D, and E, and 1 ounce each C, F, and G.

GAUGE: 7 dc = 2"; 2 rows = 1".

Note: Yoke and cap sleeves are worked in one piece starting at neck edge.

YOKE: Starting at neck edge with A, ch 47 to measure about 13". **1st row (right side):** Sc in 2nd ch from hook and in each ch across (46 sc). Break off; turn. **2nd row:** Place marker in 10th st and 37th st. With B, make lp on hook, y o, dc in each sc up to marker, work 2 dc in marked st (inc made), inc in each of next 5 sc, dc in next 16 sc, inc in each of next 5 sc, inc in 2nd marked st, dc in remaining 9 sc (58 dc, counting ch-3 as 1 dc); ch 3, turn. **3rd row:** Skip first dc, dc in next 9 dc, * inc in next dc, skip next dc, inc in each of next 6 dc, skip next dc, inc in next dc *, dc in next 18 dc. Repeat from * to * once; dc in remaining 10 dc (70 dc); ch 3, turn. **4th row:** Skip first dc, dc in each of next 10 dc, * inc in next dc, skip next dc, inc in each of next 10 dc, skip next dc, inc in next dc *, dc in each of next 20 dc. Repeat from * to * once; dc in remaining 11 dc (90 dc). Break off; turn. **5th row:** With C, make lp on hook, y o, dc in first 12 dc, * inc in next dc, skip next dc, inc in each of next 18 dc, skip next dc, inc in next dc *, dc in each of next 22 dc. Repeat from * to * once; dc in each of remaining 12 dc (126 dc); ch 3, turn. **6th row:** Skip first dc, dc in next 12 dc, * inc in each of next 2 dc, dc in next 34 dc, inc in each of next 2 dc *, dc in next 24 dc. Repeat from * to * once; dc in remaining 13 dc (134 dc). Break off. **7th row:** With D, make lp on hook, y o, dc in first 14 dc, * inc in next dc, dc in next 38 dc, inc in next dc *, dc in next 26 dc. Repeat from * to * once; dc in remaining 14 dc (138 dc); ch 3, turn. **8th row:** Skip first dc, dc in each dc across, increasing in 2nd st of first and 3rd inc and in first st of 2nd and 4th inc (142 dc); ch 3, turn. **9th and 10th rows:** Repeat 8th row, changing to A on 10th row (150 dc). Ch 3, turn at end of 10th row. **11th row:** Skip first dc, dc in each dc across, increasing in first st of first and 3rd inc and in 2nd st of 2nd and 4th inc (154 dc). Break off; turn. **12th row:** With E, make lp on hook, y o, dc in each dc across, working incs as for 11th row (158 dc); ch 3, turn. **13th row:** Repeat 11th row (162 dc). Break off; turn.

To Divide for Body: With F, make lp on hook, y o, dc in first 19 dc for right front, ch 3 for underarm, skip next 44 dc for right sleeve, dc in next 34 dc for back, ch 3 for underarm, skip next 44 dc for left sleeve, dc in remaining 19 dc for left front (72 dc). Break off.

LARGE GRANNY SQUARES: Each large square measures 3″.

Square No. 1: Starting at center with A, ch 4; sl st in 4th ch from hook to form ring. **1st rnd:** Ch 3, 2 dc in ring, (ch 1, 3 dc in ring) 3 times; ch 1, sl st in top of ch-3. Break off A. **2nd rnd:** With G, make lp on hook, y o, * work 3 dc in next ch-1 sp, ch 1, 3 dc in same sp (corner made), ch 1. Repeat from * 3 times more; join with sl st in top of first dc. **3rd rnd:** Sl st across next 2 dc and in first ch-1 sp, ch 3, work 2 dc in same sp, ch 1, 3 dc in same sp, * ch 1, 3 dc in next ch-1 sp (shell made), ch 1, work corner in next corner sp. Repeat from * twice more; ch 1, shell in next sp, ch 1; join. Break off.

Work 6 more granny squares in same manner in the following colors:

Square No. 2: A, B, B.
Square No. 3: A, D, D.
Square No. 4: A, G, G.
Square No. 5: A, B, B.
Square No. 6: A, D, D.
Square No. 7: A, G, G.

To Join Squares: Holding 1st and 2nd squares with wrong sides facing, working through top lps only, whipstitch squares together along one edge. Join 3rd square to 2nd, 4th to 3rd, and so on, to form strip.

With wrong side of strip facing you, pin one long edge to last F row of smock, easing to fit. Whipstitch strip to yoke.

LOWER BORDER: 1st row: With D, make lp on hook, y o and dc evenly across lower free edge of strip; ch 3, turn. **2nd row:** Skip first dc, dc in each dc across. Break off D. Work evenly in dc for 3 rows more, working 2 rows C and 1 row B. Break off.

EDGING: 1st row: Starting at neck edge with A, make lp on hook and sc in each st along neck edge, marking first and last sc; continue to sc, evenly spaced, along front and lower edges, working sc, ch 1 and sc in lower front corners. Break off. **2nd row:** With wrong side facing you, using A, make lp on hook, y o, dc over side of marked sc at neck edge, dc in each sc along front and lower edges, working 3 dc in each ch-1 corner sp and ending with dc over side of other marked sc. (**Note:** Sts along neck edge between markers remain free.) Break off.

With right side facing you, using E, make lp on hook, y o, dc in each dc along front edge to within corner dc, 3 dc in corner dc, * ch 2, skip next dc, sc in next dc. Repeat from * along lower edge to within next corner dc, ch 2, work 3 dc in corner dc, dc in each remaining dc along front. Break off.

SMALL GRANNY SQUARES: Each small square measures 2″. Work as for 1st and 2nd rnds of large granny square, working squares in the following colors:

Square No. 1: G and A.
Square No. 2: B and C.
Square No. 3: A and E.

Join squares to form strip as for large strip. Use wrong side of strip as right side. Following photograph for placement and working through back lps only, whipstitch strip between front edges of smock.

COLLAR: 1st row: With right side facing you, using A, work 2 dc in each A sc along neck edge; ch 3, turn. **2nd row:** Skip first dc, dc in each dc across. Break off; turn. **3rd row:** With E, work dc in each dc across. Break off; turn. **4th row:** With F, work sc in first st, * ch 2, skip next st, sc in next st. Repeat from * across. Break off.

FINISHING: Sleeve Edging: 1st rnd: With right side facing you, using F, work as for 4th row of collar, working around sleeve opening; join with sl st to first sc. **2nd rnd:** Sl st in next

Monk's Cord For Tyrolean Smock

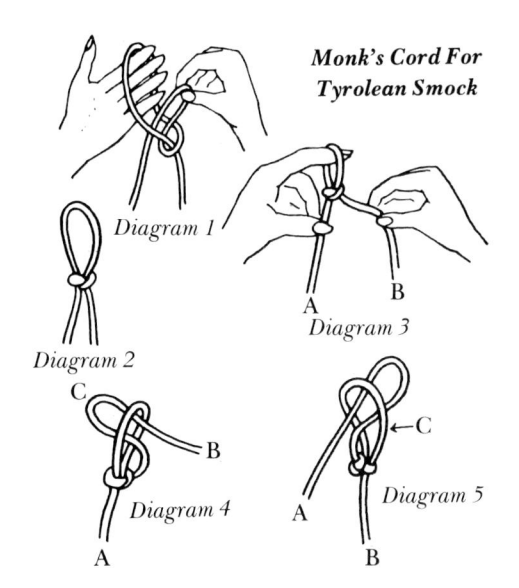

Diagram 1
Diagram 2
Diagram 3
Diagram 4
Diagram 5

ch-2 sp, sc in same sp, * ch 2, sc in next ch-2 sp. Repeat from * around; join. Break off.

Cord: Cut 8-yard length of F. Following diagrams, make monk's cord as follows: Fold yarn in half over left hand. Cross back strand across front and bring loop through (Diagram 1). Holding on to loop, pull front strand to tighten (Diagram 2). Hang loop on left index finger, holding end that slides easily (A) in left hand and other end (B) in right hand (Diagram 3). Insert a loop (C) of B strand through loop on finger (Diagram 4); pull A to tighten. Insert loop of strand A through loop C (Diagram 5) and pull B to tighten. Continue in this manner, alternating Diagrams 4 and 5 for desired length. Lace cord through sps on last row of front edging and tie in bow.

Here are two sweater sets—one for a girl and one for a boy. The girl's short-sleeved cardigan tops her long-sleeved turtleneck. Not to be outdone by the girl's version, the boy's set (page 186) features a wide-banded sleeveless vest over a long-sleeved, skinny-stripe V-neck pullover.

Girl's Sweater Set

SIZES: 6 [8—10]. Pullover measures 12" [13"—14"] across back at underarms, 16½" [16¾"—17"] from back of neck to lower edge. Cardigan measures 13" [14"—15"] across back at underarms, 17½" [18"—18½"] from back of neck to lower edge.

MATERIALS: For set: Bear Brand Winsom Orlon acrylic, 4 (2-ounce) skeins electric blue No. 14 (color E), 2 skeins each cyclamen No. 363 (C), bronze No. 38 (B), orange No. 91 (O), and rosy pink No. 342 (R). **For pullover or cardigan only:** 2 skeins orange (O), 1 skein each cyclamen (C), bronze (B), electric blue (E), and rosy pink (R). Aluminum crochet hook size G (or Canadian hook No. 9) *or the size that will give you the correct gauge;* 5 buttons ⅝" in diameter.

GAUGE: 5 sts (ch-1's and sc's) = 1"; 5 rows = 1".

Pullover

BACK AND SLEEVES: Work as for back and sleeves of pullover from Boy's Sweater Set (p. 187), working border in O and working remainder of pattern in 2 rows each C, B, E, R, and O.

FRONT: Work as for back of boy's pullover until armholes measure 4¾" [5¼"—5¾"].

To Shape Neck and Shoulders: 1st row: Work across first 19 [19—21] sts; turn. **2nd row:** Sl st in first 2 sts, work across; ch 1, turn. **3rd row:** Work across to within last 2 sts; turn. **4th row:** Repeat 2nd row, omitting ch-1; turn (13 sts). **5th row:** Sl st in first 4 sts, work across; ch 1, turn. **6th row:** Work across to within last 4 sts; turn. **7th row:** Sl st in first 2 sts, work across; ch 1, turn. **8th row:** Work across to

FINISHING: Sew shoulder, side, and sleeve seams. Sew in sleeves. **Neckband:** With A, ch 16. Work as for border on back until piece, when stretched slightly, fits around neck. Sew ends together to form ring. Sew neckband in place and fold in half to outside.

Cardigan

FRONT AND BACK: Work as for vest from Boy's Sweater Set (p. 187), working border with O and remainder of pattern in 8 rows each C, B, E, R, and O.

SHORT SLEEVE: Starting at lower edge with B, ch 48 [52—56]. **1st row:** Sc in 2nd ch from hook, (ch 1, skip next ch, sc in next ch) 23 [25—27] times (47 [51—55] sts); ch 1, turn. Work 8 rows each B and E. Sleeve should measure about 3" from beg.

To Shape Cap: Continue in stripe pattern, working 8 rows each R, O, and C and, *at the same time*, shape cap as follows: **1st row:** Sl st in first 4 sts, work across to within last 4 sts; turn. **2nd through 4th rows:** Work even. **5th row:** Sl st in first 2 sts, work across to within last 2 sts; turn. Repeat 2nd through 5th rows 3 times more; then work even for 0 [2—4] rows. (Repeat 5th row, work 1 row even) twice; repeat 5th row once more (11 [15—19] sts). Break off.

FINISHING: Sew shoulder, side, and sleeve seams. Sew in sleeves. Work neckband in O, as for boy's vest, placing buttonholes on right front instead of left. Sew neckband in place. Sew on buttons.

within last 2 sts. Break off. Skip center 11 sts, attach yarn to next st, ch 1, sc in same place; work other side of neck and shoulder to correspond.

Boy's Sweater Set

SIZES: 6 [8—10]. Pullover measures 12" [13"—14"] across back at underarms, 16½" [16¾"—17"] from back of neck to lower edge. Vest measures 13" [14"—15"] across back at underarms, 17½" [18"—18½"] from back of neck to lower edge.

MATERIALS: For set: Bear Brand Winsom Orlon acrylic, 4 (2-ounce) skeins Pompeii (rust) No. 339 (color P), 2 skeins each bronze No. 38 (B), green turquoise No. 331 (G), orange No. 91 (O), and electric blue No. 14 (E). **For pullover or vest only:** 2 skeins Pompeii (P), 1 skein each bronze (B), green turquoise (G), orange (O), and electric blue (E). Aluminum crochet hook size G (or Canadian hook No. 9) *or the size that will give you the correct gauge;* 5 buttons ⅝" in diameter.

GAUGE: 5 sts = 1"; 5 rows = 1".

Pullover

BACK: Border: (**Note:** Border is worked vertically.) Starting at side edge with P, ch 11. **1st row:** Sc in 2nd ch from hook and in each ch across (10 sc); ch 1, turn. **2nd row:** Working in back lp of each st, sc in each sc across; ch 1, turn. Repeat 2nd row until border measures 12" [13"—14"] when stretched slightly. Break off P, attach B, and ch 1. Do not turn but work along one long edge (top edge) of border and start body of pullover as follows: **1st row:** Sc in same place as last sc, (work ch 1 and sc) 30 [32—34] times evenly spaced along top edge of border (61 [65—69] sts); ch 1, turn. **2nd row:** Sc in first sc, * ch 1, sc in next sc. Repeat from * across. Break off B, attach E; ch 1, turn. Repeating 2nd row for pattern, work in stripes of 2 rows each E, O, G, and P. Repeat last 5 stripes for pattern until piece measures 10½" or desired length to underarms, omitting ch-1 on last row.

To Shape Armholes: Next row: Sl st in first 2 sts, continue across in pattern to within last 2 sts (2 sts dec at beg and end of row); turn. Dec 2 sts at beg and end of every row 2 [3—3] times more. Work even on 49 [49—53] sts until armholes measure 5½" [6"—6½"], omitting ch-1 on last row, ending at arm edge.

To Shape Shoulders: 1st row: Sl st in first 4 sts, work in pattern to within last 4 sts; turn. **2nd row:** Work 1 row even. Repeat 1st and 2nd rows once more. **5th row:** Sl st in first 4 [4—6] sts, work in pattern to within last 4 [4—6] sts (25 sts for back neck). Break off.

FRONT: Work as for back until piece measures 9½" or 1" less than desired length to underarms.

To Shape V-Neck and Armhole: Next row (side edge): Work across first 29 [31—33] sts; ch 1, turn. **Following row (dec row):** Sl st in first 2 sts (neck edge), work in pattern across; ch 1, turn. At neck edge repeat dec row every 4th row 5 times more and, *at the same time,* when piece measures same length as back to underarms, shape armhole as follows: **1st row:** At side edge, sl st in first 2 sts, work across. **2nd row:** Work across to within last 2 sts; turn. **For size 6 only:** Repeat first row once more. **For sizes 8 and 10 only:** Repeat first and 2nd rows once more. **For all sizes:** Work even on 11 [11—13] sts until piece measures same as back to shoulders, ending at arm edge and omitting ch-1 on last row.

To Shape Shoulder: 1st row: Sl st in first 4 sts, work across; ch 1, turn. **2nd row:** Work 1 row even. **3rd row:** Sl st in first 4 sts, work across remaining 3 [3—5] sts. Break off.

Skip center 3 sts, attach yarn to next sc and work other side to correspond.

SLEEVES: Cuff: (**Note:** Cuff is worked vertically.) With P, ch 11. Work same as for back border, repeating 2nd row 24 times (26 rows in all). (Cuff should measure 7", stretched slightly.) Break off P, attach B and ch 1. Sc in same place as last sc, (work ch 1 and sc) 14 times evenly spaced across top of cuff (29 sts); ch 1, turn. Continuing in pattern and color sequence as for back, inc 2 sts (to inc 2 sts work sc, ch 1, and sc in 1 sc) at beg and end of row every 1" 4 [5—6] times. Work even on 45 [49—53] sts until sleeve measures about 13½" or desired length to underarm, ending with same color stripe as on back and omitting ch-1 on last row.

To Shape Cap: 1st row (dec row): Sl st in first 2 sts, work across to within last 2 sts; turn. **2nd row:** Work even. Repeat 1st and 2nd rows once more, then repeat 1st row once again. Dec every 4th row twice. Work 2 rows even. Dec next 2 rows (17 [21—25] sts). Break off.

FINISHING: Sew shoulder, side, and sleeve seams. Sew in sleeves. **Neckband:** With P, crochet a chain to measure around neck. **1st row:** Sc in 2nd ch from hook and in each ch across; ch 1, turn. **2nd row:** Pull up lp in each of next 2 sc, y o hook and draw through all 3 lps on hook (1 sc dec), sc in each sc to within last 2 sc, dec 1 sc; ch 1, turn. Repeat last row twice more. Sew ends of neckband tog to form center front seam. Sew neckband in place.

Vest

BACK: Border: Work as for back of pullover until border measures 12" [13"—14"] when stretched slightly. Break off P, attach B and ch 1. Do not turn but work along one long edge (top edge) of border and start body of vest as follows: **1st row:** Sc in same place as last sc, (work ch 1 and sc) 32 [34—36] times evenly spaced along top edge of border (65 [69—73] sts); ch 1, turn. **2nd row:** Sc in first sc, * ch 1, sc in next sc. Repeat from * across. Repeating 2nd row for pattern, work in stripe pattern of 8 rows each B, E, O, G, and P as already established until piece measures 11½" or desired length to underarms, omitting ch-1 on last row.

To Shape Armholes: 1st row: Sl st in first 4 sts, work across in pattern to within last 4 sts; turn. **2nd row:** Sl st in first 2 sts, work across to within last 2 sts; turn. Repeat last row 1 [2—2] times more. Work even on 49 [49—53] sts until armholes measure 5½" [6"—6½"], omitting ch-1 on last row, ending at arm edge.

To Shape Shoulders: 1st row: Sl st in first 4 sts, work in pattern to within last 4 sts; turn. **2nd row:** Work even. Repeat 1st and 2nd rows once more. Then repeat 1st row once again (25 [25—29] sts remain for back neck). Break off.

LEFT FRONT: Border: Work as for back until piece measures 6½" [7"—7½"] when stretched slightly. Break off P, attach B and ch 1. Do not turn but work along one long edge (top edge) of border and start body of vest as follows: **1st row:** Sc in same place as last sc, (work ch 1 and sc) 14 [15—16] times evenly spaced along top edge of border (29 [31—33] sts); ch 1, turn. Work even in pattern and stripe pattern for back until piece measures same as back to underarm, ending at side edge and omitting ch-1 on last row.

To Shape Neck and Armhole: 1st row: Sl st in first 4 sts, work across. **2nd row:** Dec 2 sts (neck edge), work across to within last 2 sts; turn. **3rd row:** Sl st in first 2 sts, work across; ch 1, turn. At neck edge dec 2 sts every 1" [1"—¾"] 3 [4—5] times more. Work even on 13 sts until armhole measures same as back to shoulder, ending at arm edge.

To Shape Shoulder: 1st row: Sl st in first 4 sts, work across; ch 1, turn. **2nd row:** Work even. **3rd row:** Sl st in first 4 sts, work across remaining 5 sts. Break off.

RIGHT FRONT: Work as for left front, reversing shaping.

FINISHING: Sew shoulder and side seams. **Neckband:** With P, crochet a chain to measure from lower edge of left front, around neck to lower edge of right front. **1st row:** Sc in 2nd ch from hook and in each ch across; ch 1, turn. Mark band for 5 buttonholes on left front, placing the first 1" from lower edge, the last at beg of neck shaping, and the others evenly spaced between. **2nd row:** * Sc in each sc to marker, ch 2, skip next 2 sc. Repeat from * 4 times more, sc in each sc across; ch 1, turn. Work 1 row sc, working sc in each ch st of buttonholes. Work 1 more row sc. Break off. Sew neckband in place. Sew on buttons. **Armband:** With P, crochet a chain to measure around armhole. **1st row:** Sc in 2nd ch from hook and in each ch across; ch 1, turn. **2nd row:** Sc in each sc across; ch 1, turn. Repeat 2nd row twice more. Break off. Sew ends of armband together to form ring. Sew in place. Make other armband in same manner.

Drawstring Skirt

In colorful pink, plum, and turquoise stripes, in shell pattern, for a pretty young lady.

SIZE: Fits 19" waist. Length is 10".
MATERIALS: Knitting worsted, 4 ounces turquoise (color T), 2 ounces each hot pink (H) and plum (P); aluminum crochet hook size G (or Canadian hook No. 9) *or the size that will give you the correct gauge.*
GAUGE: 4 sc = 1"; 4 sc rows = 1".
2 shells = 1½"; 2 shell rows = 1".

Starting at waist with H, ch 75 to measure 19". Join with sl st to form ring. **1st rnd:** Ch 1, sc in each ch around (74 sc); sl st in ch-1.

Break off; attach P, ch 1. **2nd rnd:** Sc in each sc around; join, ch 1. **3rd rnd:** Sc in each sc around, increasing 6 sc evenly spaced (80 sc); join. Break off P; attach T, ch 1. **4th rnd:** Sc in each sc around; join, ch 1. **5th rnd:** Sc in each sc around, increasing 7 sc evenly spaced (87 sc); join. Break off T. **6th rnd:** With P, form a lp on hook; work 3 dc in first sc on 5th row (shell made), ch 1, skip next 2 sc, * 3 dc in next sc, ch 1, skip next 2 sc. Repeat from * around (29 shells); join. Break off. **7th rnd:** Form a lp on hook, * work 3 dc in next sp, ch 1. Repeat from * around; join. Repeating 7th rnd for shell pattern, work 1 more rnd with P, 5 rnds H, 9 rnds T. Do not break off on last rnd.

PICOT EDGING: * Sc in center dc of next shell, ch 2, sc in side of last sc worked (picot made), ch 1, dc in same center dc of same shell, ch 2. Repeat from * around; join. Break off.

FINISHING: Waistband: 1st rnd: With H, form a lp on hook, sc in any sc on first rnd, * ch 1, skip next sc, sc in next sc. Repeat from * around; join. Break off.

DRAWSTRING: Working with 1 strand each of T and H, crochet a 30" chain. Break off. Weave through ch-1 sps of waistband. With P, make two tassels 2" long and fasten one to each end of drawstring.

Accessories

Snappy Envelope

This snappy shoulder bag is quick and easy to make, looks great in bright red and turquoise knitting worsted.

SIZE: 6" x 8".

MATERIALS: Knitting worsted, 2 ounces turquoise, 1 ounce red; aluminum crochet hook size H (or Canadian hook No. 8), *or the size that will give you the correct gauge.*

GAUGE: 7 sc = 2"; 4 rows = 1".

Beginning at side edge with turquoise, ch 46 to measure about 12½". **1st row:** Sc in 2nd ch from hook and in each sc across (45 sc); ch 1, turn. **2nd row:** Sc in each sc across; ch 1, turn. Repeat last row until piece measures approximately 7½" from beg. Break off.

EDGING: Fold one end of piece over 4¾" for front of bag and pin sides.

1st rnd: With right side facing you, attach red at one corner of flap. Working sc evenly

Shoulder Bag

For the little girl with a sweet tooth. Decorated with crocheted lollipops and real lollipop sticks.

SIZE: 6½" in diameter.
MATERIALS: Aunt Lydia's heavy rug yarn, 1 (70-yard) skein red No. 120, small amounts national blue No. 715 and sunset orange (yellow) No. 550 for lollipops; aluminum crochet hook size G (or Canadian hook No. 9) *or the size that will give you the correct gauge;* 2 lollipop sticks.
GAUGE: 7 dc = 2".
FIRST CIRCLE: Starting at center with red, ch 5. Join with sl st to form ring. **1st rnd:** Ch 3, work 12 dc in ring (13 dc, counting ch-3 as 1 dc); sl st in top of ch-3. **2nd rnd:** Ch 3, dc in same place as sl st, 2 dc in each dc around (26 dc); sl st in top of ch-3. **3rd rnd:** Ch 3, 2 dc in same place as sl st, * dc in next dc, 2 dc in next dc. Repeat from * around, ending with dc in last dc (40 dc); sl st in top of ch-3. **4th rnd:** Ch 3, dc in next dc, 2 dc in next dc, * dc in each of next 2 dc, 2 dc in next dc. Repeat from * to within last dc, 2 dc in last dc (54 dc); sl st in top of ch-3. **5th rnd:** Ch 1, sc in each dc around; join. Break off.
SECOND CIRCLE: Work as for first circle.
JOINING: Holding circles together with wrong sides facing, crochet around ¾ of circles, working sc through both thicknesses. Leave remaining section open for top of bag. Do not break yarn. **Shoulder Strap:** Ch 85 to measure about 24"; sl st in opposite end of opening, positioning strap correctly so that it will not twist. Sc in each st along chain to opposite end; join with sl st. Break off.
LOLLIPOPS (make 1 blue, 1 orange): Repeat directions through first rnd of circle. Break off. Following photograph for placement, sew crossed lollipop sticks and lollipops to one side of bag.

Watchband

Worked in single crochet, this colorful watchband is simple enough for a child to make.

MATERIALS: Coats & Clark's Speed-Cro-Sheen (100 yards), 1 ball watermelon No. 122; steel crochet hook No. 1 (or Canadian hook No. 0); one 1" round buckle.

Ch 36 to measure 8". **1st row:** Sc in 2nd ch from hook (mark this end), sc in each ch across to within last ch, work 3 sc in last st. Work a sc in each st along opposite side of chain. Ch 1, turn. **2nd row:** Sc in each sc across one side only to within last 3 sc, working 2 sc in each of next 3 sc, then sc in each sc across opposite side. Break off.

FINISHING: Sew buckle in place at marked end, folding end over bar and prong.

Funny Puppet Mittens

Give a performance while you keep your hands warm: ferocious alligator meets busy bumblebee. Made of knitting worsted.

Busy Bumblebee

SIZE: Child's 4 to 6 years.

MATERIALS: Knitting worsted, 2 ounces each yellow and black, small amounts white, red, and lavender; aluminum crochet hook size F (or Canadian hook No. 10) *or the size that will give you the correct gauge;* tapestry needle.

GAUGE: 5 sc = 1"; 4 rows = 1".

Starting at fingertips with yellow, ch 4. Join with sl st to form ring. **1st rnd:** Ch 1, work 7 sc in ring; join with sl st to ch-1. **2nd rnd:** Ch 1, 2 sc in each sc around (14 sc); join. **3rd rnd:** Ch 1, * 2 sc in next sc, sc in next sc. Repeat from * around (21 sc); join. **4th rnd:** Ch 1, * 2 sc in next sc, sc in each of next 2 sc. Repeat from * around (28 sc); join. **5th rnd:** Ch 1, sc in each sc around; join. Repeat 5th rnd twice more. Break off yellow; attach black to first sc. **8th rnd:** Ch 2, h dc in each sc around (28 h dc, counting ch-2 as 1 h dc); join. Repeat 8th rnd 6 times more in the following color sequence: 1 rnd black, 2 rnds yellow, 2 rnds black, 1 rnd yellow. **15th rnd:** With yellow, ch 7, skip next 7 h dc, sl st in next h dc (opening for thumb), ch 2, h dc in each of next 20 h dc, sc in each of next 7 ch (28 sts, counting ch-2 as 1 st); join. Repeat 8th rnd 10 times in the following color sequence: 2 rnds black, (2 rnds yellow, 2 rnds black) twice. Break off (wrist edge).

THUMB: Attach yellow with sl st to one end of thumb opening. **1st rnd:** Ch 1, sc in each st around (14 sc); join. **2nd rnd:** Ch 1, draw up lp in each of next 2 sts, y o hook and draw through all 3 lps on hook (1 sc dec), sc in each sc around to within last 2 sc, dec 1 sc; join. **3rd and 4th rnds:** Work even. **5th rnd:** Ch 1, sc in each sc around, decreasing 1 sc (11 sc). **6th rnd:** Work even. Repeat 5th and 6th rnds once more, then repeat 6th rnd again. **10th rnd:** Ch 1, sc in each sc around, decreasing 3 sts as evenly spaced as possible; join. Repeat 10th rnd once more (4 sc). Break off, leaving 12" end. Thread end in tapestry needle, weave through remaining 4 sts, pull up and break off.

SMALL WINGS (make 2): With white, ch 8. **1st rnd:** Sc in 2nd ch from hook and in each of next 5 ch, 3 sc in next ch; working along opposite side of chain, sc in each of next 6 ch, sl st in next sc. **2nd rnd:** Ch 2, h dc in each of next 6 sc, 3 h dc in next sc, h dc in each of next 7 sc, h dc in next sl st; join. Break off.

LARGE WINGS (make 2): With white, ch 10. **1st rnd:** Sc in 2nd ch from hook and in each of next 7 ch, 3 sc in next ch; working along opposite side of chain, sc in each of next 8 ch, sl st in next sc. **2nd rnd:** Ch 2, h dc in each of next 8 sc, 3 h dc in next sc, h dc in each of next 9 sc, h dc in next sl st, sl st in ch-2. **3rd rnd:** Ch 2, h dc in each of next 8 h dc, (2 h dc in next h dc) 3 times; h dc in each of next 10 h dc, h dc in next sl st; join. Break off. Make another mitten and wings in same manner.

FINISHING: Fold mittens so that thumbs are on opposite sides of palms. Hold a small and a large wing together and sew 2 pairs to back of each mitten, following photograph for position. With red, work satin-stitch eyes on 10th row. To form stinger, with white, crochet 1" chain and sew in position. To form mouth, with lavender, work small straight stitches on inside of thumb. With black, crochet 36" chain. Sew one end of chain to each mitten.

Ferocious Alligator

SIZE: 6 to 10 years.

MATERIALS: Knitting worsted, 4 ounces green, small amounts red, white, and blue; aluminum crochet hook size F (or Canadian hook No. 10) *or the size that will give you the correct gauge;* tapestry needle.

GAUGE: 5 sc = 1"; 5 rows = 1".

HAND (UPPER JAW): Starting at fingertips (snout of alligator) with green, ch 3. Join with sl st to form ring. **1st rnd:** Ch 1, work 8 sc in ring; join with sl st to ch-1. **2nd rnd:** Ch 1, sc in each sc around; join. **3rd rnd:** Ch 1, * 2 sc in next sc, sc in next sc. Repeat from * around (12 sc); join. Repeat 2nd rnd 3 times more. **7th**

rnd: Ch 1, * sc in each of next 3 sc, 2 sc in next sc. Repeat from * around (15 sc); join. Repeat 2nd rnd twice more. **10th rnd:** Ch 1, * sc in each of next 2 sc, 2 sc in next sc. Repeat from * around (20 sc); join. Repeat 2nd rnd once more. **12th rnd:** Ch 1, sc in each sc around, increasing 6 sc as evenly spaced as possible (26 sc); join. Repeat 2nd rnd 4 times more. **17th rnd:** Ch 1, sc in each sc around, increasing 7 sc as evenly spaced as possible (33 sc); join. Work even until piece measures 5″ from beg. **Next rnd:** Work to within last 5 sc, sc in next sc and place marker, sc in each of next 4 sc; join. Do not break off.

THUMB (LOWER JAW): Ch 1, sc in each of next 10 sc, ch 10, turn, skip last 10 sc, sl st in ch-1 at beg of rnd to form ring; turn. **1st rnd:** Ch 1, sc in each of next 10 sc, sc in each of next 10 ch (20 sc); join with sl st to ch-1. **2nd rnd:** Ch 1, sc in each sc around; join. Repeat 2nd rnd once more. **4th rnd:** Ch 1, * sc in each of next 3 sc, dec 1 sc as follows: Draw up lp in each of next 2 sts, y o, draw through all 3 lps on hook. Repeat from * around (16 sc); join. Repeat 2nd rnd until thumb measures 3″. **Next rnd:** Ch 1, sc in each sc around, decreasing 2 sts as evenly spaced as possible; join. Repeat last rnd 4 times more (6 sc). Break off, leaving 9″ end. Thread end in tapestry needle, draw thread through each remaining st, pull tight and break off.

Following stitch diagram, and photograph for placement, with red, embroider satin-st tongue on inner side of thumb (make each st the height of 1 sc, working back and forth in rows). With white, embroider satin-st teeth along sides of tongue and on palm.

TOP OF HAND: 1st rnd: Attach green to marked st, ch 1, sc in same place as sl st, sc in each of next 4 sc. Work 10 sc along base of thumb, sc in each free sc around hand (33 sc); join. **2nd rnd:** Ch 1, sc in each sc around, increasing 3 sts as evenly spaced as possible (36 sc); join. **3rd rnd:** Ch 1, sc in each sc around; join. **4th rnd:** Ch 1, sc in each of next 20 sc, 2 h dc in each of next 6 sc to start alligator eye, sc in each of next 4 sc, 2 h dc in each of next 6 sc for other eye; join. **5th rnd:** Ch 1, sc in each of next 20 sc, dc in each of next 12 h dc, sc in each of next 4 sc, dc in each of next 12 h dc; join. **6th rnd:** Ch 1, sc in each of next 20 sc, h dc in each of next 12 dc, sc in each of next 4 sc, h dc in each of next 12 dc; join. **7th rnd:** Ch 1, sc in each of next 20 sc, (dec 1 h dc) 6 times; sc in each of next 4 sc, (dec 1 sc) 6 times; join. Work even until piece measures 8″ from beg. **Next rnd:** Ch 1, sc in each sc around, decreasing 8 sts evenly spaced (28 sc); join. Work even for 3 rnds more. Break off. Work 2nd mitten in same manner.

FINISHING: Following photograph, work blue and white eyes in satin stitch. With green, make 45″ chain and attach an end to inside of each mitten at wrist.

Toys

Four Soft Foam-Filled Blocks

In various sizes and bright colors to keep baby amused. Some are made of solid granny squares, others are multicolored or two-toned.

SIZES: Finished blocks measure:
  No. 1: 4½" square
  No. 2: 2" square
  No. 3: 3½" square
  No. 4: 2½" square

MATERIALS: Bear Brand Winsom Orlon acrylic yarn, 1 (2-ounce) skein each white No. 330, red No. 332, yellow No. 302 and blue No. 292; steel crochet hook No. 0; 18" square of ½"-thick polyurethane foam; tapestry needle.

BLOCK NO. 1: Square: Starting at center with white, ch 4. Join with sl st to form ring. **1st rnd (right side):** Ch 3, work 2 dc in ring, (ch 1, work 3 dc in ring) 3 times, ch 1; join with sl st to top of ch-3. Break off. **2nd rnd:** Make lp on hook with red, y o, insert hook in any ch-1 sp and complete dc; in same sp work 2 more dc, ch 1 and 3 dc for first corner, * ch 1, in next sp work 3 dc, ch 1 and 3 dc (another corner). Repeat from * twice more, ch 1; join. Break off. **3rd rnd:** Make lp on hook with yellow, work first corner in any corner sp, * ch 1, 3-dc shell in next sp, ch 1, work corner in next corner sp. Repeat from * twice more, ending ch 1, shell in next sp, ch 1; join. Break off. **4th rnd:** With blue, work first corner in any corner sp, * ch 1, shell in next sp. Repeat from * to next corner, ch 1, work corner in next corner sp. Continue around in pattern; join. Break off. **5th rnd:** With white repeat last rnd.

Edging: With right side of square facing you, working through back lps only, sc with red in each st around, working 3 sc in each corner sp; join with sl st to first sc. Break off. Unblocked square should measure about 4".

Work 5 more squares in same manner.

Assembling: Holding two squares with right sides facing you, using matching-color yarn and tapestry needle, whipstitch squares together along one side. Join 3rd square to 2nd, and 4th to 3rd, so that piece forms strip, then join ends of strip to form ring. Matching corners, join 5th square around one edge of ring to form square cup shape.

Finishing: Cut nine 4½" squares of foam and fit inside block. Join remaining square to close block.

BLOCK NO. 2: Square No. 1: Work as for 1st and 2nd rnds of Block No. 1, working 1st rnd in red, 2nd rnd in blue. **Squares No. 2, 3 and 4:** Work as for Square No. 1. **Squares No. 5 and 6:** Work in same manner, working 1st rnd in blue, 2nd rnd in red.

Edging: With yellow work as for Block No. 1. Unblocked squares should measure about 1½".

Assembling and Finishing: Work as for Block No. 1, using four 2" squares of foam for stuffing.

BLOCK NO. 3: To change colors: Work dc to point where 2 lps are on hook. With new color make lp on hook and complete dc. Break off old color, leaving a 3" end. Crochet over ends to conceal them.

Square No. 1: With white ch 4. Join with sl st to form ring. **1st rnd:** Ch 3, work 2 dc in ring, ch 1, work 3 dc in ring, changing to blue on last dc; break off white. With blue ch 1, work 3 dc, ch 1 and 3 dc in ring, ch 1; join to top of ch-3. Break off. **2nd rnd:** With white make lp on hook and work 3 dc in last ch-1 sp (half of first corner made); ch 1; in next ch-1 sp work 3 dc, ch 1 and 3 dc (2nd corner), ch 1, work 3 dc in next ch-1 sp, changing to blue on last dc (half of 3rd corner). With blue ch 1, work 3 dc in same sp to complete 3rd corner, ch 1, in next ch-1 sp work 3 dc, ch 1 and 3 dc (4th corner), ch 1, in same sp with first 3 dc work 3 dc and ch 1, join to top of first dc (first corner completed). Break off. **3rd rnd:** With white make lp on hook, work half of first corner in last ch-1 sp, ch 1, 3 dc in next sp (first shell made), ch 1, 2nd corner in next sp, ch 1, shell in next sp, ch 1, 3rd corner in next sp (half white, half blue), ch 1, shell in next sp, ch 1, 4th corner in next sp, ch 1, shell in next sp, ch 1, complete first corner. Break off. **4th rnd:** Work as for 3rd rnd, working 1 more shell in each ch-1 sp between corners.

Edging: Work as for Block No. 1, working in colors to match square halves. Unblocked square should measure about 3".

Work remaining squares as for first square with the following colors:

Square No. 2: Blue and yellow
Square No. 3: Yellow and red
Square No. 4: Red and white
Square No. 5: Yellow and white
Square No. 6: Red and blue

Assembling and Finishing: Work as for Block No. 1, matching colors and using seven 3½" square pieces of foam.

BLOCK NO. 4: Work 6 squares as for Block No. 1 through 3rd rnd, working each square in one color only as follows: Do not break off at end of rnd but sl st into first ch-1 sp, ch 3, then continue in pattern as given. Work 2 squares each red, blue, and yellow.

Edging: With white, work as for Block No. 1. Unblocked squares should measure about 2½".

Assembling and Finishing: Work as for Block No. 1, using five 2½" squares of foam for stuffing.

Zoo Animals to Cuddle

These delightful creatures—elephant, tiger, and lion—take their bodily form from an egg-shaped stocking container. Enclose a couple of beans in the container to make them rattle, then cover in single crochet. Their felt faces are sewn on afterward.

SIZE: Each animal measures 5½".

MATERIALS: Coats and Clark's Wintuk sock and sweater acrylic yarn: for elephant, 1 (2-ounce) skein each red No. 905, yellow No. 230, and royal blue No. 845; for tiger, 1 skein each yellow and blue; for lion, 1 skein each red and yellow (**note:** one skein of each color will do for color requirements for all 3 animals); scraps of turquoise, orange, green, lavender, and purple felt; 1 container from L'eggs panty hose for body of each animal; steel crochet hook No. 0 *or the size that will give you the correct gauge;* tapestry needle; plastic glue; fabric glue; matching-color yarn for stuffing; a few beans or pebbles for rattle.

GAUGE: 7 sts = 1"; 7 rows = 1".

GENERAL DIRECTIONS: The body of each animal is worked in 2 sections. Each section is slipped over half a L'eggs container and 2 sections are seamed together. The animals are hand washable.

To Change Colors: Work to within last sc of first color, draw up lp in next sc, y o hook with new color and complete st.

Elephant

See General Directions.

BODY: Front Section: Starting at front with red, ch 2. **1st rnd:** Work 6 sc in 2nd ch from hook. Do not join, but mark beg of each rnd. **2nd rnd (inc rnd):** Work 2 sc in each sc around (12 sc). **3rd rnd (inc rnd):** Sc in each sc, increasing 6 sc evenly spaced around (18 sc). **4th through 8th rnds:** Repeat 3rd rnd (48 sc). **9th rnd:** Sc in each sc around.

Continue to work even until piece fits over smaller half of container. Break off.

Back Section: Work as for front section until piece fits over pointed half of container, leaving about 15" length of yarn to sew sections together.

LEGS (make 4): 1st rnd: Starting at bottom with red, ch 2, work 7 sc in 2nd ch from hook. **2nd rnd (inc rnd):** Work 2 sc in each sc around (14 sc). **3rd rnd:** Working in back lp only, sc in each sc around. **4th rnd:** Sc in each sc around.

Continue to work even until leg measures about 1″ in length. Break off.

EARS (make 2): Starting at narrow end with yellow, ch 6. **1st row:** Sc in 2nd ch from hook and in each ch across; ch 1, turn. **2nd row (inc row):** Work 2 sc in first sc, sc in each sc to within last sc, 2 in last sc (7 sc); ch 1, turn.

Repeat 2nd row twice more (11 sc), then work even until piece measures about 1½″ from beg. Mark first and last sts of last row. Break off.

Border: 1st rnd: Starting in right marked st with red, work 3 sc in this st (corner made), sc in each st across to within left marked st, work another corner; continue to sc evenly around remainder of ear. **2nd and 3rd rnds:** Sc in each sc around, working corner in center sc at each corner. Break off.

TAIL: With red, ch 10 to measure about 1½″. **1st row:** Sc in 2nd ch from hook and in each ch across. Break off.

Tassel: Cut four 2″ lengths of red yarn. Hold tog and fold in half. Insert folded end through end of tail and draw ends through loop; tighten.

TRUNK: Starting at end with yellow, ch 2. **1st rnd:** Work 4 sc in 2nd ch from hook. Attach red; break off yellow. **2nd rnd (inc rnd):** With red, work 2 sc in each sc around (8 sc). Sc in each sc around until piece measures about 2½″ long. **Last rnd (inc rnd):** Sc in each sc, increasing 4 sc evenly spaced around. Break off.

BLANKET: Starting at one end with blue, ch 11 to measure about 1½″. **1st row:** Sc in 2nd ch from hook and in each ch across; ch 1, turn. **2nd row:** Sc in each sc across; ch 1, turn.

Continue to work even until piece measures about 6″ when slightly stretched. Break off.

Tassels (make 14): Cut two 2″ lengths of yellow yarn. Following directions for tail tassel, fasten 7 tassels to blanket ends.

FINISHING: Place a few pebbles or beans in container, close container and, following manufacturer's directions, seal with plastic glue. (Be sure to seal well so that water won't seep in when animal is washed.) Fit crocheted pieces of body over container. Thread yarn end in tapestry needle and sew body sections together.

Following photograph, sew ears, tail, and blanket in place. Stuff trunk and feet with matching-color yarn and sew in place.

Features: From felt cut 2-tone turquoise-and-green eyes, a smiling lavender mouth, and 2 orange cheeks; glue in place with fabric glue.

Tiger

See General Directions.

BODY: Front Section: Starting at nose with red, ch 2. **1st rnd:** Work 6 sc in 2nd ch from hook. Attach yellow; break off red. **2nd through 8th rnds:** With yellow, work as for elephant (48 sc). **9th rnd:** Sc in each sc around. Attach blue; drop yellow. **10th and 11th rnds:** With blue, work sc in each sc around. Drop blue; pick up yellow. **12th and 13th rnds:** With yellow, work sc in each sc around. Drop yellow; pick up blue.

Repeat last 4 rows for stripe pattern until piece fits over pointed half of container, ending with a yellow stripe. Break off.

Back Section: Work as for front section, working with yellow only on 1st through 9th rnds, then work in stripe pattern until piece fits over other half of container, ending with a blue stripe. Break off, leaving about 15″ length of yarn to sew sections together.

LEGS (make 4): Using yellow, work as for elephant's legs.

EARS (make 2): Starting at center with yellow, ch 2. **1st row:** Work 6 sc in 2nd ch from hook; ch 1, turn. **2nd row:** Work 2 sc in each sc across (12 sc); ch 1, turn. **3rd row:** Sc in each sc across. Break off.

TAIL: Starting at tip with yellow, ch 2. **1st rnd:** Work 6 sc in 2nd ch from hook. **2nd through 5th rnds:** With yellow, work sc in each sc around. Attach blue; drop yellow. Working even, work 2 rnds blue, 2 rnds yellow, 2 rnds blue, 3 rnds yellow. Break off.

FINISHING: Follow first paragraph of finishing for elephant.

Following photograph, sew ears in place. Stuff tail and legs with matching yarn and sew in place.

Topknot: Make several loops with blue yarn and tack to center of head between ears.

Features: Work as for elephant's features.

Lion

See General Directions.

BODY: Front Section: Starting at nose with red, ch 2. **1st rnd:** Work 6 sc in 2nd ch from hook. Attach yellow; break off red. With yellow, work as for elephant through 8th rnd (48 sc). **9th rnd:** Sc in each sc around. Attach red, break off yellow; ch 1, turn.

Looped Fringe for Mane: 1st rnd (wrong side): You will need 1½" x 3" strip of cardboard. Holding crocheted piece at lower edge of cardboard, y o cardboard from back to front, pull up lp in next sc, y o hook and draw through both lps on hook, * insert hook in next sc, y o cardboard, pull up lp, y o hook and draw through both lps on hook. Repeat from * around, sliding completed lps from cardboard. **2nd rnd:** Sc in each sc around.

Repeat last 2 rnds twice more. Attach yellow at end of last rnd; break off red. Turn. **7th rnd (right side):** With yellow, sc in each sc around.

Continue to work even until piece fits over pointed half of container. Break off.

Back Section: With yellow, work as for 1st through 8th rnds of front section. **9th rnd:** Sc in each sc around.

Continue to work even until piece fits over other half of container. Break off, leaving about 15" length of yarn to sew sections together.

LEGS (make 4): Work as for elephant's legs.
EARS (make 2): Work as for tiger's ears.
TAIL: Starting at tip with red, ch 2. **1st rnd:** Work 6 sc in 2nd ch from hook; ch 1, turn. **2nd rnd (wrong side):** Work as for first rnd of looped fringe. **3rd rnd:** Sc in each sc around. Attach yellow; break off red. Turn. **4th rnd (right side):** Sc in each sc around.

Continue to work even until tail measures about 1½". Break off.

FINISHING: Follow first paragraph of finishing for elephant.

Following photograph, sew ears in place. Stuff tail and legs with matching-color yarn and sew in place.

Features: Work as for elephant's features, making mouth orange and cheeks purple.

Three lovable, huggable friends never to be parted with—Panda Bear, Tootsie Turtle, and Mr. Mouse. They are worked in single crochet in sections that are then joined together. In Orlon acrylic knitting worsted for easy washability.

Panda Bear

SIZE: 16" tall.
MATERIALS: Knitting worsted (Orlon acrylic), 4 ounces each white (color W) and black (B); aluminum crochet hook size H (or Canadian hook No. 8), *or the size that will give you the correct gauge;* 2 moving sew-on eyes or buttons ½" in diameter; Poly-fil or any washable stuffing.
GAUGE: 3 sc = 1"; 7 rnds = 2".
BACK OF HEAD: Starting at center with W, ch 2. **1st rnd:** Work 6 sc in 2nd ch from hook. Do not join rnds, but mark beg of each rnd. **2nd rnd:** Work 2 sc in each sc around (12 sc). **3rd through 11th rnds:** Sc in each sc around, increasing 6 sts evenly spaced. Do not work increases directly above increases of previous rnd. Sc in each sc around for 2 rnds (66 sc). Piece should measure about 6½" in diameter. Do not break off.

Work short rows as follows: **1st short row:** Ch 1, sc in each of next 56 sc. Do not work across remaining sts for neck. Break off. **2nd and 3rd short rows:** With same side of work facing you, sc in each sc of last row. Break off.

FRONT OF HEAD: Work as for back of head until 13th rnd is completed (66 sc). Work even in sc for 1 rnd more, then repeat 1st and 2nd short rows.

Note: Label small sections as you work to simplify assembling.

EAR (make 4): With B, work as for back of head until 5th rnd is completed (30 sc). **6th rnd:** Sc in each sc around. Break off.

EYE PATCH (make 2): With B, work first 2 rnds of back of head (12 sc). **3rd rnd:** * (Work 2 sc in next sc) 3 times; sc in each of next 3 sc. Repeat from * once more (18 sc). **4th rnd:** * 2 sc in next sc, (sc in next sc, 2 sc in next sc) twice; sc in each of next 4 sc. Repeat from * once more; sl st in next sc (24 sc). Break off.

SNOUT: With W, work first 3 rnds of back of head (18 sc). Work even in sc for 2 rnds. **6th and 7th rnds:** Sc in each sc around, increasing 6 sc evenly spaced (30 sc). Sc in each sc around for 2 rnds. Join with sl st in next sc and break off.

NOSE: With B, work first 2 rnds of back of head. Sc in each sc around for 1 rnd. Join and break off.

FOOT (make 2): Starting at center of bottom with W, ch 7. **1st rnd:** Work 3 sc in 2nd ch from hook, sc in each of next 4 ch, work 3 sc in last ch; working along opposite side of chain, sc in each of next 4 sts. **2nd rnd:** (Work 2 sc in each of next 3 sc, sc in each of next 4 sc) twice. **3rd rnd:** 2 sc in next sc, (sc in next sc, 2 sc in next sc) twice; sc in each of next 5 sc. Repeat from * once more. **4th rnd:** * Sc in next sc, 2 sc in next sc, sc in each of next 2 sc, 2 sc in next sc. Repeat from * around, sc in last sc. Join and break off W (36 sc). Continue as follows for leg:

LEG: 1st rnd: With B, sc in back lp only of each sc around (36 sc). Working in both lps of each sc, work even in sc for 3½" from first rnd, decreasing 6 sts on last rnd. Join and break off. **For ridge:** Hold piece with white section toward you. With B, working through both thicknesses of last W rnd and first B rnd of leg, sc in each st around. Join and break off.

ARM (make 2): Work as for foot and leg.

TAIL: With B, make 2 pieces as for ear.

BODY: Make one with W for front and one with B for back. Starting at center, ch 8. **1st rnd:** Work 3 sc in 2nd ch from hook, sc in each ch across, 5 sc in last ch. Working along opposite side of starting chain, sc in each ch across, work 2 sc in same ch where first 3 sc were worked (20 sts). **2nd rnd:** Sc in each sc around. **3rd rnd:** Sc in each sc around, increasing 5 sts evenly spaced at each end of oval (10 sts increased). Repeat last 2 rnds 6 times more (there are 90 sc at end of 15th rnd). Work even in sc for 1 rnd. Break off. At one end of oval, mark center 5 sts for neck edge. **1st short row:** Starting at st after last marker, sc in each sc around to first marker, do not work sts marked for neck. Break off. Repeat 2nd and 3rd short rows of back of head.

FINISHING: Sew head sections together and sew body sections together, matching sts of last short rows and leaving opening at neck. Sew eyes securely to eye patches, then sew patches in place. Sew nose to snout, stuff snout and sew in place. Sew 2 ear pieces together for each ear, leaving an opening. Stuff ears, sew opening closed and sew in place. Stuff head and body, then join at neck. Stuff arm sections and foot-and-leg sections, pinch top edges together and sew in place. Sew tail sections together, leaving opening; stuff and sew opening closed. Sew in place at rear of body. With B, chain about 3". Break off. Sew in place below snout for mouth.

Tootsie Turtle

SIZE: 15" across body and head.

MATERIALS: Knitting worsted (Orlon acrylic), 4 ounces antique gold (color G), 2 ounces jade green (J), 1 ounce chartreuse (C), small amount of black; aluminum crochet hook size H (or Canadian hook No. 8), *or the size that will give you the correct gauge;* 2 moving sew-on eyes or buttons ½" in diameter; paper-towel tube (remove tubing to wash); Poly-fil or any washable stuffing.

GAUGE: 3 sc = 1"; 7 rnds = 2".

BODY: Under Section: Starting at center with G, ch 8. **1st rnd:** Work 3 sc in 2nd ch from hook, sc in each of next 5 ch, work 3 sc in last ch; working along opposite side of ch, sc in each of next 5 sts; join with sl st in first sc. **2nd rnd:** Work 2 sc in same sc as sl st, work 2 sc in each of next 2 sc, sc in each of next 5 sc, work 2 sc in each of next 3 sc, sc in each of next 5 sc; join as before. **3rd rnd:** Work 2 sc in same sc as sl st, (sc in next sc, 2 sc in next sc) twice; sc in each of next 6 sc, 2 sc in next sc, (sc in next sc, 2 sc in next sc) twice; sc in each of next 6 sc; join. **4th rnd:** Sc in same sc as sl st, sc in next sc, * 2 sc in next sc, sc in each of next 3 sc, 2 sc in next sc, sc in each of next 2 sc. Repeat from * around, ending last repeat with 2 sc in last sc (8 sts inc); join.

Continue to sc in each sc around, increasing 8 sts as evenly spaced as possible in each rnd until 12th rnd is completed (do not work increases over those in previous rnds). **Last rnd:** Sc in each sc around (100 sc); join and break off.

Top Section: Using C, work as for under section until 2nd rnd is completed. Break off C; make lp on hook with J. Always change color in same manner. With J, repeat 3rd and 4th rnds (36 sc). Break off J.

Place six markers in work, one at each end of oval and two on each side, evenly spaced between first two. Continue to work in striped pattern as established (2 rnds C, 2 rnds J) and sc in each sc around, increasing 1 st at each of the 6 markers every rnd until 14th rnd is completed. Increases should always fall in approximately the same places. Break off C. **15th rnd:** With J, sc in each sc around, increasing 4 sts evenly spaced (100 sc). With J, sc evenly around for 3 rnds more. Join and break off.

FOOT (make 4): Starting at center of bottom with G, ch 5. **1st rnd:** Work 3 sc in 2nd ch from hook, sc in each of next 2 ch, work 3 sc in last ch; working along opposite side of chain, sc in each of next 2 sts. Mark beg of rnds. **2nd rnd:** (Work 2 sc in next sc, sc in next sc) 5 times. **3rd and 4th rnds:** Sc around, increasing 5 sc evenly spaced; join with sl st in next sc. **5th rnd:** Ch 1, sc in back lp only of each sc around (25 sc). Working in both lps of each sc, work even in sc for 2 rnds. Put a marker in work in center st at one end of oval for toe shaping. **Next rnd:** Sc around to within 2 sts of marker, draw up a lp in each of next 3 sts, y o and draw through all lps on hook (2 sts dec), sc to end of rnd. Repeat last rnd 3 times more. Join and break off. **For ridge:** With G, working around free lps of 5th rnd and also through 6th rnd, sc in each st around. Join and break off.

HEAD: Top Section: With G, ch 7. **1st rnd:** Work 3 sc in 2nd ch from hook, sc in each of next 4 sts, work 3 sc in last ch; working along opposite side of chain, sc in each of next 4 sts. **2nd rnd:** (Work 2 sc in each of next 3 sc, sc in each of next 4 sc) twice. **3rd rnd:** * 2 sc in next sc, (sc in next sc, 2 sc in next sc) twice; sc in each of next 5 sc. Repeat from * once. **4th rnd:** * Sc in next sc, 2 sc in next sc, sc in each of next 2 sc, 2 sc in next sc. Repeat from * around, sc in last sc (36 sc). Work even in sc for 3 rnds. Join and break off.

Lower Section: Starting at top edge with G, ch 36. Join with sl st to form ring. **1st rnd:** Sc in same ch as sl st and in each ch around (36 sc). Work 1 rnd even. Put a marker in any sc for neck shaping. Dec 2 sts (in same manner as for toe shaping on foot) before marker and 2 sts after marker every rnd for 4 rnds (20 sc). Join and break off.

NECK: With G, ch 20. Repeat first 2 rnds of lower section (20 sc). Work even in sc until piece is 3" from beg. Join and break off.

TAIL: With G, ch 4; join. Sc evenly around for 2". Dec 1 st; then sc evenly around for 1", turn, sc evenly along length of tail. Break off. Mark this end for joining to body.

FINISHING: Join head sections with shaping at one end of oval; stuff. Cut paper-towel tube the same length as neck section. Sew neck to lower section of head; insert tube and stuff. For eyelashes, cut four 1" lengths of black yarn. Using two for each eye, sew eyes in place securely with lashes behind eyes. With black, crochet a 3½" chain for mouth and sew in place.

Sew both sections of body together, stuffing before opening becomes too small. For ridge, with J, crochet one rnd of sc around edge.

Stuff each foot; then pinch top edge together and sew to body. Sew marked end of tail to body. Place head-and-neck section on body and sew.

Mr. Mouse

SIZE: 9" tall.

MATERIALS: Knitting worsted (Orlon acrylic), 3 ounces medium gray (color G), 1 ounce baby pink (P), small amounts of black and white; aluminum crochet hook size G (or Canadian hook No. 9), *or the size that will give you the correct gauge;* 2 moving sew-on eyes or buttons ½" in diameter; Poly-fil or any washable stuffing.

GAUGE: 7 sc = 2"; 4 rnds = 1".

BACK OF BODY: Starting at center with G, ch 7. **1st rnd:** Work 3 sc in 2nd ch from hook, sc in each of next 4 ch, work 3 sc in last ch; working along opposite side of chain sc in each of next 4 sts. Do not join rnds, but mark beg of each rnd. **2nd rnd:** (Work 2 sc in each of next 3 sc, sc in each of next 4 sc) twice. **3rd rnd:** * 2 sc in next sc, (sc in next sc, 2 sc in next sc) twice; sc in each of next 5 sc. Repeat from * once. **4th rnd:** (Sc in each of next 2 sc, 2 sc in next sc) 3 times; sc in each of next 5 sc, 2 sc in next sc, (sc in each of next 2 sc, 2 sc in next sc) twice; sc in each of next 5 sc (32 sc).

Continue to sc in each sc around, increasing 3 sts evenly spaced at each end of oval (6 sts increased on each rnd) until 9th rnd is completed. Sc in each sc around for 3 rnds (62 sc). Join with sl st in next sc and break off.

FRONT OF BODY: With P, work as for back of body until 9th rnd is completed. Break off P; attach G. With G, work even in sc for 3 rnds. Join and break off.

HEAD (make 2): Starting at center with G, ch 2. **1st rnd:** Work 6 sc in 2nd ch from hook. Do not join rnds. **2nd rnd:** Work 2 sc in each sc around (12 sc). **3rd through 5th rnds:** Sc in each sc around, increasing 6 sts evenly spaced. Do not work increases directly above increases of previous rnd. **6th rnd:** Sc in each sc around. **7th rnd:** Inc 6 sts as before. Repeat last 2 rnds once more. Work even on 42 sc for 3 rnds more. Join and break off.

FOOT (make 2): Starting at center of bottom with G, ch 10. **1st rnd:** Work 3 sc in 2nd ch from hook, sc in each of next 7 ch, work 3 sc in last ch; working along opposite side of chain, sc in each of next 7 sts. **2nd rnd:** (Work 2 sc in each of next 3 sc, sc in each of next 7 sc) twice. **3rd rnd:** Sl st across next 7 sts for heel shaping; ch 1, sc in each of next 5 sc, 2 sc in next sc, (sc in each of next 2 sc, 2 sc in next sc) twice; sc in each of next 6 sc, sl st in next sc (increased end is for toe shaping). **4th rnd:** Ch 1, sc in only back lp of each sl st and each sc around (29 sc). Working in both lps of each sc, work even in sc for 1 rnd. Join and break off.

With P, make two more pieces in same manner until 3rd rnd is completed for top section. Join and break off.

To join, matching toe and heel shapings, place P section on top of G section. With G, working through both thicknesses of last G rnd and last P rnd, sl st in each sc around, stuffing leg before opening is too small. Join and break off. Repeat with other pair of P and G sections.

ARM (make 2): Starting at top edge, with G, ch 5. **1st rnd:** Work 3 sc in 2nd ch from hook, sc in each of next 2 ch, work 3 sc in last ch; working along opposite side of chain, sc in each of next 2 sts (10 sc). Stuff arm as you crochet, completing stuffing before last rnd. Sc in each sc around for 2½". **Next rnd:** For thumb, y o hook, draw up a lp in next st, y o and draw through 2 lps on hook, (y o hook, draw up a lp in same st, y o and draw through 2 lps) 3 times; y o and draw through all lps on hook, sc in each sc around. Omitting thumb st, sc in each sc around (9 sc) for 3 rnds more. **Last rnd:** Dec 4 sc. Break off.

SNOUT: With G, work first 3 rnds of head (18 sc). Work even in sc for 2 rnds. **6th and 7th rnds:** Sc in each sc around, increasing 6 sc evenly spaced. Join and break off. **Nose:** With P, work first rnd of head (6 sc). Join and break off.

EAR: Make 2 with P for front section and 2 with G for back section. Starting at lower edge, ch 2. **1st row:** Work 3 sc in 2nd ch from hook, ch 1, turn. **2nd row:** Work 2 sc in first sc, sc in each sc across, ch 1, turn (1 sc increased). Repeat 2nd row 5 times more. **Last row:** Sc in each sc across (9 sc). Break off. **Edging:** Work with G on all four sections. Sc evenly around all 3 sides of ear section for 2 rnds, working 3 sc in each corner st. Join and break off.

To join, place P section on top of G section. With G, working through both thicknesses of last rnd on each, sl st in each sc around. Do not stuff ears. Repeat with other pair of P and G sections.

HAT: Starting at center with black, work as for head until 4th rnd is completed. Pull ½" of yarn through center on right side of hat. Sc in each sc around for 1 rnd. Dec 6 sc evenly around next rnd. Join and break off.

TAIL: Using 2 strands of G, make a chain 9" long. Break off. To make tail curl, wet end of chain, wind around a pencil and leave until thoroughly dry.

FINISHING: Sew corresponding pieces together to form head and body, leaving opening for stuffing. Stuff and close opening. Sew head to body. Sew nose to snout, stuff snout and sew in place. Sew eyes securely in place. Sew on ears, hat, arms, and feet. Sew tail to back of body. **Whiskers:** Cut three lengths of white yarn, each 5½" long. Draw through snout.

The Three Bears

Favorite characters come alive in this crochet version of a popular children's story. Papa Bear is 16" tall, Mama Bear is 14" tall, and Baby Bear is 11". All three are worked in an Orlon acrylic knitting worsted-weight yarn.

SIZES: Papa Bear: 16" tall. Mama Bear: 14" tall. Baby Bear: 11" tall.

MATERIALS: For each bear: Bear Brand Win-Knit (Orlon acrylic yarn, knitting-worsted weight), 1 (4-ounce) skein camel No. 457 (color C), small amounts baby pink (P); aluminum crochet hook size H (or Canadian hook No. 8) *or the size that will give you the correct gauge;* steel crochet hook No. 0; scraps of black and white felt for eyes; polyester or any washable stuffing; 1 ounce each green and white sport yarn for collar, tie, apron, and bib; 1 ounce each blue and white mohair for baby blanket.

GAUGE: 4 sc = 1"; 9 rnds = 2" (with knitting worsted on size H hook and without stretching).

Note: Label small sections as you work to simplify assembling.

Papa Bear

Note: Right side is always facing you as you work.

BACK OF HEAD: Starting at center with size H hook and C, ch 2. **1st rnd:** Work 6 sc in 2nd ch from hook. Do not join rnds, but mark beg of each rnd. **2nd rnd:** Work 2 sc in each sc around (12 sc). **3rd through 11th rnds:** Sc in each sc around, increasing 6 sc evenly spaced (do not work increases directly above increases of previous rnd). **12th rnd:** Sc in each sc around, increasing 4 sc evenly spaced (70 sc). Sc in each sc around for 2 rnds. Piece should measure about 8" in diameter, stretched. Join with sl st in next sc and break off.

FRONT OF HEAD: Work as for back of head.

BACK OF EAR (make 2): With size H hook

and C, work as for back of head through 5th rnd (30 sc). Join and break off.

FRONT OF EAR (make 2): Work as for back of ear, working first 3 rnds with P and next 2 rnds with C.

SNOUT: Work as for back of head through 7th rnd (42 sc). Work 1 rnd even. Join and break off.

NOSE: With P, work as for back of head through first rnd. Sc in each sc for 1 rnd. Join and break off.

BACK OF BODY: Starting at center with size H hook and C, ch 6. **1st rnd:** Work 3 sc in 2nd ch from hook, sc in each of next 3 ch, work 3 sc in last ch; working along opposite side of chain, sc in each of next 3 ch (12 sc). Do not join rnds, but mark beg of each rnd. **2nd rnd:** * Work 2 sc in each of next 3 sc, sc in each of next 3 sc. Repeat from * once more (18 sc). **3rd rnd:** * Work 2 sc in next sc, sc in each of next 2 sc. Repeat from * around (24 sc). **4th rnd:** * Work 2 sc in next sc, sc in each of next 3 sc. Repeat from * around (30 sc). Piece should measure about 2½" across width of center, stretched. **5th through 14th rnds:** Sc in each sc around, increasing 6 sts on each rnd as evenly spaced as possible (do not work increases directly above increases of previous rnd). **15th rnd:** Sc in each sc around, increasing 4 sc evenly spaced (94 sc). Work even for 2 rnds. Piece should measure about 9" across width of center, stretched. Join and break off.

FRONT OF BODY: Work as for back of body.

LEG (make 4): Starting at bottom of paw with P, work as for back of body through 4th rnd (30 sc). Join and break off P. Continue as follows to complete leg: **5th rnd:** With C, sc in back lp only of each sc around (30 sc). Working in both lps of each sc, work even in sc for 3½" from first C rnd. Join and break off. **For Ridge:** With paw facing you, using C and working through both thicknesses of last P rnd and first C rnd of leg, sc in each st around. Join and break off.

FINISHING: With wrong sides together, using C and working through 1 lp only of corresponding sts, sl st head sections together, leaving opening at neck. Repeat for body sections. **For Eyes:** Cut circles of felt, 2 black ⅜" in diameter and 2 white ¾" in diameter; sew in place. Sew nose to snout. Sew snout to head, stuffing snout as you sew. Following photograph, embroider mouth with P. With C, sl st 2 ear pieces together for each ear, leaving an opening. Pad ears lightly and close opening; sew in place. Stuff head and body, then join at neck. Stuff legs; pinch top edges together and sew in place.

COLLAR: Starting at neck edge with No. 0 hook and white sport yarn, ch 36 to measure about 7". **1st row:** Dc in 4th ch from hook, dc in each of next 2 ch, * 2 dc in next ch, dc in each of next 4 ch. Repeat from * across (40 dc, counting ch-3 as 1 dc); ch 3, turn. **2nd row:** Skip first dc, dc in each of next 3 dc, * 2 dc in next dc, dc in each of next 5 dc. Repeat from * across (46 dc); ch 3, turn. **3rd row:** Skip first dc, dc in each of next 3 dc, * 2 dc in next dc, dc in each of next 6 dc. Repeat from * across (52 dc). Break off. Starting at left neck corner, work 1 row sc along left front edge, lower edge, and right front edge, working 3 sc in lower corners. Break off.

TIE: Starting at bottom point with No. 0 hook and green sport yarn, ch 2. **1st row:** Work 2 sc in 2nd ch from hook; ch 1, turn. **2nd row:** Sc in first sc, 2 sc in next sc; ch 1, turn. **3rd row:** Sc in each sc to last sc, 2 sc in last sc; ch 1, turn. Repeat last row 5 times more (9 sc). **9th row:** Sc in each sc across; ch 1, turn. Repeat 9th row 9 times more, or until tie measures about 3¼" from beg. **19th row:** Skip first sc, sc in each sc across; ch 1, turn. Repeat 19th row 3 times more (5 sc). Work row of sc around outer edges, working 3 sc at corners. Join and break off. Tack collar and tie in place.

Mama Bear

BACK OF HEAD: Work as for back of Papa Bear's head through 10th rnd. Sc in each sc around for 2 rnds (60 sc). Piece should measure about 7" in diameter when stretched. Join and break off.

FRONT OF HEAD: Work as for back of head.

EARS (make 2): Work as for Papa Bear's ears.

SNOUT: Work as for back of Papa Bear's head through 6th rnd (36 sc). Work 1 rnd even. Join and break off.

NOSE: Work as for Papa Bear's nose.

BACK OF BODY: Work as for back of Papa Bear's body through 13th rnd (84 sc). Work 2 rnds even. Join and break off.

FRONT OF BODY: Work as for back of body.

LEG (make 4): Starting at bottom of paw with P, work as for back of Papa Bear's body through 3rd rnd (24 sc). **4th rnd:** * Work 2 sc in next sc, sc in each of next 5 sc. Repeat from * around (28 sc). Join and break off P. Continue as follows to complete leg: **5th rnd:** With C, sc in back lp only of each sc around (28 sc). Working in both lps of each sc, work even in sc for 3" from first C rnd. Join and break off. Work ridge as on Papa Bear's leg.

FINISHING: Work as for Papa Bear, making circles for eyes 3/8" and 5/8" in diameter.

APRON: Starting at upper edge with No. 0 hook and white sport yarn, ch 14. **1st row:** Dc in 4th ch from hook and in each ch across (12 dc, counting turning ch as 1 dc); ch 3, turn. **2nd row:** Skip first dc, dc in each dc across; ch 3, turn. Repeat 2nd row once more, ending with ch 1, turn. **4th row:** Sc in each st across; ch 1, turn. Repeat 4th row once more, ending with ch 3, turn. **6th row:** Dc in first sc and in each sc across to last sc, 2 dc in last sc (2 dc inc—14 dc); ch 3, turn. Repeat 6th row 3 times more (20 dc), omitting ch-3 at end of last row. Break off. **Edging:** Attach yarn to side of first sc on 4th row, ch 3, dc in same place, work 14 dc along side of lower half of apron to lower corner (dc's form ruffle), continue ruffle with 2 dc in each dc along lower edge, work 14 dc along other side edge of lower half of apron; work sc evenly spaced around top, working 3 sc in top corners. Join and break off. **Ties:** Crochet a chain about 12" long, sc in 2nd ch from hook and in each ch across; sl st to one corner of apron. Break off. Make 2nd tie in same manner and attach to other corner of apron. **Pocket:** Ch 7, sc in 2nd ch from hook and in each of next 5 ch (6 sc); ch 1, turn. Work 4 rows even in sc. Break off. Sew pocket in place. Tie apron around neck and tack in place.

Baby Bear

BACK OF HEAD: Work as for back of Papa Bear's head through 8th rnd (48 sc). Sc in each sc around for 2 rnds. Piece should measure about 5¾" in diameter when stretched. Join and break off.

FRONT OF HEAD: Work as for back of head.

BACK OF EAR (make 2): Work as for back of Papa Bear's ear through 4th rnd (24 sc).

FRONT OF EAR (make 2): Work as for front of Papa Bear's ear through 4th rnd.

SNOUT: Work as for back of Papa Bear's head through 5th rnd (30 sc). Work 1 rnd even. Join and break off.

NOSE: Work as for Papa Bear's nose.

BACK OF BODY: Work as for back of Papa Bear's body through 10th rnd (66 sc). Sc in each sc around for 3 rnds. Join and break off.

FRONT OF BODY: Work as for back of body.

LEG (make 4): Starting at bottom of paw with P, work as for back of Papa Bear's body through 2nd rnd (18 sc). Join and break off P. Continue as follows to complete leg: **3rd rnd:** With C, sc in back lp only of each sc around (18 sc). Working in both lps of each sc, work even in sc for 2½" from first C rnd. Join and break off. Work ridge as on Papa Bear's leg.

FINISHING: Work as for Papa Bear, making circles for eyes ¼" and ½" in diameter.

BIB: Starting at lower edge with No. 0 hook and white sport yarn, ch 7. **1st row:** Sc in 2nd ch from hook and in each sc across (6 sc); ch 1, turn. **2nd row:** Work 2 sc in first sc, sc in each sc across to last sc, 2 sc in last sc (8 sc); ch 1, turn. Repeat 2nd row twice more. Work even on 12 sc until piece measures 2½" from beg. Break off. Work 1 row sc evenly spaced along curved edges. Break off. **Ties:** Make 2 chains about 5½" long. Attach one to each upper corner of bib. Tie bib around neck.

BLANKET: With size H hook and blue mohair, ch 31 to measure about 10". **1st row:** Dc in 4th ch from hook and in each ch across (29 dc, counting turning ch as 1 dc); ch 3, turn. **2nd row:** Skip first dc, dc in each dc across; ch 3, turn. Repeat 2nd row until piece measures 10" from beg, omitting ch-3 at end of last row. Break off. **Ruffle:** With white mohair, work 2 dc in each dc, or over post of each dc, around, working 6 dc in each corner. Join and break off.

Porky Pig

Flowered and pink, to delight any child. The crocheted posies are appliquéd on. In synthetic knitting worsted.

SIZE: About 12" long.
MATERIALS: Synthetic knitting worsted, 4 ounces pink for pig, small amounts of purple, rose, and lavender for flowers and green for leaves; aluminum crochet hook size H (or Canadian hook No. 8) *or the size that will give you the correct gauge;* 2 moving sew-on eyes or buttons ½" in diameter (or cut eyes from felt, if desired); polyester for stuffing.
GAUGE: 4 sc = 1".
BODY: Starting at tail end, ch 4. Join with sl st to form ring. **1st rnd:** Work 6 sc in ring. Do not join, but work around spiral fashion and mark beg of rnds. **2nd rnd:** 2 sc in each sc around. **3rd rnd:** * Sc in each sc around, increasing 6 sc evenly spaced, being careful not to work increases directly over those on the previous rnd. Repeat last rnd 7 times more (60 sc). Work 18 rnds even. **29th rnd:** * Sc in next 8 sc; pull up lp in each of next 2 sc, y o hook and draw through 3 lps on hook (1 sc decreased). Repeat from * around. **30th rnd:** * Sc in next 7 sc, dec 1 sc. Repeat from * around. Work 7 more rnds in this manner, decreasing 6 sts evenly spaced and being careful not to work decreases directly over those on previous rnd (6 sc). Break off, leaving 6" end. Stuff; sew opening closed.
HEAD (make 2 pieces): Work as for body through 8th rnd (48 sc). Work 2 rnds even. Break off.
SNOUT: Work as for body through 3rd rnd (18 sc). **4th rnd:** Working through back lps only, sc in each sc around. Working through both lps, work 2 rnds even. Break off.
EAR BACK (make 2): Starting at tip, ch 2. **1st row:** Work 3 sc in 2nd ch from hook; ch 1, turn. **2nd row:** Sc in each sc across; ch 1, turn. **3rd row:** 2 sc in first sc, sc in each sc to last sc, 2 sc in last sc; ch 1, turn. (Work 2 rows even, repeat 3rd row) three times (11 sc). Break off.
EAR FRONT (make 2): Work same as for back.
Sl st sides of ears together, leaving edges along last row open.
FRONT LEGS (make 2): Starting at center of bottom, work as for body through 4th rnd (24 sc). Work 8 rnds even. Break off. With bottom of foot facing you, form lp on hook. Work 1 sc over each sc of 4th rnd to form ridge; join. Break off.
BACK LEGS (make 2): Work as for body through 4th rnd. Work 5 rnds even. Break off. Make ridge as for front legs.
FINISHING: Sew head pieces together, leaving opening for stuffing. Stuff and sew opening closed. Sew snout to face and feet to body, following photograph for position and stuffing softly. Pad ears and sew to head. Sew eyes to face. Sew head in place.
TAIL: Ch 13, work 2 sc in 2nd ch from hook

and in each ch across. Break off. Sew tail in place.

FLOWERS (make 1 purple, 2 lavender, and 2 rose): Starting at center, ch 12. Join with sl st to form ring. **1st rnd:** * 2 dc in each of next 2 ch, sl st in next ch. Repeat from * 3 times more. Break off.

LEAVES (make 7): Ch 10. **1st rnd:** Sl st in 2nd ch from hook, * sc in next ch, h dc in next ch, dc in each of next 3 ch, h dc in next ch, sc in next ch *, 3 sc in last ch. Working along opposite side of starting ch, repeat from * to * once; join. Break off. Sew flowers and leaves to back of pig.

For Men

Sweaters

Sweatermates for Men

In shades of blue sparked with red and off-white. Sleeveless vest is crocheted in dazzling diagonals, the V-neck, button-front cardigan in horizontal stripes.

SIZES: Small (36–38) [medium (40–42)—large (44–46)]. Vest measures 18½" [20½"—22½"] across back at underarms, 24" [24½"—25"] from shoulder to lower edge. Cardigan measures 19" [21"—23"] across back at underarms, 27" [27½"—28"] from back of neck to lower edge.

MATERIALS: For cardigan: Brunswick Germantown knitting worsted (100% wool), 4 (4-ounce) skeins thunderstorm (blue) No. 4231 (color A), 3 skeins royal No. 412 (B), 1 skein each scarlet No. 421 (C) and Monhegan-Aran No. 4301 (winter white, D). **For vest:** 2 skeins each thunderstorm No. 4231 (A) and royal No. 412 (B), 1 skein each scarlet No. 421 (C) and Monhegan-Aran (D). Aluminum crochet hook size H (or Canadian hook No. 8) *or the size that will give you the correct gauge;* 5 buttons ⅝" in diameter; tapestry needle.

GAUGE: 9 sts (sc's and ch-1's) = 2"; 4 rows = 1".

Vest

Note: The vest is worked on the bias and it is very important to get the exact stitch and row gauge for proper fit.

BACK: Starting at lower right corner with A, ch 2. **1st row (right side):** Work sc, ch 1 and sc in 2nd ch from hook; ch 1, turn. **2nd row:** Work sc, ch 1 and sc in first sc (inc made), ch 1, inc in next sc; ch 1, turn. **3rd row:** Sc in first sc, * ch 1, sc in next sc. Repeat from * across; ch 1, turn. Mark last sc worked for lower edge. **4th row:** Inc in first sc, ch 1, * sc in next sc, ch 1. Repeat from * to within last sc, inc in last sc; ch 1, turn. Using a different color marker, mark last sc worked for side edge. Repeating 3rd and 4th rows for pattern, work in stripe pattern of 4 rows A, 1 row D, 4 rows B, 1 row D, 4 rows A, 1 row C, 4 rows B, 1 row D, 4 rows A, 1 row D, 4 rows B, and 1 row C until side edge measures 13" from beg, ending at side edge and omitting ch-1 on last row; turn.

To Shape Right Armhole: Next row: Keeping in stripe pattern as established, at side edge, sl st in first sc and in ch-1, work across in pattern. **Following row (lower edge):** Inc in first sc, work across; turn. Repeat last 2 rows 2 [3—4] times more, then repeat 3rd and 4th rows of back until lower edge measures 18½" [20½"—22½"] from beg, ending at lower edge.

To Shape Left Side: 1st row (lower edge): Pull up a lp in each of first 2 sc, y o hook and pull through all 3 lps on hook (2 sts dec), work across in pattern to within last st, inc in last st; ch 1, turn. **2nd row:** Work even. Repeat last 2 rows until right armhole measures 6" [6½"—7"]; then dec 2 sts at beg of every row until left side measures 13" from beg, ending at left side edge and omitting ch-1 on last row; turn.

To Shape Left Armhole: (Note: Armhole shapings will not be symmetrical.) **Next row:** Sl st over first 6 [8—10] sts, sc in next sc, work across; turn. Continue to dec 2 sts at beg of every row until no sts remain. Break off.

Yoke: 1st row: With right side facing you, attach A to upper right corner of back, sc in same place, (ch 1, skip about ½" along upper edge, sc in next sc) 33 [35—37] times evenly spaced across (67 [71—75] sts); ch 1, turn. **2nd row:** Sc in first sc, * ch 1, sc in next sc. Repeat from * across; ch 1, turn. Repeat 2nd row 6 times more, omitting ch-1 on last row.

To Shape Shoulders: 1st row: Sl st in first 4 sts, sc in next sc, * ch 1, sc in next sc. Repeat from * to within last 4 sts; turn. Repeat first row once more. **3rd row:** Sl st in next 4 [6—6] sts; sc in next sc, (ch 1, sc in next sc) 3 [3—4] times; ch 1, turn. **4th row:** Sc in first sc, (ch 1, sc in next sc) 3 [3—4] times. Break off. Skip center 29 sts; attach A to next sc, sc in same place, (ch 1, sc in next sc) 3 [3—4] times; ch 1, turn. **Next row:** Sc in first sc, (ch 1, sc in next sc) 3 [3—4] times. Break off.

FRONT: Work same as back to yoke, placing marker for side edge on first sc of 4th row so that stripe pattern will be reversed.

Yoke: 1st row: With right side facing you, attach A to upper left corner of front, sc in same place, (ch 1; skip about ½" along upper edge, sc in next st) 11 [12—13] times (23 [25—27] sts); turn. **2nd row (neck edge):** Sl st in first 2 sts, work across in pattern; ch 1, turn. **3rd row:** Work across in pattern to within last ch-1 and sc (19 [21—23] sc); ch 1, turn. Work 5 rows even, ending at arm edge and omitting ch-1 on last row; turn.

To Shape Shoulder: 1st row: Sl st in first 4 sts, sc in next sc, (ch 1, sc in next sc) 7 [8—9] times; ch 1, turn. **2nd row:** Sc in first sc, (ch 1, sc in next sc) 5 [6—7] times; turn. **3rd row:** Sl st in first 4 [6—6] sts, sc in next sc, (ch 1, sc in next sc) 3 [3—4] times; ch 1, turn. **4th row:** Sc in first sc, (ch 1, sc in next sc) 3 [3—4] times. Break off. Attach A to upper right corner of front and work other yoke and shoulder to correspond.

WAISTBAND: (Note: Waistband ribbing is worked vertically.) Starting at side edge with A, ch 15. **1st row:** Sc in 2nd ch from hook and in each ch across (14 sc); ch 1, turn. **2nd row:** Working in back lps only, sc in each sc across; ch 1, turn. Repeat 2nd row for rib pattern until piece measures 37" [39"—41"] when stretched slightly. Break off.

FINISHING: Sew shoulder and side seams. Sew ends of ribbing to form ring. Sew to lower edge of back and front. With right side facing and using B, work 1 row of sc, ch 1 pattern around neck and armhole edges and along lower edge of ribbing.

Cardigan

BACK: Border: Work as for waistband on vest until piece measures 19" [21"—23"] when stretched slightly. Break off A; attach B and ch 1. Do not turn, but work along one long edge (top edge) of border as follows: **1st row (right side):** Sc in same place as last sc, (work ch 1 and sc) 42 [47—51] times evenly spaced along top edge of border (85 [95—103] sts); ch 1, turn. **2nd row:** Sc in first sc, * ch 1, sc in next sc. Repeat from * across; ch 1, turn. Repeating 2nd row for pattern, work in stripe pattern of 4 rows B, 1 row D, 4 rows A, 1 row D, 4 rows B, 1 row C, 4 rows A, 1 row D, 4 rows B, 1 row D, 4 rows A, and 1 row C until piece measures 17½" or desired length to underarm, omitting ch-1 on last row.

To Shape Armholes: 1st row: Sl st in first 4 sts, sc in next sc, work across in pattern to within last 4 sts; turn. **2nd row:** Sl st in first 2 sts, sc in next sc and work across to within last 2 sts; turn. Repeat last row 1 [2—3] times more. Work even on 69 [75—79] sts until armholes measure 8½" [9"—9½"], omitting ch-1 on last row.

To Shape Shoulders: 1st row: Sl st in first 4 [6—8] sts, sc in next sc, work across to within last 4 [6—8] sts; turn. **2nd row:** Sl st in first 6 sts, sc in next sc, work across to within last 6 sts; turn. Repeat 2nd row twice more (25 [27—27] sts). Break off.

LEFT FRONT: Border: Work as for waistband on vest until piece measures 9" [10"—11"] when stretched slightly. Break off A, attach B and ch 1. Do not turn, but work along one long edge (top edge) of border as follows: **1st row:** Sc in same place as last sc, (work ch 1 and sc) 20 [23—25] times evenly spaced along top edge of border (41 [47—51] sts); ch 1, turn. Mark last sc for front edge. Continue in pattern and stripes as for back until piece measures 16½" or 1" less than back to underarm, ending at front edge and omitting ch-1 on last row.

To Shape Neck: Next row (dec row): Sl st in first 2 sts, sc in next sc, work across. Continuing in established pattern, repeat dec at front edge every 1½" 4 [5—5] times more and, *at the same time,* when piece measures same as back to underarm (ending at side edge with same color stripe as back), shape armhole as follows:

To Shape Armhole: Starting at side edge, sl st in first 4 sts, sc in next sc, work across; then at arm edge, sl st in first 2 sts every other row 2 [3—4] times more. Work even until armhole measures same as back to shoulder, ending at arm edge and omitting ch-1 on last row.

To Shape Shoulder: 1st row: Sl st in first 4 [6—8] sts, sc in next sc, work across; ch 1, turn. **2nd row:** Work across first 13 sts; turn. **3rd row:** Sl st in first 6 sts, sc in next sc, work across; ch 1, turn. **4th row:** Work across first 7 sts. Break off.

RIGHT FRONT: Work as for left front, reversing shaping.

SLEEVES: Cuff: Work as for border on back until piece measures 9" when stretched slightly. Break off A, attach B and ch 1. Do not turn, but work along one long edge (top edge) of cuff as follows: **1st row:** Sc in same place as last sc, (work ch 1 and sc) 21 times (43 sts); ch 1, turn. Working in pattern and stripes as for back, inc 2 sts at beg and end of row every 2½" [2"—1¾"] 6 [7—8] times (to inc 2 sts, work sc, ch 1 and sc in sc). Work even on 67 [71—75] sts until sleeve measures 19¾" or desired length to underarms, ending with same stripe row as on back and omitting ch-1 on last row.

To Shape Cap: 1st row: Sl st in first 4 sts, sc in next sc, work across to within last 4 sts; turn. **2nd row (dec row):** Sl st in first 2 sts, sc in next sc, work across to within last 2 sts; turn. Repeat dec row every 3rd row 7 [8—9] times more, then every row 4 times more (11 sts remain). Break off.

FINISHING: Sew shoulder, side, and sleeve seams. Sew in sleeves.

Front and Neck Band: 1st row: Attach A to lower corner of right front edge, sc in same place, work ch 1 and sc evenly spaced along right front edge, around neck, and along left front edge to lower corner; ch 1, turn. **2nd row:** Sc in first sc, * ch 1, sc in next sc. Repeat from * across; ch 1, turn. Mark right front for 5 buttons, the first 1½" from lower edge, the last at beg of neck shaping, the others evenly spaced between. **3rd row:** Work as for 2nd row, making 5 buttonholes along left front opposite markers as follows: Ch 3, skip next sc, sc in next sc. **4th row:** Repeat 2nd row, working ch 1, sc and ch 1 over ch-3 lps. Break off.

Edging: With B, work 1 row of sc-and-ch-1 pattern along front bands, neck, and lower edge of border, working 3 sc in each corner at front. With B, work 1 row of sc-and-ch-1 pattern around lower edge of each cuff. Following photo and stitch diagram on page 40, with B, embroider 1 row of chain stitch along inner edge of front and neck band. Sew on buttons.

Lumber Jacket

The burgundy, rust, and taupe textured waffle pattern is produced by overstitching as you go. Breast-pocket flaps are not just for show. Zips up the front.

SIZES: Small (36–38) [medium (40–42)—large (44–46)]. Jacket measures 19″ [21″—23″] across back at underarms, 21″ [21½″—22″] from back of neck to lower edge.

MATERIALS: Bear Brand Winsom Orlon acrylic, 6 [7—7] (2-ounce) skeins burgundy No. 8 (color A), 2 [3—3] skeins each Pompeii (copper) No. 339 (B) and mushroom No. 333 (C); aluminum crochet hook size F (or Canadian hook No. 10) *or the size that will give you the correct gauge;* 20″ [20″—22″] separating zipper; 2 buttons ¾″ in diameter.

GAUGE: In pattern, 9 sts = 2″; 6 rows = 1″.

BACK: Border: (**Note:** Border is worked vertically.) Starting at side edge with A, ch 11. **1st row:** Sc in 2nd ch from hook and in each ch across (10 sc); ch 1, turn. **2nd row:** Working in back lps only, sc in each sc across; ch 1, turn. Repeat 2nd row until piece measures 19″ [21″—23″] when stretched slightly. Ch 1, do not turn or break off but continue to work along one long edge (top edge) of border and start body of sweater as follows: **1st row (right side):** Work 86 [95—104] sc evenly spaced along top edge of border; ch 1, turn. **2nd row:** Sc in each sc across; drop A, attach B; ch 1, turn. **3rd row:** With B, sc in each sc across; ch 1, turn. **4th row:** With B, sc in each sc across; drop B, pick up A; ch 1, turn. **5th row (right side):** With A, sc in first 2 sc, * y o hook, insert hook from right to left under post of next A sc three rows below, y o and draw lp through, (y o and draw through 2 lps on hook) twice (long post dc made), skip next sc on last row, sc in next 2 sc. Repeat from * across. **6th row:** With A, sc in each sc and dc across; drop A, attach C;

ch 1, turn, **7th and 8th rows:** With C, repeat 3rd and 4th rows. **9th and 10th rows:** Repeat 5th and 6th rows. Drop A, pick up B; ch 1, turn. Repeat 3rd through 10th rows for pattern until piece measures 12½" or desired length to underarm, ending with a 6th or 10th pattern row and omitting ch-1 on last row.

To Shape Armholes: 1st row: Sl st in first 4 sts, work in pattern to within last 4 sc (8 sts dec); ch 1, turn. **2nd row:** Work even, omitting ch-1; turn. **3rd row:** Sl st in first st, work in pattern to within last st; ch 1, turn. **4th row:** Repeat 2nd row. Repeat 3rd and 4th rows 2 [4—6] times more. Work even on 72 [77—82] sts until armholes measure 9" [9½"—10"], ending with a 6th or 10th pattern row and omitting ch-1 on last row; turn.

To Shape Shoulders: 1st row: Sl st in first 8 sts, work in pattern across next 15 [17—19] sts; ch 1, turn. **2nd row:** Work across first 15 [17—19] sts; turn. **3rd row:** Sl st in first 8 sts, work across next 7 [9—11] sts; ch 1, turn. **4th row:** Work across 7 [9—11] sts. Break off. Skip center 26 [27—28] sts for back of neck, attach yarn in next st, sc in same place, and work other side to correspond.

RIGHT FRONT: Pocket Lining: With A, ch 23. **1st row:** Sc in 2nd ch from hook and in each ch across (22 sc); ch 1, turn. **2nd row:** Sc in each sc across; ch 1, turn. Repeat 2nd row until piece measures 5½" from beg. Mark last row worked. **Flap:** Repeat 2nd row 7 times more. **8th row:** Pull up lp in each of first 2 sts, y o and draw through all 3 lps on hook (1 st dec), work across to within last 2 sts, dec 1 st; ch 1, turn. **9th row:** Sc in each st across; ch 1, turn. Repeat last 2 rows once more. **12th row:** Work as for 8th row to within center 3 sts, ch 3, skip center 3 sts for buttonhole, complete row. Repeat 9th row once, then 8th and 9th rows once more. Break off.

Border: Work as for border on back until piece measures 9½" [10½"—11½"] when stretched slightly. Ch 1, do not turn or break off but continue to work along one long edge (top edge) of border as follows: **1st row:** Work 44 [47—50] sc evenly spaced along top edge of border; ch 1, turn. Work in pattern as for back until piece measures same as back to underarms, ending with a 6th or 10th pattern row and omitting ch-1 on last row; turn.

To Shape Armhole: 1st row: Sl st in first 3 sts, work across in pattern; ch 1, turn. **2nd row:** Work even, omitting ch-1; turn. **3rd row:** Sl st in first st, work across; ch 1, turn. **4th row:** Repeat 2nd row. Repeat 3rd and 4th rows 3 [4—5] times more and, *at the same time,* when 1" above beg of armhole shaping (ending with a 5th or 9th pattern row), insert pocket lining as follows:

Pocket: Mark 9th and 31st sts from front edge on last row. **Next row (wrong side):** Work in pattern to within first marked st; fold pocket lining along marked row to form flap on right side, then sc in each of next 22 sc along fold row of lining, then, starting with other marked st, continue in pattern across; ch 1, turn. Continue in pattern. When armhole shaping is completed, work even on 37 [39—41] sts until armhole measures 8" [8½"—9"], ending at front edge with a 4th or 8th pattern row and omitting ch-1 at end of last row; turn.

To Shape Neck and Shoulder: 1st row (neck edge): Sl st in first 7 sts, work across; ch 1, turn. **2nd row:** Work across to within last 3 sts; turn. **3rd row:** Sl st in next 2 sts, work across; ch 1, turn. **4th row:** Work across to within last 2 sts, dec 1 st; ch 1, turn. **5th row:** Dec 1 st, work across; turn. **6th through 9th rows:** Repeat 1st through 4th rows of back shoulder shaping. Break off.

LEFT FRONT: Work to correspond to right front, reversing all shaping.

SLEEVES: Cuff: (Note: Cuff is worked vertically.) With A, ch 19. **1st row:** Sc in 2nd ch from hook and in each ch across (18 sc); ch 1, turn. Continue as for border on back until piece measures 9" when stretched slightly. Ch 1, do not turn or break off but continue along one long edge (top edge) of border as follows: **1st row:** Work 50 sc evenly spaced along top edge of border; ch 1, turn. Work in pattern as for back, increasing 1 st (to inc 1 st work 2 sc in 1 sc) at beg and end of row every 1" 9 [11—13] times. Work even on 68 [72—76] sts until sleeve measures 19" or desired length to underarms, ending on same pattern row as for back and omitting ch-1 at end of last row.

To Shape Cap: 1st row: Sl st in first 3 sts, work in pattern to within last 3 sts; ch 1, turn. Work as for 2nd through 4th rows of back armhole shaping. Repeat 3rd and 4th rows 12 [13—14] times more, then repeat 3rd row 13 [14—15] times (10 sts). Break off.

FINISHING: Sew shoulder, side, and sleeve seams. Sew in sleeves. Sew pocket lining in place.

Collar: Starting at neck edge with A, ch 66 to measure about 16″. **1st row:** Work sc in 2nd ch from hook and in each sc across; ch 1, turn. **2nd row:** Work 2 sc in first sc, sc in each sc to within last sc, 2 sc in last sc; ch 1, turn. **3rd row:** Sc in each sc across; ch 1, turn. Repeat 2nd and 3rd rows 7 times more, then repeat 3rd row 4 times. Break off. Pin collar to neck edge, easing to fit. Sew in place.

With right side facing you, using A, work 1 row of sc evenly spaced up right front edge, around collar, and down left front edge. Work 1 row sc around free edge of each pocket flap. Sew buttons in place. Insert zipper.

Casual Coat

So easy to make—just one long stretch of colorful stripes, all done in single crochet. Low patch pockets finish it off.

SIZES: Small (36–38) [medium (40–42)—large (44–46)]. Sweater measures 20″ [22″—24″] across back to underarms.

MATERIALS: Bernat Sesame Germantown knitting worsted, 6 (2-ounce) skeins new camel No. 4013 (color A), 5 skeins each autumn gold No. 4010 (B), Roman gold No. 4107 (C) and 4 skeins walnut No. 4116 (D); aluminum crochet hook size G (or Canadian hook No. 9) *or the size that will give you the correct gauge.*

GAUGE: 4 sts (sc's and ch-1's) = 1″; 4 rows = 1″.

BACK: Starting at lower edge with B, ch 81 [89—97] to measure 20″ [22″—24″]. **1st row (right side):** With B, sc in 3rd ch from hook, * ch 1, skip 1 ch, sc in next ch. Repeat from * across (80 [88—96] sc's and ch-1's); ch 2, turn. **2nd row:** Sc in first ch-1 sp, * ch 1, skip next sc, sc in next ch-1 sp. Repeat from * across; ch 2, turn. **3rd row:** Work as for 2nd row, changing to color D on last sc; ch 2, turn. (**Note:** To change colors, work to within last sc of old color, insert hook in next sc, y o and draw lp of old color through st, then draw up lp of new color through both lps on hook. Break off old color, leaving 3″ end.) Continue to repeat 2nd row, working in stripe pattern of 2 rows D, 3 rows C, 4 rows A, and 3 rows B until piece measures 22" from beg or desired length to underarms.

To Shape Armholes: 1st row (dec row): Sl st across first 6 [6—8] sts (6 [6—8] sts dec), work across in pattern to within last 6 [6—8] sts; ch 1 to turn. (Note: Ch-1 does not count as a ch-1 sp.) **2nd row (dec row):** Sl st across first 2 sts (2 sts dec), ch 2 (counts as first st), continue in pattern across; ch 1, turn.

Repeat 2nd row (dec row) every row 3 [5—5] times more (60 [64—68] sts). Work even on 60 [64—68] sts until armholes measure 9" [9½"—10"].

To Shape Shoulders: 1st row: Keeping in stripe pattern, sl st across first 4 [6—6] sts, place marker, work across next 10 sts; turn. **2nd row:** Dec 2 sts (neck edge), work across remaining sts to marker; turn. **3rd row:** Sl st across next 4 sts, work across remaining sts. Break off. Skip next 32 [32—36] sts for back neck. Work other shoulder to correspond.

RIGHT FRONT: With B, ch 35 [39—43] sts to measure 8½" [9½"—10½"]. Work as for back until piece measures same as back to underarm, ending with a wrong-side row (34 [38—42] sts).

To Shape Neck and Armhole: 1st row (neck edge): Sl st across first 2 sts (2 sts dec at neck edge), work in pattern across to last 6 [6—8] sts (6 [6—8] sts dec for armhole); ch 2, turn. Continue to work in pattern, decreasing 2 sts at armhole edge every other row 4 [5—6] times more and, *at the same time*, continue to dec 2 sts at neck edge every 3¾" twice more (14 [16—16] sts remain). Work even until piece measures same as back to shoulder, ending at armhole edge.

To Shape Shoulder: Work same as for back shoulder shaping through 3rd row.

LEFT FRONT: Work as for right front, reversing shaping.

SLEEVES: With B, ch 39 to measure 9½". **1st row:** Work same as for back (38 sts). Continuing in pattern, inc 2 sts (to inc 2 sts, sc in first ch-1, ch 1, sc in same sp) at beg of row every 1" 11 [13—15] times (60 [64—68] sts). Work even until sleeve measures 19" [19¼"—19½"] from beg, or desired length to underarm, ending with same color stripe as back and front.

To Shape Cap: 1st row: Sl st across first 6 [6—8] sts, work across to within last 6 [6—8] sts; ch 1, turn. Dec 2 sts at beg of every other row 12 [13—13] times. Then dec 2 sts at beg and end of every row 3 times, omitting last ch-2. Break off.

POCKET (make 2): With B, ch 21 to measure 5". Working in pattern as for back, work even until pocket measures 6½". Break off.

FINISHING: Sew side, shoulder, and sleeve seams. Sew in sleeves.

Border: With right side facing you, attach C at lower corner of right front edge. Work a row in pattern evenly spaced around front and neck edges. Continuing to work in pattern, work 2 more rows C, 2 rows D, and 3 rows B. Break off.

Following photograph, sew pockets in place.

Zip-Front Battle Jacket

Body is worked in variegated Orlon and nylon yarn in long single crochet. Solid-color cuffs and waistband are of knitting worsted.

SIZES: Small (36–38) [medium (40–42)—large (44–46)]. Jacket measures 19" [21"—23"] across back from side seam to side seam and about 25" [25"—27"] from back of neck to lower edge of waistband.

MATERIALS: Bernat Big Berella Bulky (Orlon and nylon) 9 [9—10] (4-ounce) balls pearl ombré No. 8619; 3 [3—4] ounces Oxford gray knitting worsted; aluminum crochet hooks sizes F and H (or Canadian hooks No. 10 and No. 8) *or the size that will give you the correct gauge;* 20" [20"—22"] heavyweight separating-type zipper.

GAUGE: In pattern st with size H hook: 5 sts = 2".

BACK: Starting at lower edge above waistband, with pearl ombré and size H hook, ch 50 [54—58] loosely to measure about 19" [21"—23"]. **1st row:** Sc in 2nd ch from hook and in each ch across (49 [53—57] sts); ch 1, turn. **2nd row:** Sc in each sc across; ch 1, turn. **3rd row (right side):** Sc in first sc, * insert hook in next sc 2 rows below and work sc (long sc made), sc in next sc. Repeat from * across; ch 1, turn. **4th row:** Sc in first sc, * sc in next long sc, sc in next sc. Repeat from * across; ch 1, turn.

Repeating 3rd and 4th rows for pattern, work even until piece measures 10½" [10½"—12½"] from beg or 3" less than desired length to underarm (3" waistband will be added later); ch 1, turn.

To Shape Armholes: 1st row: Sl st across first 3 [3—4] sts, ch 1, continue across row in pattern as established to within last 3 [3—4] sts; ch 1, turn. **2nd row (dec row):** Skip first sc, work across row in established pattern to within last sc (do not work in last sc); ch 1, turn. Repeat dec row 1 [2—2] times more.

Work even in pattern on 39 [41—43] sts until armholes measure 9" [9¼"—9½"] from beg; ch 1, turn.

To Shape Shoulders: 1st row: Sl st across first 6 [6—7] sts, ch 1, work across row to within last 6 [6—7] sts; ch 1, turn. **2nd row:** Sl st across first 7 sts, ch 1, work across row to within last 7 sts (13 [15—15] sts remain for back of neck). Break off.

LEFT FRONT: Working as for back, ch 26 [28—30]. Work even in pattern on 25 [27—29] sts until piece is same length as back to armholes, ending with a wrong-side row.

To Shape Armhole: next row: Sl st across first 3 [3—4] sts, ch 1, work across row; ch 1, turn. **Following row:** Work across row to within last sc; ch 1, turn (1 st dec). Dec 1 st at armhole edge 1 [2—2] times more. Work even in pattern on 20 [21—22] sts until armhole measures 6" [6¼"—6½"] from beg, ending at front edge.

To Shape V-Neck: Dec 1 st at front edge every row 7 [8—8] times. Work even, if necessary, on 13 [13—14] sts until armhole measures same as back armhole to shoulder, ending at arm edge.

To Shape Shoulder: 1st row: Sl st across first 6 [6—7] sts, ch 1, work across; ch 1, turn. **2nd row:** Work across row (7 sts). Break off.

RIGHT FRONT: Work as for left front, ending with a right-side row before armhole shaping, then complete to correspond.

SLEEVES: Starting at lower edge above cuffs (cuffs will be added later), with pearl ombré and size H hook, ch 32 loosely to measure about 12½". Working as for back, work even in pattern on 31 sts for 6", ending with a right-side row; ch 1, turn.

Next row (inc row): Working in pattern, work 2 sc in first and last sc (2 sts increased); ch 1, turn.

Following row (right side): Work long sc in first sc, sc in next sc, work long sc, continue across in pattern, ending with long sc in last sc; ch 1, turn.

Being careful to keep pattern as established, repeat inc row every 4" [2½"—2"] 2 [3—4] times more. Work even on 37 [39—41] sts until sleeve measures 15½" [15¾"—16"] from beg or 2½" shorter than desired length to underarm (2½" cuff will be added later); ch 1, turn.

To Shape Cap: Repeat 1st and 2nd rows of back armhole shaping, then work even in pattern for 3 [2—3] rows. **Next row:** Repeat dec row. Continue to work in pattern and repeat dec row every 4th row 4 times more, then repeat dec row every other row 4 [5—6] times (11 [11—9] sts remain). Break off.

FINISHING: Sew side, shoulder, and sleeve seams. Sew sleeves in place. Use knitting worsted and size F hook only from now on.

WAISTBAND: 1st row: Working along lower edge of cardigan, work 1 sc in each st of foundation chain. **2nd row:** Ch 1, turn; sc in each sc across. Repeat last row until waistband measures 3". Break off.

CUFFS: 1st rnd: Working around lower edge of sleeve, sc in each st of foundation chain. Continue to sc in each sc around for 2½", then sl st in next 2 sts. Break off.

NECKBAND: With right side facing you and taking in edge slightly, sc evenly across neck edge. **Next row (dec row):** Ch 1, turn, skip first sc, sc in each sc across to last sc, do not work in last sc. Repeat dec row until piece measures 1¾" from beg. Break off.

Work 1 row of sc evenly along both front edges and neckband edge. Break off. Sew in zipper.

Vest in Basket-Weave Stitch

A classic V-neck vest worked in navy and red knitting worsted in the not-so-classic basket-weave stitch.

SIZES: 40 [42—44—46]. Sweater measures 20" [21"—22"—23"] across back at underarms, 23" [24"—25"—26"] from shoulder to lower edge.

MATERIALS: Coats & Clark's knitting worsted, 4 [4—5—5] (4-ounce) skeins geranium No. 912, 1 skein navy No. 858; aluminum crochet hooks sizes E and H (or Canadian hooks No. 11 and No. 8) *or the size that will give you the correct gauge.*

GAUGE: In pattern st on size H hook: 4 sts = 1"; 9 rows = 3".

BACK: Border: (Border is worked vertically.) With navy and size E hook, ch 10. **1st row:** Sc in 2nd ch from hook and in each ch across (9 sc); ch 1, turn. **2nd row:** Working in back lp of each st, sc in first sc and in each sc across; ch 1, turn. Repeat 2nd row until border measures 18" [19"—20"—21"] slightly stretched. Break off navy; attach red and work across one long edge (top edge) of border with size H hook as follows: **1st row:** Ch 3, work 81 [85—89—93] dc as evenly spaced as possible across edge (82 [86—90—94] dc, counting ch-3 as 1 dc); ch 3, turn. **2nd row:** Skip first dc, * y o hook, insert hook from front to back around post of next dc, y o hook and draw lp through, (y o hook and draw through 2 lps on hook) twice (front dc made), work front dc around next dc; y o hook, insert hook from back to front around post of next dc, y o hook and draw lp through, (y o hook and draw through 2 lps on hook) twice (back dc made), work back dc around next dc. Repeat from * across, dc in turning ch; ch 3, turn. **3rd row:** Repeat 2nd row. **4th row:** Skip first dc, * work back dc around each of next 2 dc, work front dc around each of next 2 dc. Repeat from * across, dc in turning ch; ch 3, turn. **5th row:** Repeat 4th row. Repeating 2nd through 5th rows for pattern, work even until piece measures 13" [13½"—14½"—15"] from beg or desired length to underarm.

To Shape Armholes: 1st row: Sl st in first 7 sts, ch 3, work in pattern to within last 6 dc; turn. **2nd row:** Sl st in first 5 sts, ch 3, work in pattern to within last 4 dc; turn. **3rd row:** Sl st in first 3 sts, ch 3, work to within last 2 dc; turn. Repeat last row 2 [2—3—3] times more. Work even on 50 [54—54—58] sts until armholes measure 6½" [7"—7"—7½"].

To Shape Neck: 1st row: Work across first 21 [23—23—25] sts; turn. **2nd row:** Sl st in first 4 [5—5—5] sts, ch 3, work across; ch 3, turn. **3rd row:** Work across to within last 2 [3—3—3] sts; ch 3, turn. Work even on 16 [16—16—18] sts until armholes measure 10" [10½"—10½"—11"]. Break off. Skip center 8 sts, attach yarn and work other side to correspond.

FRONT: Work same as back until 3rd row of armhole shaping has been completed.

To Shape Neck: 1st row: Sl st in first 3 sts, ch 3, work in pattern over next 26 [28—30—32] sts; place marker on next st; turn. **2nd row:** Sl st in first 2 sts, ch 3, work across to within last 2 dc; turn. **3rd row:** Sl st in first 3 sts, ch 3, work across to within ch-3 (21 [23—25—27] dc); turn. **For sizes 40 and 42 only: 4th row:** Sl st in first 2 sts, ch 3, work across; ch 3, turn. **5th row:** Work across to within last st; turn. Repeat 4th and 5th rows once more for size 40, twice more for size 42, then repeat 4th row again. **For sizes 44 and 46 only: 4th row:** Sl st in next 2 sts, ch 3, work across to within last 3 dc, ch 3; turn. **5th row:** Work across to within last st; turn. **6th row:** Sl st in next 2 sts, ch 3, work across; ch 3, turn. Repeat 5th and 6th rows once more, then repeat 5th row again. **For all sizes:** Work even on 16 [16—16—18] sts until armhole measures same as back to shoulders. Break off. Attach yarn to marked st and work other side to correspond.

FINISHING: Sew shoulder and side seams.

Note: Work with navy and size E hook from now on.

ARMBANDS (make 2): With navy and size E hook, ch 7. **1st row:** Sc in 2nd ch from hook and in each ch across (6 sc); ch 1, turn. **2nd row:** Working in back lp of each st, sc in first sc and in each sc across; ch 1, turn. Repeat 2nd row until piece fits around armhole. Break off. Sew ends together. Sew to armhole.

NECKBAND: Starting at center front V, ch 2. **1st row:** Work 3 sc in 2nd ch from hook, ch 1, turn. (Note: Work in back lps only throughout.) **2nd row:** Sc in first sc, 3 sc in next sc, sc in next sc; ch 1, turn. **3rd row:** Sc in first 2 sc, 3 sc in next sc, sc in next 2 sc; ch 1, turn. **4th row:** Sc in first 2 sc, 2 sc in next sc, 4 sc in next sc, 2 sc in next sc, sc in next 2 sc; ch 1, turn. **5th row:** Sc in each of next 6 sc (leave remaining 6 sc to be worked over for other section of border), mark next sc; ch 1, turn. **6th row:** Sc in each sc across; ch 1, turn. Repeat 6th row until piece fits from front V to center back neck. Break off. Attach yarn to marked st on 4th row. Ch 1, sc in same st and in each st across (6 sc); ch 1, turn. Repeat 6th row to match first section; sew center back seam. Break off. Sew border around neck.

Decorating with Crochet

Extravagant Afghan

In exuberant colors, with textural rows of popcorns, deeply fringed at two sides. In bulky wool yarn.

SIZE: Approximately 48" x 54" without fringe.

MATERIALS: Bucilla Multi-Craft (100% bulky acrylic) yarn, 36 ounces lavender (color (A), 28 ounces purple (B), 8 ounces orange (C), 36 ounces green (D), 4 ounces black (E), 4 ounces red (F), 4 ounces turquoise (G); approximately 6 yards each blue and green sport-weight yarn for embroidery; aluminum crochet hook size K (or Canadian hook No. 4), *or any size that will give you the correct gauge.*

GAUGE: 5 sc = 2".

With D, ch 136 to measure about 54". **Pattern A: 1st row:** Sc in 2nd ch from hook and in each ch across (135 sc). Ch 3, turn. **2nd row:** Skip first sc, dc in each sc across (ch-3 counts as 1 dc). Break off D; attach B. (**Note:** Always change colors as follows: Break off old color, leaving a 3" end. Tie on new strand, with knot close to work. Ch 1, turn.) **3rd row:** With B, working in back lp only, sc in each dc across, sc in top of ch-3. Break off B, attach F. Working in both lps, work 2 rows F. Break off F, attach E. Work 1 row E. Break off E, attach B. Working in back lp only, work 2 rows of sc. Break off B, attach D. **9th through 17th rows:** Working even in sc pattern and working in back lps only, work 2 rows D, 1 row C, 2 rows D, 2 rows B, 2 rows D. Break off. Do not turn work. Last row worked is a right-side row.

Pattern B: 1st row (popcorn row): With right side of work facing you, with B, make a lp on hook and attach yarn with a sc in first sc of last row, sc in next sc, y o, pull lp up in next sc, y o, pull through 2 lps on hook, (y o, pull lp up in same st, y o, pull through 2 lps on hook) 4 times; y o, pull through all 6 lps on hook (one popcorn made), * sc in each of next 2 sc, popcorn in next sc, repeat from * across row (45 popcorns). Break off B, attach D. Ch 1, turn. **2nd row:** * Sc in top of popcorn, sc in next 2 sc, repeat from * across (135 sts). Ch 1, turn. **3rd row:** Sc in each sc across (135 sc). Break off D, attach B. Ch 1, turn. **4th through 13th rows:** Working in back lps only for next 10 rows, sc in each sc across. Work 2 rows B, 1 row D, 4 rows B, 2 rows C, 1 row B. Break off B, attach A. Ch 1, turn.

Pattern C: 1st row: With A, work sc in each sc across. Ch 1, turn. **2nd row (popcorn row):** * Sc in each of next 2 sc, popcorn in next sc. Repeat from * across row. Ch 1, turn. **3rd row:** * Sc in top of popcorn, sc in each of next 2 sc, repeat from * across. Ch 1, turn. Repeat 2nd and 3rd rows twice more. **8th row:** With A, working in back lp only, sc in each sc across. Break off A, attach G. Ch 1, turn. **9th row:** With G, working in back lp only, sc in each sc across. Break off G, attach A. Ch 1, turn. **10th row:** Repeat 2nd row. Break off A, attach G. Ch 1, turn. **11th row:** With G, repeat 3rd row. Break off G, attach A. Ch 1, turn. **12th row:** With A, sc in each sc across. Break off A, attach B. Ch 1, turn.

Pattern D: 1st through 5th rows: Working in back lp only, sc in each sc across. Work 1 row B, 1 row D, 1 row B, 1 row C, 1 row D. Ch 1, turn. **6th row:** Work 1 sc, 2 h dc in first sc (first side shell made), skip next 2 sc, work 1 sc and 2 h dc in next sc (2nd side shell made), * skip next 2 sc, work sc and 2 h dc in next sc. Repeat from * across row, ending by skipping 1 sc and working sc and 2 h dc in last sc (last side shell made). Ch 1, turn. **7th row:** * Work side shell in next sc, skip 2 h dc. Repeat from * across (46 side shells). Ch 2, turn. Repeat 7th row twice more. Ch 1, turn. **10th row:** Skip 2 h dc, sc in each st across row, skip last st (135 sc). Break off D, attach A. Ch 1, turn. **11th through 13th rows:** Working in back lp only, sc in each sc across. Work 1 row A, 1 row D, 1 row A. Ch 1, turn. **14th and 15th rows:** Repeat 2nd and 3rd rows of pattern C from * to *. Break off A, attach D. Ch 1, turn. **16th through 20th rows:** Working in back lp only, sc in each sc across. Work 1 row D, 1 row A, 3 rows D. Break off D, attach A. Ch 1, turn.

Repeat pattern C in reverse by beginning with the last row and working backward to the first row, then repeat patterns B and A in the same manner.

FINISHING: With crochet hook or tapestry needle and 2 strands (about 1½ yards) each blue and green sportweight yarn, backstitch over 1st row of F sc on each side of afghan. With B, backstitch over 2nd row of F sc on each side of afghan.

FRINGE: Cut 2 strands of D to measure 18" and, beginning on one end at post of first row of D sc, knot the 2 strands over post of sc. Continue along end, matching the color of the fringe to the color of each row. Work remaining end in same manner.

Superwarm Afghan

In an interlocking stitch in red, blue, and sea green.

SIZE: 48" x 66".

MATERIALS: Bear Brand Win-Knit (knitting worsted-weight Orlon acrylic yarn), 5 (4-ounce) skeins each of seafoam No. 472 (color A), Spanish tile No. 431 (B), and royale No. 466 (C); aluminum crochet hook size H (or Canadian hook No. 8) *or the size that will give you the correct gauge.*

GAUGE: 5 dc groups of 2 overlapping rows = 2".

Note: Draw up first lp of each dc about ½" unless otherwise specified.

Starting at one end with A, ch 120 to measure approximately 48". **1st row:** Dc in 4th ch from hook, * skip next ch, work 2 dc in next ch (dc group made). Repeat from * across (59 dc groups made, counting turning ch as 1 dc). Do not break off A; attach B. (**Note:** Do not break off old color at end of row.) With A and B together, ch 3, turn. **2nd row:** With B only, work 2 dc in each unworked ch of foundation ch to last dc group, dc in turning ch. Attach C. With B and C together, ch 3, turn. **3rd row:** With C only, working in row below into color A, work 1 dc in top of turning ch, 2 dc in first dc of each dc group across. Pick up A. With C and A together, ch 3, turn. **4th row:** With A only, working in row below into color B, work 2 dc in first dc of each dc group across, work regular dc in turning ch of previous row. Pick up B. With A and B together, ch 3, turn. **5th row:** With B only, working in row below into color C, work 1 dc in top of turning ch, 2 dc in first dc of each dc group across. Pick up C. With B and C together, ch 3, turn.

6th row: With C only, working row below into color A, work 2 dc in first dc of each dc group across, work regular dc in turning ch of previous row. Pick up A. With C and A together, ch 3, turn. **7th row:** With A only, working in row below into color B, work 1 dc in top of turning ch, 2 dc in first dc of each dc group across. Pick up B. With B and A together, ch 3, turn. **8th row:** With B only, working in row below into color C, work 2 dc in first dc of each dc group across, work regular dc in turning ch of previous row. Pick up C. With B and C together, ch 3, turn.

Repeat 3rd through 8th rows for pattern until afghan measures 66" or desired length, ending with an A row.

FINISHING: With A, working into last B row made, work 2 sc in first dc of each dc group across. Break off. Attach A to foundation ch. Work 1 sc in 2nd ch, skip 1 ch, * 2 sc in next ch, skip next ch. 1 sc in next ch. Repeat from * across. Break off.

Hexagon Afghan

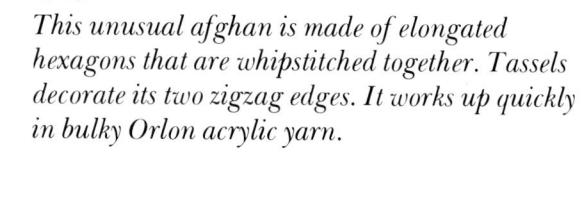

This unusual afghan is made of elongated hexagons that are whipstitched together. Tassels decorate its two zigzag edges. It works up quickly in bulky Orlon acrylic yarn.

SIZE: About 48" x 60" without tassels.
MATERIALS: Bernat Big Berella Bulky Orlon acrylic yarn, 2 (4-ounce) skeins magenta No. 8528 (color A), 4 skeins each old gold No. 8509 (B) and scarlet No. 8533 (C), 5 skeins tartan mix (green) No. 8576 (D) and 6 skeins royal No. 8550 (E); aluminum crochet hook size I (or Canadian hook No. 7) *or the size that will give you the correct gauge.*
GAUGE: Each motif measures 14" long from point to point.
Note: Always work with right side of piece facing you.
MOTIF (make 28): Starting along center with A, ch 16 to measure about 5". **1st rnd:** Work 2 dc in 4th ch from hook (first shell made), ch 1, 3 dc in same ch (another shell made), (skip 3 ch, ch 1, shell in next ch) twice; ch 1, skip 3 ch, in last ch work shell, ch 1, shell, ch 1 and shell; working along opposite edge of foundation chain, (skip 3 ch, ch 1, shell in next ch) 3 times, ch 1; join with sl st to top of ch-3. Break off. **2nd rnd:** With B, make lp on hook, in center dc of first shell work shell, ch 1 and shell (inc group made), * ch 1, work inc group in next ch-1 sp, ch 1, (work shell in next ch-1 sp, ch 1) 3 times, inc group in next ch-1 sp, ch 1, inc group in center dc of next shell. Repeat from * once more, omitting last inc group (3 inc groups at each short end, 3 shells along

each long edge); join. Break off. **3rd rnd:** With C, make lp on hook, work inc group in first sp, ch 1, shell in next sp, ch 1, inc group in next sp, ch 1, (work shell in next sp, ch 1) 4 times; (inc group in next sp, ch 1, shell in next sp, ch 1) twice; inc group in next sp, ch 1, (work shell in next sp, ch 1) 4 times; inc group in next sp, ch 1, shell in next sp, ch 1; join. Break off. **4th rnd:** With D, make lp on hook, work inc group in first sp, ch 1, (shell in next sp, ch 1) 11 times, inc group in next sp, ch 1, (shell in next sp, ch 1) 11 times; join. Break off. **5th rnd:** With E, make lp on hook, work shell in first sp, ch 1, (shell in next sp, ch 1) 3 times; * shell in center dc of next shell, ch 1, (shell in next sp, ch 1) 6 times; shell in center dc of next shell, ch 1 *, (shell in next sp, ch 1) 7 times. Repeat from * to * once more, (shell in next sp, ch 1) 3 times; join. Break off.

HALF MOTIF (make 4): Starting at straight edge with A, ch 21 to measure about 7″. **1st row:** Work shell in 5th ch from hook, (skip 3 ch, ch 1, shell in next ch) 3 times; skip 3 ch, ch 1, sc in last ch. Break off. **2nd row:** With B, make lp on hook and, over turning ch at beg of last row, work dc, ch 1 and inc group, ch 1, (work shell in next sp, ch 1) 3 times; inc group in next sp, ch 1, dc in last sc. Break off. **3rd row:** With C, make lp on hook, work dc in first dc, ch 1, shell in first sp, ch 1, inc group in next sp, ch 1, (shell in next sp, ch 1) 4 times; inc group in next sp, ch 1, shell in next sp, ch 1, dc in last dc. Break off. **4th row:** With D, make lp on hook and work dc in first dc, ch 1, shell in first sp, ch 1, (shell in next sp, ch 1) 10 times; dc in last dc. Break off. **5th rnd:** With E, make lp on hook, work shell in first sp, ch 1, (shell in next sp, ch 1) twice; shell in center dc of next shell, ch 1, (shell in next sp, ch 1) 6 times; shell in center dc of next shell, ch 1, (shell in next sp, ch 1) 3 times. Continue by working along side of last 3 rows as follows: Work shell and ch-1 over post of each of next 3 dc, then, working along outer edge of foundation chain, work shell and ch-1 in base of each of first 4 shells made on motif; finish by working shell and ch-1 over post of each of next 3 dc, ch 1; join. Break off.

JOINING: Hold 2 motifs together with right sides facing. Whipstitch together along one long edge, working through one lp only of each st (ridges formed on right side). Following diagram, make 3 strips with 6 motifs each

Hexagon Afghan

and 2 strips with 5 motifs and 2 half motifs each. Following diagram, sew strips together in same manner as for motifs.

TASSELS (make 12): Combining all colors for each tassel, cut about thirty 14″ strands. Fold in half. Tie tightly about 1½″ from folded end. Tie one tassel to each point along zigzag edges of afghan.

Bedspread

A simple but time-consuming project, this sunny bedcover. But the individual hexagons are small, so take them along wherever you go, and before you know it, a field of flowers will brighten your bedroom.

SIZE: Approximately 87″ x 101″.
MATERIALS: Coats & Clark's Pearl Cotton No. 5 (50-yard balls), 90 balls main color (MC), 95 balls white, 7 balls contrasting color (CC); aluminum crochet hook size C (or Canadian hook No. 13), *or the size that will give you the correct gauge.*
GAUGE: Each hexagon = 3½″.
HEXAGON: Make 259 with MC, 300 with white, 50 with 2 colors (rnds 1 through 4 in MC, rnd 5 in CC). Ch 5, join with sl st to form a ring. **Rnd 1:** Ch 3, 1 dc into ring, ch 1, * 2 dc,

ch 1, repeat from * 4 times more, join with sl st in 3rd ch of starting ch 3. **Rnd 2:** Ch 3, 1 dc in next dc, * 1 dc, ch 2, 1 dc in ch-1 sp, skip next dc, 1 dc in next dc, repeat from * 5 times, ending last repeat with 1 dc in ch-1 sp, ch 1, join with sl st in 3rd ch of starting ch-3—6 dc groups with 3 dc in each. **Rnd 3:** Ch 3, 1 dc in ch-1 sp to the right, dc in each of next 2 dc, * 2 dc, ch 2, 2 dc in ch-2 sp, skip next dc, dc in each of next 2 dc, repeat from * 5 times more, ending last repeat with 2 dc in ch-2 sp, ch 2, join with sl st in 3rd ch of starting ch-3—6 dc groups with 6 dc in each. **Rnd 4:** Ch 3, 1 dc in ch-2 sp to the right, dc in each of next 5 dc, * 2 dc, ch 2, 2 dc in ch-2 sp, skip next dc, dc in each of next 5 dc, repeat from * 5 times more, ending last repeat with 2 dc in ch-2 sp, ch 2, join with sl st in 3rd ch of starting ch-3—6 dc groups with 9 dc in each. **Rnd 5:** Ch 3, 1 dc in ch-2 sp to right, dc in each of next 8 dc, * 2 dc, ch 1, 2 dc in ch-2 sp, skip next dc, dc in each of next 8 dc, repeat from * 5 times more, ending last repeat with 2 dc in ch-2 sp, ch 1, join with sl st in 3rd ch of starting ch-3—6 dc groups with 12 dc in each.

FINISHING: Assembling: Sew 6 white hexagons around each 2-color hexagon to form posy motif. Join posies by sewing to one row of MC hexagons. Posies should fall in alternating rows of 5 and 6 across (9 rows in all, beginning and ending with 6-posy rows), to form a zigzag pattern (see photograph).

Cozy Afghan

A cascade of wavy stripes in a multitude of colors. Worked in sport yarn.

SIZE: Approximately 66" wide by 84" long.

MATERIALS: Sport yarn, 14 ounces each white, red, yellow, green, orange, brown, gold, navy (this does include fringe); aluminum crochet hook size D (or Canadian hook No. 12), *or the size that will give you the correct gauge.*

GAUGE: 13 sts = 3".

Note: Pattern is divisible by 26 + 2; to make spread wider, increase by 26 dc; to make narrower, decrease by 26 dc.

Start with any color desired and change colors every 2 rows. Use all 8 colors, then repeat sequence every 16 rows.

Note: Change color at the end of the row when you work the last dc: draw up lp of new color through last 2 lps of dc, then continue to work next row.

With first color, ch 290 loosely. **Row 1:** Dc in 3rd ch from hook and in each ch across—288 dc. **Row 2:** Ch 2, 1 dc in first dc, * 2 dc in next st (1 inc), 1 dc in each of next 10 dc, (2 dc tog [1 dec]), twice, 10 dc, 2 dc in next st (1 inc), repeat from *, end 1 dc, turn. Repeat this row for entire length of bedspread.

FINISHING: Fringe both sides of bedspread with yarn color to match edge stripe.

Crossover Granny Pillow

Made up of four 9" squares that are sewn together. Then the four corners are folded over to the center front to get this unusual effect.

SIZE: Approximately 13" square.

MATERIALS: Knitting worsted, 2 ounces each orange (color O), green (G), purple (P), and red (R); aluminum crochet hook size J (or Canadian hook No. 6) *or the size that will give you*

2 dc in each dc around; sl st in top of ch-3 (24 dc, counting ch-3 as 1 dc). Break off. **3rd rnd:** With G, work 2 sc in last sl st, work 2 sc in each dc around (48 sc); sl st in first sc. Break off. **4th rnd:** With P, work 2 dc, ch 1 and 2 dc in any sc (corner made), * skip next sc, sc in next 9 sc, skip next sc, work 2 dc, ch 1 and 2 dc in next sc (another corner). Repeat from * twice more; skip next sc, sc in next 9 sc; sl st in top of first dc. Break off. **5th rnd:** With R, work sc, ch 1 and sc in any ch-1 sp (corner), * sc in next 13 sts, work sc, ch 1 and sc in next ch-1 sp (corner). Repeat from * twice more; sc in next 13 sts; sl st in first sc. Break off. **6th rnd:** With P, work sc, ch 1 and sc in a ch-1 sp, * sc in next 15 sts, work sc, ch 1 and sc in next ch-1 sp. Repeat from * twice more; sc in next 15 sts; sl st in first sc. Break off. **7th rnd:** With O, work sc, ch 1 and sc in a ch-1 sp, * sc in next 17 sts, work sc, ch 1 and sc in next ch-1 sp. Repeat from * twice more; sc in next 17 sts; sl st in first sc. Break off. **8th rnd:** With R, sc in each st around; sl st in first sc. Break off.

Make 3 more blocks in same manner, working 7th rnd on 2 of the blocks with G instead of O.

Sew blocks together to form square. Fold each corner of square to center so that corners meet. Sew touching sides together, leaving an opening large enough to insert pillow.

PILLOW: Cut 2 squares of red cotton ½" larger on all sides than crocheted cover. Stitch together along 3 sides. Turn and stuff. Sew opening closed. Insert pillow in crocheted cover and sew remaining seam.

the correct gauge; tapestry needle; ½ yard 36"-wide red cotton for pillow lining; Dacron or kapok for stuffing.

GAUGE: Each block measures 9" square without stretching.

BLOCK: Starting at center with O, ch 6. Join with sl st to form ring. **1st rnd:** Ch 3, work 11 dc in ring; join with sl st to top of ch-3. **2nd rnd:** Ch 3, work dc in same place as ch-3, work

Pyramid and Zigzag Pillows

In luscious shades of fuchsia, pink, orange, yellow, and brown knitting worsted. They are made in rectangles folded crosswise, so pattern shows on front and back.

Pyramid Pillow

SIZE: Approximately 13½" by 13½".
MATERIALS (for 2 pillows): Knitting worsted, 2 ounces each pink, orange, yellow, fuchsia, brown; aluminum crochet hook size F (or Canadian hook No. 10) *or the size that will give you the correct gauge.*

GAUGE: 21 dc and 12 rows = 4".

Note: When crocheting triangles, it is necessary to crochet over the yarn that is not being used. All dc are inserted through both threads of st, not into sp.

With orange, ch 143. **Row 1:** Skip 2 ch, dc in each ch—141 dc, turn. **Row 2:** With pink, ch 2, 1 dc, * with orange, 19 dc, with pink 1 dc, repeat from * to end of row, turn. **Row 3:** With pink, ch 2, 2 dc, * with orange, 17 dc, with pink, 3 dc, repeat from * , ending last repeat with pink, 2 dc, turn. **Row 4:** With pink, ch 2, 3 dc, * with orange, 15 dc, with pink, 5 dc, repeat from *, ending last repeat with pink, 3 dc, turn. **Row 5:** With pink, ch 2, 4 dc, * with orange, 13 dc, with pink, 7 dc, repeat from *, ending last repeat with pink, 4 dc, turn. **Row 6:** With pink, ch 2, 5 dc, * with orange, 11 dc, with pink, 9 dc, repeat from *, ending last repeat with pink, 5 dc, turn. **Row 7:** With pink, ch 2, 6 dc, * with orange, 9 dc, with pink, 11 dc, repeat from *, ending last repeat with pink, 6 dc, turn. **Row 8:** With pink, ch 2, 7 dc, * with orange, 7 dc, with pink, 13 dc, repeat from *, ending last repeat with pink, 7 dc, turn. **Row 9:** With pink, ch 2, 8 dc, * with orange, 5 dc, with pink, 15 dc, repeat from *, ending last repeat with pink, 8 dc, turn. **Row 10:** With pink, ch 2, 9 dc, * with orange, 3 dc, with pink, 17 dc, repeat from *, ending last repeat with pink, 9 dc, turn. **Row 11:** With pink, ch 2, 10 dc, * with orange, 1 dc, with pink, 19 dc, repeat from *, ending last repeat with pink, 10 dc, turn. **Row 12:** With pink, ch 2, 141 dc. **Rows 13 and 14:** With fuchsia, ch 2, 141 dc, turn. **Row 15:** With brown, ch 2, 141 dc, turn. **Row 16:** With fuchsia, ch 2, 1 dc, * with brown, 19 dc, with fuchsia, 1 dc, repeat from *, ending row with fuchsia, 1 dc, turn. **Rows 17 thru 25:** Same as rows 3 thru 11, working fuchsia and brown, each row beginning and ending with fuchsia. **Row 26:** With fuchsia, ch 2, 141 dc, turn. **Rows 27 and 28:** With yellow, ch 2, 141 dc, turn. **Row 29:** With orange, ch 2, 141 dc, turn. **Rows 30 thru 40:** Same as rows 2 thru 12, with the same colors. Fasten off.

FINISHING: Fold piece in half, right sides out. Sew the two ends and part of the third side. Insert pillow form or stuffing. Sew opening closed.

Zigzag Pillow

SIZE: Approximately 12" by 12".
MATERIALS: See Pyramid Pillow, p. 230.
GAUGE: From top point of zigzag to top point of zigzag = 3".

With yellow, ch 100. **Row 1:** Skip 3 ch, work 3-group st over next 3 ch (**group st:** * y o, insert hook in the next st, y o and draw through, y o, draw through 2 lps on hook, repeat from * twice [4 times for 5-group st], y o, draw through all 4 [6] lps on hook), * 1 dc in each of next 9 sts, 5 dc in next st, 1 dc in each of next 9 sts, 5-group st over next 5 sts, repeat from *, ending last repeat with 3-group st, ch 3, turn. **Row 2:** Work a 3-group st, * 1 dc in each of next 9 sts, 5 dc in next st, 1 dc in each of next 9 sts, 5-group st, repeat from *, ending last repeat with 3-group st, ch 3, turn. Repeat Row 2 for pattern throughout, working 4 rows more with yellow. **Rows 7 through 12:** With brown. **Rows 13 through 16:** With fuchsia. **Rows 17 through 20:** With pink. **Rows 21 through 26:** With orange. Repeat Rows 1 through 26 again in color sequence. Continue with yellow until pillow cover measures approximately 24". Fasten off.

FINISHING: Fold piece in half and sew uneven edges first with a straight line very close to points of design. Sew second side and part of third. Stuff with pillow form or stuffing. Sew opening closed.

Pink Scallops

This pillow couldn't be simpler to make—single and double crochet plus a shell-stitch border, in bright-colored knitting worsted. Good project for leftover yarns.

SIZE: 10" x 12" without ruffle.

MATERIALS: Knitting worsted, 1 ounce each medium blue (color M), watermelon (W), green (G), yellow (Y), and fuchsia (F); aluminum crochet hook size H (or Canadian hook No. 8), *or the size that will give you the correct gauge;* 2 pieces gold felt 12" x 14"; kapok or Dacron for stuffing.

GAUGE: 3 dc = 1".

Starting at center with M, ch 9. **1st rnd:** Work 4 h dc in 3rd ch from hook and in each of next 5 ch, 5 h dc in next ch; working along opposite side of chain, work h dc in each of next 5 ch; join with sl st to top of ch-2. **2nd rnd:** Ch 2, work 3 h dc in next h dc (mark 2nd h dc with pin), h dc in next h dc, 3 h dc in next h dc, h dc in next 7 h dc, 3 h dc in next h dc, h dc in next h dc, 3 h dc in next h dc, h dc in next 6 h dc (28 h dc, counting ch-2 as 1 h dc); join. Break off. **3rd rnd:** With W, form lp on hook, work 3 h dc in marked h dc, h dc in next 3 h dc, 3 h dc in next h dc, h dc in next 9 h dc, 3 h dc in next h dc, h dc in next 3 h dc, 3 h dc in next h dc, h dc in next 9 h dc; join. **4th rnd:** Ch 3, 3 dc in next h dc (shell made), dc in next 5 h dc, shell in next h dc, dc in next 11 h dc, shell in next h dc, dc in next 5 h dc, shell in next h dc, dc in next 5 h dc, shell in next h dc, dc in next 10 h dc; join. Break off. **5th rnd:** With G, work sc in center dc of first shell, * shell in next dc, sc in next dc, skip next dc, shell in next dc, skip next dc, sc in next dc, shell in next dc, sc in next dc, (shell in next dc, skip next dc, sc in next dc, skip next dc) 3 times; shell in next dc, sc in next dc. Repeat from * once more, omitting last sc; join. Break off. **6th rnd:** With Y, work 5 dc in first sc made on last rnd (first corner), * sc in center dc of next shell, (3-dc shell in next sc, sc in center of next shell) twice; 5-dc shell in next sc (corner), sc in center dc of next shell, (3-dc shell in next dc, sc in center dc of next shell) 3 times; work corner. Repeat from * once more, omitting last corner; join. Break off. **7th rnd:** With F, work 3 dc in center dc of first corner, * dc in each st to center dc of next corner, 3 dc in center dc. Repeat from * twice more, dc in each dc to end (72 dc); join. Break off. **8th rnd:** With M, work 3 h dc in center st of first corner, work h dc in each st around, working 3 h dc in center st of each corner (80 h dc); join. Break off. **9th rnd:** With G, repeat last rnd, working dc instead of h dc (88 dc). **10th rnd:** With Y, repeat 8th rnd, working sc instead of h dc (96 sc). Break off. **11th rnd:** With W, repeat 8th rnd, working dc instead of h dc (104 dc). Break off. **12th rnd:** With M, repeat 8th rnd, working dc instead of h dc (112 dc). Break off. **13th rnd:** With Y, repeat 8th rnd, working sc instead of h dc (120 sc). Break off.

PILLOW: Center and baste crocheted piece on one felt piece, stretching it to measure about 10" x 12". Trim felt edges, leaving ½" all around for seams. Cut 2nd felt piece same size. Pin felt pieces together with crochet sandwiched between. Machine stitch around, catching crochet in stitching and leaving opening along one side. Turn, stuff, and sew opening closed.

SCALLOPED EDGING: With F, work sc in any st on edge, * skip next st, work 5 dc in next st, skip next st, sc in next st. Repeat from * around, skip next st; join. Break off.

Chair Seat

It looks like needlepoint, doesn't it? Chair seat in traditional grapevine and leaf pattern is worked in unstretchy single crochet with needlepoint and crewel wool to give a luxurious tapestry look.

SIZE: Crochet measures 21" x 24" to cover chair seat approximately 17" deep and 20" wide. Crochet can be enlarged by extending the background borders.

MATERIALS: Bucilla Needlepoint and Crewel Wool, 49 (30-yard) cards light taupe No. 143 (A—background color), 11 cards bronze No. 49 (B), 3 cards each light bronze No. 21 (L), purple No. 31 (P), violet No. 30 (V), and dark turquoise No. 65 (T); steel crochet hook No. 1 (or Canadian hook No. 0) *or the size that will give you the correct gauge.*

GAUGE: 6 sc = 1"; 6 rows = 1".

Note: Each square on chart represents 1 sc. The border, worked in background color (shaded area), is not shown on chart. Follow color key for marked areas. Only one grape in each group is marked. Make others the same color. Always change colors as follows: Sc in each sc to within last sc of old color, insert hook in last sc, draw up loop (2 loops on hook), attach new color and draw loop of new color through both loops on hook. In areas where 2 colors alternate frequently, carry color not in use across top of piece and work over it, otherwise break off old color leaving 5" end for weaving through wrong side.

Starting at front edge with A, ch 146 to measure about 24". **1st row:** Sc in 2nd ch from hook and in each ch across (145 sc); turn. **2nd row:** Sc in each sc across; ch 1, turn. Repeat 2nd row 12 times more for border.

Start pattern as follows: **1st row (right side):** Sc in first 14 sc for border, place pin in work as marker between last sc worked and next sc, work 13 more sc, attach B and work 3 sc, work 25 A sc, 3 T sc, 12 A sc, 1 T sc, 33 A sc, 1

Color Key
B bronze
V violet
L light bronze
T dark turquoise
P purple

B sc, 9 A sc, 3 T sc, 15 A sc, place marker in work as before, work remaining 13 A sc for border; ch 1, turn. **2nd row:** Work 13 A sc to marker; follow chart from 2nd row, reading from left to right to marker, work remaining 14 A sc. Continue to follow chart until it has been completed, working from right to left on right-side rows and from left to right on wrong-side rows and working the border sts before the first marker and after the 2nd marker in A only.

Note: Move markers from row to row as you work. After chart has been completed, work 14 rows with A only for border.

FINISHING: Weave in all ends. Block piece carefully by dampening it, then stretching and pinning it to a padded board, lining up the rows evenly so that they do not ripple. Allow to dry thoroughly before unpinning. Fold and staple or baste piece over chair seat; slip seat in chair frame.

Special Setting to Fit Round Tables

A center piece and matching place mat. Worked mostly in double crochet and chain-two pattern. In mercerized bedspread cotton.

MATERIALS: 1 (550-yard) ball mercerized bedspread cotton (or crochet cotton size 10) in beige (1 ball will make 1 place mat and 1 center piece); No. 5 steel crochet hook (or Canadian hook No. 2½), *or the size that will give you the correct gauge.*

GAUGE: 9 sc = 1"; 4 rows = 1".

Place Mat

SIZE: Place mat measures 10½" deep.

Starting at inner edge, ch 72 to measure approximately 8". **1st row:** Dc in 4th ch from hook and in each ch across (70 dc, counting ch-3 as 1 dc); ch 3, turn. **2nd row:** Dc in 2nd dc and in each of next 8 dc (first dc-group made), * ch 1, dc in each of next 10 dc (another dc-group made). Repeat from * across (7 groups made, separated by ch-1 sp); ch 3, turn. **3rd row:** Dc in 2nd dc and in each of next 8 dc, * ch 2, dc in each of next 10 dc. Repeat from * across; ch 3, turn.

4th row: Dc in 2nd dc and in each of next 8 dc, * ch 2, dc in ch-2 sp, ch 2, dc in each of next 10 dc (2 sp between groups). Repeat from * across; ch 3, turn.

5th row: Work even across first group, * ch 2, (dc in next sp, ch 2) twice; dc in each of next 10 dc (3 sp between groups). Repeat from * across; ch 3, turn.

6th row: Work even across first group, * ch 2, (dc in next dc, ch 2) twice; dc in each of next 10 dc. Repeat from * across; ch 3, turn.

7th row: Dc in 2nd dc and in each of next 2 dc, y o, draw up lp in next st, y o, draw through 2 lps on hook, y o, draw up lp in next st (4 lps on hook), y o, draw through 2 lps on hook, y o, draw through remaining 3 lps (1 dc dec), dc in remaining dc of group (9 dc in group), * ch 3, (dc in next dc, ch 3) twice; dc in each of next 4 dc of next group, dec 1 dc, dc in remaining 4 dc. Repeat from * across (3 sp between 9-dc groups); ch 3, turn. **8th—10th rows:** Work even in pattern. **11th row:** Dec 1 dc in center of first dc group, * ch 3, dc in next dc, ch 3, dc in next sp, ch 3, dc in next dc, ch 3, work dec in center of next dc group. Repeat from * across (4 sp between 8-dc groups); ch 3, turn. **12th row:** Dc in each dc of first group, * ch 3, (dc in next dc, ch 3) three times; dc in each dc of next group. Repeat from * across (4 sp between 8-dc groups); ch 3, turn. **13th—19th rows:** Work even in pattern. **20th row:** Working in pattern, dec 1 dc in first group, * ch 3, dc in next dc, (ch 3, dc in next sp) twice; ch 3, dc in next dc, ch 3, dec 1 dc in next group. Repeat from * across (5 sp between 7-dc groups); ch 3, turn. **21st row:** Dc in each dc of first group, * ch 3, (dc in next dc, ch 3) 4 times; dc in each dc of next group. Repeat from * across (5 sp and 7-dc groups); ch 3, turn.

22nd—29th rows: Work even in pattern. **30th row:** Working in pattern, dec 1 dc in first group, * ch 3, dc in next dc, (ch 3, dc in next sp) 3 times; ch 3, dc in next dc, ch 3, dec 1 dc in next group. Repeat from * across (6 sp between 6-dc groups); ch 3, turn. **31st row:** Dc in each dc of first group, * ch 4, (dc in next dc, ch 4) 5 times; ch 4, dc in each dc of next group. Repeat from * across (6 sp between 6-dc groups); ch 3, turn. **32nd—39th rows:** Work even in pattern. **40th row:** Working in each dc and ch st, work dc in each st across (216 dc); ch 3, turn. **41st row:** Dc in 2nd dc and in each dc across; ch 3, turn. **42nd row:** Dc in 2nd dc and in each dc across. Break off.

Center Piece

SIZE: 15" in diameter.

Starting at center, ch 10. Join with sl st to form ring.

1st rnd: Ch 3, work 29 dc in ring; join with sl st in top of ch-3 (30 dc, counting ch-3 as 1 dc). **2nd rnd:** Ch 3, dc in same place as sl st, 2 dc in each dc around (60 dc); join with sl st to top of ch-3. **3rd rnd:** Ch 3, dc in each dc around (60 dc); join. **4th rnd:** Ch 3, dc in same place as sl st, * dc in next dc, 2 dc in next dc. Repeat from * around, ending with dc in last dc (90 dc). **5th rnd:** Ch 3, dc in 2nd dc and in each dc around; join. **6th rnd:** Ch 3, dc in 2nd dc and in each dc around, increasing 30 dc evenly spaced (120 dc); join. **7th rnd:** Work even around; join. **8th rnd:** Repeat 6th rnd (150 dc). **9th rnd:** Ch 3, dc in 2nd dc and in each of next 8 dc (first dc-group made, ch-3 counts as 1 dc), ch 1, * dc in each of next 10 dc (another dc-group made), ch 1. Repeat from * around (15 dc-groups made, separated by ch-1 sp); join. **10th rnd:** Ch 3, work even across first group, ch 2, * work dc in each dc of next group, ch 2. Repeat from * around; join. **11th rnd:** Ch 3, work even across first group, ch 2, * work dc in sp, ch 2, work dc in each dc of next group. Repeat from * around, ending in pattern (2 sp between each group); join. **12th rnd:** Ch 3, dc in 2nd dc and in each of next 2 dc, y o, draw up lp in next st, y o, draw through 2 lps on hook, y o, draw up lp in next st (4 lps on hook), y o, draw through 2 lps on hook, y o, draw through remaining 3 lps (1 dc dec), dc in remaining dc of group (9 dc in group), * ch 2, dc in next dc, ch 2, dc in each of next 4 dc of next group, dec 1 dc, dc in remaining 4 dc. Repeat from * around, ending in pattern (2 sp between 9-dc groups); join. **13th and 14th rnds:** Work even in pattern. **15th rnd:** Dec 1 dc in first group, * ch 2, (dc in next sp, ch 2) twice; dec 1 dc in next group. Repeat from * around, ending in pattern (3 sp between 8-dc groups); join. **16th rnd:** Ch 3, work even across first group, * ch 2, (dc in next dc, ch 2) twice; dc in each dc of next group. Repeat from * around, ending in pattern; join. **17th rnd:** Work even in pattern. **18th rnd:** Ch 3, dec 1 dc in first group, * ch 2, (dc in next sp, ch 2) 3 times; dec 1 dc in next group. Repeat from * around, ending in pattern (4 sp between 7-dc groups); join. **19th rnd:** Ch 3, work even across first group, * ch 2, (dc in next sp, ch 2) 4 times; dc in each dc of next dc group. Repeat from * around, ending in pattern; join. **20th rnd:** Ch 3, dec 1 dc in first group, * ch 3, (dc in next dc, ch 3) 4 times; dec 1 dc in next group. Repeat from * around, ending in pattern (5 sp between 6-dc group); join. **21st rnd:** Work even in pattern. **22nd—25th rnds:** Work even in pattern, working ch-4 sp instead of ch-3 sp. **26th rnd:** Ch 3, working in each dc and ch st, work dc in each st around (450 dc); join. **27th and 28th rnds:** Ch 3, dc in 2nd dc and in each dc around. Join. Break off.

Four Fruits Tablecloth

An ordinary square tablecloth made special with these crocheted set-in place mats, each of which is worked in a different fruit motif. A filet border is worked in four separate strips and sewn on.

SIZE: Tablecloth measures 52" square. Each fruit motif measures 8½" x 12½". Hem border measures 1½" wide. Cloth size is adjustable.

MATERIALS: D.M.C. pearl cotton No. 5, 22 (53-yard) balls orange No. 741; steel crochet hook No. 2 (or Canadian hook No. 1) *or the size that will give you the correct gauge;* purchased linen tablecloth, color-matched to pearl cotton.

GAUGE: 5 sp and 5 bl = 3"; 5 rows = 1½".

FRUIT MOTIFS: Starting at base, ch 85. **1st row (mark for right side):** In 5th ch from hook work joined dc as follows: Y o and pull up lp in ch, y o and draw through 2 lps on hook, y o and pull up lp in same ch, y o and draw through 2 lps on hook, y o and draw through all 3 lps on hook (joined dc made), dc in next ch (1st bl completed); * ch 1, skip next ch, dc in next ch (sp made), joined dc in next ch, dc in next ch (another bl made). Repeat from * across (21 bl, 20 sp); ch 4, turn. **2nd row:** Skip first dc and joined dc, dc in next dc (sp made over bl); * work joined dc in next sp, dc in next dc (bl made over sp); ch 1, skip joined dc, dc in next dc (sp made over bl). Repeat from * across, ending last repeat with dc in turning ch; ch 3, turn. **3rd row:** Work joined dc in first sp, dc in next dc (first bl made over sp); * work 1 sp, 1 bl. Repeat from * across; ch 4, turn. **4th row:** Repeat 2nd row. **5th row:** Work 1 bl, (1 sp, 1 bl) twice; work joined dc in next joined dc, dc in next dc (bl made over bl); work 31 more bl; (1 sp, 1 bl) twice; ch 4, turn. **6th row:** (Work 1 sp, 1 bl) twice; 1 more bl, 31 sp, 2 bl, 1 sp, 1 bl, 1 sp; ch 3, turn. **7th row:** Work 1 bl, then (1 sp, 1 bl) twice; ch 1, dc in next dc (sp made over sp); work 30 more sp, 1 bl, (1 sp, 1 bl) twice; ch 4, turn.

Starting with 8th row (wrong side) of apple chart, and working wrong-side rows from left to right and right-side rows from right to left, follow chart to top. Break off.

Working border as for apple motif, make 1 motif each of cherries, grapes, and pear.

Motif Edging: Work edging around each motif as follows: With right side facing you, starting in upper left corner of motif, work 3 sc over post of first dc (X on apple chart); * work sc and sl st over each end st across to lower left corner, in corner work 3 sc, sc in each st across base, 3 sc in corner sp. Repeat from * once more across right side and top edge, omitting last corner; join with sl st to first sc. Break off.

HEM BORDER: The hem border is worked in 4 strips and sewn together at corners.

Border Strips (make 4): Starting at narrow end, ch 14. **1st row:** Work joined dc in 5th ch from hook, dc in next ch (first bl made); (work 1 sp, 1 bl) twice; ch 4, turn. **2nd row:** Work 1 sp, (1 bl, 1 sp) twice; ch 3, turn. **3rd row:** Work 1 bl, (1 sp, 1 bl) twice; ch 4, turn. **4th row (mark beg of row for inside edge):** Repeat 2nd row. **5th row:** Work 1 bl, (1 sp, 1 bl) twice; ch 3, turn. **6th row:** Work 2 bl, 1 sp, 1 bl, 1 sp; ch 3, turn. Repeat 5th and 6th rows until strip measures 50½" or desired length, ending with 6th row.

Matching checkerboard pattern and inside edges at corners, sew strips together to form square, being careful not to twist strips.

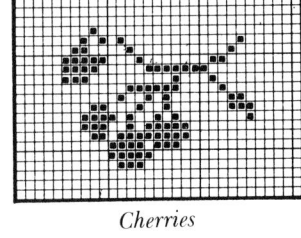

Apple

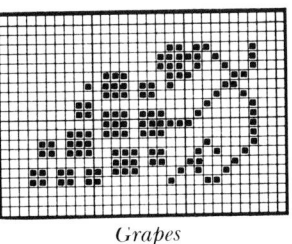

Cherries

Grapes

Pear

Outer Border Edging: Work as for Motif Edging, always working over end sts.

Inner Border Edging: Work sc in st at center of any inner edge, then * work as for Outer Border to corner sp, skip corner sp, sc in next sp. Repeat from * around; join with sl st in first sc. Break off.

ASSEMBLING and FINISHING: Block motifs to same size.

For 52" cloth (see note below for other sizes), measure 9¾" up from lower edge of tablecloth and 19" in from left side edge; mark a dot. Measure 18¼" up from lower edge and 19" in from left side and mark another dot. Draw a light line from dot to dot. Place left edge of any motif against this line and mark other edges of motif on cloth. Following photograph, place other motifs on cloth and mark positions. Remove motifs. Mark another rectangle ½" inside each placement rectangle. Cut out the smaller rectangle. Place a motif over each opening and sew to tablecloth along outer lines. Clip ½" linen (under motif) at corners and press back. Overcast raw linen edge to prevent raveling and tack in place. Sew hem border on tablecloth.

Note: If tablecloth is a different size, find center and arrange motifs around center point as in photograph. Mark placement and finish as specified above.

Elegant Tablecloth

More elegance in filet crochet. Nine squares make up this beautiful tablecloth in a delicate rose pattern.

SIZE: Approximately 51" x 51" without fringe.

MATERIALS: Coats & Clark's Knit-Cro-Sheen, 18 (250-yard) balls. Steel crochet hook No. 6 (or Canadian hook No. 3) *or the size that will give you the correct gauge.*

GAUGE: Each motif is approximately 17" x 17".

MOTIF (make 9): Ch 169. **Row 1:** 1 dc in 7th ch from hook, * ch 2, skip 2 ch, 1 dc in next ch, repeat from * across—55 meshes. **Row 2:** Ch 4 to turn all rows and ch 2, dc in 3rd ch of turning ch-4 to end all rows (first 2 ch counts as 1 dc), 1 dc in next dc and in each dc across, filling mesh with 2 dc or working ch-2 between dc according to the chart. Continue in pattern, following chart and detail for openwork center.

FINISHING: Sew motifs together in 3 rows of 3 motifs each.

Fringe: Wrap yarn around 8" cardboard, cut one end. To knot tassels around edge, use 4 stands of yarn, insert folded end through mesh, insert crochet hook into loop formed and pull all strands through.

⊠ **Block** — *Dc in dc, 2 dc over ch-2 lp, dc in dc (if the mesh is filled with dc on previous row, work dc in each dc).*

□ **Space** — *Dc in dc, ch 2, skip 2 dc or ch-2, dc in next dc.*

Row 10 — *Dc in dc, 5 dc in ch-5 lp, dc in next dc.*

Row 9 — *Dc in dc, 3 dc in ch-4 lp, ch 5, 3 dc in next ch-4 lp, dc in next dc.*

Row 8 — *Ch 4, insert hook under ch-9 and ch-5, y o and pull through ch-4, dc in next dc.*

Row 7 — *Dc in dc, ch 9, skip 3 dc, ch 5 and 3 dc, dc in next dc.*

Row 6 — *Dc in dc, ch 5, skip 5 dc, dc in next dc.*

Row 5 — *Dc in dc, 5 dc over ch-2, dc, ch 2, dc in next dc.*

Openwork Center

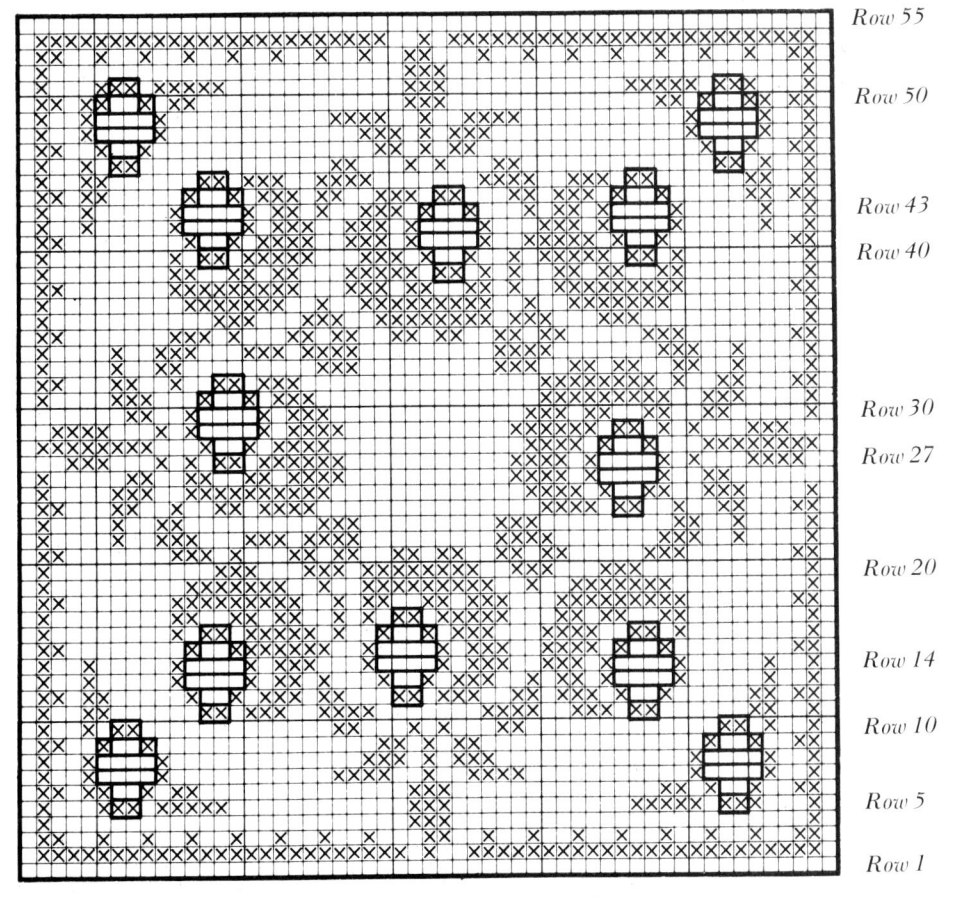

Bed-Linen Decorations: For Sheets and Shams

Lacy border of filet crochet on sheet and corners of pillow sham add a loving touch to any bedroom. This idea may be applied to almost any bed-linen pattern.

SIZES: Sheet-edging strip measures 5" x 72"; length is adjustable. Each pillow-sham corner measures 9" x 9" x 12".

MATERIALS: D.M.C. pearl cotton No. 5 in Wedgwood No. 799: **for sheet edging,** 9 (53-yard) balls; **for pillow-sham corners,** 5 balls. Steel crochet hook No. 2 (or Canadian hook No. 1) *or the size that will give you the correct gauge;* 1 Wamsutta Ultracale "Bachelor Buttons" top sheet (twin size) and pillow sham (standard size).

GAUGE: 4 sp = 1½"; 5 rows = 1½".

Sheet Border

Starting at narrow end, ch 38. **1st row:** Work joined dc in 5th ch from hook as follows: Y o and pull up lp in ch, y o and draw through 2 lps on hook, y o and pull up lp in same ch, y o and draw through 2 lps on hook, y o and draw through all 3 lps on hook (joined dc made), dc in next ch (bl completed); ch 1, skip 1 ch, dc in next ch (sp made); (work 1 bl, 1 sp) 7 times, then 1 bl; ch 4, turn. **2nd row:** Skip first dc and joined dc, dc in next dc (sp made over bl); ch 1, dc in next dc (sp made over sp); ch 1, skip joined dc, dc in next dc (sp made over bl); work 14 more sp; ch 3, turn. **3rd row:** Work joined dc in first sp, dc in next dc (bl made over sp); work 6 sp, 3 bl, 6 sp; joined dc in next sp, dc in top of turning ch; ch 4, turn. **4th row:** Work 6 sp, 1 bl; work joined dc in next joined dc, dc in next dc (bl made over bl); work 1 sp, 2 bl, 6 sp; ch 3, turn.

Starting with 5th row, follow chart, on page 241, to Y, then repeat from X to Y 24 times more or for width of sheet. **Next row:** Work 1 bl, (1 sp, 1 bl) 8 times. Do not break off.

Picot Trim: * Ch 4, sc in 3rd ch from hook (picot made), ch 1; working across long side, skip 1 row, sc over end st of next row. Repeat from * across long side, ending with sc over end st on 1st row made; working across width, (ch 4, sc in 3rd ch from hook, ch 1, sc in next joined dc) 9 times; ch 4, sc in 3rd ch from hook, ch 1, sc over other end st of 1st row. Work across other length and width in same manner, ending with sl st in base of ch-4. Break off.

Finishing: Block strip a few inches at a time.

Sheet Border

Pillow-Sham Corner

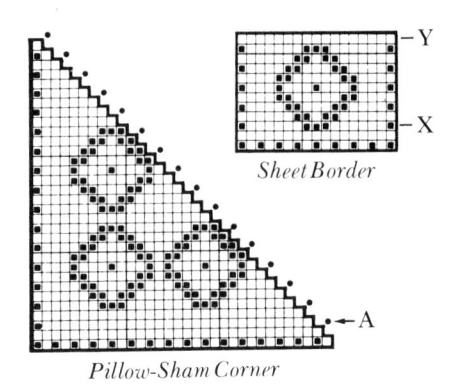

Sew to sheet 1¼" from top edge, lining with white fabric if print is too bold.

Pillow-Sham Corners

Make 4.

Ch 68. **1st row (right side):** Dc in 6th ch from hook (sp made); (work 1 bl, 1 sp) 15 times; 1 bl; ch 4, turn. **2nd row:** Work 31 sp, do not work over last sp (1 dec made); to make picot (dot A on chart), ch 3, turn, sl st in last dc worked. **3rd row:** Sl st in first sp and in next dc (1 dec made over sp), ch 4, make 29 sp, 1 bl; ch 4, turn. **4th row:** Work 29 sp; work picot.

Starting with 5th row and working right-side rows from right to left and wrong-side rows from left to right, follow chart for pillow-sham corner through 10th row, continuing to work decreases and picots as established. **11th row:** Sl st in joined dc and in next dc (1 dec made over bl); ch 3, make 2 bl, (3 sp, 2 bl) 3 times; 4 sp, 1 bl; ch 4, turn.

Starting with 12th row, follow chart to top. After picot on last row, sl st in corner sp; do not break off.

Picot Trim: Work as for picot trim on sheet border across 9" sides only. Break off.

Finishing: Mark a 9" square on blocking surface and block pieces, using corners of square as a guide. Sew one triangle to each corner of sham, inside ruffle, lining with white fabric if desired.

Filet Café Curtain

Old-fashioned filet crochet will add a new, nostalgic look to your home. Usually worked in cotton, it is surprisingly simple to learn. Its lacy look is obtained by combining filled-in squares, worked in double crochet, with spaces bridged by chain stitches. It's easy to make up your own design by using graph paper and charting out a design in the same way you would a cross-stitch or needlepoint pattern, each square representing one stitch.

This lovely café curtain consists of four squares that are crocheted together. Loops along one edge slide over a narrow rod.

SIZE: About 22" square.

MATERIALS: D.M.C. pearl cotton No. 5, 11 (53-yard) balls natural No. 822; steel crochet hook No. 2 (or Canadian hook No. 1) *or the size that will give you the correct gauge.*

GAUGE: Each square measures about 10½".

CAFÉ SQUARES (make 4): Ch 76. **1st row:** In 5th ch from hook work joined dc as follows: Y o and pull up lp in ch, y o and draw through 2 lps on hook, y o and pull up lp in same ch, y o and draw through 2 lps on hook, y o and draw through all 3 lps on hook (joined dc made), dc in next ch (bl completed); joined dc in next ch, dc in next ch (another bl made); ch 1, skip next ch, dc in next ch (sp made). Work 31 more sp, 2 bl; ch 3, turn. **2nd row:** Skip first dc, joined dc in first joined dc, dc in next dc (bl made over bl); work 1 more bl; joined dc in next sp, dc in next dc (bl made over sp); work 1 more bl, ch 1, dc in next dc (sp made over sp); work 27 more sp, 3 bl, joined dc in next joined dc, dc in top of turning ch (last bl made); ch 4, turn. **3rd row:** Skip first dc and joined dc, dc in next dc (sp made over first bl); work 3 bl, 9 sp, 4 bl, 2 sp, 4 bl, 9 sp, 3 bl, ch 1, skip first joined dc, dc in top of turning ch; ch 4, turn. **4th row:** Work

1 sp, 2 bl, ch 1, skip next joined dc, dc in next dc (sp made over bl); work 9 more sp, 4 bl, 2 sp, 4 bl, 10 sp, 2 bl, 1 sp; ch 4, turn. **5th row:** Work 11 sp, 2 bl; ch 2, skip next joined dc, sc in next dc, ch 2, skip next joined dc, dc in next dc (V-st made over 2 bl); work 1 more V-st, 2 bl, 2 V-sts, 2 bl, 11 sp; ch 4, turn. **6th row:** Work 11 sp, 2 bl; (ch 3, dc in next dc) twice (2 large sp made over 2 V-sts); 2 bl, 2 large sp, 2 bl, 11 sp; ch 4, turn. **7th row:** Work 9 sp, 2 bl, 1 V-st; ch 2, skip 1 ch, sc in next ch, ch 2, skip 1 ch, dc in next dc (V-st made over large sp); work 5 more V-sts, 2 bl, 9 sp; ch 4, turn.

Starting with 8th row, follow chart, above, through 10th row. **11th row:** Work 6 sp, 4 bl, 1 sp; in large sp work joined dc, dc and joined dc, dc in next dc (2 bl made over large sp); 5 V-sts, 2 bl, 1 sp, 4 bl, 6 sp; ch 4, turn. Starting with 12th row, follow chart to top. Break off.

ASSEMBLING: Trim: Work around square 1 as follows: Starting at X on chart, sl st in 1st dc; working along left side (see chart), * ch 5, skip first row, sc in lower corner of next row, (ch 5, skip 1 row, sc in lower corner of next row) 17 times; ch 7, sl st in same place as last sc made for corner lp. Continuing around square, repeat from * 3 times more; break off.

To join squares 1 and 2, place square 2 to the right of square 1 and line up the squares so that rows are aligned. **Joining Trim:** Starting at X on square 2, sl st in 1st dc; ch 3, join with sl st to 4th ch of ch-7 corner lp at upper right corner of square 1; ch 3, sl st in same place as first sl st on 2nd square (corners joined). Working along left side of square 2 and right side of square 1, * ch 2, sl st in 3rd ch of corresponding ch-5 on square 1, ch 2, skip 1 row on square 2, sc in lower corner of next row. Repeat from * across to corner; ch 3, sl st in 4th ch of next ch-7 corner lp on square 1 (mark this ch st on square 1), ch 3, sl st in same place as last sc. Work trim on remaining 3 sides of square same as trim for square 1, omitting last corner and ending with sl st in base of ch-3; break off.

To join squares 2 and 3, turn work so that square 2 is at upper left. Line up square 3 to the right of square 2 and work in same manner as before, joining 2nd corner in marked ch. Complete trim on remaining 3 sides of square 3. Break off.

To join square 4 to squares 3 and 1, turn work so that square 3 is at upper left and line up square 4 in wedge between squares 3 and 1. Join as before along left side and bottom of square 4. Complete trim on remaining 2 sides of square 4. Break off. Large square formed.

FINISHING: Work edging as follows: Sl st in 4th ch of ch-7 at upper right corner of curtain; working across top of curtain, (ch 4, sc in 3rd ch of next ch-5 lp of trim, * ch 3, sc in center ch of next lp. Repeat from * to next corner; ch 4, sc in 4th ch of ch-7 corner). Repeat directions in parentheses on 3 remaining sides of curtain, ending with sc in base of 1st ch-4; do not break off. **Top Loop Border:** Ch 10, sc in next sc, * ch 9, sc in next sc. Repeat from * across to sc before corner; ch 10, sc in corner. Break off.

Block curtain. Slide curtain rod through top loop border as shown in photograph or turn curtain upside down and attach small curtain rings to straight edge.

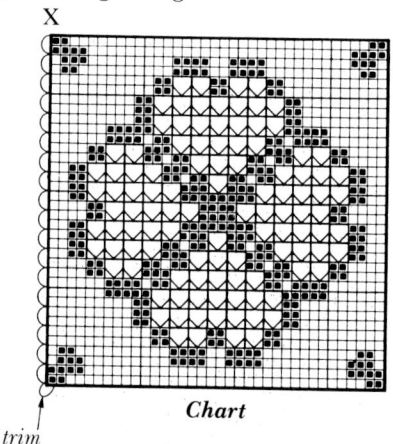

Chart

Café Curtains and Valance

In crochet cotton, made of curtain rings covered with tightly worked single crochet, alternated with vertical strips of crocheted rectangles. Fringe is knotted to single-crochet border.

SIZE: Length and width are adjustable.
MATERIALS: Lily Daisy mercerized crochet cotton No. 10 ecru, 1 (300-yard) skein will make approximately 30 rings and 30 rectangles; 1″ plastic rings; steel crochet hooks No. 6 and No. 7 (or Canadian hooks No. 3 and No. 3½), *or the sizes that will give you the correct gauge*.
GAUGE: 4 joined rings = 5″; 4 joined rectangles = 5″.
Note: Use thread double throughout and work tightly for best results. Rings are worked with No. 6 hook and rectangles with No. 7 hook.

CURTAIN: First Ring Strip: First Ring: 1st rnd (right side): With No. 6 hook, work 33 sc around ring. **2nd rnd:** Sc in each sc around, marking 16th and 24th sc; join with sl st to first sc. Break off.

Second Ring: 1st rnd: Work as for first rnd of first ring. **2nd rnd:** Sc in each of next 7 sc, drop lp from hook, with right side of first ring facing you, insert hook in 16th sc of ring, insert hook in dropped lp, insert hook in next sc on 2nd ring and draw up a lp, y o and draw thread through both lps and through sc on hook (joining completed), sc in each sc around, marking 24th and 32nd sc; join. Break off.

Third Ring: 1st rnd: Repeat first rnd of first ring. **2nd rnd:** Sc in each of next 7 sc, join as before to 24th sc on last ring, sc in each sc around, marking 24th and 32nd sc; join. Break off.

Make and join rings for desired length of curtain, allowing 2″ for band and fringe at lower edge and 2″ for band and rod rings at upper edge.

First Rectangle Strip: First Rectangle: 1st row: With No. 7 hook, * ch 11, sc in 2nd ch from hook and in each ch across (10 sc); ch 1, turn. **2nd row:** Working in back lp of each st, sc in each sc across; ch 1, turn. **3rd, 4th, and 5th rows:** Repeat 2nd row, joining to ring at end of 5th row as follows: Ch 1, turn. Drop lp from hook, insert hook on right side in 32nd sc on last ring on strip, pull dropped lp through the sc (joining completed). **6th row:** Sc in each sc across (first rectangle completed); turn; be sure that thread is behind and to left of lp on hook. Do not break off but repeat from * on first row, joining each rectangle to corresponding ring until the same number of rectangles as rings has been completed. Break off.

Second Ring Strip: First Ring: 1st rnd: Work as for first rnd of first ring. **2nd rnd:** Sc in each of next 7 sc, drop lp from hook, insert hook on right side in corresponding corner lp of last rectangle and draw dropped lp through (joining completed), sc in each sc around, marking 16th and 24th sc; join. Break off.

Second Ring: 1st rnd: Work as for first rnd of first ring. **2nd rnd:** Sc in each of next 7 sc, join to 16th sc of last ring, * sc in each of next 7 sc, join to corresponding corner lp on next rectangle, sc in each sc around, marking 24th and 32nd sc; join. Break off.

Continue to make and join rings in this manner to end of strip. Complete curtain in established pattern, alternating strips of rectangles and rings for desired width, ending with a ring strip.

Top Band: 1st row: With right side facing you, attach thread to 3rd sc to right of center top sc on top right corner ring, ch 5, skip 2 sc, sc in next (top) sc, * ch 13, in top corner of next rectangle, ch 13, sc in top center of sc of next ring. Repeat from * across to last ring, ch 3, skip 2 sc, dc in next sc; ch 1, turn. **2nd row:** Work 3 sc over ch-3 lp, sc in next sc, * work 13 sc over next ch-13 lp, sc in next sc. Repeat from * across, ending with 4 sc over ch-5 lp; ch 1, turn. **3rd, 4th, and 5th rows:** Sc in each sc across; ch 1, turn. Omit ch-1 on last row. Break off. Work band across lower edge in same manner.

Fringe: Wrap double strand of thread around and around a 2" piece of cardboard. Cut strands at one edge (4" lengths of thread). Take 2 strands and fold in half. Draw folded end through first sc on lower band, draw ends through lp and pull tightly. Tie a knot of double thread in each sc across.

Rod Rings: Mark edge of top band for about 7 rings, evenly spaced, for rod. Crochet around a ring as before. At end of 2nd rnd, join to a marked sc on top band. Make and join a ring at each mark.

VALANCE: Make and join strips in same manner as for curtains, working the number of rings and rectangles on each strip for desired width of valance and the number of strips for desired length. Trim top and bottom edges as for curtains, joining about 14 rings for rod across top.

Rug-in-the-Round

Worked with one strand of knitting worsted and one strand of cotton-and-rayon rug yarn for strength. A contemporary rug with the old-fashioned good looks of a rag rug. It is 45" in diameter but the size is adjustable. To keep the rug from slipping use an antiskid rug coating in the form of a liquid rubber to be painted on the back of the rug.

SIZE: About 45" in diameter.
MATERIALS: Coats and Clark's ombré knitting worsted, 2 (3½-ounce) skeins purple No. 985 (color A), 1 skein each orange No. 980 (B), green No. 970 (C), blue No. 960 (D); Coats and Clark's cotton-and-rayon rug yarn, 6 (70-yard) skeins sapphire blue No. 89 (D), 4 skeins burnt orange No. 137 (E), 2 skeins amethyst No. 140 (F); aluminum crochet hook size K (or Canadian hook No. 4) *or the size that will give you the correct gauge.*

Note: To keep rug from slipping, you can use Saf-T-Bak antiskid rug backing, a liquid rubber to be painted on back of rug, available from Sears, Roebuck and Co.

GAUGE: 3 sts = 1"; 2 rnds = 1".

To Change Colors: Work to within last st,

draw up lp in last st, break off old colors, leaving 4" end. Pick up new colors and complete st. Continue with new colors, working over ends of old colors to conceal them.

RUG: (Work with 2 strands yarn throughout, using 1 strand each knitting worsted and rug yarn.) Starting at center with B and F, ch 4. Sl st in 4th ch from hook to form ring. **1st rnd:** Work 8 sc in ring. Do not join rnds but work around and around in spiral fashion, marking beg of each rnd. **2nd rnd:** Work 2 sc in next sc (inc made), work 2 sc in each sc around (16 sc). **3rd rnd:** * Sc in next sc, 2 sc in next sc. Repeat from * around (24 sc). **4th rnd:** Repeat 3rd rnd (36 sc). **5th rnd:** Sc in each sc around, increasing 8 sc as evenly spaced as possible (44 sc). Piece should measure about 5" in diameter.

Continue to work in same manner, increasing as often as necessary to keep rug flat and being careful not to work increases over increases of previous rnd. Work in the following color sequence: 1" more with B and F, 4½" B and E, 5½" C and E, 6" A and D, 3" D and F.

Rug can be made larger if desired.

Coasters

A quickie stocking-stuffer: red coasters of rug yarn to make in a jiffy.

SIZE: 4" in diameter.
MATERIALS: Rug yarn, 2 ounces or 50 yards; 1" plastic rings; aluminum crochet hook size H (or Canadian hook No. 8), *or the size that will give you the correct gauge.*
GAUGE: 4 sts (ch's and dc's) = 1".

1st rnd: Work 17 sc around plastic ring, sl st to first sc, ch 4. **2nd rnd:** Working in back lps only, * dc in next sc, ch 1, repeat from * around (17 dc's), sl st to 3rd ch of ch-4. **3rd rnd:** * Skip ch-1, sc in next dc, ch 4, repeat from * around, sc in base of ch-4. Break off.

Candy Pockets

There's a special joy in making your own holiday decorations. Here are two made of knitting worsted to trim the tree.

Basket

SIZE: Circle measures 3¾" in diameter.
MATERIALS: Knitting worsted, small amounts of hot pink, lavender, and orange; aluminum crochet hook size H (Canadian hook No. 8) *or the size that will give you the correct gauge.*

CIRCLE: Starting at center with hot pink, ch 4. Join with sl st to form ring. **1st rnd:** Ch 1, work 8 sc in ring. Join with sl st to ch-1. **2nd rnd:** Ch 1, 2 sc in each sc around. Join (16 sc). **3rd rnd:** Ch 1, * 2 sc in next sc, sc in next sc. Repeat from * around. Join (24 sc). Break off. **4th rnd:** Attach lavender to sl st of last rnd. Ch

yarn 24 times around a 3″ piece of cardboard. Remove cardboard and tie yarn together ½″ below one folded edge. Cut other end. Sew tassel in place.

Star

SIZE: Width of star measures 5″.

MATERIALS: Knitting worsted, small amounts of purple, lime, and turquoise; aluminum crochet hook size H (Canadian hook No. 8) *or the size that will give the correct gauge.*

STAR: Starting at center with purple, ch 4. Join with sl st to form ring. **1st rnd:** Ch 1, work 6 sc in ring. Join with sl st to ch-1. **2nd rnd:** * Ch 5, skip 2 ch, sc in each of next 3 ch, sc in next sc (1 spoke made). Repeat from * 5 times more (6 spokes made). Break off. **3rd rnd:** Attach lime to top of one spoke. Ch 3, sc in same place, * work sc in base of next 2 sc, skip next sc, h dc in sc at base of spoke, skip next sc, sc in each of next 2 sc, work sc, ch 2 and sc in top of spoke. Repeat from * around, ending last repeat with sl st in base of ch-3 at beg of rnd. Break off. **4th rnd:** Attach turquoise in ch-3 space at end of lime point. Ch 3, sc in same place, * sc in each of next 3 sc, skip h dc, sc in each of next 3 sc, work sc, ch 2 and sc in point. Repeat from * around, ending repeat with a sl st in sc at beg of rnd. Break off.

Make another star in same manner.

FINISHING: Starting at one point, overcast stars together along 8 edges, leaving 4 edges (1 point) open. Attach turquoise at one free point, ch 15 for handle; join to other free point. Break off.

1, working in back loop only, sc in each sc around. Join (24 sc). **5th rnd:** Repeat 3rd rnd (36 sc). Break off. **6th rnd:** Attach orange to sl st. Ch 1, working in back loop only, * work 2 sc in next sc, sc in each of next 2 sc. Repeat from * around. Join (48 sc). Break off.

Make another circle in same manner.

FINISHING: With wrong sides of circles together, join them by working sc through both layers of next 36 sc, working through back loop of each sc. Ch 24 for handle and join to opposite side of opening. **Tassel:** Wind orange

Cat Nest

Who could be cozier than this feline friend in its own warm little nest? Made of heavy rug yarn. Wears and washes well.

MATERIALS: Aunt Lydia's heavy rug yarn (70-yard skeins), 1 skein each beige No. 210 and dove gray No. 261, 2 skeins dark red No. 254; aluminum crochet hook size H (or Canadian hook No. 8) *or any size that will give you the correct gauge.*

GAUGE: 3 dc = 1″.

With beige, ch 4. Join with sl st to form ring.

1st rnd: Ch 2, work 9 h dc in ring (10 h dc counting ch-2 as one h dc). Join with sl st to ch-2. **2nd rnd:** ch 2, work 1 h dc in same place as sl st, * work 2 h dc in next h dc. Repeat from * around. Join (20 h dc counting ch-2 as 1 h dc). **3rd rnd:** Ch 3, work 1 dc in same place as sl st, * work 2 dc in next h dc. Repeat from * around. Join (40 dc). **4th rnd:** Ch 3, work 1 dc in same place as sl st, * work 1 dc in next dc, 2 dc in next dc. Repeat from * around, ending with 1 dc. Join (60 dc). Continue to work in dc's, inc 12 sts as evenly spaced as possible on each of next 5 rnds (120 dc at end of last rnd). (Piece should measure approximately 12" across.) Break off beige. Attach red. **10th through 12th rnds:** With red, dc in each dc around. Break off red. Attach beige. **13th rnd:** With beige, dc in each dc around. Break off beige. Attach gray. **14th and 15th rnds:** With gray, dc in each dc around. Break off gray. Attach beige. **16th rnd:** With beige, sc in each dc around. Break off beige. Attach red. **17th and 18th rnds:** With red, sc in each sc around. Break off red. Attach gray. **19th rnd:** With gray (working in back lp only), sc in each sc around. Mark this round. **20th through 22nd rnds:** Sc in each sc around. Break off gray. Attach red. **23rd rnd:** With red, dc in each sc around. Break off. Fold marked row over to inside of nest.

Fruit Centerpiece

Life is but a bowl of charmingly crocheted strawberries, grapes, oranges, apples, and carrots. Worked mostly in single crochet using knitting worsted. What a whimsical way to set a table!

MATERIALS: Knitting worsted-weight yarn: You will need about 1 ounce of fruit color (red for apple and strawberries, orange for carrot and orange, lavender for grapes) and small amounts yarn for trimmings (2 shades green for leaves and stems, brown for grape stem, white for strawberry seeds); aluminum crochet hook size H (or Canadian hook No. 8) *or the size that will give you the correct gauge;* matching yarn for stuffing; tapestry needle.

GAUGE: 3 sc = 1"; 3 rnds = 1".

GENERAL DIRECTIONS: To inc 1 sc, work 2 sc in 1 sc. Do not join rnds but mark beg of each rnd. Stuff fruit with matching-color yarn so that stuffing will not show through stitches.

Decorating with Crochet

French knot

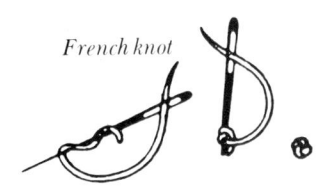

Apple

See General Directions.

Starting at bottom with red, ch 4. Join with sl st to form ring. **1st rnd:** Ch 2, work 9 h dc in ring (10 h dc, counting ch-2 as 1 h dc). **2nd rnd (inc rnd):** Work 2 sc in each h dc around (20 sc). **3rd rnd:** Sc in each sc around. **4th rnd (inc rnd):** Sc in each sc around, increasing 4 sc evenly spaced (24 sc). **5th through 12th rnds:** Sc in each sc around. **13th rnd:** * Sc in next sc, skip next sc. Repeat from * around, ending with sc in last sc. Stuff. **14th rnd:** Repeat 13th rnd. **15th rnd:** Sl st in each st around. Break off.

Leaf: 1st row: With dark green, work 3 sc along top edge of apple; turn. **2nd row:** Sl st in first sc, ch 3, work 2 dc in same place as sl st, 4 dc in next sc, 3 dc in next sc; ch 1, turn. **3rd row:** Sc in each of next 3 dc, h dc in next dc, 3 dc in next dc, h dc in each of next 2 dc, sc in each of next 3 dc. Break off.

Stem: With light green, sl st in top edge of apple directly below leaf joining. **1st row:** Ch 8, sc in 2nd ch from hook and in each ch across; turn. **2nd row:** Sc in each sc across. Break off. Close top opening of apple with 2 or 3 sts.

Orange

See General Directions.

Starting at bottom with orange, ch 4. Join with sl st to form ring. Work as for apple through 8th rnd. **9th rnd:** Repeat 13th rnd of apple. Stuff. **10th rnd:** Repeat 13th rnd of apple. **11th rnd:** Sl st in each st around. Break off.

Tiny Leaves: Using tapestry needle, and alternating light green and dark green yarn, work a cluster of French knots at top of orange (see diagram).

Large Strawberry

See General Directions.

Starting at bottom with red, ch 3. Join with sl st to form ring. **1st rnd:** Ch 2, work 5 h dc in ring (6 h dc, counting ch-2 as 1 h dc). **2nd rnd (inc rnd):** Work 2 sc in each h dc around (12 sc). **3rd and 4th rnds:** Sc in each sc around. **5th rnd (inc rnd):** Sc in each sc around, increasing 4 sc evenly spaced (16 sc). **6th rnd:** Sc in each sc around. Repeat 5th and 6th rnds 3 times more (28 sc). **13th rnd:** * Sc in next sc, skip next sc. Repeat from * around (14 sc). Stuff. **14th rnd:** Repeat 13th rnd (7 sc). **15th rnd:** Sl st in each sc around; join. Close opening with 2 or 3 sts and break off.

Leaves: With light green ch 9. Join with sl st

to form ring. **1st rnd:** (Ch 2, sc in ring) 4 times. **2nd rnd:** (Sl st in next ch-2 sp, ch 3, work 6 dc in same sp) 4 times; sl st in base of first ch-3. **3rd rnd:** Sc in top of each ch-3, in each dc and in each sl st around. **4th rnd:** Sc in each sc around. Break off. Sew starting ring on leaves to top of strawberry.

Stem: With dark green, sl st in center top of strawberry, ch 7, sc in 2nd ch from hook and in each ch across. Break off, leaving a 12″ end. Thread end in tapestry needle and work a long st over each indentation between leaves.

Seeds: With tapestry needle and white yarn, work French-knot seeds (see diagram) on strawberry.

Small Strawberry

See General Directions.

Starting at bottom with red, ch 3. Join with sl st to form ring. **1st rnd:** Ch 2, work 5 h dc in ring (6 h dc, counting ch-2 as 1 h dc). **2nd rnd (inc rnd):** Sc in each h dc, increasing 2 sc evenly spaced (8 sc). **3rd rnd:** Sc in each sc around. **4th rnd (inc rnd):** Repeat 2nd rnd (10 sc). **5th rnd:** Work even. **6th rnd:** Sc in each sc, increasing 5 sc evenly spaced (15 sc). **7th and 8th rnds:** Repeat 3rd rnd. Stuff. **9th rnd (dec rnd):** * Sc in next sc, skip next sc. Repeat from * around, ending with sc in last sc (8 sc). **10th rnd:** Sl st in each st around. Close opening and break off.

Leaves: 1st rnd: With dark green, sc into side of any sc on 9th rnd, * ch 2, skip next sc, sc into next sc. Repeat from * around, ending with sc into last sc. **2nd rnd:** (Sl st in next ch-2 sp, ch 3, work 4 dc in same sp) 3 times; sl st in base of first ch-3. Break off.

Stem: With light green, sl st in center top of strawberry, ch 5, sc in 2nd ch from hook and in each of next 3 ch. Break off.

Seeds: See Large Strawberry.

Carrot

See General Directions.

Starting at lower end with orange, ch 4. Join with sl st to form ring. **1st rnd:** Ch 2, work 5 h dc in ring (6 h dc, counting ch-2 as 1 h dc). **2nd rnd:** Sc in each h dc around. **1st inc rnd:** Sc in each sc around, increasing 3 sc evenly spaced (9 sc). **Next rnd:** Sc in each sc around. Continue to work even until piece measures 3″ from beg. Stuff. **2nd inc rnd:** Sc in each sc around, increasing 2 sc evenly spaced (11 sc). Work even until piece measures 5″ from beg. Stuff. **3rd inc rnd:** Sc in each sc around, increasing 2 sc evenly spaced (13 sc). Work even until piece measures 8″ from beg. Stuff. **Last rnd:** * Sc in next sc, skip next sc. Repeat from * around, ending with sc in last sc (7 sc); join with sl st to first sc. Close opening and break off.

First Leaf: 1st row: Using dark green and working into side of each sc on last row of carrot, work sc into first sc, 2 sc into each of next 2 sc; turn. **2nd row:** Sl st in first sc, ch 3, dc in same place as sl st, 2 dc in each of next 4 sc; ch 1, turn. **3rd row:** Sc in each of next 3 dc, dc in each of next 4 dc, sc in each of next 3 dc. Break off. **2nd Leaf:** With light green, work as for first leaf in each of next 3 sc at top edge of carrot.

Make other carrots in different shades of orange.

Grapes

See General Directions.

Grapes (make 20): Starting at center bottom with lavender, ch 3. Join with sl st to form ring. **1st rnd:** Ch 3, work 6 dc in ring (7 dc, counting ch-3 as 1 dc). **2nd rnd:** Sc in each dc around. Stuff. **3rd rnd (dec rnd):** * Sc in first sc, skip next sc. Repeat from * around, ending with sc in last sc (4 sc). Break off, leaving 3″ end.

Stem: Starting at left end with dark brown, ch 5. Join with sl st to form ring; ch 1. **1st rnd:** Sc in each ch around. **2nd rnd:** Sc in each sc around. Repeat 2nd rnd, stuffing as you go, until stem measures about 8″ from beg.

Following photograph, sew some grapes to stem and some to other grapes to form bunch.

Cachepot

Everyday jute twine from the hardware store, worked in half-double and treble crochet stitches, gives this cachepot its strong textural effect.

SIZE: 11½" in diameter, 12" high, or it can be made to fit your planter.

MATERIALS: Heavy jute twine (available in hardware stores), 10 (125-yard) balls; aluminum crochet hook size J (or Canadian hook No. 6) *or the size that will give you the correct gauge;* tapestry needle.

GAUGE: 3 tr = 1"; 1 tr row = 1".

BOTTOM: Starting at center, ch 12. Join with sl st to form ring. **1st rnd:** Ch 3, work 13 dc in ring; join with sl st to top of ch-3. **2nd rnd:** Ch 3, work dc in same place as ch-3, work 2 dc in each dc around (28 dc, counting ch-3 as 1 dc); join. **3rd rnd:** Ch 3, * 2 dc in next dc, dc in next dc. Repeat from * around; 2 dc in last dc (42 dc); join. **4th rnd:** Ch 3, * 2 dc in next dc, dc in each of next 2 dc. Repeat from * around, ending with dc in last dc; join (56 dc). Continue increasing 14 dc evenly spaced on every rnd in this manner until bottom measures 11½" in diameter or fits your planter. Break off.

SIDE: Starting vertically along side, ch 37, or a chain the height of the flowerpot plus 5 ch sps. **1st row (right side):** Tr in 5th ch from hook and in each ch across (34 tr, counting turning ch as 1 tr); ch 2, turn. **2nd row:** Skip first tr, h dc in each tr across and in top of ch-4 (34 h dc, counting ch-2 as 1 h dc); ch 4, turn. **3rd row:** Skip first h dc, tr in back loop of each h dc across and in top of ch-2; ch 2, turn. Repeat 2nd and 3rd rows until piece is long enough to fit around bottom piece, ending with h dc row. Break off, leaving 25" end. Thread end in tapestry needle and sew first and last rows together.

RIDGES: Work across each h dc row as follows: Make loop on hook, y o, with right side facing you, insert hook under post of first h dc on a row and draw yarn through, y o, draw through all 3 loops on hook. Continue in this manner, working h dc over post of each h dc across. Break off. Sew bottom piece in place.

Room Divider

(See photograph on page 251.)

If you know the four basic stitches you can make this airy panel for a room divider: chain, single and double crochet, and slip stitch. Cotton thread combines with wooden beads.

MATERIALS: Coats and Clark's Speed-Cro-Sheen (100% cotton thread), 11 (100-yard) balls Nu Ecru; steel crochet hook No. 1 (or Canadian hook No. 0) *or the size that will give you the correct gauge;* 161 wooden beads, 25 mm; 1" x 1" pine stock strips, two 82" lengths for uprights and four 22" lengths for crosspieces; staple gun or tacks and hammer; drill or eye screws.

GAUGE: 16 dc = 3" when stretched.

STRIPS FOR TOP AND BOTTOM PANELS (make 11): Ch 114 to measure approximately 22" for basic chain. **1st row (right side):** Sc in 2nd ch from hook and in each ch across (113 sc); turn. **2nd row:** Sl st in first st, ch 3, dc in next st and in each st across (113 dc, counting ch-3 as 1 dc); turn. Repeat 2nd row 3 times more. Break off. Strip should measure about 22" when stretched.

To Join Strips: With right side facing you, attach thread to first dc on last dc row; ch 13 for bar, remove hook; with right side of another strip facing you, insert hook in first st of basic chain and draw dropped lp through, y o hook and draw through both lps on hook, skip first ch of bar, sl st in each of next 11 ch, sl st in st where thread was attached, * sl st in each of next 4 dc, ch 14 for bar, remove hook, skip next 3 sts on basic chain, join to next st, skip first ch of bar, sl st in each of next 12 ch, sl st in same st where bar was started. Repeat from * across, ending with a ch-13 bar in last st. Break off (29 bars).

Join 6 strips in all in this manner for top panel of screen and 5 strips for bottom panel.

STRIPS FOR SIDE PANELS (make 24): 1st row (right side): Ch 18 to measure about 3" for basic chain. Sl st in 2nd ch from hook and in each ch across (17 sc); turn. **2nd row:** Sl st in first st, ch 3, dc in each st across (17 dc, counting ch-3 as 1 dc); turn. Repeat 2nd row 3 times more. Break off. Strip should measure about 3" when stretched. Joining as before, join 12 strips each to form 2 side panels.

Attach a side panel to lower edge of top panel as follows: With right side of side panel facing you, attach thread to first dc on last dc row; ch 13 for bar, join to first st of basic chain on lower edge of top panel, then complete bar. Continue as before, making 4 more bars, the next 3 with ch-14 and the last one with ch-13. Break off.

Attach thread to 2nd side panel as before, ch 13 for bar, skip 79 center sts of basic chain on lower edge of top panel and join to next st; complete bar. Make 4 more bars as before. Break off.

Join side panels to top edge of bottom panel as follows: With right side of bottom panel facing you, attach thread to first dc on last dc row; ch 13 for bar, join to first st on basic chain at lower edge of right side panel; complete bar. Continue as before, making 4 more bars. Break off. Join lower edge of left side panel to opposite end of bottom panel, leaving free the center 79 dc at top edge of bottom panel. Break off.

BORDER: Keep work as flat as possible when working border so that edge will not cup or ruffle. Work across long side edge as follows: **1st row:** With right side of piece facing you, attach thread in a corner st, work a row of sc, evenly spaced, across long edge; turn. **2nd row:** Sl st in first st, ch 3, work dc in each sc across. Break off. Work across opposite outside edge and the two long inside edges of opening in same manner.

FINISHING: Join 4 pine strips by gluing and stapling or gluing and nailing them together to form a 24" by 82" frame. Place crocheted piece wrong side up on frame. Tack or staple crochet at corners and at center of each side to frame. Continue tacking at 3" intervals all around.

On each of the remaining 2 crosspieces make a center mark about 4½" in from each end; then make 5 more marks evenly spaced between. Using a fine bit, drill a hole completely through crosspiece at each mark or screw a screw eye at each mark. Attach crosspieces to frame between uprights behind lower edge of top panel and upper edge of bottom panel, making sure the screw eyes or holes face toward center opening. Staple or tack crochet to crosspieces.

With thread double, cut 7 lengths to fit center opening from crosspiece to crosspiece, allowing extra for knotting between beads and at ends. String 23 beads on each double thread, knotting at even intervals so that beads will not slip. Attach each beaded string to crosspieces by knotting ends in screw eyes or by running ends through holes and knotting on other side of crosspieces.

Rag Rug

Use up your old sheets, shirts, or whatever remnants you may have lying around the house. The project is quick and easy to do, the end result always a surprise.

To crochet a rag rug, decide first on the size and colors you want. Then invade your leftover fabric supply, if you have one. If not, you will have to shop for remnants. The rug is made of cotton fabrics, which should be colorfast and preshrunk. You will also need a crochet hook (probably size K) and a pair of scissors.

To estimate how much fabric you will need: the rug shown in a 35" by 62½" size required approximately 6 yards of each of 6 colors, or about 36 yards total. Exact yardage will depend on how loosely or tightly you crochet and on whether you wish a larger or smaller rug.

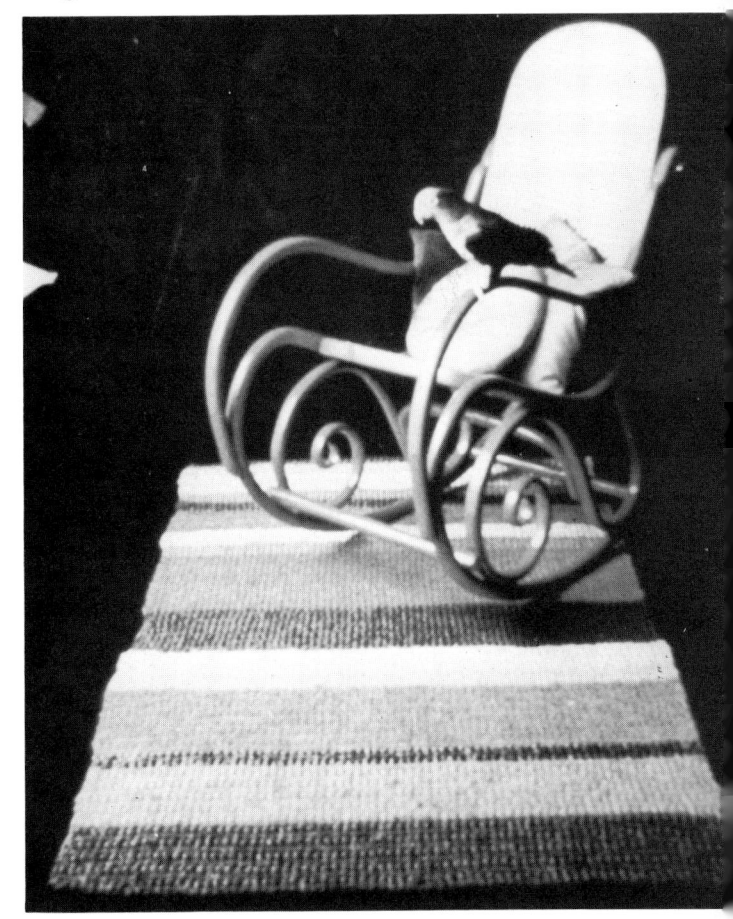

To start, tear or cut strips of fabric ½" wide. Unless your fabric is very sturdy, such as twill, it is much easier and quicker to tear it. Snip the fabric with your scissors ½" in from the edge at the selvage and tear to, but not through, the opposite selvage. At that place, measure ½" along the selvage and snip the selvage again. Tear back to the starting selvage. Continue in this manner until all the fabric is torn. All your fabric will be in one continuous, but zigzagged, ½" wide strip.

There is no gauge for crocheting with rags. You simply chain to the width desired. Work entire rug even in single crochet, inserting through both loops of previous row, and chaining one to turn. Continue to the desired length of the rug. The hook you use will be determined not by the gauge but by what seems to work best for you with your fabrics. Size K is a good large size for most rag rugs.

To change colors or strips, tie the two strips together and hold ends to back of work. When rug is complete, cut ends short and sew to underside of rug, taking care that stitches do not show on right side. For this striped rug always change colors at the end of the row. Work off the last loops of last stitch with the new color.

When your rug is the length you want it, fasten off and sew the last end to the back. Then spread the completed rug on a large table or the floor and cover it with very damp towels. Allow to dry thoroughly. The rug will lie smooth and flat.

Romantic Mirror Frame

Could also double as a sentimental picture frame. The ruffle is one long stretch of single crochet and chain loops in crochet cotton. It is gathered to fit with a narrow velvet ribbon. Little blossoms are strewn here and there for a bit of nostalgia.

SIZE: 2" wide.
MATERIALS: Mercerized crochet cotton size 10, one (200-yard) ball white; steel crochet hook No. 9 (or Canadian hook No. 4½) *or the size that will give you the correct gauge;* 1 yard ¼"-wide brown velvet ribbon; 6 appliqué flowers; framed mirror with stand, 5" x 7" or desired size; piece of cardboard 7" x 9" or 2" larger than mirror; white glue.
GAUGE: 4 loops = 1".

Starting at one end, ch 25. **1st row:** Sc in 4th ch from hook, * ch 3, skip next 2 ch, sc in next ch. Repeat from * across (8 lps); ch 3, turn. **2nd row:** Work sc over first lp, * ch 3, sc over next lp. Repeat from * across (8 lps); ch 3, turn. Repeat 2nd row until piece measures 52" or length needed, when gathered, to fit around mirror. Break off.

Starting 1 lp in from long edge, weave ribbon under 2 lps and over 4 lps along edge. Gather to fit around mirror. Tie in bow. Sew ends of crochet together. Cut center from cardboard to make 1"-wide frame around mirror; round off corners. Glue frame to mirror, then ruffle to frame. Glue appliqués in place as shown in photograph.

Yarn Sources

If you have difficulty in obtaining any of the yarns specified for the projects included in this book, you can write to the following addresses for mail orders:

American Thread
(for Aunt Lydia's Rug Yarn):
Richfield Yarn Products
469 Central Avenue, Jersey City, N.J. 07307

Bear Brand, Bucilla, and Fleisher's:
Merchandise Mailing Service
Box 144, East Meadow, N.Y. 11554

Brunswick:
Windyways, Brandwood Station
Greenville, S.C. 29610

Bernat:
Art Needlecraft, Inc.
Box 394, Uxbridge, Mass. 01569

D.M.C.:
Boutique Margot
26 West 54th Street, New York, N.Y. 10019

Kentucky Yarns:
Edgemont Yarn Service
RR 2, Box 14, Maysville, Ky. 41056

Reynolds:
International Creations
Box 55, Great Neck, N.Y. 11023

Unger:
Scandinavian Import Corp.
P.O. Box 347, Madison Square Station,
New York, N.Y. 10010

Write directly to the following manufacturers for the location of your nearest dealer:

Coats and Clark's:
75 Rockefeller Center
New York, N.Y. 10019

Columbia Minerva:
295 Fifth Avenue
New York, N.Y. 10016

Frederick J. Fawcett:
129 South Street
Boston, Mass. 02111

Lilly Mills Co.:
Shelby, N.C. 28150

Spinnerin:
230 Fifth Avenue
New York, N.Y. 10001

Yarn Industries:
P.O. Box 595
Pageland, S.C. 29728

Nan Biasiny, Needlework Consultant

Photo Credits
J. Arnold, 147
N. Barr, 70, 105, 128
L. Caron, 158
D. Dorot, 137, 139
F. Eberstadt, 40
S. Forlano, 112
F. Gill, 181, 182, 183
P. Levy, 81, 86, 88, 91, 132
G. Lunardi, 38, 46, 75, 161
J. Malignon, 32, 45, 98, 160,
A. Maucher, 27, 29, 148, 156
S. Owen, 200
M. Reinhardt, 140
C. Schiavone, 33, 35, 36, 43,
    48, 55, 57, 58, 62, 65, 68,
    73, 77, 83, 104, 108, 117,
    139, 172, 238, 240, 242, 249
S. Svensson, 122, 125
Woman's Day Studio, 150,
    151, 153, 154, 204, 220,
    230, 233, 243, 245, 247,
    248, 251, 254

Design Credits
M. Acardi, 45
M. Ake, 81, 86, 91
L. O. Blood, 33, 40, 51, 98,
    238, 242
B. Bodenstein, 225
N. Brown, 36, 147, 174, 176,
    177, 180, 189
S. Burrows, 38, 46, 75
C. Castagnoli, 179, 190
I. Cedrins, 191
Claudia, 170
Clodagh, 93, 112, 132
G. Cornish, 120
K. Curry, 230
S. De Gaetano, 150, 151, 200,
    204, 207
E. Dobbins, 195
M. Dutkus, 57
S. Flaccomio, 148
J. Ford, 197
K. Fox, 27
R. Fox, 232
C. Hasselriis, 135
R. Jacksier, 167
S. Jacobs, 32, 137

B. Johnson, 161
J. Kennedy, 245
D. Lee, 146, 158, 171
E. Loeb, 43, 48, 55, 62, 65, 68,
    83, 88, 104, 105, 108, 117,
    122, 125, 128, 169, 186,
    211, 220, 240
L. Maeda, 73
H. Maris, 223
C. Maxwell, 247
J. Mayer, 70, 77, 214
B. Muccio, 153
I. Nissen, 192, 246
P. Saperston, 35, 139
A. Schiff, 192, 193
D. Schwartz, 140
L. Sherman, 249
R. Tawfik, 110
N. Tobier, 42
M. Varon, 160
P. Webster, 154
M. Weinman, 58, 216
W. White, 235
T. Wood, 172, 181, 182, 183
Woman's Day Staff, 156, 233,
    243, 248, 251, 254